ON TEMPORAL AND SPIRITUAL AUTHORITY

NATURAL LAW AND
ENLIGHTENMENT CLASSICS

Knud Haakonssen
*General Editor*

Robert Bellarmine

# On Temporal and Spiritual Authority

On Laymen or Secular People

On the Temporal Power of the Pope.
Against William Barclay

On the Primary Duty of the Supreme Pontiff

## Robert Bellarmine

Edited, Translated, and with an Introduction
by Stefania Tutino

*Political Writings of Robert Bellarmine*

LIBERTY FUND

This book is published by Liberty Fund, Inc., a foundation established to encourage study of the ideal of a society of free and responsible individuals.

The cuneiform inscription that serves as our logo and as a design element for Liberty Fund books is the earliest-known written appearance of the word "freedom" (*amagi*), or "liberty." It is taken from a clay document written about 2300 B.C. in the Sumerian city-state of Lagash.

Frontispiece: "Portrait of St. Robert Bellarmine." Anonymous, first half of the seventeenth century. Rome, Chiesa di Sant'Ignazio.

3rd printing (2023)

Library of Congress Cataloging-in-Publication Data

Bellarmino, Roberto Francesco Romolo, Saint, 1542–1621.
[Selections. English. 2012]
Spiritual authority; On laymen or secular people; On the temporal power of the Pope, against William Barclay; On the primary duty of the Supreme Pontiff: political writings of Robert Bellarmine / Robert Bellarmine; edited, translated, and with an introduction by Stefania Tutino.
p. cm. — (Natural law and Enlightenment classics)
Includes bibliographical references and indexes.
ISBN 978-0-86597-716-7 (hc) — ISBN 978-0-86597-717-4 (pbk.)
1. Popes—Temporal power. 2. Christianity and politics—Catholic Church. 3. Catholic Church—Doctrines. I. Tutino, Stefania. II. Title.
BX1810.B45 2012
262'.132—dc23                                    2011040777

LIBERTY FUND, INC.
11301 North Meridian Street
Carmel, Indiana 46032
libertyfund.org

# CONTENTS

# INTRODUCTION

## Overview

Robert Bellarmine was one of the most influential theologians and political theorists in post-Reformation Europe.[1] Born in 1542, Bellarmine entered the Society of Jesus in 1560 and began his studies at the Roman College. In 1569 he was sent to Louvain, where he divided his time between preaching and teaching theology, acquiring a distinguished reputation for both. In 1576 he was called back to Rome to the chair of *Controversiae,* that is, to teach the course on the leading theological controversies between Protestants and Catholics, at the Roman College, of which he became rector in 1592. The lectures soon grew into one of Bellarmine's major works, the *Disputationes de controversiis Christianae fidei,* or simply *Controversiae.*[2] Here the doctrine of the pope's authority to intervene indirectly in temporal matters when those touched spiritual issues (*potestas papalis indirecta*) found its first and fullest development, even though Bellarmine later modified specific points several times.[3]

Bellarmine's intellectual efforts gained him a more central position within the Roman Curia but he also encountered dangerous setbacks. In 1587 he became a member of the Congregation of the Index and in 1598

1. For more details on Bellarmine's biography see Brodrick, *Robert Bellarmine;* Godman, *Saint as Censor;* Motta, *Bellarmino;* Tutino, *Empire of Souls.* In 1613 Bellarmine wrote an autobiography, whose manuscript copy can be found in APUG 1460 and which was printed posthumously in Rome in 1675.

2. Three volumes, Ingolstadt, 1586–89; there were several revised editions during Bellarmine's life.

3. For a complete list of Bellarmine's published works and their different editions, see Sommervogel, *Bibliothèque,* vol. 1, cols. 1151–1254.

became one of the *consultores* of the Inquisition.[4] Meanwhile, the implications of the doctrine of *potestas indirecta* angered Pope Sixtus V, who often opposed the Society of Jesus because he thought the Society's doctrines diminished the authority of the bishop of Rome.[5] In 1589–90 Sixtus moved to put volume 1 of *Controversiae* on the Index of Prohibited Books while Bellarmine was in France on a diplomatic mission.[6] However, the Congregation of the Index and, later, the Society of Jesus resisted this. In 1590 Sixtus died, and with him the project of the Sistine Index also died.[7]

After the death of Sixtus, Bellarmine's star rose higher and higher, especially during the pontificate of Clement VIII. In 1599 he was appointed cardinal and soon after became one of the pope's main advisers on the so-called controversy *de auxiliis*. This most delicate controversy of the early modern Catholic Church began in 1588 with the publication of the Spanish Jesuit Luis de Molina's *Concordia liberi arbitrii cum gratiae donis* [The Concordance of Free Will with the Gifts of Grace], considered by many theologians, and especially Dominicans, to have a Pelagian flavor.[8] The controversy caused a dangerous breach within the Church concerning the role of grace in human salvation, a key doctrinal division between Protestants and Catholics. The controversy ended only in 1607, when Pope Paul V avoided an official decision and commanded Jesuits and Dominicans to remain in "internal" theological debates and to avoid further public contention. During the long debate Bellarmine demonstrated his skills of intellectual and political diplomacy: despite being a Jesuit, he did not side completely with Molina and worked to avoid the scandal

---

4. On Bellarmine's role in the Congregations of the Inquisition and of the Index, see Godman, *Saint as Censor,* and Frajese, *La nascita dell'Indice,* pp. 127ff.

5. On some of these controversies see Pastor, *History of the Popes,* vol. 21, pp. 145–78. Also see Mostaccio, "Gerarchie," pp. 109–27.

6. See Le Bachelet, "Bellarmin à l'Index," pp. 227–46, which, however, does not take into account sources in the Archive of the Congregation of the Index that were not yet open at the time of his research. Some of the documents from the Index have been published by Godman, *Saint as Censor,* pp. 435ff. passim.

7. The main documentary evidence of the affair involving Bellarmine and the Index can be found in ACDF, Index, Diarii I, fols. 39r–v; ACDF, Index, Protocolli B, fol. 152r; ACDF, Index Protocolli DDD, fols. 423r–424v; ACDF, Index, Diarii I, fols. 39v–42v. Cf. Godman, *Saint as Censor,* pp. 134–36, and Frajese, *La nascita dell'Indice,* pp. 131–33.

8. See "Pelagius" in Biographical Notes.

that an open, authoritative condemnation of either position would have caused the Catholic Church.[9] His relationship with Clement VIII was not smooth, however, and certain implications of Bellarmine's political theory put him at odds with the pope, as the third text of this selection shows.

The beginning of the seventeenth century marked a shift in Bellarmine's intellectual interests from theory to political dynamics. The cardinal was increasingly engaged in some of the most important political controversies, all linked to his theological views. Bellarmine contributed to the controversy of the Republic of Venice versus the Roman See. This concerned the *Interdetto*, that is, excommunication ordered by Pope Paul V in 1606 against Venice as an act of retaliation for a series of laws issued in 1604–5. Those laws attacked clerical exemption from civil jurisdiction by claiming that two clergymen guilty of secular crimes should be put on trial in a civil tribunal and forbade churches from being built and ecclesiastical properties from being alienated without the Venetian Senate's approval.[10] Aside from the specific legislative measures, the issue at stake was the extent of the jurisdictions of the secular state of Venice and of the Roman See.

The authors who wrote in defense of Venice, especially Paolo Sarpi, who was probably the most effective supporter of the cause of the Republic, often mentioned Bellarmine as an author whose doctrine would indeed support the Venetian laws, as it was Bellarmine who, after all, had written against the direct power of the pope in temporal affairs.[11] The Jesuit cardinal responded in a number of pamphlets defending his own doctrine, for example *Risposta di Bellarmino alle opposizioni di F. Paolo Sarpi Servita* and *Risposta del Card. Bellarmino al Trattato delli sette theologi di Venezia* (both Rome, 1606).

Another noteworthy element in this controversy is that Bellarmine's position again caused problems in Rome, where some theologians thought it more effective to reply to the Venetian controversy not by stressing the

9. For more details on Bellarmine's role in the controversy *de auxiliis*, see Motta, *Bellarmino*, pp. 441ff.

10. See Bouwsma, *Venice and Republican Liberty*; Cozzi, *Paolo Sarpi*, pp. 235–81; Wootton, *Paolo Sarpi*; Frajese, *Sarpi Scettico*, especially pp. 247ff.

11. On the specific arguments used by Sarpi against Bellarmine out of the cardinal's own doctrine, see Frajese, "Regno ecclesiastico e Stato moderno," pp. 273–339.

indirect power of the pope in temporal matters, but by reinforcing the plenitude of power of the papacy *tout court,* in temporal as well as in spiritual matters.[12] Indeed, in 1607 Bellarmine decided to publish a revision of his own published works in order to clarify certain points of his doctrine, including the exemption of the clergy, which he thought had been misinterpreted by people like Sarpi and used against the Roman See.

In those years another political controversy involved Bellarmine's doctrine of the *indirecta potestas* even more profoundly, namely the debate over the Oath of Allegiance, promulgated by James VI and I in 1606 after the Gunpowder Plot. The oath was offered to the king's Catholic subjects to test their loyalty in temporal matters, but it also laid a heavy mortgage on the profession of their faith, namely to renounce as "impious and heretical" the Catholic doctrine that the pope could depose a heretical sovereign and absolve his subjects from their duties of obedience. This mixture of a declaration of political loyalty with a theological statement rejecting the pope's power in temporal matters was intended to extend James's temporal jurisdiction over his Catholic subjects a little beyond simple political obedience. This struck at the heart of Bellarmine's doctrine, which was introduced precisely to extend the pope's spiritual jurisdiction beyond simple spiritual authority, and indirectly into political matters. Bellarmine published numerous responses to James, Lancelot Andrewes, and William Barclay: his work against the last of these is the second and major text of this selection.[13] Once again, his intervention caused much controversy in both the Protestant and the Catholic worlds, as we will see.

By the second half of the 1610s it was clear that the doctrine of Bellarmine, perhaps the most visible theologian in Rome, was becoming very problematic. On the one hand, many considered it the ultimate bulwark of papal authority in temporal matters, affecting not only Protestant monarchies like England, but also, and more dangerously from the point of

---

12. On this different approach to the Venetian question, see Taucci, *Intorno alle lettere,* pp. 96ff.

13. On the controversy over the Oath of Allegiance and the roles of Barclay and Bellarmine, see, among others, Sommerville, "Jacobean Political Thought"; Questier, "Loyalty, Religion and State Power," pp. 311–29; Höpfl, *Jesuit Political Thought,* pp. 321ff.; and Tutino, *Law and Conscience.*

view of the Roman See, Catholic monarchies with a tradition of strong secular authority, such as those of France. On the other hand, many in Rome thought Bellarmine's doctrine insufficiently papalist by rendering the temporal authority of the pope only an indirect one. For these reasons, in the last year of his life the cardinal avoided the political arena and concentrated on his role as censor of books and opinions, a role that nevertheless kept him in the spotlight. For example, in 1616 he wrote the precept prohibiting Galileo Galilei from publicly teaching Copernicanism, the central accusation against Galileo during the second phase of his trial in 1632–33.[14] Bellarmine also maintained his impressive scholarly production.

In 1621 Bellarmine participated in the conclave that elected Gregory XV. However, his health was rapidly deteriorating, and in September of that year the cardinal died. Bellarmine was not canonized until 1931, although attempts at canonization started as early as 1627 and were reproposed throughout the seventeenth, eighteenth, and nineteenth centuries. This long delay reflects both the complexity of Bellarmine's views and the complexity of the context in which they were discussed.

## On Laymen

The first text in this edition is one of the *Controversiae, On Laymen,* part of the *Controversia de Ecclesia militante, On the Militant Church,* that is, the Church on earth. This work has three parts: on laymen, on the clergy, and on monks. It was part of the first volume of the *Controversiae,* the one that Sixtus V wanted to include in the Index.

The controversy on laymen presents a crucial theoretical basis for Bellarmine's theory of the *potestas indirecta.* His arguments supporting the indirect power of the pope in temporal matters were a theoretical and historical response to the growing strength of both the Protestant territorial churches and the early modern states. They hinge on two ideas. The first is that political government is firmly grounded in natural and divine law and thus to an extent autonomous with respect to the Catholic Church.

14. The literature on the relationship between Bellarmine and Galileo is plentiful. A good starting point that focuses on Bellarmine's role is Godman, *Saint as Censor,* pp. 214ff.

In other words, the political authority of sovereigns of the pre-Christian and non-Christian world was as legitimate as that of Christian princes. If this were not the case and if the Christian commonwealth were identical with the political commonwealth, the pope would have direct control not only over the souls but also over the bodies of Christians, who would be both political subjects and members of the Church of Rome.

The second key idea is that political government is not completely separate from the Christian Church: there is a point where the temporal and the spiritual spheres merge. That point is humanity's ultimate end, the attainment of eternal life. This is a spiritual matter entrusted to the pope for the sake of which the temporal sovereign of a Christian realm must obey the pope as a superior, since in this respect the sovereign needs the spiritual counsel of the pope, just as his subjects do. Otherwise, temporal and spiritual authority would be completely separate and the pope would have no authority at all over Christian princes in temporal matters.

A large part of the controversy on laymen is devoted to the first of these premises: that political authority derives from natural and divine law. This doctrine had constituted one of the main arguments of the neo-Thomist School of Salamanca (the "Second Scholastic"), led by the Dominican Francisco de Vitoria. Vitoria and his pupils argued that government came from the law of God in order to refute the Protestant view that the legitimacy of government depended on God's grace. The neo-Thomists rejected a Protestant reading of Augustine, according to which government was both the punishment and the remedy for humankind after the fall. On the contrary, for them the tendency to live in society was "natural," proceeding from the law of nature, which was both the expression of God's will and the manifestation of human rationality.[15]

An important corollary is that not only pagan princes, but even "wicked men," as Bellarmine puts it in chapter 8, can hold legitimate political authority. It would be unfortunate to assume the contrary, that legitimate authority resides only in sovereigns graced by God: "Since grace and jus-

15. For an introduction to the political views of the neo-Thomists, see Giacon, *La seconda scolastica*, and Skinner, *Foundations*, vol. 2, pp. 135ff. On Vitoria's political theories, see the introduction in Vitoria, *Political Writings*.

tice are entirely secret. . . . if grace were the title to sovereignty, it would follow that no sovereignty would be certain." Another corollary is that every sovereign, including heretics and pagans, issues civil laws that are binding in conscience (*On Laymen,* chap. 11).

Despite differences, sometimes very significant, Bellarmine's account of the origin of temporal authority agrees with Vitoria's arguments; in fact, both doctrines were supposed to be on the Sistine Index. The reason why Sixtus V saw them as dangerous can be found, for example, in chapter 17. In that chapter Bellarmine wrote that once we ground political authority in natural law and affirm that political laws made by any sovereign are binding in conscience, "three errors" may arise. The first is one made by those who, "attributing too much to the magistrates," argue that kings should be "not only the protectors and defenders of religion but also its judges and teachers." Against this error, and referring the reader to his *Controversia de summo Pontifice*—which the pope also wanted to place on the Index—Bellarmine responded that "kings have the first place among Christians as Christian men, that is, as citizens of the earthly city, not as fellow citizens among the saints and servants of God, nor as members of the Church. For in this last respect the bishops have the first place, and the chief is the Supreme Pontiff." While this response was a denial that the Christian Church and the political government were absolutely separate, it allowed a degree of autonomy to the latter with respect to the former and therefore, according to Sixtus, was not forceful enough in defending the pope's supremacy and his *plenitudo potestatis.*

When Bellarmine, by contrast, discussed the other two errors, that the prince should not interfere in religion at all, and that the prince should seek peace and concord between Catholic and Protestant subjects rather than defending the one true religion, he offered responses that the Roman hierarchy did not question but instead embraced as very effective tools in the fight against the heretics.[16] For example, Bellarmine stated strongly not only that no concord can be found or should ever be fostered among Protestants and Catholics (chap. 19), but also that heretical books must be

16. For example, when the Society of Jesus wanted to defend Bellarmine to avoid inclusion of his works in the Index, it used precisely the argument of his effectiveness against heretics: see ACDF, Index, Protocolli DDD, fols. 424r–v at fol. 424v.

eliminated (chap. 20) and that heretics themselves can and should receive spiritual as well as corporeal punishments, including death (chap. 21).

In a sense, then, the controversy on laymen demonstrates both how powerful Bellarmine's theory of the indirect power of the popes was as an argument against heretics and, at the same time, how high a price the political and theological structure of post-Tridentine Catholicism would have to pay to adopt this argument.

## On the Temporal Power of the Pope

King James's Oath of Allegiance of 1606 is an extraordinarily important document. It was certainly meant to split the English Catholic community by separating good loyalist Catholics from traitors, but it also had implications in a much wider context. James's attempt to shift the boundaries of sovereign authority was, in fact, a useful way to strengthen a Protestant king's power over his Catholic subjects. Additionally it could be a handy weapon to strengthen the power of any king, including Catholic ones, against the influence of the pope. James understood the cross-confessional implications of his act, and in the second edition of his *Triplici nodo triplex cuneus,* a defense of his oath, he added a dedicatory epistle to all the sovereigns of Christendom, both Protestant and Catholic.[17] The long and complex controversy over the Oath of Allegiance presented texts that defended or attacked the king from both English and European perspectives, but probably no text had as much impact in Europe as William Barclay's *De potestate Papae,* published posthumously in 1609.

Barclay was a well-known jurist who was born in Scotland in 1546 and lived there until 1571, when he moved to France and remained there until his death in 1608.[18] Barclay's most famous work is the treatise *De regno et regali potestate,* in which he polemicizes against George Buchanan's

17. *A premonition to all most mightie monarches, kings, free princes and states of Christendome* (1st ed. of *Triplici nodo* was published in 1608, even though the date of publication appeared as 1607; 2nd ed., which included the *Premonition,* appeared in 1609). See James VI and I, *Political Works of James I.*

18. For a biography of Barclay see *Oxford Dictionary of National Biography,* s.v. Barclay, William.

theories of the right to resistance, especially rejecting the legitimacy of tyrannicide defended by the *monarchomachs,* a term Barclay coined.[19] For this contribution Barclay was cited by John Locke as the main champion of the divine right of kings.[20]

Barclay's *De potestate Papae* was dedicated to Pope Clement VIII, and Barclay insisted that his criticism came from within the Church. He attacked Bellarmine's fundamental argument that political authority and ecclesiastical authority were at once separate and united in the Christian commonwealth. The separation that Bellarmine had introduced was not at all limited, Barclay suggested, nor had the historical advent of Christianity merged what used to be separate. Indeed, the separation between ecclesiastical and political authority had never been and could never be bridged by the pope's authority because it was of divine law: "One needs to know that those two authorities by which the world is kept in order, that is, the ecclesiastical and the political, are *iure divino* separated and distinguished, so that even if both come from God, each is confined within its own boundaries, and the one cannot legitimately invade the other's territory."[21] No one can dispense in matters of divine law, and not even the pope should presume to transgress boundaries set up by this law. While the primacy of the pope's supreme spiritual authority was not questioned, such authority could not intervene in politics even for the sake of consciences and the attainment of eternal life, for which spiritual punishments and censures were more than enough.

Bellarmine's *On the Temporal Power of the Pope. Against William Barclay* (Rome, 1610) is important for many reasons. First, it elucidates the development of the cardinal's thinking on papal authority in temporal matters and its complex implications. Faced with Barclay's arguments, Bellarmine needed to defend the pope's temporal authority, both direct and indirect,

---

19. *Monarchomachs* (literally, those who fight against monarchs) was a term used pejoratively by Barclay to describe a group of Calvinist political theorists who opposed monarchical absolutism and maintained that a sovereign who had become a tyrant may in certain cases be resisted and even removed. On Barclay's role in the debate against the monarchomachs, see J. H. Burns, "George Buchanan and the Anti-Monarchomachs," in Philipson and Skinner, eds., *Political Discourse,* pp. 3–22.

20. Locke, *Two Treatises of Government,* pp. 419–35.

21. Barclay, *De potestate Papae,* pp. 5–6.

as the one true Catholic doctrine, showing that, despite some disagreement on how this authority played out, Catholic theorists were unanimous in defending its existence. At the same time, however, Bellarmine needed to defend and restate his own views on the indirect character of papal authority against both Barclay and the Catholic theologians who supported the pope's direct authority in temporal matters. Bellarmine needed to do this without undermining the unity that he claimed the Catholic world presented in maintaining that the pope had some authority in the temporal sphere. For this reason, he also needed to clarify and, in certain cases, to modify and retract earlier statements that could open the way for Barclay's antipapalism, as had happened a few years before with Sarpi. Thus, on the one hand Bellarmine retained his theoretical cornerstone regarding the relationship between political and ecclesiastical authority. As he wrote in chapter 7, "The spiritual or ecclesiastical commonwealth and the temporal or political commonwealth are both two and one: two parts, one total, just as the spirit and the flesh joined together at the same time constitute one man, indeed they are one man." On the other hand, pushed by Barclay, Bellarmine was forced, for example, to restate his own opinion on the exemption of the clergy in a more clearly "papalist" sense.[22]

The treatise against Barclay is not only important for an understanding of the evolution of Bellarmine's thinking and its implications for Catholic political theory and theology, but also for the considerations it contains on many theoretical and historical issues that are crucial to seventeenth-century debates over the relationship between the Christian Church and the Christian commonwealth. For example, if Bellarmine was right in stating that the Christian commonwealth merged political and ecclesiastical authority, albeit only partly, why did not Christ himself exercise any political influence? Why did the primitive Church tolerate so many persecutions by heretical emperors if it could depose them? Why would any

---

22. For example, in the *Controversia de clericis,* one of the three parts of the *Controversia de ecclesia militante,* Bellarmine had written that clergymen's exemption from the princes' jurisdiction was not *iure divino* and that the apostles were *de iure* and *de facto* subject to the Roman emperors. He had already modified this opinion in 1599 starting from the Venice edition of the *Controversiae* and again in the 1607 *Recognitio.* In chapter 3 of his treatise against Barclay he was obliged to go over the issue once more by admitting the past mistake and declaring that the apostles were solely *de facto* subject to the Roman rulers, as they had been exempted *de iure* from their jurisdiction.

prince want to become Christian, thus submitting himself to another authority? What was the relation between the pope's spiritual authority and his role as sovereign of a temporal realm? Such questions arise from the core issues of early modern political thought: what is the origin of temporal government, and what is its relationship to spiritual authority? These issues cut across confessional boundaries and override the Catholic/Protestant dichotomy. In this respect, Bellarmine's treatise against Barclay was both the catalyst for and the expression of a series of dramatic events in the political history of Europe that involved precisely the process of theoretical definition and historical development of the early modern nation-states.

Bellarmine's *On the Temporal Power of the Pope. Against William Barclay* appeared soon after the publication of Barclay's treatise, and it caused a great stir not only in Britain but also in the Catholic world, especially in France. The situation of the Catholic Church in France was already difficult owing to strong Gallican and antipapalist influences, but it deteriorated dramatically after King Henri IV of Navarre was murdered on May 14, 1610, by a French Catholic zealot, François Ravaillac. The assassination of the king, moreover, hardened the anti-Jesuit sentiments that were already prominent following the Society's expulsion by Henri in 1594, and these sentiments had not softened after the order's rehabilitation in 1603.[23] Thus Bellarmine's book immediately became a paradigm of the dangers that the supporters of papal authority, especially the Jesuits, represented for the French monarchy in the wake of the assassination of Henri IV. That is why the book was subject to the unusual and potentially dangerous humiliation of being condemned by a sudden and unexpected *arrêt* (ruling) of the Parlement de Paris in the fall of 1610.[24]

## On the Primary Duty of the Supreme Pontiff

The division within the Catholic camp that Bellarmine's theory provoked is indeed one of the clearest indicators of its relevance in early modern Eu-

---

23. On the relationship between the Society of Jesus and the French monarchy in this period, see Nelson, *The Jesuits and the Monarchy.*

24. The engrossing and fast-moving crisis of the fall of 1610 can be followed in the diplomatic dispatches from the Papal Nuncio in Paris to Rome, in ASV, Segreteria di Stato, Francia 54, fols. 147r and following.

rope. Bellarmine's *potestas indirecta* did not simply reaffirm papal authority against the heretical denial of any such authority in spiritual or temporal matters. Rather, it did so in a manner that would allow the pope to retain his preeminence in a European context in which the Protestant churches as well as the increasingly strong European monarchies, both Protestant and Catholic, could jeopardize it. If the pope wanted to maintain supreme spiritual authority, he had to give up direct control over European subjects and concentrate on indirect direction of politics. While the first two texts in this edition clearly show the political and theoretical implications of Bellarmine's theory, the third text deals with Bellarmine's views on the dynamics of power within the Roman Curia. This is a memorandum, *On the Primary Duty of the Supreme Pontiff*, which Bellarmine gave to Pope Clement VIII in late September or early October 1600. It was never published but circulated widely in manuscript form.[25]

The memorandum concerned the need that Bellarmine saw for implementing a key aspect of Church governance that was decided at the Council of Trent, namely the enforcement of bishops' residency in their dioceses. This was necessary, according to the cardinals at Trent, to ensure an effective chain of communication from Rome to the periphery of the Catholic world.[26] Bellarmine framed the issue of episcopal residency in the context of the relationship between the pope's spiritual authority and the papacy's political interests. Bellarmine began his memorandum

25. This text, accompanied by the pope's response, was edited by Le Bachelet in his *Auctarium Bellarminianum*, pp. 513–18. For the dating of the memorandum and more-detailed information on the Roman background of the reception of the text, see Jaitner, "De officio primario Summi Pontificis." Many copies were made of the manuscript. The one on the basis of which Le Bachelet edited the text and from which I have made the translation can be found in APUG 373, fols. 160r–164v. I have located the following additional copies of the text (all with small variations of no relevance for our purpose), and there may be many others: BAV, Barb. Lat. 2628, fols. 58r–61r, Barb. Lat. 1191, fols. 1r–6v, Vat. Lat. 7398, fols. 218r–223v and fols. 226r–234v, Ottoboni Lat. 2416, fols. 42e–47r and fols. 53–61v; ARSI, Opp. Nn.243, vol. 1 fols. 42r–47v and fols. 53r–61v, Opp. Nn.252A, unfoliated; APUG 373, fols. 216r–220r. The manuscript also circulated outside of Italy: a copy, including the pope's response, can be found at the BL, Add. Mss. 48121, fols. 577r–589v.

26. For a good introduction on the discussion over episcopal residency at the Council of Trent and its significance for post-Reformation Catholicism, see Prosperi, *Il Concilio di Trento*, pp. 154ff.; and Hsia, *World of Catholic Renewal*, pp. 111ff.

by stating: "The Supreme Pastor has three roles [*personae*] in the Church of God: he is the pastor and rector of the universal Church, the bishop assigned to the city of Rome, and a temporal prince of an ecclesiastic dominion. But among all his duties the care for the universal church is in first place; indeed this is his first, unique, and greatest duty." One of the ways in which the pope could fulfill such a duty was by making sure that the appointment of bishops was made for spiritual reasons, not for political and economic gain, as "churches should be provided with good prelates, and not prelates with good churches."

Similarly, Bellarmine took issue with the bishops who served as apostolic nuncios and who, because of their international engagements, "have not seen their churches for many years." This practice sacrificed the spiritual interest of the Catholic Church to the political interest of the papacy, and Bellarmine suggested that a shift in priorities on the part of the pope would benefit the spiritual supremacy to which he, as "pastor and rector of the universal Church," was entitled and which should be his primary concern. In the text we have included the pope's far from warm response to each issue raised by Bellarmine, and we see that Clement was not willing to give up his direct political authority in the administration of the Roman Church over his own house, so to speak. "Regarding nuncios," the pope replied, "we think that it is most appropriate that the nuncios are bishops, because they command bishops and they have a greater authority with the princes and peoples."

Bellarmine understood perfectly well that the Church of Rome was not just a spiritual institution, but he thought that the future of its supremacy depended on its spiritual authority and he tried to redefine how much political authority it could afford without losing its spiritual primacy. For the pope, such redefinition might indeed be historically and theoretically necessary, but it was costly for the day-to-day political and administrative interests of the Church. When Bellarmine suggested that a bishopric had become a job to be grabbed rather than a duty to be fulfilled, the pope replied that theory was very well, but the "practical aspects" of running the Catholic Church could not be carried out from spiritual considerations, especially when it came to administering the Church's provinces through the bishops.

The contrast between Clement VIII and Bellarmine in this text complements the other controversies over the theory of the *potestas indirecta* involving Protestant monarchies, Catholic monarchies, and central protagonists of the Roman Curia. This is because Bellarmine's *potestas indirecta* was a profound and far-reaching attempt at reconsidering and reshaping the universal Church's self-understanding and internal operation as well as its universal, "catholic" role with respect both to the Protestant churches and to secular authority. Neither the Roman Church nor the European monarchies embraced Bellarmine's theory wholeheartedly, which is a further testament to the dominant place that Bellarmine's theory occupies in the historical and theoretical process of defining the boundaries between power over bodies and power over consciences.

# NOTES ON THE TRANSLATION

*On Laymen* and *On the Temporal Power of the Pope* are translated from the texts in Bellarmine's *Opera omnia*.[1] For the memorandum to Clement VIII, *On the Primary Duty of the Supreme Pontiff*, I have used Le Bachelet's *Auctarium Bellarminianum* as the text of reference for my translation, as well as the original manuscript used by Le Bachelet and other copies of the manuscript that I located.

Many of Bellarmine's works were reprinted during his lifetime, some several times, and he personally corrected and oversaw the reissuing of some of them, particularly the *Controversiae*. For obvious reasons, I have not accounted for all the corrections from the 1580s to the late 1610s, but since one of the most interesting aspects of Bellarmine's doctrine of the *potestas indirecta* is its development, I have made an exception for the corrections that Bellarmine made in 1608 to a copy of the Venice 1599 edition of the *Controversiae*.[2] Thus, I have identified Bellarmine's modifications concerning the controversy on the laymen in italic text and have indicated the specific reference in the footnotes. I have noted only important conceptual points and changes that could be useful for elucidating his

1. *Ven. Cardinalis Roberti Bellarmini Politiani S.J. Opera omnia*, ed. J. Fèvre, 12 vols. (Paris: Vivès, 1870–74).

2. Bellarmine's corrections, in his own handwriting, to the 1599 edition of the *Controversiae* can be found at the Archive of the Pontificia Università Gregoriana, APUG 1363–1366. Those corrections were made because the cardinal decided to donate that copy of the work to the Roman College, his alma mater, and he wanted the college to have a correct and updated version of the work (the accompanying letter to the rector of the Roman College, dated 12 December 1608, can be found at the beginning of APUG 1363 unfoliated). All those corrections were implemented in subsequent editions of the work.

arguments or their context. I have not noted corrections of typographical errors and the like.

All the translations of Bellarmine's quotations are my own. However, a few of the books from which Bellarmine quoted are available in English, and those English translations have been indicated in the Index of Works Cited by Bellarmine. Whenever possible, I have checked Bellarmine's (and Barclay's) quotations against the modern editions of these works, and I have occasionally found that some of the references given do not match those in the modern editions and that a few typographical errors have crept into the quotations. These references have been silently corrected in the text, and the revised quotations have been inserted in square brackets. The same procedure has been followed in the cases of incorrect biblical references.

Bellarmine, of course, used the Vulgate Bible, but I have taken all biblical quotations from the King James Version, since it is likely to be more familiar to readers of this edition. Many arguments in the present texts involve controversy over translation issues. I have given a detailed explanation in the footnotes for every passage in which a contested reading of particular verses of the Bible was involved.

The intended audience of Bellarmine's texts was prelates and churchmen, all of whom would be familiar with the distinctive formal style used by the church hierarchy in addressing religious controversies. Lengthy parenthetical phrases, complex syntax, copious and often redundant use of quotations, and devotion of entire pages and sections to the listing of sources and authorities were common elements. These elements, far from rendering the texts unnecessarily complex and difficult to read, conferred polemical effectiveness on the works and bestowed scholarly and theological prestige on their authors. I have preserved, whenever possible and appropriate, Bellarmine's style of writing; thus, the syntactical structure of my translation is more complex than is common in current English.

Translating Bellarmine's Latin presented a familiar dilemma of how to balance literal accuracy with readability. I tried to stay close to Bellarmine's Latin, not only to reproduce accurately his arguments but also to give a sense of the tone and format that were characteristic of early modern controversies and that were integral to the arguments made. While modern readers may not share the stylistic preferences of the early modern era, they may nevertheless appreciate the traces of Bellarmine's writing style as cues to a different historical and cultural period.

Bellarmine and his contemporaries buttressed their arguments with long and erudite lists of authors and works. Information on the authors referred to by Bellarmine can be found in the Biographical Notes. Complete publication information for works cited in the footnotes can be found either in the Index of Works Cited by Bellarmine or in the Bibliography of Works Cited by the Editor.

Stefania Tutino

# BIOGRAPHICAL NOTES

These notes include all the authors to whom Bellarmine refers. More information and suggestions for further readings can be found in the *Dictionnaire de droit canonique,* the *Dictionnaire de théologie catholique,* the *Oxford Dictionary of the Christian Church,* and the *Oxford Classical Dictionary.*

Ado of Vienne (d. ca. 875), ecclesiastical historian, author of a chronicle of the world and of a martyrology.

Adrian VI (Adrian of Utrecht) (1459–1523), pope; Cardinal Inquisitor of Aragón, Navarre, Castile, and León; viceroy to Spain for Emperor Charles V; and author of a commentary on Lombard's *Sententiae* and a text of *Quodlibeta.*

Aegidius Bellamera (Giles de Bellemère) (ca. 1342–1407), canonist and bishop of Avignon, author of various commentaries on the canon law.

Aerius of Pontus (fourth century), Christian presbyter who questioned some Christian tenets and practices such as the primacy of bishops over laymen and the prayers for the dead.

Agatho (d. 681), pope; under his pontificate the Sixth Ecumenical Council was held in Constantinople in 680–81.

Agrippa von Nettesheim, Heinrich Cornelius (1486–1535), German humanist scholar and author of *De vanitate scientiarum,* a work skeptical of humanistic and historical studies.

Aimoinus of Fleury (tenth century), monk and author of a history of the Franks.

Alexander of Hales (d. 1245), Franciscan theologian and author of several works, including an unfinished *Summa universae theologiae.*

Alexander of St. Elpidio (d. 1326), Augustinian monk and author of a number of theological and ecclesiological treatises in which he defended the pope's primacy over the Church with arguments very similar to those of his fellow Augustinian, Giles of Rome, whose work he often referred to.

Alexius I Comnenus (ca. 1048–1118), Byzantine emperor who participated in the first crusade.

Alfonso Alvarez Guerrero (d. 1574), Portuguese jurist who served in Italy under Charles V, ending his legal career as president of the supreme tribunal in Naples before quitting it to become a priest and, in 1572, bishop of Monopoli. In a series of important works he attacked the authority of the pope in temporal matters and defended the superiority of the council over the pope; these writings included the *Thesaurus Christianae religionis* and *De modo et ordine generalis concilii celebrandi.*

Almain, Jacques (ca. 1480–1515), theologian at the University of Paris and author of several works on ecclesiology (*De potestate ecclesiastica et laica, Libellus de auctoritate ecclesiae, Quaestio resumptiva*) and a commentary on the fourth book of Peter Lombard's *Sententiae.*

Alvarus Pelagius (ca. 1275–1352), Franciscan friar, bishop of Silves in Portugal, and scholar of canon and civil law. His works include *De statu et planctu ecclesiae* and *Speculum regum* dedicated to King Alfonso XI of Castile.

Ambrose (ca. 340–97), bishop of Milan from 374. One of the most influential Fathers of the Church and often quoted for his engagement in his pastoral duty, he wrote extensive homilies on the Bible, treatises on ecclesiastical and ecclesiological matters, and works against Arianism and on ethics, among them *De officiis ministrorum,* from which Bellarmine often quotes.

Anastasius, Flavius (ca. 430–518), Byzantine emperor.

Anastasius II, pope between 496 and 498.

Anselm of Canterbury (d. 1109), saint and Father of the Church. He was a prominent theologian and author of many theological, philosophical, and devotional treatises and is well known for his "ontological proof" of God's existence.

Anselm of Lucca (ca. 1035–86), bishop, canonist, and author of exegetical works. He supported vigorously Pope Gregory VII against Emperor Henry IV.

Anthimus (sixth century), patriarch of Constantinople and a supporter of the Monophysite heresy.

Antonino of Florence (1389–1459), archbishop of Florence, saint, and a Dominican theologian. He was the author of *Summa theologica moralis* and other Scholastic works, as well as a historical work, the *Chronicon,* from the beginning of the world until the year 1360.

Antonius Cordubensis (d. 1578), Spanish Franciscan theologian and author of *Quaestionarium theologicum.*

Apelles (second century), adherent of Gnosticism.

Aquinas, Thomas. *See* Thomas Aquinas.

Aretius, Benedictus (1522–74), Protestant theologian who wrote in support of Valentino Gentile's execution.

Aristotle (384–22 B.C.), the most authoritative ancient Greek philosopher during the Middle Ages as the result of Aquinas's interpretation of Aristotle's philosophy. Aristotle's *Politics* became the basis of the Scholastic understanding of the nature, origin, and aim of the political commonwealth.

Arius (d. 336), heresiarch and founder of Arianism, a heresy that refused to consider the Son to be of the same essence and substance as the Father.

Astesanus from Asti, or Astiensis (d. 1330), Franciscan monk and author of *Summa de casibus,* or *Summa Astensis,* a collection of cases of conscience containing many references to canon and civil law and meant to serve as a manual for priests.

Athanasius (d. 373), bishop of Alexandria, saint, and Father of the Church; he was the author of many anti-Arian works.

Aufreri, Etienne (Stephanus Aufrerius) (ca. 1458–1511), jurist, president of the inquests in the parliament of Toulouse, and author of a number of legal and ecclesiological works.

Augustine (354–430), bishop of Hippo beginning in 396 and Doctor of the Church. His *Confessions* is often considered the first autobiography in Western literature. His writings include more than one hundred treatises and commentaries, more than two hundred letters, and more than five hundred sermons. Among his works the *De civitate Dei,* a historical, philosophical, and theological reflection on the relation between temporal and secular authority, the meaning of history, and the significance of pagan philosophy and its relationship with Christian theology, is especially important. Among Augustine's many contributions to Christian thought is his theology of grace, with influenced Luther and Calvin. Bellarmine engaged deeply with Augustinianism and its view on grace, particularly when dealing with the delicate controversy *de auxiliis,* an issue that pitted members of Bellarmine's own order, the Society of Jesus, against members of the Dominican Order.

Baconthorpe, John (Bacon) (d. 1346), an English Carmelite theologian and the author of numerous works, including a series of commentaries on the Gospel and a relatively influential commentary on Lombard's *Sententiae.*

Baldus de Ubaldis (ca. 1327–1400), professor of law in Pisa, Perugia, Florence, and Pavia, where he also taught canon law. He was one of the most important jurists of his time and wrote a number of commentaries on canon and Roman law.

Balsamon, Theodore (twelfth century), Byzantine canonist.

Bañez, Domingo (1528–1604), Dominican theologian and pupil of Francisco de Vitoria. He was professor of theology at the University of Salamanca, and his works include a commentary on Aquinas's *Summa.* He took part in the controversy *de auxiliis* against Molina.

Baronius, Cesare (1538–1607), cardinal and author of the influential *Annales Ecclesiastici,* covering up to the year 1198. This work was directed against the "Magdeburg Centuries" (1559–74), the first universal Protestant church history (cf. Matthias Flacius Illyricus).

Bartolus from Sassoferrato (ca. 1313–57), professor of law in Pisa and Perugia and one of the most influential jurists of his time. He wrote commentaries on almost the entire *Corpus iuris civilis.*

Basil the Great (ca. 330–79), saint, bishop, and Doctor of the Church. He was the author of many exegetical, moral, and homiletic works.

Bernard of Clairvaux (ca. 1090–ca. 1153), saint and author of, among other writings, numerous sermons and a small treatise titled *De consideratione,* on the duty of the pope, which contained many passages that Bellarmine and other theologians used as key references in works on papal authority.

Bernold of Constance (d. ca. 1100), historian and continuator of Hermann Contractus's chronicle.

Beza, Théodore (1519–1605), French reformer, collaborator, and successor of Calvin in Geneva. In his *De hereticis a magistratu puniendis,* a defense of Calvin's execution of Servetus, and in *De iure magistratum,* Beza offers an important exposition of the Calvinist theory of resistance.

Bibliander, Theodorus (Theodor Buchmann) (1506–64), a Swiss reformer and famous linguist, who published a Hebrew grammar, a Latin translation of the Koran, and works of biblical exegesis.

Biel, Gabriel (ca. 1420–95), professor of theology and author of an influential commentary on Peter Lombard's *Sententiae.* Biel was well known as a representative of Nominalist thought.

Biondo, Flavio (1392–1463), Italian humanist and historian who authored a number of important works, including a trilogy on Roman history and architecture and *Historiarum decades,* a history of the world since the end of the Roman Empire.

Bonaventure (1221–74), saint and theologian of Augustinian inclinations. He wrote an extensive commentary on Peter Lombard's *Sententiae,* together with many other mystical, theological, and ecclesiological works. His writings, especially the mystical ones, have been translated repeatedly, but some appear to be lost.

Boniface (ca. 675–754), saint and archbishop of Mainz. He was a Christian missionary in the Frankish empire and became known as the "Apostle of Germany."

Boniface VIII (ca. 1235–1303), pope (1294–1303) and key figure in the question of papal authority. During his controversy with King Philip the Fair of France, the pope issued a series of bulls, such as the *Unam sanctam,* which became crucial for the following debate over the pope's plenitude of power. Boniface's concern with canon law resulted in a collection of *Decretales,* the *Liber sextus,* to be added to the five books of Gregory IX (*Decretales Gregorii IX,* 1234).

Bozio, Francesco (d. 1635), Oratorian Father under whose name the treatise *De temporali ecclesiae monarchia* appeared in 1602, although much of the work must be attributed to Tommaso Bozio, his brother and fellow Oratorian. This treatise was one of the most vigorous assertions of the absolute authority of the pope in both temporal and spiritual matters.

Brenz, Johannes (1499–1570), one of the leaders of the Reformation in Germany.

Burchard of Ursperg (d. ca. 1230), monk and author of a well-known chronicle, which was for a long time attributed to Konrad of Lichtenau, his successor as abbot of Ursperg.

Cajetan (Tommaso de Vio) (1469–1534), cardinal and general of the Dominicans. Cajetan was a well-known theologian whose works included a commentary on Aquinas's *Summa,* which became a classic reference for Scholastic theologians.

Cassander, George (1513–66), Flemish humanist and promoter of religious peace between Protestants and Catholics. His anonymous treatise, *De officio pii viri,* which advocated religious toleration, pleased neither Catholics nor Protestants.

Castaldi, Ristoro (Restaurus Castaldus) (d. 1564), a professor of law in Perugia and Bologna.

Castro, Alfonso de (ca. 1495–1558), Franciscan friar, jurist, theologian, and author of many works, including *De iusta haereticorum punitione.*

Cedrenus, George (eleventh century), Byzantine historian and author of a chronicle covering the period from the creation to his own times.

Charlemagne (ca. 742–814), king of the Franks. He was crowned Holy Roman Emperor by Pope Leo III on Christmas day in the year 800. The role of the pope in the transfer of the empire, the *translatio imperii,* from Rome to the Franks, was a key polemical weapon in the medieval and early modern discussion of papal authority in temporal matters.

Chrysostom, John (ca. 347–407), one of the most influential doctors and preachers in the Greek Church, becoming bishop of Constantinople in 398. He was a prolific writer, and Bellarmine quotes often from his numerous homilies or commentaries on the New Testament (more than fifty of those homilies were dedicated to the Acts of the Apostles).

Cicero, Marcus Tullius (106–43 B.C.), philosopher and orator. Cicero's eclectic moral and political philosophy was much quoted by Christian authors in Bellarmine's time, and humanist scholars regarded his style as achieving one of the highest peaks of Latin prose.

Clarus, Julius (Giulio Claro) (ca. 1525–75), Italian humanist and jurist, an expert in civil and penal law.

Cochlaeus, Johann (1479–1552), prolific Catholic controversialist.

Conradus Brunus (Konrad Braun) (ca. 1491–1563), Catholic theologian and canonist, who wrote a number of anti-Protestant works. His *De legationibus* was a treatise on the legal obligations and rights of ambassadors.

Constantine the Great (ca. 280–337), Roman emperor who converted to Christianity and whose Edict of Milan, or Edict of Constantine, promulgated in 313, allowed Christians freedom of worship. The "Donation of Constantine" was supposed to be a document by which the emperor gave to Pope Sylvester I temporal authority over Italy, and as such it was widely quoted in the medieval debate over the pope's plenitude of power and his rights in temporal matters. Lorenzo Valla, an Italian humanist (ca. 1405–57), proved the document to be a forgery. Today scholarship is able to date the forged document to a period between the second half of the eighth century and the first half of the ninth.

Covarrubias y Leiva, Diego de (1512–77), Spanish jurist and theologian, pupil of Vitoria and professor at Salamanca. He was the author of many ecclesiological and theological treatises.

Cujas, Jacques (also known as "Jurisconsultus") (1522–90), an important French jurist and author of a commentary on Roman law.

Cyprian (d. 258), saint and bishop of Carthage, whose works include numerous epistles and a treatise against Novatian titled *De Catholicae Ecclesiae unitate*.

Cyprianus Benetus Aragonensis (d. 1522), a Dominican professor of theology and author of several theological and ecclesiological treatises.

Cyril of Alexandria (d. 444), Doctor of the Church and author of many works, including numerous commentaries on the Old and New Testaments and various theological and apologetic treatises and sermons.

Diocletian, Aurelius Valerius (ca. 245–312), Roman emperor who in 303 ordered the destruction of the Christian churches and thus started a bitter persecution.

Dionysius the Areopagite, an Athenian whom Paul converted to Christianity (Acts 17:34) and to whom was attributed a series of theological treatises. This attribution has been discarded: the works have been dated to between the end of the fifth century and the beginning of the sixteenth century, and the author is now known as "pseudo-Dionysius." Most often quoted by medieval and early modern theologicians are his works *De coelesti hierarchia* and *De ecclesiastica hierarchia*.

Dionysius of Alexandria (d. 265), bishop and Father of the Church, mainly known to us through Eusebius, which see.

Dionysius (Denys), the Carthusian (ca. 1402–71), monk and theologian, author of numerous works ranging from mystical writings to ecclesiological treatises and exegetical commentaries on the Bible.

Dodechinus (end of twelfth century to beginning of thirteenth century), continuator of Marianus Scotus's chronicle.

Domitian (Titus Flavius Domitianus) (51–96), Roman emperor and a fierce persecutor of the Christians.

Driedo, John (ca. 1480–1535), theologian at the University of Louvain and author of, among other works, *De gratia et libero arbitrio, De libertate Christiana,* and *De ecclesiasticis scripturis et dogmatibus.*

Duns Scotus, John (ca. 1265–1308), Scottish-born Franciscan theologian who taught in England, France, and Germany. His philosophy departed from Aristotelianism in important points and embraced many Augustinian elements.

Durand, Guillaume (Durandus) (ca. 1235–96), bishop of Mende and author of numerous theological, liturgical, and juridical works, including the *Rationale divinorum officiorum* and the *Speculum iudiciale.*

Durandus of St. Pourçain (Durandus de Sancto Porciano) (ca. 1270–1334), Dominican theologian of Nominalist tendencies and author of *De origine iurisdictionis,* a treatise supporting the *plenitudo potestatis* of the pope.

Einhard (ca. 775–840), courtier and historian whose works include a biography of Charlemagne.

Epiphanius of Salamis (d. ca. 403), bishop and author of many theological and apologetic works against the heresies of his time, in particular *Panarion* ("cabinet of medicine"), a multivolume catalog of about eighty heresies.

Eucherius (d. ca. 449), saint and theologian; author of various homilies and theological works.

Eunomius (fourth century), disciple of Aetius and founder of Eunomianism, a heretical sect that shared many tenets with Arianism.

Eusebius (ca. 260–340), bishop of Caesarea, a historian, and a prolific commentator on the Bible. His best-known works, which Bellarmine refers to often, are *De vita Constantini, Historia ecclesiastica* (translated into Latin by Rufinus), and the *Chronicle,* partially translated into Latin by Jerome.

Eustathius of Sebaste (fourth century), monk involved in the Arian and semi-Arian debates.

Eutyches (fifth century), heresiarch after whom is named the Euthychian or Monophysite heresy. This heresy rejected Nestorianism's insistence on Christ's double person and held that Christ's human nature was incorporated by his divine nature so as to almost disappear.

Evagrius (d. after 594), called "Scholasticus" to distinguish him from Evagrius Ponticus, a fourth-century author of important ascetical works. He wrote a *Historia ecclesiastica,* which was intended as a continuation of Eusebius's *Historia.*

Faber Runcinus, Johannes (Jean Faure) (d. ca. 1340), jurist and author of a series of commentaries on Justinian's *Institutiones* and of a *Breviarium* on Justinian's Code.

Felino Maria Sandeo (Felinus) (ca. 1444–1503), professor of canon law in Ferrara and Pisa and author of a series of commentaries on the *Liber extra* (cf. Raymond of Peñafort).

Fitzralph, Richard (Armachanus) (ca. 1295–1360), archbishop of Armagh and author of *Summa in quaestionibus Armenorum,* a treatise against Greek and Armenian doctrines, and of *De pauperie salvatoris,* on poverty.

Gaguin, Robert (ca. 1433–1501), French humanist and historian of France.

Galen (second century), Greek physician and natural philosopher.

Gambari, Pietro Andrea (Gambarinus) (1480–1528), professor of canon law in Bologna and author of several juridical treatises.

Gaudentius (end of fourth century to beginning of fifth century), Donatist bishop of Thamugada.

Gelasius I (d. 496), pope and saint, prolific author whose letters are frequently referred to by Bellarmine.

Gellius, Aulus (second century), Roman author of the multivolume *Noctes Atticae*, an eclectic collection of anecdotes and miscellaneous information.

Génebrard, Gilbert (1535–97), Benedictine monk and professor of Hebrew in Paris who first opposed, then endorsed, the accession of Henri of Navarre to the throne of France. He was the author of numerous works of ecclesiology and exegesis, including an edition of the works of Origen.

Gennadius (late sixth century), Roman nobleman who was appointed prefect of the African province of the Roman empire by Emperor Mauritius and who was one of Gregory I's correspondents.

Gentile, Giovanni Valentino (1520–66), Italian humanist who propagated antitrinitarian doctrines in central and eastern Europe. He was executed in Berne.

Geoffrey of Viterbo (ca. 1120–96), member of the court of Emperor Henry VI and author of historical works and a *Speculum regum,* dedicated to Henry and his father, Frederick.

Gerson, Jean (1363–1429), theologian and chancellor of the University of Paris. He was a supporter of the conciliarist theory at the Council of Constance and is the author of *De potestate Ecclesiae, De unitate Ecclesiae, De vita spirituali animae,* and other works.

Giles of Rome (Aegidius Romanus) (Egidio Colonna) (ca. 1247–1316), Augustinian monk, general of Augustinian Order (1292–95), and professor of theology at Paris. He was closely linked to Pope Boniface VIII, who conferred on him the title of archbishop of Bourges and whose political and theological positions Giles defended in *De regimine principum* and *De ecclesiastica potestate,* which became a key reference for the following debates on papal authority.

Giovanni of Anagni (d. ca. 1457), professor of canon law in Bologna and author of influential commentaries on the *Decretales*.

Glycas, Michael (twelfth century), Byzantine historian who wrote a chronicle from the creation to the death of Emperor Alexius Comnenus.

Gratian (ca. 359–83), Roman emperor.

Gratian (d. before 1150), jurist from Bologna and author of a compilation of texts known as the *Concordia discordantium canonum,* or *Decretum Gratiani,* which constitutes the bulk of canon law.

Gregory I (Gregory the Great) (ca. 540–604), pope from 590 onward, was extremely influential in asserting the religious, political, and social power of the Church after the fall of the Western Roman Empire. He was instrumental in converting the king of the Lombards. He was the author of many commentaries on the Bible, especially the much cited *Moralia* on the Book of Job, and of an equally well-known treatise on the duties of bishops, *De cura pastorali* or *Liber regulae pastoralis.*

Gregory VII (Hildebrand of Soana) (ca. 1020–85), pope from 1073 and protagonist in the investiture controversy against Emperor Henry IV. He was also the supposed author of the *Dictatus papae* (1075), a series of propositions that strongly assert the preeminence of the pope both within the Church and with respect to the political authority, and of numerous epistles.

Gregory of Nazianzus (ca. 325–89), saint and Doctor of the Church. His works include several orations which Bellarmine quotes often, as well as poetic works.

Gregory of Tours (ca. 538–ca. 94), saint and bishop. He wrote theological and historical works; among the latter his *Historia Francorum* is often quoted by Bellarmine.

Gregory of Valencia (ca. 1540–1603), Jesuit professor of theology in Ingolstadt and Rome and author of a very influential commentary on Aquinas's *Summa,* the *Commentariorum theologicorum tomi quatuor* (1591). He was closely involved in the controversy *de auxiliis,* as the chosen spokesman for the Jesuit position in the early phase of the controversy.

Henry II (972–1024), Holy Roman Emperor and saint.

Henry IV (1050–1108), Holy Roman Emperor excommunicated by Gregory VII in 1076 in the context of the investiture controversy.

Henry of Ghent (d. 1293), a Scholastic philosopher and theologian whose many works include a *Summa* (incomplete) and a series of *Quodlibeta.*

Hermann Contractus (1013–54), monk and author of a universal chronicle as well as a variety of theological, poetical, and mathematical works.

Hervé de Nedellec (Hervaeus Natalis) (ca. 1260–1323), general of the Dominicans and author of the hierocratic treatise *De potestate ecclesiastica papali.*

Hessels, Jean (Joannes from Louvain) (1522–66), theologian and author of many works of controversy against Protestants, as well as a catechism.

Hilary of Poitiers (d. 368), bishop and saint, vigorous opponent of Arianism and author of several exegetical and apologetic works.

Hincmar (ca. 806–82), archbishop of Reims and author of several theological, devotional, and historical works.

Holcot, Robert (ca. 1290–1349), English Dominican theologian and author of a well-known commentary on the Book of Wisdom.

Honorius (d. 423), Roman emperor. He was the son of Theodosius I, who, at his death in 395, divided the empire into western and eastern parts and gave Honorius the western part.

Hosius of Cordova (ca. 256–358), bishop and one of the most important and vocal opponents of the Arian heresy although he was rumored to have slipped into philo-Arian positions late in life.

Hostiensis (Henricus de Segusio) (d. 1271), cardinal bishop of Ostia and professor of canon law in Paris. He was the author of a number of theological and juridical works, including a *Summa* and a series of commentaries on canon law.

Hugh of St. Victor (ca. 1096–1141), monk and theologian whose works include *De sacramentis Christianae fidei,* in which he explained his theory that the *ecclesia* should be distinguished from the order of the clergy, as an organism composed of both laymen and clergy, just as man is composed of body and soul. As the soul must rule the body, so in the *ecclesia* the ecclesiastical part must rule, and even establish, the secular part.

Hydatius (fourth century), bishop of Mérida and one of the opponents of the heretic Priscillian.

Illyricus, Matthias Flacius (1520–75), Lutheran reformer and one of the most influential historians among the Centuriators of Magdeburg, authors of the *Ecclesiastica historia* (the "Magdeburg Centuries").

Innocent I (d. 417), pope and author of many epistles to which Bellarmine often refers.

Innocent IV (Sinibaldo Fieschi) (d. 1254), pope and professor of canon law in Bologna. He was the author of a very influential commentary on the five books of Gregory's *Decretales.*

Irenaeus (late second to early third centuries), saint and Father of the Church. He wrote many works in Greek, of which only a few are extant in their entirety in later Latin translations; the rest survive only in fragments reported by others.

Isidore of Seville (ca. 560–636), saint and bishop of Seville. He wrote a widely popular *Etymologiae,* an encyclopedic work arranged as a dictionary on several branches of knowledge.

Isidoro from Milan (Isidoro Isolani) (d. 1528), Dominican theologian and pupil of Silvestro Mazzolini da Prierio, prolific author of theological and ecclesiological works, and of the *Revocatio Martini Lutheri Augustiniani ad Sanctam sedem,* published anonymously in Cremona in 1519.

Ithacius (fourth century), bishop of Ossanoba and opponent of Priscillian.

Ivo of Chartres (ca. 1040–1115), saint and celebrated canonist and theologian. His works include the *Decretum* and the *Panormia,* which were the key references for canon law until Gratian.

James VI and I (1566–1625), king of Scotland as James VI, and, from 1603, king of England and Ireland as James I. He promulgated the 1606 Oath of Allegiance and defended it in his own writings, in particular the *Triplici nodo, triplex cuneus,* to which Bellarmine responded on several occasions.

Jean de Selve (Joannis de Selva) (1475–1520), influential politician and expert on canon and civil law. He was the author of *De beneficio* (1504), often reprinted during the sixteenth and seventeenth centuries.

Jean Quintin (Haeduus) (ca. 1509–61), professor of canon law at the university of Paris and author of several commentaries on the *Corpus iuris canonici.*

Jerome (ca. 340–420), saint and Father of the Church. He wrote the Latin translation of the Bible known as *Vulgata,* which the Council of Trent reasserted as the only allowed version of the Bible. Famously gifted as a linguist, he wrote many commentaries on the Bible and treatises against heresies, especially Pelagianism.

Jerome of Prague (1379–1416), follower of Jan Hus and burned with him at the Council of Constance.

Johannes Andreae (ca. 1270–1348), famous jurist and professor of both canon and civil law in Bologna.

John of Capistrano (1385–1456), saint, Franciscan friar, and author of many ecclesiological and theological treatises, including *De auctoritate papae,* often referred to by Bellarmine.

John the Deacon (Johannes Hymonides) (ninth century), monk and deacon of the Roman Church, author of a biography of Gregory the Great.

Josephus, Flavius (ca. 37–100), Jewish historian and author of *Jewish Antiquities, Jewish War,* and *Against Apion,* all written in Greek.

Jovian (ca. 330–64), Roman emperor, successor of Julian the Apostate.

Julian, Flavius Claudius, "the Apostate" (d. 363), Roman emperor who abandoned the Christian religion and attempted to restore paganism in Rome.

Justinus, Marcus Junianus (third century), Roman historian, author of the *Epitoma historiarum Philippicarum.*

Karlstadt (Carlstadt) (Andreas Bodenstein) (1486–1541), Protestant reformer and erstwhile collaborator of Luther, who soon disagreed with important Lutheran doctrinal and liturgical points. For example, Karlstadt denied the real presence of Christ in the Eucharist and rejected infant baptism.

Krantz, Albert (ca. 1450–1517), German Catholic historian whose works include the well-known *Hamburgenses historiae* and *Metropolis, sive historia de ecclesiis sub Carolo Magno in Saxonia.*

Lambert of Hersfeld (ca. 1024–d. after 1077), Benedictine monk and historian, author of a chronicle of the world from the Creation to the year 1077 and of a history of Germany.

Latomus, Jacobus (Jacques Masson) (1475–1544), professor of theology at Louvain and opponent of Erasmus against whose theology and philological method he wrote *De trium linguarum et studii theologici ratione dialogus* (1519). He wrote several other theological works against Protestant doctrine and ecclesiology.

Ledesma, Martin (d. ca. 1575), Dominican professor of theology at the University of Coimbra, pupil of Vitoria, and author of an influential commentary on Peter Lombard's *Sententiae*.

Leo I (Leo the Great) (d. 461), pope and saint, author of numerous sermons to which Bellarmine often refers.

Leo Ostiensis (Marsicanus) (ca. 1045–1115), Benedictine monk and bishop of Ostia, author of a chronicle of the monastery of Monte Cassino.

Liberatus of Carthage (sixth century), author of an important anti-Nestorian work, *Breviarium causae Nestorianorum*.

Licinius, Galerius Valerius (ca. 260–325), Roman emperor, defeated by Constantine in 314.

Livy (Titus Livius) (59 B.C.–17 A.D.), one of the most influential Roman historians, thanks to his history of Rome from its foundation to his own days, *Ab urbe condita*. He was much admired during the Renaissance and subsequently, and the subject of Machiavelli's *Discorsi sopra la prima deca di Tito Livio*.

Louis IX (1214–70), king of France and saint, usually known as St. Louis.

Louis the Pious (778–840), king of the Franks and Holy Roman Emperor.

Lucius (second century), semilegendary Christian king of Britain.

Marcellus of Ancyra (fourth century), bishop and great opponent of Arianism.

Marcian (d. 457), Eastern Roman Emperor from 450.

Marcion (second century), founder of the heretical sect of Marcionites. Rejecting the Old Testament, they believed that Jesus was not the son of the God of the ancient Covenant, but of the "good" God of the Gospel.

Marianus Scotus (ca. 1028–ca. 1082), Irish monk and author of a *Chronicon* covering the period from the beginning of the Christian era until 1082.

Martin of Tours (ca. 316–97), saint, bishop, and vigorous opponent of the Priscillian heresy.

Martinus of Lodi (Garatus) (mid-fifteenth century), professor in Pavia and Siena, author of several treatises on both civil and canon law.

Masson, Jean Papire (Papirius Massonius) (1544–1611), French historian and author of a history of France titled *Annales,* in four volumes, published in 1578, and a series of biographies of popes, *De vitis Episcoporum urbis,* censored by Bellarmine in 1592.

Matthew Paris (ca. 1200–ca. 1259), Benedictine monk, author of *Chronica maiora,* a history of the world from creation to the year of his death.

Mayron, Francis (ca. 1280–1327), Franciscan theologian, pupil of Duns Scotus, author of many theological treatises and a commentary on Peter Lombard's *Sententiae.*

Mazzolini da Prierio, Silvestro (Sylvester Prierias) (ca. 1460–1523), Dominican theologian and Master of the Sacred Palace, author of an influential *Summa Sylvestrina.*

Melanchthon, Philip (1497–1560), one of Luther's main collaborators and a well-known humanist scholar. He was the author of the *Loci communes* (1521), commonly considered the first systematic exposition of Lutheran theology. He also drafted the Augsburg Confession of 1530.

Miguel de Aninyon (Aniñón) (d. 1596), professor of law and author of the *Tractatus de unitate ovilis et pastoris,* published in 1578.

Molina, Luis de (1535–1600), Jesuit and one of the most important and controversial theologians of his day. His works include *Concordia liberi arbitrii cum gratiae donis* (1588), which stirred the controversy *de auxiliis;* a commentary on several parts of Aquinas's *Summa;* and *De iustitia et iure,* a classic text of neo-Thomist political and moral theology, only published in full posthumously.

Montserrat, Guillem (late fifteenth century), Catalan jurist and author of a historical work, *De successione regum.*

Nauclerus, Johannes (ca. 1425–1510), historian and jurist, author of a chronicle covering the period from the Creation to 1500 by generations.

Navarrus (Martin de Azpilcueta) (ca. 1491–1586), jurist and theologian, author of a series of commentaries on canon law and an influential manual for confessors, *Manual de confessores y penitentes* (1560).

Nestorius (fifth century), heresiarch and founder of Nestorianism, a heresy that implies some distinction between the divine Christ and the human Christ.

Netter, Thomas (Waldensis) (ca. 1370–1430), Carmelite friar, author of *Doctrinale antiquitatum fidei catholicae* against John Wyclif.

Nicephorus Callistus (late thirteenth century to early fourteenth century), Byzantine historian, author of *Historia ecclesiastica,* in eighteen books, covering until 610.

Nicholas of Cusa (Cusanus) (ca. 1401–64), philosopher and theologian. Initially he supported the conciliarist view but later changed his mind and accepted the office of papal legate (1440–47). In 1449 he was appointed a cardinal by Pope Nicholas V.

Nicholas of Lyra (ca. 1270–1340), Franciscan friar and biblical exegete. His *Postillae* represents a key reference for literal biblical exegesis.

Oecolampadius (Johann Heusegen) (1482–1521), Swiss reformer close to Zwingli's position on the Eucharist and a gifted humanist scholar who collaborated with Erasmus on Erasmus's edition of the New Testament.

Optatus of Milevis (fourth century), saint and bishop who vigorously opposed the Donatist heresy with a treatise written as a response to Parmenianus, the Donatist bishop of Carthage.

Origen, Adamantius (ca. 185–ca. 255), Father of the Church and important Neoplatonist interpreter of Christian doctrine, some of whose ideas were later declared heretical by the Christian Church. Origen's works include *De principiis,* extensive commentaries on the Bible, and numerous homilies.

Otto I (Otto the Great) (912–73), Holy Roman Emperor.

Otto of Freising (ca. 1111–58), bishop and historian, author of a history of the world from creation to 1146 and of a history of Emperor Frederick I.

Panvinio, Onofrio (1530–68), monk of the Order of the Augustinian Hermits and author of numerous works, including a revision and continuation of Platina's *Liber de vita Christi et omnium pontificum.*

Parmenianus (fourth century), Donatist leader, successor of Donatus as bishop of Carthage.

Paulus Aemilius Veronensis (Paolo Emilio da Verona) (ca. 1455–1529), Italian historian and author of a history of the French kings titled *De rebus gestis Francorum,* left unfinished.

Paulus Diaconus (Paul the Deacon) (ca. 720–99), a Benedictine monk and historian. He was the author of the *Historia gentis Longobardorum* and *Historia Romana,* which run up to the time of Justinian.

Paulus Orosius (b. ca. 380–d. after 418), Christian apologist and historian. He wrote, among other works, a *Historia adversus paganos* that was supposed to complement Augustine's *De civitate Dei.*

Pelagius (late fourth to early fifth centuries), founder of the heresy of Pelagianism, which denied that original sin had made it impossible for humans to attain salvation without grace, but assumed that even after Adam's fall human will was perfectly capable of wanting and accomplishing good. Pelagianism was vigorously attacked by Augustine, among others.

Peter Lombard (ca. 1100–1160), professor of theology at Paris, author of four books of *Sententiae* that represented a summa of Catholic theology. Before Aquinas's *Summa,* Lombard's *Sententiae* was the standard textbook of theology.

Petilianus (late fourth to early fifth centuries), Donatist bishop.

Petrus Bertrandus (Pierre Bertrand) (ca. 1280–1349), cardinal bishop of Autun and professor of canon and civil law in Avignon, Montpellier, Paris, and Orléans; author of several works of theology and jurisprudence, including *De iurisdictione ecclesiastica et saeculari, De origine iurisdictionis,* and a commentary on the *Liber sextus.*

Petrus de Ancharano (ca. 1333–1416), canon lawyer and jurist, pupil of Baldus de Ubaldis, and author of many commentaries on the canon law.

Philippus Caesar (Philip the Arab) (third century), Roman emperor (244–49); according to some Christian historians, including Eusebius, the first Christian emperor.

Pierre de la Palude (Paludanus) (ca. 1277–1342), patriarch of Jerusalem and Dominican theologian and canonist, whose works include the well-known *De causa immediata ecclesiasticae potestatis,* in which he defended the *plenitudo potestatis* of the pope.

Pietro del Monte (ca. 1390–1457), Venetian bishop of Brescia and humanist scholar, author of many ecclesiological works.

Pighius, Albert (Pigghe) (ca. 1490–1542), theologian and mathematician, whose works include a series of treatises in support of papal authority against Marsilius of Padua and a ten-volume treatise titled *De libero hominis arbitrio et divina gratia.*

Platina (Bartolomeo Sacchi) (1421–81), Italian humanist and historian, author of the well-known *Liber de vita Christi et omnium pontificum,* under the patronage of Pope Sixtus IV.

Pole, Reginald (1500–1558), cardinal and papal legate in England, a leading Catholic reformer and author of an important work on the role of the pope, *De summo pontifice.*

Priscillian (fourth century), heretic who gave the name to Priscillianism, a series of heretical doctrines under Gnostic influence.

Protagoras of Abdera (fifth century B.C.), Greek sophist and protagonist in two Platonic dialogues, the *Protagoras* and the *Theaetetus;* commonly considered the leading example of the Sophists' ethical relativism and religious agnosticism.

Raymond le Roux (Rufus) (sixteenth century), expert on canon and civil law and jurist at the parliament in Paris, author of a treatise against Du Moulin (1553).

Raymond of Peñafort (ca. 1175–1275), general of the Dominicans and a great canonist. He was in charge of the commission set up by Pope Gregory IX to complement and correct the main collection of Decretals, the *Quinque compilationes antiquae,* and he collected and edited the *Liber extra* of decretals, the resulting work known as *Decretales Gregorii IX* of 1234 (cf. Boniface VIII). He was also the author of an important manual for confessors titled *Summa de poenitentia, sive casuum.*

Regino of Prüm (d. ca. 915), Benedictine abbot and author of a universal chronicle.

Richard of Middleton (Ricardus de Mediavilla) (d. ca. 1305), Franciscan theologian and author of an influential commentary on Peter Lombard's *Sententiae.*

Roger of Hoveden (d. ca. 1201), chronicler and one of the king's clerks under Henry II. His *Annals* covered the history of England from 732 to 1201.

Rufinus, Tyrannius (Rufinus of Aquileia) (ca. 345–410), theologian best known as translator into Latin of Origen's *De principiis* and Eusebius's *Historia.*

Sander, Nicholas (1530–81), English theologian at the University of Louvain, author of *De visibili monarchia ecclesiae,* a treatise defending papal authority in temporal matters, and of the unfinished *De schismate Anglicano,* a historical work on the progress of the Reformation in England.

Sebadius (Sabadius or Foebadius) (fourth century), bishop of Agen and author of a treatise against Arianism, *Contra Arianos.*

Servetus, Michael (1511–53), Spanish physician, theologian, and humanist who elaborated an anti-Trinitarian theology and argued for a form of religious toleration. Hated with equal vigor by Protestants and Catholics alike, Servetus was executed in Geneva by order of Calvin.

Sigebert of Gembloux (ca. 1035–1112), Benedictine monk and historian and author of a *Chronicon* of the history of the world.

Simancas, Jacobus (Didacus) (1513–83), theologian, canonist, and bishop successively of Ciudad Rodrigo, of Badajoz, and of Zamora, whose works include *De Catholicis institutionibus.*

Socrates Scholasticus (fifth century), historian of the Christian Church who continued Eusebius's *Historia ecclesiastica* until the middle of the fourth century.

Soto, Domingo de (1494–1560), Dominican theologian and one of Vitoria's most famous students. His most important work is *De iustitia et iure,* a treatise on jurisprudence and political philosophy.

Sozomen, Salminius Hermias (d. ca. 447), historian of the Church and author of *Historia ecclesiastica,* which covers the period between the emperor Constantine and the beginning of the reign of Theodosius II.

Suetonius Tranquillus, Gaius (ca. 70–after 130), author of biographies of twelve Roman emperors from Augustus to Domitian, *De vita caesarum,* full of anecdotes and gossip about the private lives of the emperors as well as valuable historical information. His other works are lost.

Suger (ca. 1081–1151), abbot of St. Denis, author of historical works and a memoir of his experiences as abbot, *Liber de rebus in administratione sua gestis.*

Sulpicius Severus (ca. 360–ca. 420), Christian chronicler and writer whose works include a biography of St. Martin and a *Chronicorum libri duo,* or *Historia sacra,* covering the time from the creation of the world until the year 400.

Surius, Laurentius (1522–78), Carthusian monk whose numerous treatises include *Commentarius brevis,* a chronicle of the history of the world from 1500 to 1564, and a collection of lives of the saints, *De probatis sanctorum historiis.*

Sylvanus of Tarsus (fourth century), bishop and associate of Eustathius of Sebaste.

Tertullian (ca. 160–ca. 220), Father of the Church and author of vigorous polemical and apologetic treatises, in particular *Apologeticus,* much quoted by Bellarmine, and *De corona,* on a Christian soldier who disobeyed his pagan commander, which Bellarmine quoted when dealing with the question of just war.

Themistius (ca. 317–after 385), Greek philosopher and panegyrist.

Theodoretus (ca. 393–ca. 457), bishop of Cyrus and prolific author. Bellarmine refers often to his commentaries on books of the Old Testament and to his *Historia ecclesiastica,* which starts with the beginning of the Arian heresy.

Theodosius I (ca. 346–95), Roman emperor who issued the Edict of Thessalonica in 380, declaring Christianity the religion of the empire. He vigorously defended the Christian religion against Arians and pagans.

Theodosius II (ca. 401–50), Roman emperor who commissioned the collection of law known as the Codex Theodosianus, which later used and partly incorporated the Justinian code.

Theophanes (mid-eighth century to beginning of ninth century), saint and author of a chronicle covering the period between 284 and 813.

Theophilus of Alexandria (d. 412), patriarch of Alexandria, accused of philo-Origen positions.

Theophylactus (ca. 1050–1109), archbishop of Ohrid, in Bulgaria, and a theologian, author of numerous exegetical works and epistles.

Thomas Aquinas (ca. 1225–74), probably the most influential theologian and philosopher of the Middle Ages. His philosophy was profoundly reworked in early modern Europe by Francisco de Vitoria and the so-called Second Scholastics, or School of Salamanca. Aquinas's works include *Summa theologiae,* a Christianized version of Aristotelian philosophy and the backbone for much of early modern Catholic theology; the *Quodlibeta,* a set of theological and ecclesiological questions and answers in typical Scholastic fashion; and numerous *Opuscula,* small works on specific doctrinal questions. Many of Bellarmine's theological works are discussions of aspects of Thomism and of their political and theological implications.

Torquemada, Juan de (1388–1468), Dominican canonist and cardinal whose works include a commentary on Gratian's *Decretum* and *Summa de ecclesia,* which exerted great influence on neo-Thomist theologians.

Toschi (Tuschi), Domenico (1535–1620), cardinal from 1599, scholar of canon law and author of an eight-volume collection of *Practicarum conclusionum iuris in omni foro frequentiorum* (1605–8).

Trionfo, Agostino (Augustinus Triumphus Anconitanus) (ca. 1243–1328), monk of the Order of the Hermits of St. Augustine and author of *Summa de potestate ecclesiastica,* which defended papal sovereignty on the basis of a political Augustinianism similar to that of Giles of Rome.

Trithemius (Johann Heidenberg) (1462–1516), Benedictine abbot of Sponheim, scholarly polymath whose works range from natural science to biography and devotional treatises.

Tudeschis, Nicholas de (Panormitanus) (1386–1445), Benedictine archbishop of Palermo and one of the most important canonists of his time. He wrote extensive commentaries on the *Liber extra* and the other collections of decretals.

Ulrich of Strasbourg (mid-thirteenth century), Dominican theologian, pupil of Albert the Great, author of *Summa de bono.*

Valens (d. 378), Roman emperor who converted to Arianism.

Valentinian I (d. 375), Roman emperor and, according to Augustine, a follower of Christianity.

Valentinian II (d. 392), Roman emperor, son of Valentinian I and brother of Gratian.

Valerius Maximus (first century), Roman historian, author of *Factorum et dictorum memorabilium libri novem,* a collection of anecdotes regarding famous Greek and Roman figures, which was supposed to exemplify the spectrum of human vices and virtues and which was widely used in the schools of rhetoric.

Vázquez de Menchaca, Fernando (1512–69), professor of law at the University of Salamanca, author of *De successionum creatione, progressu et resolutione* and *Controversiarium illustrium usuque frequentium libri tres,* both on common and public law.

Vigilius (ca. 353–405), martyr and saint, bishop of Trent who strongly opposed the Arian heresy.

Vignier, Nicholas (ca. 1530–96), French historian whose works include *Bibliothèque historiale* and a *Sommaire* of French history.

Vincent of Lérins (Vincentius Lirinensis) (fifth century), saint and author of *Commonitorium adversus profanas novitates,* a summary of the main tenets of the Christian faith based on the tradition of the Fathers.

Vitoria, Francisco de (ca. 1483–1546), Dominican theologian and founder of the so-called School of Salamanca, or Second Scholastic, an original interpretation of the doctrine of Thomas Aquinas. Vitoria published nothing during his life, but the manuscripts of his lectures have been published after his death in several editions. Vitoria greatly influenced two generations of theologians and jurists, including Francisco Suárez, Domingo de Soto, and Bellarmine, although the Jesuit's political theory differed from the Dominican's in many points.

Wild, Johann (1497–1554), also known under his Latinized name "Ferus," a Franciscan friar and author of an extensive series of commentaries on the Old and New Testaments.

William of Tyre (ca. 1127–90), archbishop of Tyre and author of a number of historical works.

Zeno (d. 491), Eastern Roman emperor from Isauria under whom the *Henotikon,* or "act of unity," was issued in an attempt to solve peacefully the monophysite controversy.

Zonaras, Joannes (eleventh–twelfth centuries), Byzantine chronicler and canonist.

# ABBREVIATIONS AND
# FREQUENTLY CITED WORKS

ACDF: Archivio della Congregazione per la Dottrina della Fede, Rome.

APUG: Archivio della Pontificia Università Gregoriana, Rome.

ARSI: Archivum Romanum Societatis Iesu, Rome.

ASV: Archivio Segreto Vaticano, Rome.

BAV: Biblioteca Apostolica Vaticana, Rome.

BL: British Library, London.

PG: J. P. Migne, ed., *Patrologia Graeca,* 161 vols., Paris, 1857–66.

PL: J. P. Migne, ed., *Patrologia Latina,* 221 vols., Paris, 1844–55 and 1862–65.

*Conciliorum oecumenicorum decreta:* G. Alberigo, P. P. Joannou, C. Leonardi, P. Prodi with H. Jedin, eds., *Conciliorum oecumenicorum decreta,* Basel: Herder, 1962.

*Corpus iuris civilis:* P. Krueger, T. Mommsen, R. Schoell, W. Kroll, eds., *Corpus iuris civilis,* 3 vols., Berlin: Weidmann, 1954.

*Corpus iuris canonici:* A. L. Richter and E. Friedberg, eds., *Corpus iuris canonici,* 2 vols., Graz: Akademische Druck u. Verlagsanstalt, 1959.

# ACKNOWLEDGMENTS

I would like to thank the staffs of the various archives where I worked in order to complete this work. In particular, I would like to thank Dr. Daniel Ponziani and Monsignor Alejandro Cifres, respectively Archivist and Director of the Archivio della Congregazione per la Dottrina della Fede, along with the rest of the staff of the archive; Prof. Martín M. Morales S.J., Director of the Archivio della Pontificia Università Gregoriana; Dr. Mario Brunello, Dr. Nicoletta Basilotta, and all the staff of the Archivum Romanum Societatis Iesu; and Dr. Giovanni Castaldo and all the staff of the Archivio Segreto Vaticano. Last but certainly not least, I am very grateful to Diana Francoeur, of Liberty Fund, for her editorial help and to Professor Knud Haakonssen for his knowledgeable and insightful comments and for his immense patience.

*On Laymen or Secular People*

## ✂ CHAPTER I ✂

# Summary of the entire disputation

We have discussed two branches of the Church, the clergymen and the monks, and it remains for us to talk about the third, the laymen or secular people, and at the same time about the branches which are severed from the Church, that is, the heretics, all of which things can be subsumed in a disputation on the political magistrate.

This entire disputation is contained in six questions. First, we must deal with political authority itself, then with its duty in political matters, and third with its duty in matters of religion.

On the first point there are two questions. The first is whether this authority is good and therefore lawful for Christians, and the second whether it can be lost through sin.

On the second point there are two questions. First, on the duty of the magistrate in preserving the commonwealth from the citizens' wickedness through laws and sentences both civil and penal, that is, whether it is lawful for Christians to make laws, administer justice, and punish the guilty with the sword, which are the acts proper to the magistrate. The second, on the duty of the magistrate in protecting the commonwealth from external enemies, that is, whether it is lawful for Christians to wage wars, and to this we add—almost as a corollary, because of Luther—whether it is lawful to fight against the Turks.[1]

---

1. Luther's position on the war against the Ottoman Empire was complex and two-fold. From an exegetical and eschatological perspective, Luther believed that the Turks were the Antichrist or servants of the devil employed to destroy Christ's Church. However, he also believed that the Muslim threat was a punishment coming from God

3

On the third point there are two further questions. The first is whether the care of religion pertains to the magistrate or whether he can allow everybody to believe what they want. The second question is whether the magistrate must punish the heretics sentenced and condemned by the Church in their writings and in their possessions and in their persons, even to the point of punishing them with death.

---

for the sins of his Church, and in this sense the war against the Turks was a strong polemical tool that Luther used against the Roman Catholics. Indeed, Luther had first mentioned the question of the war against the Turks in his defense of the fifth of his ninety-five theses, which asserted that the pope could not remit God's punishment. The threat coming from the Ottoman Empire to Christianity, Luther argued, was precisely a sign of God's wrath, and therefore the pope could not remove it by waging war against it. Luther dealt with the issue of the war against the Turks in many texts over a long period of time, from his 1529 *Vom Kriege widder die Türcken* to the 1541 *Vermanunge zum Gebet wider den Türcken.*

# The first question, whether the political authority is good and lawful for Christians, is proposed [2]

Among the chief heretical beliefs of the Anabaptists and Antitrinitarians of our time there is one that says that it is not lawful for Christians to hold magistracy and that among Christians there must not be power of capital punishment, etc., in any government, tribunal, or court. The ministers in Transylvania who oppose the trinity and the incarnation and infant baptism declared in 1568 in Alba Julia the differences between the true Christ and the false Christ, and the seventh difference is that the false Christ has in His Church kings, princes, magistrates, and swords; the true Christ cannot allow anything like this in His Church.[3]

Their arguments are these, or certainly can be these: first, from Scripture, Matthew 17: "And when they were come to Capernaum, they that

2. From here until the end of chapter 13 Bellarmine offers his own explanation of a tenet that was a key component of Francisco de Vitoria's and the Second Scholastics' theory of law. In opposition to the Protestants' grounding of political authority in God's grace, Vitoria, his pupils, and Bellarmine here try to demonstrate that it is an emanation of God's law. Consequently, while for Luther and Calvin only those endowed with God's grace could be just political leaders, for these Catholic theorists the political order arises directly out of the law of nature to which all humans, both those endowed with God's grace and those deprived of it, respond. See the introduction to Vitoria's *Political Writings*. For an analysis of the neo-Thomists' political theories see Giacon, *La seconda scolastica*, and Skinner, *Foundations*, vol. 2, pp. 135ff.

3. Bellarmine is referring to a series of Antitrinitarian writings published together in *De falsa et vera unius Dei, patris, filii et spiritus sancti cognitione libri duo* (Albae Juliae, 1568). For a general introduction on the religious and political context of Transylvanian and Polish Antitrinitarianism see R. R. Betts, "Poland, Bohemia and Hungary," in Elton, *The Reformation*.

received tribute money came to Peter, and said, Doth not your master pay tribute? etc."[4] And Luke 22: "The kings of the Gentiles exercise lordship over them; and they that exercise authority upon them are called benefactors,"[5] Romans 13: "Owe no man any thing, but to love one another,"[6] 1 Corinthians 7: "Ye are bought with a price; be not ye the servants of men,"[7] 2 [1] Corinthians 8: "One Lord,"[8] Ephesians 4: "One Lord, one faith, one baptism, one God."[9]

Second, arguments from examples: very many princes abuse their authority, and not only are they not useful to the commonwealth, but they are indeed a nuisance, as is clear at the very beginning of the world in the case of Cain (Genesis 4) and of the sons of God (Genesis 6) who took different wives and were corrupted by every evil, and because of them the flood followed. The same in the case of Nimrod, Pharaoh, Nebuchadnezzar, Saul, Rehoboam, and others: indeed, after the division of the kingdom, of all the kings of Israel not one was good.

Third, arguments from the final cause, for the Jews were allowed a magistrate because of the imperfection of the time: the Jews were all children and therefore had to be ruled by somebody else, as is clear from Galatians 4. But we are perfect men, and "our anointing teacheth us of all things," to keep with the biblical language.

Fourth, arguments from the efficient cause, for this authority was introduced by God, but it was usurped by men in a tyrannical way: Who made Nimrod king? Who Nebuchadnezzar? Who Alexander? Who Julius Caesar? Who the others? This is the reason why that pirate who replied to Alexander, "I am called a pirate because I go around in a small boat, you are called an emperor because you plunder the world with a big fleet," is praised (Augustine, *De civitate Dei,* book 4, chapter 4, from Cicero, *De republica,* book 3).[10]

4. Matthew 17:24.
5. Luke 22:25.
6. Romans 13:8.
7. 1 Corinthians 7:23.
8. 1 Corinthians 8:6.
9. Ephesians 4:5–6.
10. This is the chapter in which Augustine explains how kingdoms without justice are like bands of robbers.

Fifth, arguments from the origin, for God created man free, and subjection was introduced through sin; therefore once we are freed from sin through Christ, we must be freed also from subjection. The antecedent is clear, as in Genesis 1 it is not said "have dominion over men," but "have dominion over the fish of the sea."[11] Likewise the woman is now subjected to the man only by a political subjection, but this was introduced through sin, as is clear from Genesis 3 "[thy husband] shall rule over thee."[12] Moreover, before the flood the first one who founded a city and started a political kingdom was Cain, as Augustine deduced in book 15 of *De civitate Dei*, chapter 1, out of Genesis 4; and after the flood the first was Nimrod (Genesis 10).

Finally, the Fathers clearly teach this. Augustine in *De civitate Dei*, book 19, chapter 15, says that God, having made man a rational creature, in His image, did not want him to dominate except over irrational creatures, not over another man but over beasts. Hence the first just men were made shepherds of flocks rather than kings of men, so that God could demonstrate from this what the order of the creatures required and what the punishment of sins demanded. Gregory in his *Moralia*, book 21, chapter 11 [15], says that nature made all men equals; but through varying degrees of merits, a secret dispensation places some after some others. Indeed that very difference which arose from vice has been rightly ordered by the divine counsels so that, since not every man walks the path of life in the same manner, one may be ruled by another; and he says similar things in *De cura pastorali*, part 2, chapter 6.

Not only all Catholics, especially blessed Thomas in *Opusculum* 20, and all philosophers detest this heresy, but also Philip Melanchthon in *Loci communes*, the chapter on the civil magistrate, and John Calvin in book 4 of his *Institutiones*, chapter 20, most aggressively and broadly oppose it, and so does Luther himself in *De visitatio Saxonica*,[13] although

---

11. Genesis 1:26.

12. Genesis 3:16.

13. The visitation was a traditional practice of the Christian Church, reinforced at the Council of Trent, according to which an ecclesiastical superior—usually the bishop—was in charge of making regular visits to the parishes of his diocese in order to assess the

the Anabaptists took as a pretext his own words in *De Babylonica captivitate ecclesiae*, the chapter on baptism.[14] We will refute this heresy with five arguments, for the principles of our adversaries are that many: first, from the Scriptures; second, from the examples of saints; third, from the final or necessary cause; fourth, from the efficient cause; and fifth, from origin.

---

status of their clergy and to report possible cases of abuse to Rome. The early Lutheran Church, facing the difficult task of ensuring that the Reformed doctrines were correctly implemented, borrowed the same practice of the visitation but substituted for the bishop a commission of jurists, theologians, and administrators, usually controlled by the political authority. The Saxon visitation, which started in 1527 and lasted for three years, was the first example of such a procedure in the Lutheran Church.

14. Luther's *The Babylonian Captivity of the Church* was published in 1520, the year in which two other important works by Luther were published, *The Freedom of a Christian Man* and *An Address to the German Nobility.* In January 1521 Luther was excommunicated by Pope Leo X.

## CHAPTER 3

# The political magistrate is defended by Scripture

As to the first argument, the Scripture of the Old Testament is full of testimonies. In Exodus 22 the judges of the people are called gods by God himself and likewise in Psalm 81: "God standeth in the congregation of the mighty; he judgeth among the gods."[15] Jehoshaphat explains the rationale of this word in 2 Paralipomena[16] 19, where he says that judges administer not men's but God's justice, that is, they judge in place of God; similarly in Deuteronomy 1 Moses warns the judges of the people to judge justly since judgment is of God. And Christ in John 10: "if he called them gods, unto whom the word of God came, and the Scripture cannot be broken; Say ye of him, whom the Father hath sanctified, and sent into the world . . . etc.,"[17] where Christ means to say if God calls the princes gods, since to them has been given the divine order to judge in His place, why not with all the more reason, etc., for what others say, that all those to whom God has spoken are called gods, does not make sense. If therefore the princes are called gods, since they hold God's place, the office of the prince cannot be blamed, unless the office of God Himself is blamed.

Moreover, in Deuteronomy 17 Moses lays out the laws for the future king, and in the Book of Judges, last words of the last chapter, the Holy Spirit, wanting to express the cause of all the evils which happened at that

15. In the King James Bible this verse can be found in Psalm 82:1.

16. *Paralipomena* is the Greek name of the books that, in the King James Bible, are 1 and 2 Chronicles.

17. John 10:35–36.

time, says: "In those days there was no king in Israel: every man did that which was right in his own eyes."[18] In the same Book of Judges and in the Book of Kings here and there we read that God set up judges or princes for Israel through whom He would liberate His people (Proverbs 8: "By me kings reign").[19]

The Anabaptists reply that the Jews were allowed a magistrate because of imperfection, but in the New Testament the reasoning is different.

In fact it is the contrary, as, first of all, the Prophets predicted that all kings of the earth would become servants of Christ and of the Church, which cannot happen unless there are kings in the Church. In Psalm 2: "Be wise now therefore, O ye kings: be instructed, ye judges of the earth. Serve the Lord with fear, and rejoice with trembling. Kiss the Son, lest he be angry,"[20] according to the Hebrew expression, "Embrace the Son," whom in the same Psalm the Scripture calls Messiah; likewise in Psalm 71: "Yea, all kings shall fall down before him: all nations shall serve him."[21] Isaiah 60: "And the Gentiles shall come to thy light, and kings to the brightness of thy rising,"[22] and chapter 49: "And kings shall be thy nursing fathers, and their queens thy nursing mothers: they shall bow down to thee with their face toward the earth, and lick up the dust of thy feet";[23] which certainly we see fulfilled in Constantine, Theodosius, Charlemagne, and others who worshipped the tombs of the apostles and martyrs and enriched and protected the Church.

Moreover, Christ, preaching the gospel of the kingdom, said among other things: "Render therefore unto Caesar the things which are Caesar's" (Matthew 22),[24] and Paul in Romans 13 commands "Let every soul be subject unto the higher powers. For there is no power but of God: the powers that be are ordained of God."[25] In the same epistle he repeats

18. Judges 21:25.
19. Proverbs 8:15.
20. Psalm 2:10–12.
21. In the King James Bible this is Psalm 72:11.
22. Isaiah 60:3.
23. Isaiah 49:23.
24. Matthew 22:21.
25. Romans 13:1.

three times that the secular princes to whom tributes are paid are ministers of God, a passage which Irenaeus also uses in book 4, chapter 70.[26] Likewise in 1 Timothy 2 the apostle commands expressly to pray for the kings, and Tertullian uses this passage in *Apologeticus,* chapter 31, because the pagans falsely accused the Christians of not being willing to obey the magistrates. And certainly if the Gospel did not support the magistrate it would be necessary to pray for the destruction of kings and princes, but in Paul's epistle to Titus, chapter 3, we read: "Put them in mind to be subject to principalities and powers,"[27] and in 1 Peter 2: "Fear God. Honour the King."[28]

But, they reply, from these testimonies it is proved that it is necessary to be obedient to a pagan king, but not that it is lawful for Christians to possess kingdoms and to exercise the duty of magistrate. To which we reply, first, that it is not surprising that in the New Testament not much mention is made of the magistrates, as Christ did not come to build a political kingdom, but a spiritual and heavenly one; and likewise the apostles were occupied in spreading and propagating this spiritual kingdom, and left the political one as it was before.

Moreover, we add that even though the Scripture of the New Testament does not expressly approve the political magistrate in the Church, nevertheless this is gathered from the adduced testimonies, for if it is lawful for Christians to be subject to a pagan king, why not rather to a Christian king? And if it is lawful for a Christian to be subject, why not to rule? Being subject seems more against evangelical freedom than ruling.

Finally, if civil subjection or primacy were incompatible with Christian freedom, ecclesiastical subjection or primacy would be more incompatible, since Christian freedom pertains more to the Christian man as a citizen of the Church than as a citizen of the world, but ecclesiastical subjection or primacy is not incompatible with Christian freedom, as is clear

26. It is not clear which work by Irenaeus is being referred to here, and the task of identifying it is rendered more difficult by the complex history of the tradition of Irenaeus's works—see Biographical Notes.

27. Titus 3:1.

28. 1 Peter 2:17.

from this passage, Matthew 24: "Who then is a faithful and wise servant, whom his lord hath made ruler over his household,"[29] and from the one in Romans 12: "he that ruleth, with diligence,"[30] or that in Hebrews 13: "obey them who have the rule over you."[31] Therefore political primacy or subjection is not incompatible either. And hence the first argument is disproved.

Regarding the first passage of the Scriptures adduced against us in the previous chapter, it must be said that Christ in that passage was speaking only of Himself and most rightly proves that He, being the Son of God, the supreme King, was not obliged to pay tribute to any prince, but in another passage He Himself ordered that tribute be paid to Caesar (Matthew 22) and the apostle in Romans 13 said "tribute to whom tribute is due."[32] *Therefore even if Christ properly said about Himself "Then are the children free,"[33] nevertheless from this passage it is correctly gathered that clergymen must be free from tributes because the Son of the King is free in such a way that because of Him also his household is free, as we explained before in our* De clericis, *chapter 25.*[34]

Regarding the second passage, in this Christ instituted the ecclesiastical magistrate and He distinguished him from the political magistrate and

29. Matthew 24:45.
30. Romans 12:8.
31. Hebrews 13:17.
32. Romans 13:8.
33. Matthew 17:26.
34. The passage shown here in italic type was added by Bellarmine himself to the 1599 Venice edition of this controversy (Bellarmine's handwritten corrections can be found in APUG 1364, col. 460). The issue of the exemption of the clergy was a crucial theme for Bellarmine's theory of the *potestas indirecta* and one that put Bellarmine at odds with some members of the Roman Curia. In the work quoted here, *De clericis,* Bellarmine had in fact defended the exemption of the clergy, but he had denied that this was to be considered *de iure divino,* since the Church was not a temporal institution as Christ was never a temporal sovereign, and therefore the members of the Church were subject to the temporal prince insofar as they were parts of the temporal commonwealth (see in particular chap. 28). Soon afterward the political pressures from his adversaries in Rome made Bellarmine correct his thesis, and in 1599 he published in Venice an *Opusculum de pontificia exemptione clericorum,* in which he affirmed that the exemption of the clergy was *de iure divino,* which is the same position he took in the treatise against Barclay, chap. 34. See Frajese, "Regno ecclesiastico e Stato moderno."

from a corrupt political magistrate to whom pomp, pride, and arrogance are usually linked, and if we interpret this kind of political magistracy as being forbidden to Christians, we will not say anything absurd, for in that passage it is not ruling in general, but a particular manner of ruling that is censured.

Regarding the third passage, Paul does not mean to say that you are not permitted to be bound by any law, but that you should pay back all debts promptly, as in fact he previously said, "Render therefore to all their dues";[35] and because the debt of love, alone of all debts, can never be paid off—for we are always bound to love—he says: "Owe no man anything, but to love one another."[36]

Regarding the fourth passage, I say that to become the servant of man in that passage means to become so only for the sake of man, as in another passage in the same epistle Paul exhorts the servants to choose servitude even if they could be freed, and in Galatians 5 he says, "Serve one another."[37]

Regarding the last passage, I say that there the name of the Lord is taken properly, as it is appropriate to God only; and for this reason kings and princes are not removed, as they are not properly "Lords" but ministers of God, who is the only true Lord, as there is no higher title. In fact the true Lord has two prerogatives that do not apply to any creature. One is, that He can at will use anything of which He is the Lord and increase it, decrease it, change it, destroy it, etc. The other is that He is subject to none, does not need anything, but is sufficient in Himself for all things, as Augustine rightly notes in his commentary on Genesis, book 8, chapter 11, and deduces from Psalm 15: "Thou art my Lord, my goodness extendeth not to thee."[38] In fact, the translator of the Septuagint rendered the Hebrew word for "Lord"[39] with κύριος and Jerome with "Dominus," and this is the reason why also Augustus, as Tertullian reports in *Apologeticus*,

---

35. Romans 13:7.
36. Romans 13:8.
37. Galatians 5:13.
38. In the King James Bible this is Psalm 16:2.
39. In Hebrew in the text.

chapter 34, never permitted anybody to call him "Dominus," because he understood that that title was fitting only for God. By contrast, Domitian is reproached by Suetonius for his incredible arrogance, since in the amphitheater he was glad to hear himself saluted with the formula "Domino, et Dominae feliciter"[40] and because he ordered that this be added to his writings: "Dominus, et Deus noster, sic fieri iubet."[41]

40. "Good fortune attend to our Lord and Mistress." See Suetonius, *Life of Domitian,* chapter 13.

41. "Our Master and our God bids that this be done." See ibid.

## CHAPTER 4

# The same is defended from the examples of the Saints

The second reason is drawn from examples; for if sovereignty were evil, holy men would never exercise it. However, in Scripture we have very many examples of holy princes, such as Melchizedek king of Salem, the Patriarch Joseph who ruled over the whole of Egypt most advantageously, Moses, Joshua, almost all the judges, David, Solomon, Hezekiah, Jehoshaphat, Josiah, Daniel, Mordecai, Nehemiah, the Maccabees, and others.

In the New Testament we see in John 4 that a certain ruler believed in Christ, and yet he was not commanded to renounce his sovereignty; similarly in Acts 13 the proconsul, converted by Paul, did not abandon the magistracy because of his belief. Then we see that Emperor Philip was accepted by St. Fabian, Pope and Martyr, and by the whole Church, and he was not commanded to abandon his rule as is deduced from Eusebius's *Historia,* book 6, chapter 25 [34].

The reason why there is not a greater abundance of examples in the New Testament is that God wanted to begin his Church with poor and humble men, as is said in 1 Corinthians 1, so that the growth of the Church would not be reputed the work of man, which would have happened if it had grown through the favor of princes. Indeed, to the contrary, in the first three hundred years God wanted the Church to be oppressed with all force by rulers all over the whole world, in order thus to demonstrate that the Church was His work and that it was more powerful in suffering than they were in oppressing it.

Hence in epistle 50 [185] Augustine says that God wanted at the beginning to fulfill that part of Psalm 2: "The kings of the earth set themselves, etc.," and then later that other "Be wise now therefore, O ye kings: be instructed, ye judges of the earth,"[42] as indeed we see this fulfilled in Constantine and his successors, since we see Constantine divinely instructed and called by God with a special miracle, as Eusebius reports in book 1 of *De vita Constantini*. But if sovereignty were evil, why would Christ himself call Constantine to the Church? And, by the way, notice here a discrepancy in this story: in the *Historia ecclesiastica* of Eusebius translated by Rufinus, book 9, chapter 9, it is written that Constantine in his sleep saw the sign of the cross in the sky and then the angels said to him, "In this sign conquer"; but in *De vita Constantini*, book 1, Eusebius reports that during a journey Constantine saw, with his own eyes, the sign of the cross above the sun with the letters "In this sign conquer," and that sign was seen by the whole army. Later at night Christ appeared to Constantine and explained the mystery, and Eusebius heard all this from Constantine himself in person. Therefore it is likely that what we have in the *Historia* was added by Rufinus.[43]

Many more examples can be added, those of Jovian, Gratian, Theodosius I and Theodosius II, Charlemagne, Louis the Pious, Otto I, St. Henry the emperor, St. Louis king of France, and many others who either in Britain or in Hungary or in Bohemia or in other regions ruled in a most holy manner. To the opposing argument I say, first, that it is false that princes are for the most part evil; for we do not here discuss a particular kingdom but political sovereignty in general, and such a prince was Abraham along with others. Therefore, just as there were evil princes, such as Cain, Nimrod, Ninus, Pharaoh, Saul, Jeroboam, and other kings of Israel, so there were, by contrast, good princes, such as Adam, Noah, Abraham,

42. Psalm 2:2, 10. I have followed the numbers given in the edition of Augustine's letters in PL.

43. Bellarmine's remarks on the discrepancies in Ruffinus's and Eusebius's accounts of the conversion of Constantine are indicative of how he proceeded as censor of books. Formally appointed as *consultor* of the Congregation of the Index in 1587 but already informally involved in some of its cases since the end of the 1570s, Bellarmine saw the censure or correction of books as a means not only to punish or repress its authors, but to strengthen the Catholic faith by purging it of historical inaccuracies, as in this case.

Isaac, Jacob, Joseph, Moses, Joshua, almost all the judges, and many kings of Judah.

Second, I say that the examples of evil princes do not prove that political authority is evil, for oftentimes evil men abuse good things, but the examples of good princes rightly prove that political authority is good, since good men do not use evil things. Moreover, even evil princes often benefit more than they hurt, as is clear concerning Saul, Solomon, and others. Finally, it is more useful to the commonwealth to have an evil prince than none, for where there is none the commonwealth cannot last long, as Solomon says in Proverbs 11: "Where no counsel is, the people fall,"[44] and where there is a prince, even an evil one, the unity of the people is preserved. See blessed Thomas in *Opusculum* 20, chapter 6, book 1.

Third, I say that it is due to the wonderful providence of God that among the kings of Israel none was good, for God wanted to allow this because the rebellion of the Israelites from the tribe of Judah signified the separation of the heretics from the Church, as Eucherius teaches at the end of the third book of his commentary on the Book of Kings.[45] Just as there are both good and bad kings among Catholics, but no good king can be found among heretics, so even among the kings of Judah there were many good ones and many evil ones, but among the kings of Israel not one good one was to be found.

44. Proverbs 11:14.
45. The paternity of this commentary, which Bellarmine attributed to Eucherius, is now being questioned.

## CHAPTER 5

# The same is defended from the final cause of political authority

The third reason is drawn from the final cause. The political authority is so natural and necessary to humankind that it cannot be removed without destroying nature itself. In fact, by nature man is a social animal [*animal sociabile*]; whereas the brutes certainly are instructed by nature to be individually self-sufficient, man needs so many things that he absolutely cannot live by himself. In fact brutes are born clothed and armed, and they have an instinct for everything that is good for them, so that naturally and without anybody teaching them, they immediately know how to build nests, search for food, and provide themselves with medicines; but man is born without clothes, without a home, without food, lacking everything, and even though he has hands and reason with which he can produce all tools, nevertheless each thing requires such a long time that it is impossible that one man can be self-sufficient in everything, especially since we are born unskilled and the skills are learned more by instruction than by experience; therefore it is necessary for us to live together and help one another.

Moreover, even if man were self-sufficient insofar as living is concerned, he would still never be self-sufficient in protecting himself from the attack of beasts and thieves: for protection it is necessary to come together and to oppose the attack with joint forces. And even supposing man were self-sufficient against enemies, he would still remain unskilled and ignorant of knowledge, justice, and many other virtues, despite that we are in fact born expressly to exercise our mind and will. In fact, knowledge and skills were developed over a long time and by many, and they cannot be learned without a teacher; and justice cannot be exercised except in a society, since it is the virtue that establishes what is fair among many.

Finally, to what purpose would man be given the gift of speaking and listening, that is, of distinct understanding of words, if he must live by himself? Therefore in *Politics,* book 1, chapter 2, Aristotle rightly says that man is by nature a civil animal [*animal civile*], more than the bees and the cranes and any other animal, and whoever lives in solitude is either a beast or a god, that is, either less or more than a man. And our hermits are not an exception to this, for those who lived in complete solitude, such as Paul the first hermit, Mary Magdalene, Mary of Egypt, and others, can be said to have been something more than man, not by nature but by grace, as they were fed—not without miracle—by God, as is well known. Others, however, even if they lived in solitude, nevertheless got together frequently, and they were subject to their abbots, as we demonstrated in our disputation *De monachis.*

Now then, if human nature requires a social life, certainly it also requires a government and a ruler, as it is impossible that a multitude can last long unless there is somebody to hold it together and be in charge of the common good. As with each of us, if there were no soul holding together and unifying the parts and forces and conflicting elements out of which we are made, everything would immediately disintegrate. Hence Proverbs 11: "Where no counsel is, the people fall."[46] Thus, a society is an ordered multitude, and a confused and dispersed multitude is not called a society. What is order but a line of inferiors and superiors? Therefore we must necessarily have rulers, if a society is to be.

Because of this necessity of human nature, the third argument of the Anabaptists is disproved, as they assume what is false when they say that a political government was permitted to the Jews because of their imperfection, while it is not appropriate for us because "our anointing teacheth us of all things." For this anointing teaches first of all that it is necessary

46. Proverbs 11:14.

to have a ruler, and it is not necessary to know everything, for it is also necessary to do and produce many things which we cannot do without the help of others.

And moreover, from my discussion it is inferred that it is false when Cicero, in the first book of *De inventione,* writes that there was a time when men wandered like beasts and then were convinced by the force of a wise man's eloquence to assemble and live together. Indeed, those who want to praise eloquence use this argument even now. But in reality there was never such a time, nor could there be, for Adam was a very wise man and without a doubt he did not allow men to wander like beasts; and Cain, his son, even built an actual city, and before Cain and Adam there was no man. But it is not surprising that Cicero and other pagans say such things. The pagans thought that the world existed eternally, but they saw that all the crafts were new and were recorded for only a few years, so they suspected that for a very long time men had lived like beasts and that there was a record of the things accomplished only from the time when men started to live together. But it is certainly surprising that Christians, who learn from God's testimony that the world was not yet created six thousand years ago, and that the first men immediately started to have cities, dare to say that for a very long time men lived like beasts without a ruler and without cities.[47]

47. Bellarmine's concern with asserting that the natural condition of men was one in which a political or social form of organization already existed, and not one in which men "wandered like beasts," originated from the neo-Thomist view of political authority as emanating directly from the law of nature (on this issue see Skinner, *Foundations,* vol. 2, pp. 158ff.).

## CHAPTER 6

# The same is defended with a reason drawn from the efficient cause

The fourth reason is drawn from the efficient cause, as it is certain that political authority comes from God, from Whom nothing proceeds but the good and lawful, which Augustine proves throughout books 4 and 5 of *De civitate Dei*. As the Wisdom of God proclaims in Proverbs 8: "By me kings reign,"[48] and later: "By me princes rule,"[49] and in Daniel 2: "for the God of heaven hath given thee a kingdom, power, etc.,"[50] and Daniel 4: "thy dwelling shall be with the beasts of the field: they shall make thee to eat grass as oxen, and seven times shall pass over thee, until thou know that the most High ruleth in the kingdom of men and giveth it to whomsoever he will."[51]

But here some things have to be noted. First, political authority considered in general, without going into monarchy, aristocracy, and democracy in particular, comes immediately from God alone, since it follows necessarily from the nature of man and therefore it comes from Him Who made the nature of man. Moreover, this authority is of natural law, as it does not depend upon men's consent. In fact, whether or not they want to, men must be ruled by somebody unless they want humankind to perish, which is against the inclination of nature. But the law

48. Proverbs 8:15.
49. Proverbs 8:16.
50. Daniel 2:37.
51. Daniel 4:32.

of nature is divine law; therefore government was introduced by divine law, and this is what the apostle seems to mean when he says in Romans 13, "Whosoever therefore resisteth the power, resisteth the ordinance of God."[52]

Second, note that this authority immediately resides in the entire multitude as its subject because this authority is of divine law. But divine law did not give this authority to any particular man; therefore it gave it to all. Moreover, once we remove the positive law, there is no good reason why among many equals one rather than another should rule. Therefore this authority belongs to the entire multitude. Finally, human society must be a perfect commonwealth, and thus it must have the power to preserve itself and therefore to punish those who disrupt the peace, etc.

Third, note that this authority is transferred from the multitude to one or more by the same law of nature, for the commonwealth cannot in itself exercise this authority. Therefore the commonwealth is obliged to transfer it to one or a few, and in this way the princes' authority considered in general is also of natural and divine law, and humankind could not, even if it assembled all together, decree the contrary, that is, that there should not be princes or rulers.[53]

Fourth, note in particular that the individual kinds of government stem from the law of nations, not from the law of nature, for the appointment of kings, consuls, or other magistrates clearly depends on men's consent. And if there is a legitimate cause, the multitude can change a monarchy into an aristocracy or a democracy, and vice versa, as we read was done in Rome.

Fifth, note that from what we said it follows that while this particular authority certainly derives from God, it is by means of human deliberation and decision, like everything else that pertains to the law of nations. In fact, the law of nations is more or less a conclusion deduced from the

52. Romans 13:2.

53. This passage reproduces Vitoria's and the neo-Thomists' exposition of the efficient cause of civil power with one important variation: unlike Vitoria, Bellarmine does not differentiate between *potestas* and *auctoritas* when discussing the transferring of authority from the multitude to one or more rulers (see Vitoria's *relectio* on civil power, section 1, articles 3–5, in *Political Writings,* pp. 10–17, and the discussion of these articles in ibid., Introduction, pp. xviii–xx).

law of nature through human elaboration.[54] From this, two differences between political and ecclesiastical authority follow: one from the point of view of the subject, namely that political authority resides in the multitude, while ecclesiastical authority is directly over one man as its subject; the other from the point of view of the efficient cause, namely that political authority considered in general comes from divine law, and political authority considered in particular cases comes from the law of nations, but ecclesiastical authority is in every respect of divine law and stems immediately from God.

On this basis I reply to the fourth argument of the Anabaptists. First, this argument is proved only insofar as a specific government is concerned, not regarding general political authority itself. But here we want to establish political authority in general, not a specific form of government. Add, second, that very often kingdoms are just and unjust, from God and not from God. If we look at the people who occupy and invade kingdoms, we can get the impression that kingdoms are nothing but robber bands and unjust and therefore they do not come from God. If, by contrast, we consider that divine providence makes use of the evil intention of men and arranges it either to punish sins or to reward good works or to other good ends, then those same kingdoms are just and legitimate. In fact God sometimes by the wonderful reason of His providence takes away kingdoms from somebody and gives them to other people; and as a consequence in those cases, the one who falls from the kingdom falls most justly and the one who invades the kingdom does not possess it justly, and God Himself at the appropriate time will mete out the most just punishments for that invasion.

But God gave Palestine to the sons of Israel for a very different reason than that for which He later gave it to Salmanzar or Nebuchadnezzar. On the one hand, the sons of Israel, led by Joshua, fought against the people of Palestine with commendable obedience and, having killed them, claimed their lands for themselves. Salmanzar and Nebuchadnezzar, on the other hand, led the people of God into captivity by an execrable sacrilege, and

54. Bellarmine's view of the law of nations as a "deduction" from the law of nature distinguishes him from other neo-Thomist theologians such as Francisco de Vitoria and, especially, Francisco Suárez. See Skinner, *Foundations*, vol. 2, pp. 151–54.

they did not want to yield to the command of God but to their evil greed; nevertheless God used them toward that outcome which He wanted most rightly to be attained even if they did not know it.

St. Augustine in his work *De gratia et libero arbitrio,* chapters 20 and 21, and Hugh of St. Victor in book 1 of *De sacramentis,* section 1, chapter 29, explain this issue accurately, and testimonies from the Scriptures are not lacking, as in Isaiah 10 we read: "O Assyrian, the rod of mine anger, and the staff in their hand is mine indignation. I will send him against an hypocritical nation, and against the people of my wrath will I give him a charge, to take the spoil, and to take the prey, and to tread them down like the mire of the streets. Howbeit he meaneth not so, neither doth his heart think so; but it is in his heart to destroy and cut off nations not a few, etc."[55] There it speaks of Salmanzar and Sennacherib, who with evil intent occupied the lands of Israel; nevertheless God without their knowledge used their work to punish the Israelites.

Likewise in Isaiah 45: "Thus saith the Lord to his anointed, to Cyrus, whose right hand I have holden, to subdue nations before him; and I will loose the loins of kings, to open before him the two leaved gates; and the gates shall not be shut; I will go before thee, and make the crooked places straight: I will break in pieces the gates of brass, and cut in sunder the bars of iron: And I will give thee the treasures of darkness, and hidden riches of secret places, that thou mayest know that I, the Lord, which call thee by thy name, am the God of Israel. For Jacob my servant's sake, and Israel mine elect, I have even called thee by thy name: I have surnamed thee, though thou hast not known me."[56] From this passage it is clear that Cyrus acquired for himself the monarchy out of lust for domination, not in service of God, and yet God helped him and gave him the monarchy that he wanted, so that he might free the people of Israel from the Babylonian captivity.

In Jeremiah 27: "And now have I given all these lands into the hand of Nebuchadnezzar the king of Babylon, my servant; and the beasts of the field have I given him also to serve him. And all nations shall serve him, and his son, and his son's son, until the very time of his land come: and

---

55. Isaiah 10:5–7.
56. Isaiah 45:1–4.

then many nations and great kings shall serve themselves of him. And it shall come to pass, that the nation and kingdom which will not serve the same Nebuchadnezzar, the king of Babylon, and that will not put their neck under the yoke of the king of Babylon, that nation will I punish, saith the Lord, with the sword, and with the famine, and with the pestilence, until I have consumed them by his hand."[57] And yet who doubts that Nebuchadnezzar submitted to himself so many kingdoms with evil intent?

Ezekiel also says, chapter 29: "Son of man, Nebuchadnezzar king of Babylon caused his army to serve a great service against Tyrus: every head was made bald, and every shoulder was peeled; yet had he no wages, nor his army, for Tyrus, for the service that he had served against it,"[58] and later "I have given him the land of Egypt for his labour wherewith he served against it, because they wrought for me, saith the Lord God."[59]

Likewise the Romans wanted to enlarge their empire not for God, but for lust of glory, as blessed Augustine shows extensively in *De civitate Dei*, book 5, chapter 12. Nevertheless God allowed them to enlarge their empire, both to reward them for their good morals, as St. Augustine teaches in book 5, chapter 15, of *De civitate Dei*, and to prepare the path for preaching the Gospel through the union of all peoples under one government, as blessed Leo says in his first sermon on Peter and Paul [82].

Add also that even if at the beginning those who established kingdoms were for the most part invaders, in the course of time they or their successors become legitimate princes, since the peoples little by little give their consent. In this way the kingdom of the Franks, by everybody's consent, is now legitimate, even though at the beginning the Franks occupied Gaul unjustly. And the same can be said of the Hispanic kingdom, which began with the invasion of the Goths, and of the English kingdom, which began with the unjust occupation of the Anglo-Saxons, and of the Roman Empire itself, which was established by Julius Caesar, oppressor of his country, but which nevertheless later began to be legitimate to the point that the Lord said in Matthew 22: "Render therefore unto Caesar, etc."[60]

57. Jeremiah 27:6–8.
58. Ezekiel 29:18.
59. Ezekiel 29:20.
60. Matthew 22:21.

## ⌘ CHAPTER 7 ⌘

# The same is defended from antiquity

The fifth reason is drawn from the origin, for even if servile subjection began only after Adam's sin, there would still have been political authority even in the state of innocence. The proof is, first, that even then man would have been by nature a civil and social animal, and therefore he would have needed a ruler.

Second, there is proof from the Creation itself, as God made the woman from the man and did not create many men at the same time, but one man only, from whom all others would have been born so as to indicate the order and primacy which He wanted to be among men, as Chrysostom observes in homily 34 on the first Epistle to the Corinthians.

Third, in that state there would have been differences in gender, status, talents, wisdom, and honesty, and therefore primacy and subjection, for in human society there must be order. But a proper order implies that the inferior be ruled by the superior, the woman by the man, the younger by the older, the less wise by the wiser, and the less good by the better, and in this way it can be proved that these differences would have had a place even then.

In that state there would have been procreation, as is clear from Genesis 1: "Be fruitful, and multiply."[61] There would also be a difference in gender, which necessarily precedes procreation, and a difference in age, which necessarily follows procreation, and a difference in wisdom and honesty, which follows the difference in age, since there would not have

61. Genesis 1:28.

been perfect men in that state, but they would have had to learn and progress little by little. Certainly all would have been born in the grace of God, and with a greater intelligence than now, as Augustine teaches in *De baptismo parvulorum*, book 1, chapter 38, but without a doubt they would have not been as perfect as adults, and because of their free will some of those adults could devote themselves more to knowledge than others.

Finally, a variety of talents arises from the variation in bodies; but there would have been bodies of different dimension, form, strength, and so on, as is clear from the fact that those bodies were not exempt from the laws of nature but were dependent on food, on air to breathe, and on the influences of the celestial bodies. Accordingly, there would even then have been a variety of talents. See blessed Thomas, *Summa,* 1a, questions 96 and 105.

Fourth, among the angels there is primacy and subjection: why then would there have been none in the state of innocence? Beelzebub is, of course, called the prince of the devils (Matthew 12), and he certainly did not acquire his sovereignty by sinning but maintained that which he had before over those angels who followed him. And in Apocalypse, chapter 12, it is said: "Michael and his angels."[62] Finally Dionysius in chapter 9 of the *Hierarchia coelestis* says that the first angelic hierarchy has primacy and rules over the second, and the second over the third. Also blessed Gregory, homily 34 on the Gospel, says that the names of the principalities and dominions among the angels clearly indicate that some have primacy over others.

On the basis of these points we reply to the fifth argument, that the freedom in which we were created is not incompatible with political subjection but only with despotic subjection, that is, with true and real servitude.[63] Political subjection is different from servile subjection because one who is subject in a servile manner works for another, and one who is subject in a political manner works for himself; the servant is ruled not for his own, but for his master's advantage, while the citizen is ruled for his own

62. Revelation 12:7.
63. Bellarmine's discussion of the freedom enjoyed by men in the state of innocence, which coexisted with political subjection, singles him out, once again, with respect to the other neo-Thomists. See Skinner, *Foundations,* vol. 2, pp. 154–57.

advantage, not for the advantage of the magistrate. Likewise, by contrast, a political prince, as long as he rules the people, seeks not his own, but his people's utility, while a tyrant and master seeks not his people's utility but his own, as Aristotle teaches in his *Nicomachean Ethics,* book 8, chapter 10. Therefore, in truth, if there is any servitude in political government, he who is in charge, not the subject, is more properly called a servant, as Augustine teaches in *De civitate Dei,* book 19, chapter 14; and this is the literal meaning of what our Lord says in Matthew 20: "And whosoever will be chief among you, let him be your servant."[64] In the same way the bishops call themselves servants of their people and the Supreme Pontiff the servant of the servants of God.

To the first passage from chapter 1 of Genesis I say that it is about despotic government, as this was the way man had to dominate the fish of the sea and the fowl of the air and the other living things.

To the second one I say, the woman, both before and after sin, is partner and subject to the man: partner in procreation, and subject in government. That phrase "and he shall rule over thee"[65] does not mean every single kind of subjection, but the involuntary one, with sadness and fear, such as for the most part married women experience; as blessed Augustine teaches in his commentary on Genesis, book 11, chapter 37, where he says: "We should not believe that before sin the woman was created only to be dominated by the man and only to direct herself to serving him. The right opinion is that this servitude was meant as one of condition rather than of choice."

To the third I say, Cain was the first to have built an actual city, but from this it does not follow that political government started then, since a commonwealth and a kingdom can exist even without an actual city, and it cannot be denied that Adam's sons and grandsons were subject to him.

To the fourth I say, Augustine speaks of proper servitude, as is clear from that whole chapter, where, among other things, he says: "The condition of servitude is understood as being lawfully imposed on the sinner, etc." And it is not a problem that Augustine says there that the first just

64. Matthew 20:27.
65. Genesis 3:16.

men were made shepherds of flocks rather than kings of men, so that God could demonstrate what the order of the creatures required and what the punishment of sins demanded; for in this passage he refers to the abuse of the title of king, which is sometimes understood as a despotic government. Indeed, as Augustine himself says in *De civitate Dei*, book 5, chapter 12, a king is called such because of his rule and counsel, not because of his command and dominion; and in this sense Abraham, Isaac, and Jacob could have been called kings. Nevertheless, since human greed thinks that a king is called such because of his command and dominion, our Lord says in Luke 22: "The kings of the Gentiles exercise lordship over them";[66] hence the first just men were called shepherds of flocks rather than kings of men.

To the fifth I say, Gregory does not talk simply about political government, but of that which is accompanied by dread, sadness, fear, etc., things which are brought about by sin, and when he says that all men are equal by nature, and become unequal through sin, and therefore one has to be ruled by another, he does not mean that men are equal in wisdom and grace, but equal in the essence of humankind. From this equality it is rightly inferred that one must not dominate the other, in the way in which man dominates beasts, but only that one has to be ruled by another politically. Hence in the same passage he adds: "In fact it is against nature to be haughty or to want to be feared by another," since indeed sinners, through their sin, become similar to beasts and degenerate from the integrity of the nature in which they were created. Therefore, in the same passage Gregory says, rightly, that after sin one started to dominate the other with threats and punishment, which would not have happened in the state of innocence.

66. Luke 22:25.

# Political authority or sovereignty
# can reside in wicked men

We can easily prove our second proposition, that political authority can reside in wicked men. But first we take up the error of Richard Fitzralph, who in book 10 of *Quaestiones Armenicae* [*Summa in quaestionibus Armenorum*], chapter 4, teaches that the chief title of sovereignty is the grace of God, or justice and charity, and all the other titles are founded on this, and those who lack the justice and grace of God have no true sovereignty. In our time John Wyclif taught the same error,[67] which Thomas Netter most effectively refutes in book 2 of his *Doctrinalis,* chapters 81ff. until the end of the book, and afterward Jan Hus defended the same error, as is clear from the Council of Constance, session 15.[68]

Their arguments were three. First, from Scripture, from the Book of Hosea, 8: "They have set up kings, but not by me: they have made princes, and I knew it not: of their silver and their gold have they made them idols, that they may be cut off."[69] Here our Lord condemns the sovereignty of

---

67. On the relationship between Fitzralph's and Wyclif's theories, see J. Coleman, "Property and Poverty," in J. H. Burns, ed., *Cambridge History of Medieval Political Thought,* pp. 607–48 at pp. 644–48.

68. Session 15 of the Council of Constance (6 July 1415) contains the sentence of condemnation of Wyclif's and Hus's doctrines, together with a list of their propositions that the Church considered heretical and the sentence with which Hus was condemned to be burned. The canons and decrees of the Council of Constance as well as the other ecumenical councils since Nicaea can be found in *Conciliorum oecumenicorum decreta* (the text of the session to which Bellarmine refers is at pp. 397–408).

69. Hosea 8:4.

wicked kings, and says that He did not give it to them because they made idols for themselves. The second argument is from this passage of Ecclesiasticus 10: "The kingdom is transferred from people to people because of injustice."[70] The third argument is that there is no sovereignty but from God, and God does not in any way grant sovereignty to wicked men, because they are His enemies, and also because He would seem to approve of their abuse, for all wicked men abuse their authority.

This error is easily refuted. First, from Scriptures, Book of Wisdom [6] 4: "Sovereignty has been given to you by the Lord, and being ministers of his kingdom you have not judged rightly, etc.";[71] Isaiah 45: "Thus saith the Lord to his anointed, to Cyrus, etc.";[72] Jeremiah 27: "And now have I given all these lands into the hand of Nebuchadnezzar the king of Babylon, etc.";[73] and Daniel 2: "Thou, O king, art a king of kings: for the God of heaven hath given thee a kingdom, etc."[74] And in Romans 13 and 1 Peter 2, the apostles Peter and Paul teach that the authority of kings comes from God and we must obey them, even though at that time there were no kings but infidels.

Second, from the Council of Constance, sessions 8 and 15, where the Church condemned this error.[75]

Third, from Augustine, who in *De civitate Dei*, book 5, chapter 21, says: "Since this is the case, let us not attribute the giving of a kingdom or the power to rule to anybody but the true God, who gives beatitude in the kingdom of heaven only to the pious, but the earthly kingdom to both pious and impious, as He, Who does not wish anything unjustly, wishes." And later he says: "He Who gave power to Marius gave it to Caesar; He Who gave power to Augustus gave it to Nero; He Who gave power to the

70. Ecclesiasticus, or Book of Sirach—which for the Catholics was the last of the Sapiential books in the Old Testament—was not included in Protestant Bibles. This is my own translation of Ecclesiasticus 10:8.

71. The *Liber sapientiae*, or Book of Wisdom, was not included in Protestant Bibles. This is my own translation of *Liber sapientiae* 6:4.

72. Isaiah 45:1.

73. Jeremiah 27:6.

74. Daniel 2:37.

75. See in particular Wyclif's article 15, condemned in session 8 (4 May 1415), and articles 26–31 condemned in session 15, in *Conciliorum oecumenicorum decreta*, pp. 388–400.

Vespasii, both the father and the son, most benevolent emperors, gave it to the most cruel Domitian; and—although it is not necessary to go over all one by one—He Who gave power to the Christian Constantine gave it to Julian the Apostate."

Fourth, from reason, for the foundation of sovereignty is not grace, but nature. Since man is made in the image of God, he is provided with mind and reason, and thus he dominates inferior things, as can be deduced from the first chapter of Genesis. But human nature resides also in infidels, even though they lack grace, and therefore they can also truly hold sovereignty. Regarding this issue, since grace and justice are entirely secret and nobody knows about himself or another whether he is truly just, if grace were the title to sovereignty, it would follow that no sovereignty would be certain. From this an incredible confusion and commotion would arise among men. Moreover, their arguments do not lead to anything.

To the first argument I say, with those words God did not chastise the evil kings, but chastised the fact that the Jews wanted to have a king, even though God was their king. Indeed, as blessed Jerome explains, in this chapter 8 Hosea explains the reasons why the people of Israel were to be brought to captivity, and he says that one of those reasons was that they wanted to have a king; another reason was that they made idols for themselves. That they gravely sinned in wanting to have a king is clear from 1 Kings, chapter 12, where after Saul was elected king, Samuel speaks as follows to the people: "Now therefore stand and see this great thing, which the Lord will do before your eyes. Is it not wheat harvest to day? I will call unto the Lord, and he shall send thunder and rain; that ye may perceive and see that your wickedness is great, which ye have done in the sight of the Lord, in asking you a king."[76]

To the second I say, kingdoms are transferred from one people to another because of injustice, since God, because of the sins of the kings, often grants victory to their enemies, but they do not lose the right to govern because of the fact that they sin.

To the third I say, it is fitting God's benignity that it benefits also His

76. 1 Samuel 12:16–17. In the King James Version of the Bible, 1 Samuel corresponds to the Vulgate 1 Kings, 2 Samuel to 2 Kings, 1 Kings to 3 Kings, and 2 Kings to 4 Kings.

enemies, as we read in the Gospel of Matthew 5: "He maketh his sun to rise on the evil and on the good, and sendeth rain on the just and on the unjust."[77] This does not mean He approves of the abuse, as He does not give the kingdoms to wicked men so that they might abuse them, but so that they, incited by His benevolence, might turn away from their sin, as blessed Jerome explained in that passage of Isaiah 45: "Thus saith the Lord to his anointed, to Cyrus, whose right hand I have holden, to subdue nations before him; and I will loose the loins of kings, to open before him the two leaved gates; and the gates shall not be shut";[78] or he does so in order to reward some good works done by them, as blessed Augustine teaches in *De civitate Dei,* book 5, chapter 15; or finally he does so because sometimes the sins of the peoples might deserve it, as the same Augustine teaches in book 5 of *De civitate Dei,* chapter 19, from the passage in Job 34,[79] which says that God makes a hypocrite reign because of the sins of the people. Augustine in *De civitate Dei,* book 19, chapter 21, also says that among infidels there cannot be justice, laws, true people, or commonwealth, etc., but he calls true justice and true laws those which lead to the eternal life. See also *In [Contra] Julianum,* book 5, chapter 3.

77. Matthew 5:45.
78. Isaiah 45:1.
79. Job 34:30.

# The question of the authority of
# the magistrate is proposed

The third question follows: whether it is lawful for a Christian magistrate to establish law, administer justice, and punish the wicked. But there are two errors to refute. The first is that of the Waldensians and Anabaptists, who deny all this. Their arguments are that the obligation of the laws removes Christian freedom and that lawsuits are forbidden, in Matthew 5: "And if any man will sue thee at the law, and take away thy coat, let him have thy cloak also,"[80] and in 1 Corinthians 6: "Now therefore there is utterly a fault among you, because ye go to law one with another. Why do ye not rather take wrong? why do ye not rather suffer yourselves to be defrauded?"[81] Finally, capital punishment seems to be forbidden for Christians: Matthew 5, "Ye have heard that it hath been said, An eye for an eye, and a tooth for a tooth: But I say unto you, That ye resist not evil, etc."[82] Moreover it is clear that in the Old Testament inflicting the *poena talionis* was not permitted except to the magistrate, and therefore Christ prohibits precisely this when he says in Matthew 26: "All they that take the sword shall perish with the sword."[83]

The second error is Calvin's. Although in book 4 of the *Institutiones,* chapter 20, he proves, against the Anabaptists, that in the Church there must be civil laws, tribunals, and capital punishment, he nevertheless in

80. Matthew 5:40.
81. 1 Corinthians 6:7.
82. Matthew 5:38–39.
83. Matthew 26:52.

book 4 of the *Institutiones,* chapter 10, section 5, affirms that the civil laws do not bind in conscience, something that was taught before him by Jean Gerson in *De vita spirituali,* lecture 4, and by Jacques Almain, in *De potestate ecclesiastica,* question 1, chapter 10. These are their reasons.

First, since political authority is temporal, it has nothing to do with conscience. Second, the end of the civil laws is external peace. Third, the prince does not judge in internal matters. Fourth, since the prince cannot inflict a spiritual punishment, he cannot make subjects liable to such punishment. Fifth, the prince cannot absolve, nor can he bind. Sixth, the sin would be punished twice, once here and once in the next world. Seventh, the prince for the most part does not intend to impose an obligation under pain of sin. Eighth, we should rather violate the most pressing civil law than the least divine law, such as that of not telling an officious lie. But since the latter binds only under pain of a venial sin, consequently the former does not bind at all, for if it bound under pain of sin, and especially mortal sin, it would be necessary to avoid a mortal sin rather than a venial sin.

## CHAPTER 10

# The first proposition

Against those errors, the first proposition is this: it is lawful for a Christian prince to make laws. It is proved, first of all, because it is a prerogative of the prince to make laws, according to that passage in Proverbs 8: "By me kings reign, and princes decree justice,"[84] and Isaiah 33: "For the Lord is our judge, the Lord is our lawgiver";[85] for it is the prerogative of the king to command, and by commanding to direct. Moreover, the law is the command and rule itself, and therefore if Christians can be princes, certainly they can also make laws, and this is confirmed by Augustine, *De civitate Dei,* book 19, chapter 17, where he says: "The heavenly city, as long as it lives as a captive and pilgrim, even if it has already accepted the promise of redemption and the spiritual gift as a pledge, does not hesitate to obey the laws of the earthly city, which are directed to support the mortal life," and later "therefore this heavenly city, as long as it wanders on earth, summons its citizens from all nations in every tongue and brings together a society of pilgrims in which no attention is paid to the differences in customs, laws, and institutions, by which the earthly peace is either established or preserved. This heavenly city, however, does not annul or destroy such customs, laws, and institutions; indeed it preserves and follows them."

Second, this proposition is proved out of the necessity for the civil laws. Christians do not cease to be men and citizens, and therefore members of

84. Proverbs 8:15.
85. Isaiah 33:22.

36

the temporal commonwealth, because they are Christians; thus they must have some rule for their human actions, by which they might be directed in their affairs and social relations with other men. And the natural law is not sufficient, for it shows only the general principles, and it does not get into the specifics. Not even the evangelical law is sufficient, for it deals only with heavenly and divine matters, as is well known. Moreover, the divine political law of the Old Testament has now been abrogated, since it was only fitting for that people, the Jews, and in that state. Therefore another human rule, that is, the will of the princes, or a civil law established by the prince's authority, is necessary. Even if the will of the prince could suffice in a case where the prince is wise and the people are few, nevertheless in absolute terms it is necessary that the people be ruled by laws, not solely by the will of the prince, if the people are to be ruled justly. That the will of the prince sometimes is sufficient is obvious because kingdoms are older than laws. Justinus, in book 1 of *Epitoma historiarum,* says that once the peoples used to be governed without any laws and only by the will of the princes, and from Livy, book 3, it is evident that the Roman commonwealth for three hundred years was governed without laws. Finally, the first lawgiver is either Moses, as Josephus argues in book 2 of *Contra Apionem,* or, if not Moses, definitely Phoroneus, who was three hundred years older than Moses, as Eusebius in his *Chronicle* and Augustine in book 18 of *De civitate Dei,* chapter 3, teach. And before Phoroneus the kingdoms of the Assyrians, of Greece, of Egypt, and others were established.

Aristotle, in *Politics,* book 3, chapter 11, affirms that a people is better ruled by laws than by the prince's will alone, indeed, that this is in some sense necessary. And this is proved, first, because it is easier to find one or two good and wise men than many, and if the commonwealth has to be ruled by the will of a good prince, it will need an infinite number of good princes, so that one can succeed the other, but if it is governed by laws, it is sufficient that there once had been one or a few wise men who made the laws.

Second, those who make laws are many and they examine them diligently, while a prince is only one person and often he must judge quickly.

Third, those who made laws made judgments based on neither love nor hate, since they made judgments on hypothetical cases. The prince makes judgments on current issues, in which friendships, proximity, bribes, fears, etc., have a role; hence the judgment of the laws is a judgment of reason only, while the judgment of man is by reason and passion, that is, of man and beast.

Fourth, the judgment of the prince, even if it is most just, is hardly ever free from suspicion, envy, complaints, reproaches; while the judgment of the law is free from all of these, for indeed it is well known that the law cannot be corrupted by bribes.

Fifth, government through laws can last for the longest time unaltered, while the judgments of men often change.

Sixth, government through laws can be constructed as a system and more easily carried out; government according to the will of man cannot.

Seventh, the government of the prince is better when the prince himself does it rather than through his deputies, but government without laws necessarily requires many deputies who might make judgments according to their own will. However, when one governs by laws, the prince effectively judges everything by himself, since judgments are made according to his laws.

Third, [86] it is proved because if it were not lawful for a Christian prince to bind people with laws, this would be because of Christian freedom. Such a statement, however, cannot be made, for the law is so far from being opposed to Christian freedom that it is rather opposed to the slavery that contravenes such freedom than to the freedom itself. I show this from the very nature of Christian freedom, as Christian freedom is opposed to the slavery of sin, John 8: "Verily, verily, I say unto you, whosoever committeth sin is the servant of sin. And the servant abideth not in the house for ever: but the Son abideth ever. If the Son therefore shall make you free, ye shall be free indeed,"[87] and Romans 6: "Being then made free from sin, ye became the servants of righteousness."[88] But being cleansed from sin is said to be a freedom of a particular kind, since he who is in sin cannot want the good that is necessary to the eternal life, unless he is freed from it through grace. He certainly has free will, since he can choose one out of

86. Bellarmine is resuming the points introduced at the beginning of chapter 10.
87. John 8:34–36.
88. Romans 6:18.

many evils, and also a moral good, but he cannot choose a divine good, unless he at least begins to be freed through the prevenient grace of God, since he is taken captive by the Devil at his will, as is written in 2 Timothy 2. But the free will, freed through grace, can want and accomplish the divine good, and this freedom was even greater in the state of innocence, since man then could avoid any evil wishes, something which even just men now cannot, and it will be at its greatest in heaven, where we will not be able to have any evil wishes.

Therefore there are three degrees of freedom, just as there are three degrees of corporeal life. The first is that of the Blessed, who will be able to live so that they cannot die, and they will be able to act rightly so that they cannot sin.

The second was that of Adam and Eve in the state of innocence, who could live so that they could also never die, and they could act rightly so that they could never sin either.

The third is ours, who can only live so that we cannot help but die at some point, and who can only act so that we cannot avoid sin, even if only a venial sin. There is not a fourth degree below these three, except that of not living and not acting rightly, a degree suited for the damned. See Augustine, *De correptione et gratia,* chapter 2. Since therefore freedom consists in being able to choose good and reject evil, it is clear that the law does not oppose this freedom; it does not prevent us from choosing good and rejecting evil, but rather helps us to do so by providing the condition to exercise this freedom. The law can rightly be said to be opposed to slavery, since it cannot be fulfilled by a slave of sin. Hence Paul in Romans 3 says: "Do we then make void the law through faith? God forbid: yea, we establish the law."[89] See Augustine, *De spiritu et littera,* chapter 30.

Second, this point is also proved: the divine law does not oppose freedom; therefore the human law does not oppose freedom either. The antecedent is clear, for Adam was created free, yet a law was imposed on him not to eat from the tree of the knowledge of good and evil (Genesis 2). The consequence is proved because divine and human law are the same as far as obligation is concerned, as will be clear in the following chapter.

89. Romans 3:31.

## CHAPTER II

# The second proposition

The civil law does not bind in conscience less than the divine law, even if it is less stable and firm. To explain, divine and human law are different regarding their solidity, since divine law cannot be abrogated by man, while human law can. But regarding their obligation they are not different because both bind in conscience, under pain of either mortal or venial sin according to the gravity of the issues themselves. Thus there is not a better rule for understanding whether human law binds under pain of mortal or venial sin than to think of this law as divine and then see how it would bind.[90]

This is proved, first, because binding force is the essence of the law, as is said in *De Summo Pontifice,* book 4, chapter 16, and to bind is a necessary effect of law. Therefore, every law binds in the same way, by whomever it is made, whether by God, an angel, or a man, and among men, by a bishop, a king, or a father. The consequence is proved by analogy. Since the essence of man is to be rational and his proper characteristic is to be able to laugh, every man is reasonable and able to laugh, whether he be created by God alone, like Adam, or by God out of another human, like Eve, or procreated by men, like Cain.[91] The antecedent is clear, as law is a normative rule. However, it is a central feature of a rule to direct intrinsically in

90. In this chapter Bellarmine vigorously expresses a central tenet of the political theory of Vitoria and the other neo-Thomist theologians. See Vitoria's *relectio* on civil power, question 3, in *Political Writings,* pp. 32–44.

91. This definition of man as a reasonable creature "capax risus," or able to laugh, was first introduced by Aristotle in *De partibus animalium,* 3.10, and later repeated by Latin authors such as Quintilian and Boethius.

such a way that to deviate from it is a sin against the prescribed norm, just as to deviate from a rule in nature is called a sin of nature, as in the case of monsters, and to deviate from a rule of an art is a sin against that art.

Here it is to be noted that just as other things depend on an agent for their existence, but not for their essence, since the essences are eternal, and [regarding the question of essence] it is also possible that things participate in a certain way in the divine essence, the law also depends for its existence on the legislator, for there will be no law unless it is established by him who has authority. But for its essence, the law does not depend on the legislator, for the binding force of the law is something eternal and immutable and stems from a certain participation in the eternal law of God, which is the first and greatest rule. Blessed Augustine seems to have intended this in *Contra Faustum*, book 22, chapter 27, when he says: "A sin is something said or done or desired against the eternal law of God." In fact whoever transgresses the law, be it natural law, positive law, divine law, or human law, always sins against the eternal law, since every law participates in the eternal law. And even though it is impossible that any given true law does not come from God, since no law can be made unless by him who has authority, and there is no authority but from God (Romans 13), nevertheless if *per impossibile* a law did not come from God, it would still bind under pain of sin, just as if *per impossibile* there were a man who was not made by God, he would still be rational.[92]

The second proof is that if the law only bound because it is divine, then clearly all laws would be equally binding, for there would be the same reason for the obligation in all of them. But this is false, for the law "thou shalt not kill" is more binding than the law "thou shalt not steal," and this more than "thou shalt not lie," and this more than "thou shalt not say careless words."

Third, it is furthermore clear that a divine law is more binding the more contrary its violation is to the end of that law—namely charity. Hence it

92. This and similar formulations later in this chapter are vigorous statements of the neo-Thomist theory that the law of nature does not need any divinely revealed knowledge to be effective. They closely resemble Grotius's famous passage *etiamsi daremus* in *De iure belli et pacis*, Prolegomena 11. On the relationship between the neo-Thomist and the Grotian formulations, see Haakonssen, "Hugo Grotius," pp. 247–53.

is worse to kill than to steal, as killing is more against charity; and to say
a pernicious lie is a mortal sin, while to say an officious lie is a venial sin,
because the former is against charity and the latter is outside of the realm
of charity. But human law also has charity as its end, and it regulates the
means to this end, for when the apostle says that "the end of the com-
mandment is charity,"[93] it is meant for all commands. This is clear, for
a just civil law is either a conclusion or a determination from the divine
moral law. Therefore they have the same end, and they differ only in this:
that the human law directs human acts to external acts of love, that is, to
the peace and preservation of the commonwealth, but the divine law directs also to internal acts of charity; therefore the reason of the human and
the divine laws is the same insofar as the obligation is concerned.

But you will object: if the gravity of the sin comes from the nature of
the thing and from the relation to charity, then laws are superfluous, since
we are equally obliged before and after the law to avoid what by its own
nature harms charity and to do what is necessary to preserve charity.

I reply: the consequence is denied, for if the law does not help by prescribing or prohibiting something in general, many things which are bad
for one person will not be so for another. For example, without a law that
prohibits the carrying of arms, carrying arms will be bad for him who is
easily moved to anger and who has enemies whom he wishes to harm, but
it will not be bad for a peaceful man who wants only to defend himself.
Nevertheless if the law prohibits it, then it is bad for all, as the law does
not have to consider whether it might be good or bad for one or another,
but what is advantageous and what is not for the commonwealth. Besides,
there are many things that are necessary or harmful to the common good,
which, nevertheless, are neither good nor bad for anybody in particular,
unless they are prescribed or prohibited by law. For example, a tribute to
the king is necessary. But if there is no law, it is not necessary for me to pay,
for what I pay benefits the king little, and it does not concern me to see
what the commonwealth needs; and all people could say the same. Similarly, it is harmful to the commonwealth that gold be exported from the
province, but it is evidently not harmful to me to export my own gold;

93. 1 Timothy 1:5.

and all people could say the same. Therefore a law is necessary which, by making general prescriptions or prohibitions, can provide for the advantage of the commonwealth.

Fourth, the divine positive law binds under pain of sin, since it makes the act that it prescribes into an act of virtue, which it was not before. For if a Jew ate pork, which is prohibited in the law, though in moderation, not contemptuously but for hunger, without a doubt he would sin, but he would not sin formally against obedience, since he did not do it out of contempt and therefore against temperance; and eating pork in moderation is not in itself against temperance, but an indifferent thing. Therefore there was a law which made that abstinence a necessary act of temperance. And we see the same in human law. In fact, the divine law makes that which in itself was indifferent into an act of virtue for no other reason but that it is a rule of behavior imposed by Him Who has the authority to make prescriptions. But also man can make prescriptions and establish rules of behavior, as we showed above; therefore man can make an otherwise indifferent act into an act of virtue by his law, and accordingly divine and human laws are equal with regard to obligation.

Fifth, divine and human laws are as different as the law of the king and that of the viceroy, or the law of the Pontiff and that of his legates. But those latter cases bind in the same way and differ only in stability, and the same applies therefore to the first case also. The proposition is clear, since the Scriptures here and there attest that kings are ministers of God, and from Him they have the authority and judge in His place (Proverbs 8, Book of Wisdom 6, Romans 13, 1 Peter 2). The assumption is also clear, since the authority of the viceroy comes from the king, and that of the legate from the Pope; and the same is proved by experience and confirmed by the holy Fathers Augustine and Bernard. Augustine in his commentary on Psalm 70 says: "Where the father orders what is not against God, he has to be listened to as if he were God, etc." Now it is certain that the authority of the king is greater than the authority of a father, as Augustine himself says in sermon 6 on the word of God. Bernard, in *De praeceptis* [*praecepto*] *et dispensationibus* [*dispensatione*], says: "When someone, whether God or a man, in place of God, gives a command, the command undoubtedly has to be obeyed with the same care and carried out with the same reverence, provided that the man does not command anything contrary to God," and here he clearly says that the laws differ with respect to their content, not with respect to those who make the prescription.

But you will object that Bernard in the same passage, speaking of the commands of men, says that orders are not neglected without guilt, nor are they scorned without committing a crime, for neglect always deserves blame, and scorn must always be condemned; in this he seems to say that human law never binds under pain of mortal sin unless by reason of contempt. I reply that we are talking here of precepts about small matters in which there cannot be crime except by reason of contempt. For not even priests can bind under pain of mortal sin out of their own will.

Sixth, it is proved because the assumption that the prince can bind with respect to punishing, but not with respect to guilt, seems to imply a contradiction, since obviously punishment and guilt are related; blessed Augustine in book 1 of his *Retractationes,* chapter 9, says: "Every punishment, if it is just, is punishment of a sin," and in epistle 105 [186] and elsewhere, he says that God Himself would be unjust if He condemned an innocent. How, therefore, can the princes condemn to death those who transgress their laws if they have not committed a sin? If they have not committed any error of conscience?

You will say, how is it, then, that the rules of some religious orders bind with respect to punishment but not guilt? I reply that they are binding not as a law, but as an agreement and a pact, as purely penal laws. And it is not even a proper punishment, but the infliction of a penalty in order to aid the spirit.

Seventh, and last, it is proved from the doctrine of the apostles, for in Romans 13 Paul affirms it in many ways. First, when he says: "Let every soul be subject unto the higher powers. For there is no power but of God."[94] Second, "Whosoever therefore resisteth the power, resisteth the ordinance of God."[95] Third, "And they that resist shall receive to themselves damnation."[96] The Greek and Latin Fathers interpret this last passage as referring to eternal damnation. Fourth, "Wherefore ye must needs

94. Romans 13:1.
95. Romans 13:2.
96. Romans 13:2.

be subjects,"[97] and fifth, "Not only for wrath, but also for conscience sake."[98] Sixth, "For they are God's ministers."[99] In 1 Peter 2: "Submit yourselves to every ordinance of man for the Lord's sake,"[100] that is, not only for fear of punishment.

*These passages demonstrate sufficiently what we want, for if princes have their authority to command from God, certainly those who do not obey them offend not only the princes, but also God; and if those who resist the prince resist the ordinance of God, certainly they sin in conscience, no differently than if they had transgressed the divine laws, and if those who resist receive damnation for themselves, certainly they commit a wrong worthy of that punishment. If they of necessity are subject to individual princes not only for fear of wrath but also for conscience, how do those who are not obedient to them fail to commit a sin? Finally, if princes are God's ministers and we must obey them for God, certainly those who scorn the commands of princes scorn the majesty of God.*[101]

As for the contrary arguments, I respond as follows:

To the first, second, and third I reply that from the fact that the political authority is temporal and its end is external peace and that man does not make judgments on internal matters, it is rightly inferred that it can oblige only to perform temporal and external acts, but not that it cannot bind in conscience. For even if this rule directs only external acts, nevertheless, since it is a rule, deviating from it is committing a sin.

You will say, how can the law or temporal authority produce a spiritual effect, namely, binding the conscience? I reply that even if the political authority and its law are called temporal because of their object, which is to deal with temporal and external matters, nevertheless in themselves they are spiritual things. Besides, binding the conscience is not performing something spiritual, but only commanding another in such a way that if he does not obey, he sins; and by the testimony of his conscience he should or could understand that he is indeed committing a sin. Therefore, whoever can com-

97. Romans 13:5.
98. Ibid.
99. Romans 13:6.
100. 1 Peter 2:13.
101. The passage shown here in italic type was added by Bellarmine in the corrections he made to the Venice 1599 edition of the *Controversiae* (APUG 1364, cols. 473–74).

mand can also bind the conscience, even if he does not make judgments on internal matters or does not examine another person's conscience.

To the fourth and fifth I say that the prince cannot impose a spiritual and eternal punishment, and he cannot lift such punishment, but he can nevertheless impose an obligation under pain of such punishment, since he does it by the authority of God, Who granted him the latter and not the former. It is as if a king allowed a viceroy to impose an obligation on the subjects under pain of capital punishment but did not allow him to administer justice by himself or to pardon the punishment. Or we can say that political law binds under pain of eternal punishment not because it is the law of man, but because it is the law of the minister of God. Whoever offends a minister of God at the same time offends God, wherefore if *per impossibile* there were no God in nature, and likewise *per impossibile* there were a certain political law, this would bind in conscience, and transgressing it would be a sin, but no spiritual punishment or eternal damnation would follow the transgression.

To the sixth I say that it is not absurd that the same sin is punished by many and in many places when it offends many, for often we see that murderers have the hands cut off at the place where the murder took place, and their heads cut off at the place of public execution.

To the seventh I say that it depends on the intention of the legislator whether he wants to command in earnest and to make true laws or wants only to show what should be done without any command. But if he wants to command in earnest and make true laws, it is not in his power to exempt his law from binding under pain of mortal or venial sin, according to the importance of the matter.

To the last I say that the reason why human law gives way to divine law when they cannot both be obeyed at the same time is not that human law does not bind under pain of sin, but that it is established less firmly. For in such a case it ceases to be law, and therefore it ceases to be binding. See what we said in book 4 of *De Summo Pontifice;* and also John Driedo in book 3 of *De libertate Christiana,* Adrian in *Quodlibeta* 6, Francisco de Vitoria in the lecture on civil authority; Alfonso de Castro, book 1 of *De potestate legis poenalis,* chapter 4, and Domingo de Soto, *De iustitia et iure,* book 1, question 6, article 4.

## CHAPTER 12

# The third proposition

The conduct of public trials is not forbidden to Christians. The proof is, first, that it is a prerogative of the prince to exercise justice, for Scripture usually considers king and judge almost as synonyms: Psalm 2, "Be wise now therefore, O ye kings: be instructed, ye judges of the earth";[102] Isaiah 33, "For the Lord is our judge, the Lord is our lawgiver, the Lord is our king";[103] Jeremiah 23, "A King shall reign and prosper, and shall execute judgment and justice in the earth."[104] If, therefore, it is lawful for Christians to have a prince, why not a judge also?

Second, because the laws would have no benefit if there were no judgment, but laws must not be abolished, as we showed above, nor therefore judgments.

Third, Scripture in both Testaments admits judgments, for we read this in Deuteronomy 16: "Judges and officers shalt thou make thee in all thy gates, which the Lord thy God giveth thee, throughout thy tribes: and they shall judge the people with just judgment";[105] 1 Corinthians 6: "If then ye have judgments of things pertaining to this life, set them to judge who are least esteemed in the church. I speak to your shame. Is it so, that there is not a wise man among you? no, not one that shall be able to judge between his brethren?"[106] There the apostle admonishes the Corinthians

102. Psalm 2:10.
103. Isaiah 33:22.
104. Jeremiah 23:5.
105. Deuteronomy 16:18.
106. 1 Corinthians 6:4–5.

to appoint judges among themselves in those cases where they did not necessarily have to go to the tribunals of the pagans.

The arguments that were posed in the beginning are not difficult to disprove. To those words of Matthew 5, "And if any man will sue thee at the law, and take away thy coat, let him have thy cloak also,"[107] I reply with St. Augustine in his epistle 5 [138] to Marcellinus that this phrase must be understood to concern only the readiness of the spirit, for in the same place our Lord says: "Whosoever shall smite thee on thy right cheek, turn to him the other also."[108] Nevertheless our Lord Himself when smitten on the cheek did not turn the other, but said in John 18, "Why smitest thou me?"[109] by which example He taught how His precepts should be understood.

To the words of the apostle in 1 Corinthians 6, "There is utterly a fault among you, etc."[110] I say, first, that the word *fault* [*delictum*] in Greek is ἥττημα, which does not mean "sin" but "imperfection," and Theodoretus interprets it in this way. Second, if *fault* means "sin," as Chrysostom and Ambrose interpret this passage, and Augustine in *Enchiridion,* chapter 78, and book 2 of *De sermone Domini in monte,* chapter 15 [11] and conclusion 24 on Psalm 118, then it is called *fault* not because it is a sin in itself, but because in general it does not lack sin—either because of the end, as when a lawsuit stems from greed; or because of the means, as when a lawsuit is discussed with hatred, ill will, and quarrels; or because of injustice, as when deceits and treacheries are involved; or because of scandal, as happened to the Corinthians, whose litigations scandalized the pagans. Third, judgments are not blamed on the judge, but on those who take another man to court. Therefore, even if taking another man to court were a sin, judging would not be a sin, as judgments impose an end to quarrels, which is good.

107. Matthew 5:40.
108. Matthew 5:39.
109. John 18:23.
110. 1 Corinthians 6:7.

## ∞ CHAPTER 13 ∞

# The fourth proposition

It is lawful for the Christian magistrate to apply capital punishment to those who disturb the public peace. This is proved, first, by Scripture, for in the law of nature, the law of Moses, and the law of the Gospel we have precepts and examples regarding this. In fact, in Genesis 9 God says: "Whoso sheddeth man's blood, by man shall his blood be shed,"[111] which words cannot be taken as a prediction, for it would often be false, but must be taken as an order and a precept. Hence in the Chaldaic paraphrase it is rendered: "Whoever sheds men's blood before witnesses, by sentence of a judge his blood should be shed."[112] In Genesis 38 Judah said: "Bring her forth, and let her be burnt,"[113] whereby the Patriarch Judah as lord of the household sentenced the adulteress to death by fire.

In the law of Moses there are many precepts and examples, as Exodus 21: "He that smiteth a man, so that he die, shall be surely put to death,"[114] and Moses himself and Joshua, Samuel, David, Elias, and other most holy men killed many people. In Matthew 26: "All they that take the sword shall perish with the sword,"[115] which can be understood correctly

111. Genesis 9:6.
112. Bellarmine is referring here to the Jewish versions of the Old Testament called *Targums,* a series of translations and paraphrases in Aramaic, usually present in the early modern printed editions of the Polyglot Bibles. For a general introduction to these texts see B. J. Roberts, "The Old Testament: Manuscripts, Text and Versions," in Lampe, ed., *Cambridge History of the Bible,* pp. 1–26 at pp. 22–26.
113. Genesis 38:24.
114. Exodus 21:12.
115. Matthew 26:52.

only as: anybody who commits a murder must in turn be executed by the magistrate. Our Lord, in fact, reproached Peter not because just defense is unlawful, but because he did not so much want to defend himself or our Lord as to revenge a wrong done to our Lord, although he had no official authority, as Augustine rightly explains in his treatise 112 on John, and Cyril in his commentary on John, book 11, chapter 35. Moreover, in Romans 13 the apostle says: "But if thou do that which is evil, be afraid; for he beareth not the sword in vain: for he is the minister of God, a revenger to execute wrath upon him that doeth evil,"[116] meaning that the sword is given by God to the princes against the evildoers. Therefore if such evildoers are found in the Church, why may they not be punished with the sword?

Second, it is proved from the testimonies of the Fathers. In epistle 3 to Exuperius, chapter 3, Innocent I is asked whether it is lawful for the magistrate to use capital punishment for criminals after they have been baptized, and he replies that it is absolutely lawful. Hilary, in canon 32 to chapter 26 of Matthew, says that it is lawful to kill in two cases, if a man is fulfilling the duty of judge or if he kills in self-defense. Jerome in the commentary on chapter 22 of Jeremiah says: "To punish murderers and impious men is not shedding blood, but applying the laws." Augustine, in *De civitate Dei*, book 1, chapter 21, says: "Those who, holding a public authority, punished criminals with death did not violate that precept which says 'thou shalt not kill.'"

Last, it is proved by reason, for it pertains to the good prince, who is charged with the protection of the common good, to prevent the parts from corrupting the whole upon which they depend. Therefore if he cannot keep all parts sound, he should rather amputate a part than allow the common good to be destroyed, just as the farmers cut off bushes and twigs that block the path to the vine and the tree, and the doctor amputates the limbs that could infect the whole body.

To the argument of the Anabaptists from Matthew 5, "An eye for an eye, etc.,"[117] there are two replies. One is that since the old law was given to imperfect men, it permitted us to seek revenge, and commanded us

116. Romans 13:4.
117. Matthew 5:38.

only not to seek a greater injury than that which had been done. The reason is not that it is lawful to seek revenge, but that it is a lesser evil to seek a moderate revenge than an extreme one. Afterward Christ, Who was teaching to more-perfect men, removed such permission. Augustine interpreted the matter in this way in book 1 of *De sermone Domini in monte*, chapter 35 [19], and *Contra Adimantum*, chapter 8, and likewise Chrysostom and Hilary, but since revenge was prohibited in Leviticus 19 ("Thou shalt not avenge"),[118] and since we read in Ecclesiasticus 28 "Who wants to revenge himself will find revenge from the Lord," we might reply, more correctly, with St. Thomas, St. Bonaventure, and some others commenting on Peter Lombard's *Sententiae*, book 3, distinction 30, that when the Lord says "An eye for an eye" He does not condemn that law and neither does He prohibit the magistrate from inflicting retaliatory punishment, but He condemns the perverse interpretation of the Pharisees and prohibits the desire and seeking of revenge on the part of private citizens. In fact, in Exodus 21 and Leviticus 24 God established a holy law by which the magistrate might use retaliatory punishment on criminals, and from this the Pharisees deduced that private citizens were permitted to seek revenge; in the same manner the Pharisees deduced that it was permitted to hate one's enemies from "Thou shalt love thy friend." But Christ teaches that these are distortions of the law and that we must love also our enemies and not resist evil, but be ready if need be to turn the other cheek to the person who smites us on one side. That our Lord was speaking to private citizens is clear from the words that follow, for the Lord speaks thus: "But I say unto you, that ye resist not evil: but whosoever shall smite thee on thy right cheek, turn to him the other also."[119]

It is to be observed that when Christ said, "Resist not evil," He did not prohibit just defense but retaliation, for He commands us not to hit him who hits us, as Theophylactus rightly teaches. Also, by the person hitting is not meant he who hits to harm, but he who hits to defend himself. In brief, it is not the defense but the revenge that is prohibited, according to Romans 12: "Dearly beloved, avenge not yourselves";[120] that is, do

118. Leviticus 19:18.
119. Matthew 5:39.
120. Romans 12:19.

not seek revenge. For in Greek it is ἐκδικοῦντες, whence it follows: "But rather give place unto wrath: for it is written, Vengeance is mine; I will repay, saith the Lord."[121] Revenge is not simply forbidden if it is sought by a legitimate judge and for a good end, that is, because a criminal is to be corrected, or because his evildoing cannot be repressed and avoided in any other manner and if he were left unpunished he would continue to do harm. Therefore the only thing that is prohibited is the revenge that private citizens want to accomplish by themselves or the revenge that they seek from a judge in order to harm their enemies and to satisfy their anger and hatred.

121. Ibid.

## CHAPTER 14

# It is sometimes lawful for Christians to wage war

We now turn to the fourth question, which deals with war.[122] This discussion has three parts. First, we must demonstrate that sometimes wars are lawful for Christians. Second, we must explain the conditions of a just war. Third, because of Luther, we have to prove that Christians rightly take up arms against the Turks.

To start with the first point, it was an ancient heresy of the Manicheans to argue that war was by nature unlawful, and therefore they accused Moses, Joshua, David, and other Fathers of the Old Testament, who waged wars, of impiety, as blessed Augustine reports in *Contra Faustum,* book 22, chapters 74ff.[123] Some people brought up the same heresy in our time, and especially Erasmus who in various places, but especially in *Annotationes ad capitulos III et XXII Lucae,* argued at length that war was one of the evils that God tolerated and permitted to the ancient Jews, but that war was forbidden to the Christians by Christ and the apostles.[124]

122. Bellarmine returns to the questions that he had announced in chapter 1 at the very beginning of the work.

123. On the Augustinian doctrine of just war, which became the basis for the Christian doctrine on war and on which Bellarmine relies in this and the following chapter, see J. Barnes, "The Just War," in Kretzmann et al., eds., *Cambridge History of Later Medieval Philosophy,* pp. 771–84.

124. Erasmus voiced vigorous opposition to war in many of his works, to the point of doubting the legitimacy of the war against the Turks, for, as he wrote in *The Education of a Christian Prince* (1516), "The kingdom of Christ was created, spread and secured by very different means. Perhaps it should not be defended by other means than those which created and spread it" (ed. Jardine, p. 108). For an overview of Erasmus's antiwar stances in the context of his political activities, see Tracy, *The Politics of Erasmus.* Bellarmine's interest in Erasmus's works was not limited to the issue of just war, given

Also Cornelius Agrippa in *De vanitate scientiarum,* chapter 79, affirms that the practice of war was prohibited by Christ. So did Johann Wild in book 4 of his commentaries on Matthew, with an explanation of the passage in chapter 26: "All they that take the sword shall perish with the sword." The Anabaptists teach the same, as Melanchthon attests in his *Loci,* chapter on the magistrate. Alfonso de Castro attributed the same doctrine to Oecolampadius under the entry "war," which seems surprising to me, since Zwingli, his associate, approved of war so much that he died fighting in battle; and Calvin in book 4 of the *Institutiones,* chapter 20. Melanchthon, as quoted before, and other heretics of the time likewise teach in word and deed that war should be waged.

By contrast, just as the whole Church always taught in words and examples, we say that war by nature is not unlawful, and waging war is

---

that Bellarmine was one of the main protagonists in the debate over the inclusion of Erasmus's work in the Index of Prohibited Books at the end of the 1580s. Erasmus's works had been included in the first class of the prohibited books in the Index of 1559—which meant that it was not possible to *expurgare,* or correct, it. In the Index of 1564, however, Erasmus's work was put in both the first and the second class, that is, the class of works that could be corrected, but it was put back in the first and removed from the second in 1572. So when the Congregation of the Index, under Sixtus V, met to revise the Index—a new version would be published in 1596 under the Pontificate of Clement VIII—a discussion on Erasmus was necessary to settle whether his work could in fact be corrected or had to be considered absolutely forbidden. The discussion on Erasmus started in 1587, the year in which Bellarmine was officially appointed as *consultor* of the Congregation of the Index, and his judgment on Erasmus was positive. In his *votum,* that is, his formal opinion, on the matter, Bellarmine declared that in order for an author to be considered a heretic two things were necessary: "an error contrary to the faith and pertinacity." While Erasmus had the first, he did not have the second, for, as Bellarmine wrote, "In many of his works and especially in his *Annotationes ad Novum Testamentum* [which is the text that Bellarmine is quoting here] he declares that he does not want to assert anything contrary to the judgment of the Church." The conclusion, therefore, was that since Erasmus was not a heretic, his work should have been removed from the first class and put in the second. Bellarmine's *votum* can be found in ACDF, Index, Protocolli II, folder 2, fol. 405r (my translation). It has also been published by Godman, *Saint as Censor,* pp. 237–38, and analyzed at pp. 110–14; and by Frajese, *La nascita dell'Indice,* pp. 112ff., where further information on the subsequent vicissitudes of Erasmus's work between Inquisition and Index can be found. Bellarmine's discussion of Erasmus's arguments against war in this work, coupled with his defense of Erasmus's work in the discussions on the Index in the 1580s, should serve as a reminder that censorship, polemical writings, and political theory were, for Bellarmine, part of the same strategy for strengthening the Catholic Church's political and intellectual force.

allowed not only to the Jews but also to the Christians, provided that the conditions which we will later discuss are fulfilled. This is proved by the evidence of Scripture, in Judges 3: "Now these are the nations which the Lord left, to prove Israel by them, even as many of Israel as had not known all the wars of Canaan; Only that the generations of the children of Israel might know, to teach them war, at the least such as before knew nothing thereof."[125] These words not only show God's permission but God's absolute will. Likewise in 1 Kings 15: "Thus saith the Lord of hosts, I remember that which Amalek did to Israel, how he laid wait for him in the way, when he came up from Egypt. Now go and smite Amalek, and utterly destroy all that they have, and spare them not, etc."[126] Here also we see not a permission but a command, and the Old Testament is full of similar instances. The same in Luke 3: "And the soldiers likewise demanded of him, saying, And what shall we do? And he said unto them, Do violence to no man, neither accuse any falsely; and be content with your wages."[127] The Anabaptists, according to Melanchthon, say that John allowed the Jews war because they were imperfect and that Christ taught something entirely different.

On the contrary, since John was preparing the path for the Lord, he cannot have allowed what Christ was soon to remove. Also, the Jews could not make use of that permission, since Christ would come the same year and prohibit war, as they would have it. Moreover, men might have suspected that Christ and John did not agree with each other, which would have been truly absurd. Erasmus replies otherwise, that these commands are given to the soldiers not so that they might live well following them, but so that they might live less badly, which seems also to be Theophylactus's interpretation.

But it is otherwise, for John had said before: "Bring forth therefore fruits worthy of repentance," and "Every tree therefore which bringeth not forth good fruit is hewn down, and cast into the fire."[128] As a consequence, the repenting publicans and soldiers asked what was the good fruit they

125. Judges 3:1–2.
126. 1 Samuel 15:2–3.
127. Luke 3:14.
128. Luke 3:8, 9.

should bring forth. So either John deceived them, or soldiers can attain salvation if they fulfill what John commanded them.

Regarding Theophylactus, I say two things. First, he does not say that war is evil, but only that John exhorted the people who were innocent to do good, that is, to share their goods with the others, but he exhorted the publicans and soldiers, who were incapable of such perfection and could not do works of supererogation, to desist from evil. In fact, Theophylactus thought that for somebody who has two coats to give one to him who has none was a work of counsel and supererogation; otherwise he would not call the people innocent to whom he was speaking, and neither would he distinguish this act as good rather than evil, for if it is a command not to keep two coats, keeping them will be an evil act.

Second, Theophylactus does not correctly interpret this passage, for he calls the people innocent whom John calls a "generation of vipers" and says to "bring forth therefore fruits worthy of repentance."[129] Moreover, keeping two coats means keeping what is superfluous, as Jerome says in question 1, *Ad Hedibiam,* and it is a sin to keep what is superfluous. Furthermore, in Matthew 22 our Lord taught that the tribute to Caesar must be paid, and certainly no tribute is owed to kings for any other purpose but to sustain the army in defense of the commonwealth, which the apostle explains in Romans 13: "For this cause pay ye tribute also: for they are God's ministers, attending continually upon this very thing,"[130] that is, to punish with their sword those who disturb the public peace, for before he had said: "For he beareth not the sword in vain: for he is the minister of God, a revenger to execute wrath upon him that doeth evil."[131]

Second, it is proved by the examples of the saints who waged wars, for if war were evil, certainly it would not be waged by saints. In the Old Testament we read that Abraham, Moses, Joshua, Gideon, Samson, David, Josiah, and the Maccabees waged war with much praise. In the New Testament, Matthew 8, when the centurion said to Christ, "For I am a man under authority, having soldiers under me: and I say to this man, Go, and

129. Luke 3:7, 8.
130. Romans 13:6.
131. Romans 13:4.

he goeth; and to another, Come, and he cometh, etc.,"[132] the Lord praised him for his faith and did not command him to leave the army. In Acts 10, the same centurion, Cornelius, is called "a just man and one that feareth God"[133] so much so that he deserved to see an angel, and afterward, after being taught the path to salvation by St. Peter, he was not told to leave the army.

Subsequently, after Christ's ascension to heaven, there were always Christians in the army, even under pagan princes, some of them truly holy and beloved by God, as Tertullian teaches in *Apologeticus,* chapter 5, where he reports a great miracle performed by Christian soldiers when they were fighting under Marcus Aurelius in Germany. They would certainly not have been in the army if that was evil, and even if they were, they would not have been so beloved by God that they were even able to perform miracles. See also Eusebius, *Historia,* book 8, chapter 4, and book 9, chapter 10 [9]. Basil also teaches in *Oratio in laudem SS. 40 Martyrum* that there were many holy men in the army of pagan emperors, and likewise Gregory of Nazianzus in his first oration *In Julianum* [4], in the second part. Finally, it is established that Constantine, Theodosius, Valentinian, Charlemagne, St. Louis the king of France, St. Maurice with his legion of Thebans, and many other Christian saints waged wars, and the holy bishops never blamed them; indeed, Theodosius asked the Abbot John for advice on the outcome of the war, as Augustine reports in book 5 of *De civitate Dei,* chapter 26.

Third, it is proved because God always assists just wars, which of course He would not do if war were unlawful, for evil deeds may be allowed, but support to do evil deeds can never be given. In Genesis 14 Melchizedek said to Abram after he defeated four kings with only 318 servants, "Blessed be the most high God, which hath delivered thine enemies into thy hand."[134] In Exodus 17, answering the prayers of Moses, God gave victory to the Hebrews against Amalek; in Joshua 10, when Joshua was fighting, the sun stood still and God made great stones fall from heaven as rain

132. Matthew 8:9.
133. Acts 10:22.
134. Genesis 14:20.

and with the hailstorm of stones He killed more people than the sons of
Israel with spears and swords. In 2 Maccabees 10[135] angels appearing as
knights fought with the Maccabees, and at chapter 15 we read that God
gives victory to the worthy ones not because of the strength of the armies
but as He wishes.

Eusebius in *De vita Constantini* and in book 9 of *Historia,* chapter 9,
attests that Constantine won battles with the help of God and through
clearly proved miracles; Theodoretus in *Historia,* book 5, chapter 5, attests that the apostles St. John and St. Philip fought openly with Theodosius against his enemies; Socrates in book 7, chapter 18, writes that angels
fought for the younger Theodosius against the Saracens; on Clodoveus, see
Gregory of Tours, book 2 of the *Historia Francorum,* chapter 30; blessed
Augustine in book 5 of *De civitate Dei,* chapter 23, writes that Honorius's
army attained an incredible victory against the Goths with a divine miracle; and innumerable similar examples can be reported.

Fourth, it is proved by reason. It is lawful for the commonwealth to
defend its citizens from internal enemies of peace by eliminating them
with different kinds of punishment, and therefore it will also be lawful
to defend its citizens from external enemies by war and weapons when it
cannot be done in any other way. Since, in order to preserve themselves,
it is necessary for commonwealths to be able to keep away all their enemies, both internal and external, and since this is the law of nature, it is
certainly not credible that the ability to defend themselves was removed
through the Gospel.

Last, it is proved by the testimonies of the Fathers. Tertullian in *Apologeticus,* chapter 42, says: "We sail with you, and fight with you, and farm
with you, and trade with you."

St. Gregory of Nazianzus in his third [second] *Oratio de pace* [22] says:
"Both [the time of war and the time of peace] require some consideration,
for even though it is actually possible in some cases to fight war in accordance with God's law and authority, nevertheless for as long as we can we
should incline rather to peace as the more divine and sublime course."

---

135. The first and second books of the Maccabees were considered apocryphal and
were not included in the King James Bible.

In his homily *De nuptiis,* on John 2, St. John Chrysostom says, among
other things, "You use the army as a pretext and say that you cannot be
pious; was not the centurion a soldier, and yet his being in the army did
him no harm?"

Blessed Ambrose, sermon 7, says, "to be in the army is not a crime, but
to be in the army for the sake of pillaging is a sin." And in his *De officiis,*
book 1, chapters 40 and 41, he lists among the virtues military valor, and
he proves that our men did not lack it with many examples. Likewise in
his *Oratio de obitu Theodosii* he vigorously praises Theodosius for his ability in war.

In his epistle 5 [138] to Marcellinus blessed Augustine says: "For if
Christian discipline disapproved all wars, the soldiers in the Gospel who
were asking for advice about salvation would have been told to throw
away their weapons and to remove themselves completely from the army,
but in fact they were told not to do violence to any man, or accuse any
falsely, and to be content with their wages. So He commanded that their
pay should suffice and certainly did not prohibit them from serving in the
army." And in epistle 205 or 207 [189] to Boniface he says, "Do not think
that anybody who serves in the army cannot please God, etc." He teaches
the same in book 22 of his *Contra Faustum,* chapters 74ff., and book 6,
*Quaestiones in Iesum Nave,* question 10.

Blessed Gregory, in book 1 of the epistles, chapter 72 [epistle 74] to
Gennadius,[136] says: "Just as the Lord of victories made your excellence
shine brightly against the enemies of war in this life, so it is necessary
that the same excellence is shown against the enemies of His Church with
all vigor of mind and body, etc.," and in chapter 73 [epistle 75], "If such
prosperity had not followed your excellence in warfare as a reward of your
faith, and through the grace of the Christian religion, it would not be
such a wonder, but since you have made provisions for future victories
(God willing) not with carnal precaution, but rather with prayers, it is
something wonderful that your glory stems from God, who grants it from
above, not from earthly advice."

136. I have followed the numbers given in the edition of Gregory's letters found in
PL, vol. 77.

Gregory of Tours in *Historia,* book 5, chapter 1, says: "If only you, O kings, engaged in the same battles as your forefathers, that the heathen terrified by your union might be crushed by your strength!"

Blessed Bernard in his sermon to the soldiers, chapter 3, says: "Indeed the soldiers of Christ confidently fight the battles of their Lord, and have no fear of sinning when killing the enemies, and no fear of incurring the danger of being killed, seeing that death suffered or inflicted for Christ is not a crime but deserves a great glory."

But against this they object, first, through the Scriptures, starting with Deuteronomy 32: "To me belongeth vengeance and recompence,"[137] and Romans 12: "Dearly beloved, avenge not yourselves, but rather give place unto wrath: for it is written, Vengeance is mine; I will repay, saith the Lord."[138] I reply that the vengeance that public authorities seek is rightly called the vengeance of God, for they are ministers of God serving Him in this matter, and that is why Paul, having said, "Vengeance is mine," at the end of Romans 12, begins chapter 13 by saying, "But if thou do that which is evil, be afraid; for he beareth not the sword in vain: for he is the minister of God, a revenger to execute wrath upon him that doeth evil."[139]

Then they add this passage from Isaiah 2: "And they shall beat their swords into plowshares, and their spears into pruning hooks: nation shall not lift up sword against nation, neither shall they learn war any more,"[140] which are things predicted of the Christian era. I reply that in this passage only the perfect peace to come at the time of Christ's birth is predicted, as blessed Jerome explains, and we know that this was fulfilled at the time of Augustus. Those words "any more" do not mean "for eternity," but "for a long time." Moreover, even if that had not been fulfilled, nothing could be concluded from it, for Isaiah does not prohibit war if there are enemies who disturb us, but he predicts a time in which there will be no enemies. Therefore as long as there are enemies, war can be waged, as it can also be said that it is predicted that Christ's kingdom will be peaceful,

137. Deuteronomy 32:35.
138. Romans 12:19.
139. Romans 13:4.
140. Isaiah 2:4.

seeing that His kingdom is not of this world and does not deal with temporal matters, and in this it is distinguished from the Judaic kingdom, which had to be strengthened and preserved with war and killings.

Finally they object with these words in Matthew 5: "But I say unto you, That ye resist not evil: but whosoever shall smite thee on thy right cheek, turn to him the other also,"[141] and Matthew 26: "All they that take the sword shall perish with the sword,"[142] which are similar to Romans 12, "Recompense to no man evil for evil. Provide things honest in the sight of all men, etc."[143]

I reply that Julian the Apostate once used the same arguments against the Christians, as Gregory of Nazianzus reports in the first oration *In Julianum* [4], around the middle of the work. But first, that all these precepts or counsels are given to private citizens, for God or the apostle did not command the judge not to punish him who wronged another, but He commanded everybody to suffer patiently their wrongs. War, however, does not pertain to private revenge but to public justice, and just as loving one's enemy, which everybody must, does not prevent the judge and the executioner from doing their duty, so it does not prevent the soldiers and the emperors from doing theirs.

Moreover, even these are not always precepts to private citizens; sometimes they are precepts, sometimes advice. Precepts are always to prepare the soul, so that a man may be ready to turn the other cheek and to give away his coat to somebody who wants it rather than offend God. But such action is in fact prescribed when it is necessarily demanded by God's honor. Otherwise it is only advice, and sometimes not even that, for instance when offering the other cheek is of no use because the other person just repeats his sin. Such is the response of Gregory of Nazianzus in this passage, and Augustine's in epistle 5 [138] to Marcellinus.

Second, they can oppose our argument with three decrees of the Church. The first is in the Council of Nicaea, canon 11, where a most serious punishment is inflicted against those who return to the army after

141. Matthew 5:39.
142. Matthew 26:52.
143. Romans 12:17.

leaving it.[144] The second is in epistle 90 [167] of blessed Leo, to Rusticus, and it is found also in the canon "Contrarium, de poenitentia," distinction 5.[145] Leo says, "It is contrary to the ecclesiastical rules to return to a secular army after doing penance," and later, "He who wants to involve himself in worldly warfare is not free from the Devil's snares." The third is Gregory's canon "Falsas," same distinction, where it is said that those who adopt an activity that cannot be done without sinning are not entitled to do penance unless they abandon such activity, and Gregory gives the example of a soldier.[146]

To the first I reply that it deals with those who because they confessed their faith were deprived by Diocletian or Licinius of their sword belt, and afterward they reclaimed it, ready to deny their faith. See Zonaras and Balsamon on that canon, and Rufinus, *Historia,* book 10, chapter 6, and what we wrote on this in book 2 of *De Conciliis,* chapter 8.

To the second and third I say that it deals with those who committed many sins occasioned by their military life and who therefore needed to

144. This is canon 12, not 11, of the Council of Nicaea (text in *Conciliorum oecumenicorum decreta,* pp. 10–11).

145. This is the first of many quotations from canon law used by Bellarmine both in this work and in the treatise against Barclay. The body of canon law is composed of two parts. The first is the collection of laws made by Gratian in the twelfth century titled *Concordia discordantium canonum* or *Decretum Gratiani.* The second part is composed of five books of decretals called the *Liber extra* of Gregory IX, edited by Raymond de Peñafort and promulgated in 1234; a *Liber sextus* of decretals added by Pope Boniface VIII; the *Clementinae* of Clement V; the *Extravagantes* (until John XXII); and the *Communes.* After 1491 these books were printed as a single work, and many different editions were made until 1582, when a committee appointed by Pope Gregory XIII produced the Roman edition of the canons as the only authoritative one. Bellarmine reports faithfully the text of this canon, which he quotes in the manner that was usual for medieval and early modern theologians and jurists, that is, by indicating its first word or words. The canon in question is number 3 of the second part of Gratian's *Decretum,* causa 33, question 3, distinction 5 (the text can be found in *Corpus iuris canonici,* vol. 1, col. 1240).

146. This canon, the sixth of the second part of Gratian's *Decretum,* causa 33, question 3, distinction 5, was issued by Gregory VII at the Synod of Rome in 1078. The example of the soldier who after doing penance should return to the army only on the suggestion of the bishop was used in support of the assertion that only penances attributed according to the will of the Fathers on the basis of the nature of the crime should be considered legitimate punishments (the text is in *Corpus iuris canonici,* vol. 1, col. 1241).

do penance. In fact, those who return to military life knowing from experience that they cannot live it without sinning, are badly behaved because they themselves are evil, not the army; this is especially so when they have been commanded by a priest not to return. And that those canons do not in fact absolutely prohibit military life is clear from the ending of the canon, "Falsas," where after saying that those who come back to the army after doing penance behave badly, it is added, "unless they come back upon suggestion of their bishops to defend justice."

Third, many passages from the Fathers are set against our argument by Erasmus, and to those passages we add two, one by Tertullian and the other by Jerome. In *De corona militis,* second part [11], Tertullian asks whether military life is becoming to a Christian. And he replies: "Do we believe that it is lawful for a human oath to supersede a divine one? And to answer to another lord after Christ? Will it be lawful to live by the sword when God said that whoever takes the sword shall perish by the sword? And will a son of peace, to whom even lawsuits are not becoming, engage in battle?"

I reply that Tertullian does not condemn military life for being evil in itself. This is clear, first, from the passages above quoted from *Apologeticus,* chapters 5 and 42. Second, because in the book *De corona militis* he says that those who were soldiers before baptism can remain soldiers even after baptism, and he only teaches that he who is free must not enter military life after baptism, and he says: "Clearly, if faith afterward comes to those who have already entered military life, their situation is different from those whom John admitted to baptism, just like that very faithful centurion whom Christ approves of and Peter instructs in the Christian religion. For once the faith is accepted and sealed, one should either desert immediately or try every way possible not to do anything against God." Third, it is clear because the chief reason he gives why Christians should not serve in the army is the danger of idolatry, for almost all princes were then pagans. Therefore Tertullian judges war to be contingently evil at that time: "Will he be guarding the temples he has renounced? Will he be eating with those who displease the apostle?[147] Will he defend at night

147. Cf. 1 Corinthians 5:11.

those demons that he rejected with exorcisms during the day? Will he bear a standard opposed to the standard of Christ? etc." Moreover, his other reasons given above are only reasons of convenience, as is clear.

In the epistle to Ageruchia, *De monogamia,* Jerome says: "Once it was said to soldiers, 'Tie your sword very firmly to your thigh'; now it is said to Peter, 'Put up again thy sword into its place,' etc." But his point is that in the Old Testament wars were commanded by God and were necessary to acquire and preserve the promised land; in the New Testament not wars but peace is commanded, since weapons are not necessary to conquer the kingdom of heaven. Nevertheless, from this it does not follow that Christians, as citizens of the temporal commonwealth, cannot wage wars against those who wronged them.

Besides these, Erasmus opposes some other Fathers, and first Origen, who in *Contra Celsum,* book 2, just before the middle, says that Christ removed all wars; and in treatise 7 on Matthew, he explains in the passage of Luke 22, "He that hath no sword, let him sell his garment, and buy one,"[148] saying that this passage is harmful for those who interpret it literally, thinking that they really must sell their garment and buy a sword.

I reply that in the first passage there is nothing supporting Erasmus, for when Origen says that Christ removed all wars, he does not mean that Christ prohibited all wars, but that with His providence He brought a general peace to the world at the time of His birth. Indeed here there is something against Erasmus, for Origen says that because of God's providence it happened that with Christ's coming all were subjects of the Roman emperor, for if there had been many kings, wars would have been necessary, as some would respond to the wrongs of others. Nor is anything said against war in the following passage, for the words of God must not be understood so literally that anybody should necessarily sell his garment and buy a sword. In that figure of speech the Lord wanted only to explain that the apostles would have had the same hardship and need as those who sell their garment and buy a sword to defend themselves. But what is inferred from this against war? Because our Lord in this passage did not truly command purchase of a sword, then is He understood to have prohibited

148. Luke 22:36.

war? When Origen himself, in his homily 15 on Joshua, says that physical wars must not be waged by Christians, he means that the Christian army under the command of Christ is not a physical army against men, as was the army of the Jews under Joshua, but a spiritual one against demons. However, from this it does not follow that waging wars is unlawful for Christians as citizens of the political commonwealth.

In the same manner the arguments that Erasmus takes from Chrysostom, Basil, and Theophylactus (drawing from St. Thomas's *Catena aurea*, on Luke 22) can be disproved, since those passages show only that Christ did not order the apostles to really buy a sword.

Then he juxtaposes our arguments against those of Ambrose, who in book 10 of his commentary on Luke explains the passage "He that hath no sword, let him sell his garment and buy one." Ambrose says: "O Lord, why do you order me to buy a sword and prohibit me from striking? Why do you command me to get what you forbid me to bring out? Maybe to prepare me for an act of defense and not authorize an act of revenge, so that I would decide not to take revenge even if I could. The law does not in fact forbid to strike back and therefore perhaps He said to Peter, who was offering two swords, 'It is enough' as if this were lawful until the Gospel, so that in the law there is the knowledge of justice, and in the Gospel the perfection of virtue." I reply, first, that nothing is said in this passage against war that is waged by public authority; this passage deals with private defense or revenge. Second, even private defense, according to Ambrose's statement, does not refer to the prohibition of the precept, but to the perfection of the advice, as is clearly indicated by the words, "so that in the law there be the discipline of equity, and in the Gospel the perfection of virtue."[149]

Erasmus opposes also Augustine, who, he says, is not consistent, for while in some cases he defended war, in others he wrote against war, as in the commentary on Psalm 37 where he writes: "We must not pray for our enemies to die, but for them to amend themselves." And in epistle 5 [138] to Marcellinus he writes many things against war; indeed in epistle 158

149. Bellarmine used the same passage in chapter 19 of the treatise against Barclay when discussing whether the clergy could use the material sword in addition to the spiritual one: cf. pp. 282–85.

[133] and other places he beseeches the same Marcellinus to punish the Donatists without bloodshed.

However, Erasmus seems to have regarded those with whom he spoke as children, for what are these things to our purpose? Certainly in the commentary on Psalm 37 Augustine censured hatred of the enemy, which leads some to pray to God for their enemies' death: who denies, in fact, that it is evil to wish the enemy's death out of hatred and lust for revenge? But wishing death on one's enemy and even accomplishing it is not evil according to the order of justice, if it is done not because of hatred toward man, but because of love of justice and the common good. Indeed in epistle 5 [138] there is nothing against war, but rather something in support of it, as we quoted before, and I do not know what Erasmus was dreaming of. In epistle 158 [133] he begs the judge to pardon the wicked who were already in custody and confessed their crime, which the bishops even now are accustomed to do. But what does this have to do with war? Or should we say that whoever begs that a thief be not hung consequently prohibits war?

He also used as a counterexample St. Martin, who, as Sulpicius reports in his biography of him, said to the emperor Julian: "Let him who is to fight accept your gratuity. I am a Christian; fighting is not lawful for me." However, Erasmus did not report St. Martin's words faithfully, for he does not say "I am a Christian; fighting is not lawful for me," but "So far I have fought for you, but now allow me to be a soldier for God; I am Christ's soldier, fighting is not lawful for me." By this he did not mean simply that he was Christian, but also that he was a monk by vow and way of life, for that is what "Allow me to be a soldier for God" and "I am Christ's soldier" mean. This was the reason why Sulpicius a little earlier had written that St. Martin, after receiving baptism, continued being a soldier for two more years, not because St. Martin did not want to renounce the world immediately, but because the tribune of the soldiers, who shared the tent with him, promised to also renounce the world after his term as tribune had expired, that is, he promised St. Martin to become a monk with him. Therefore, St. Martin affirmed that war was forbidden not to a Christian, but to a monk, since he, being Christian, had remained in the army for two more years.

Finally, Erasmus urges that the weapons of the Church are the sword of the word of God, the shield of faith, the helmet of salvation, the breast-plate of justice, the darts of prayers, as the apostle teaches in Ephesians 6, and therefore Christians must not fight with swords and weapons.

I reply, first, that the apostle does not describe a war against men, but against demons, as is clear from this passage, "For we wrestle not against flesh and blood, etc."[150] Second, I say that the weapons of Christians are chiefly faith and prayers, but weapons made of iron are not unnecessary on that account, for in Exodus 17 we read that God granted victory to the Israelites against Amalek, with Moses praying and Joshua fighting, and we know that the Maccabees fought with weapons and prayers, and Augustine writes to Boniface, epistle 194 [Pseudo-Augustine 13],[151] "Seize the weapons in your hands and let the prayer resonate in the ears of the Creator." And Augustine writes to the same Boniface in epistle 205, alias 207 [189]: "Some fight against the invisible enemies by praying for you; you struggle against the visible barbarians by fighting for them."

But, they say, war is the opposite of peace, and peace is good and an effect of charity; therefore war is evil. I reply that war is the opposite of peace in such a way that it is also a means toward peace, and this is the difference between a just and an unjust war. An unjust war is the opposite of a good peace and leads to an evil peace, and therefore such war is evil; a just war is the opposite of an evil peace and leads to a good peace, just as the wounds of the surgeon are the opposite of the ill and imperfect health of sick people, but they lead to good and perfect health as their end.

150. Ephesians 6:12.
151. The text of this epistle, wrongly attributed to Augustine, together with fifteen other spurious letters between Augustine and Boniface, can be found in PL, vol. 33, col. 1098.

## CHAPTER 15

# How many and what are the conditions of a just war?

The conditions of a just war are usually four according to those who discuss these matters: legitimate authority, a just cause, a good intention, and an appropriate way of proceeding. But each one must be discussed by itself.

The first condition is legitimate authority, as St. Augustine says in *Contra Faustum,* book 22, chapter 75: "The natural order of mortals, that is suited to peace, requires that the authority and deliberation to undertake a war reside in the prince, while the soldiers owe it to peace and common safety to execute military orders." And reason proves the same, for if private citizens or anyone who has a superior are wronged by somebody, they can appeal to their superior and ask him for justice. But if princes are wronged by other princes, they do not have a common tribunal where they can complain, and therefore it is lawful for them to respond to public wrongs with war.

Moreover, this authority of declaring war resides, according to common opinion, in all princes and peoples who have no superior in temporal matters, which means all kings, the Republic of Venice, and similar entities, and also certain dukes and counts who are not subject to anybody in temporal matters, for those who are subject to others are not themselves heads of commonwealths but rather limbs. Note, however, that this authority is not required for a defensive war, only for an offensive one, for self-defense is lawful for anybody, not only for a prince, but also for a private citizen, while declaring war and invading the enemy are the prerogative of the supreme head.

The second condition is just cause, since a war cannot be declared without a cause, nor can it be declared simply for some crime, but only to ward off a wrong. Thus St. Augustine in question 10 in his *Quaestiones in Iesum Nave* says: "Just wars are usually defined as those that take revenge for a wrong done, for instance if the people or city against which war is waged neglected to give satisfaction for their people's unjust action or neglected to return what was wrongly taken away." The reason is that a prince is only a judge of his own subjects, and therefore he cannot punish all the crimes committed by others, but only those crimes that are detrimental to his subjects; for even if he is not an ordinary judge of other people, he is nevertheless the defender of his own, and by reason of this necessity he behaves in a certain sense as the judge of those who wronged his people, so that he can punish them with the sword.

Indeed, it must be observed that the cause for war must not be trivial or dubious, but important and certain, lest such war bring more harm than the hoped-for advantage. If in fact it is dubious, we must distinguish between prince and soldiers. The prince without a doubt commits a sin, for war is an act of punitive justice, and it is unjust to punish anybody for a reason not yet proved. Soldiers, however, do not commit a sin unless it is clear that the war is certainly unlawful, for subjects must obey their superior and must not discuss his commands; rather they must presume that their prince has a just cause, unless they clearly know the contrary. Likewise, when the guilt of a private citizen is dubious, the judge who condemns him sins, while the executioner who kills the condemned man does not, for the executioner is not bound to discuss the sentence of the judge, as Pope Boniface teaches in *Liber sextus*, "De regulis juris," rule 25: "Whoever does something by order of the judge appears not to behave wrongly, since he must necessarily obey,"[152] and blessed Augustine, *Contra Faustum*, book 22, chapter 75, says: "Thus it happens that a just man, if

152. The rule quoted by Bellarmine is actually the twenty-fourth rule, not the twenty-fifth, of book 5, title 12, "De regulis iuris" (text in *Corpus iuris canonici*, vol. 2, col. 1122).

perhaps he is in the army of a sacrilegious king, could rightfully fight at his command preserving the order of civic peace, both when he is certain that what he is commanded to do is not against God's precept and also when he is not certain that this is the case, for maybe the iniquity of the command makes the king guilty, but the duty to obey proves the soldier innocent."

Note, however, that this indulgence must be applied only to those soldiers who are obligated to serve their prince when he wages war, such soldiers being his subjects and also those who, even in time of peace, receive a regular salary from the prince, but not those soldiers who come from somewhere else when a war has to be fought. In fact, those who are not obliged to serve in the army cannot enter a war with a safe conscience, unless they know that the war is just. Those, however, who do not think about this, and are ready to enter a war whether it is just or not, simply to get paid, find themselves in a state of damnation.

The third condition is good intention. Since the aim of war is peace and public tranquillity, it is not lawful to undertake a war for any other end. Hence those kings and soldiers who undertake a war either to harm somebody, or to enlarge the empire, or to show their prowess in war, or for a reason other than the common good, sin gravely, even if the authority is legitimate and the cause is just. So in the epistle to Boniface (no. 207 or 205 [189]), blessed Augustine says: "The will should want peace, only necessity should bring war, so that God may free us from the necessity and preserve us in peace. For peace is not sought in order that war might be undertaken, but a war is undertaken so that peace might be acquired. Therefore you should be peaceful even when fighting, so that by winning the war you may bring those whom you conquer into the unity of peace"; and in *Contra Faustum,* book 22, chapter 74: "Lust for harming, cruelty in seeking revenge, an unpacified and implacable spirit, brutality in rebelling, lust for power, and similar things are rightly condemned in war."

But there are two things to be noted. First, since war is a means to peace, but a very serious and dangerous one, a war must not be undertaken immediately when there is cause; peace must first be sought in other less dangerous ways, such as a peaceful request to enemies for the satisfaction that they owe: Deuteronomy 20: "When thou comest nigh unto a city to fight against it, then proclaim peace unto it,"[153] and blessed Augustine, epistle 207 [189] to Boniface: "The will must want peace, only necessity should bring war."

But you will ask, if the enemy at first does not want to give satisfaction, but soon, with the war already begun, asks for peace and offers to give satisfaction, will the other be bound to desist from war? Cajetan at the entry "war" says that he is not bound to end the war when it has already begun, but he would be obliged to accept satisfaction before beginning the war. But (with the proviso of a better judgment) it seems that we must say that he who has a just cause is never bound in justice to accept satisfaction either before the beginning of the war or after, but in both cases he is bound to do so out of charity. The reason for the former is that a prince who has a just cause for war functions as judge of the other prince, who wronged him, but a judge is not bound in justice to pardon a guilty man who is condemned to death even if he offers satisfaction; nevertheless he could pardon him out of mercy, if he is the supreme judge. For example, a king is not bound to spare the life of a thief even if he gives back what he stole, but the king can out of mercy.

The reason for the latter is that war is a very grave punishment, by which not only he who sinned is punished, but many innocent people are also involved accidentally. Christian charity seems, therefore, always to demand that the war should end when he who did the wrong offers due satisfaction, unless perhaps something else is accidentally involved, for instance, if the enemy against whom one fights is such that it benefits the common good that he is subject to another or that he is completely destroyed. Such enemies were the Amorites, whom God ordered to be eliminated completely (Deuteronomy 20).

Second, it is to be noted that this third condition differs from the first two, because if those are absent, the war is unjust, but if this one is missing, the war is evil, but not properly speaking unjust. Whoever wages war without authority or just cause sins not only against charity, but also against justice, and he is not so much a soldier as a robber; but whoever

---

153. Deuteronomy 20:10.

has authority and just cause, and nevertheless fights for love of revenge or to enlarge the empire or for any other evil end, does not act against justice, but only against charity, and he is not a robber, but an evil soldier.

From this it is deduced that when only the third condition is lacking, soldiers and kings are not obliged to make any restitution but only to do penance, while when the first or the second condition is lacking, all are obliged to make restitution for damage caused, unless they are excused by an invincible ignorance. For just as a crass and guilty ignorance does not excuse from sin, so it does not excuse from restitution, as we explain in the last chapter, regarding injuries and damage inflicted. But whoever suffers from an invincible ignorance is not obliged to make restitution for as long as he suffers from such ignorance. But when he realizes that the war was unjust, he is obliged to make restitution not for the damage inflicted at the time of the war, but for anything he has gotten out of the war that was not his. If he has no possessions but has become richer by selling things, he is obliged to give back as much as he gained, for something that does not belong to him cannot be kept even if it has been acquired in ignorance and without sin; it must be given back to the owner, if he is known, or to the poor.

The fourth condition is the appropriate way of proceeding, which consists chiefly in this, that no innocent should be harmed, which John the Baptist explained in Luke 3: "Do violence to no man, neither accuse any falsely; and be content with your wages."[154] With these words John prohibits the injuries that soldiers usually inflict upon innocent people either by force or by treachery, either against their person or against their property. When he says, "Do violence to no man," he prohibits the injury that people inflict with brutal violence, as when they kill the peasants if they do not readily obey. When he says, "neither accuse any falsely," he prohibits the injury that is inflicted with treachery and calumny, as when they say that somebody is a traitor or an enemy, even if they know the contrary to be true, and with this accusation either rob him or kill him or bring him to the commander or the prefects. Indeed, when he adds, "and be content with your wages," he prohibits the injury inflicted on

154. Luke 3:14.

somebody not to their person, but to their goods, as when they rage and pillage wherever they can, or demand and extort things from those who owe them nothing.

However, it must be observed that there are three kinds of people on whom soldiers cannot inflict any damage, according to the rule of John the Baptist. The first is composed of all those who do not belong to the commonwealth of the enemies, and from this rule soldiers who inflict some damage on citizens or friendly peasants with whom they are quartered or whose land they are passing cannot be excused. And neither are they excused if they say that they have not received their pay, for this does not entitle them to the goods of private citizens. The citizen or peasant should not pay the price if the king or commander sins by not paying stipends to the soldiers, unless, for just cause, the inhabitants of a certain place are condemned to this form of punishment, that is, of providing for the soldiers, but that happens rarely. The second kind of people are those who, even if they belong to the commonwealth of the enemies in some capacity, nevertheless are exempted by the chapter "Innovamus, de tregua et pace," where it says: "We decree that priests, monks, those who live in convents, pilgrims, merchants, peasants who come or go or work in the fields, and the beasts by which they plow or bring the seeds to the field, should enjoy a fitting security."[155] Here "merchants" does not seem to mean those who live in the city of the enemies and are part of that city, but only those who are there in transit or who are going to market, but are not part of the city.

The third kind is composed of the people not suited for war, such as children, elderly people, and women, for such people, even if they can be captured and robbed since they are part of the city, nevertheless cannot rightfully be killed, unless they are killed by chance and by accident. Thus when a soldier shoots into a battalion of enemies and by chance kills a child or a woman or even a priest, he does not sin, but when he kills them intentionally and has the means, if he wishes, to avoid killing them, then he sins. In fact, natural reason teaches this, and God also commands the

155. The chapter quoted by Bellarmine is from the first book of Gregory IX's *Decretales*, title 34, chapter 2, and it was issued by Alexander III in 1179 (text in *Corpus iuris canonici*, vol. 2, col. 203).

Hebrews in Deuteronomy 20 to spare children and women, and Theodosius was gravely reproached by Ambrose because when he wanted to punish the Thessalonians, he ordered all those who were in his way to be killed
without discrimination, as Theodoretus reports in his *Historia,* book 5,
chapters 17 and 18. The fact that Moses also sometimes ordered women
and minors to be killed, as appears in Deuteronomy 2 and 3 and other
places, does not mean that the same is lawful for our soldiers, as Moses
clearly knew from God's revelation that God wanted it, and to God no
man can say, What doest thou?[156]

156. Here Bellarmine is making a reference to Job 9:12.

## CHAPTER 16

# It is lawful for Christians to
# fight against the Turks

The question of the war against the Turks could certainly have been omitted if Luther among his other paradoxes had not brought forth this proposition and attempted also to defend it: that it is not lawful for Christians to wage war against the Turks. This is clear from the article that is condemned in the bull of Pope Leo, that is, article 34.[157] Theodorus Bibliander seems to agree with Luther in *Chronologia,* table 13, where he says: "Urban, that most cruel tornado, driven by an evil spirit to indulge in homicide, started a war to regain Judea."

However, it must be observed that Luther does not say that the war against the Turks was unlawful because he thinks that every war in general is unlawful, for in the *assertio* of his article he recommends war against the Pontiff who, he says, is a most Turkish Turk, and neither does he judge in this way because he thinks that Christians have no just cause, since it is evident to everybody that the Turks occupied the lands of the Christians without any right. Every day they want to occupy more land, and it is also evident that the Turks want to eliminate all religion and to see to it that men convert from Christianity to Islam. Finally, it is evident that ancient Pontiffs such as Urban II, Paschal II, Eugene III,[158] and many others, together

---

157. The text to which Bellarmine refers and that contains article 34 is Luther's *Resolutiones disputationum de indulgentiarum virtute* (Wittenberg, 1518). This article was condemned explicitly by Pope Leo X in the bull *Exurge Domine.*

158. Pope Urban II began the first crusade in 1095, which was continued by Pascal II, Urban's successor. Pope Eugene III started the second crusade in 1145.

with general councils such as the Lateran, the Council of Lyon, the Council of Vienne, and others, declared a general war against the Muslims; and St. Bernard and other holy men in public speeches stirred the peoples to that war, and they strengthened their speech with miracles, as blessed Bernard himself indicates modestly at the beginning of book 1 of *De consideratione*. Luther does not deny any of these things, but there are three other reasons why he thought that it was not lawful to fight against the Turks.

First, because the will of God seems to be that we should be punished by the Turks as by a divine punishment, and it is not lawful for us to resist God's will. That this is indeed God's will he proves in the *assertio* of article 34, where he argues that experience shows that so far the war against the Turks has not given any benefit to the Christians.

But this first reason has little value, for even if God's will is that our sin be punished through the Turks, nevertheless it is not His will that we should not resist the Turks; indeed His will is for us to resist, which is proved from the final cause. For God does not allow the Turks to rage against us so that we may die but so that we may convert, for we are led to converting when we try to resist the Turks who are assaulting us; and by resisting we suffer, and by suffering we recognize our weakness, and hence we turn to God with our whole heart and we beg Him for help. Therefore, from the final cause for which God allows the Turks to rage against us it clearly follows that God wants us to resist the Turks. Moreover, the war of the Turks is a divine punishment just like plague, famine, heresy, the flames of sin, and such, but nobody is so foolish as to think that one should not seek a remedy against the plague, or that we should not cultivate the land so as not to die by starvation, or that we should not resist heresy.

Furthermore, it is not true, as Luther says, that experience shows that the war against the Turks brought us nothing good. Not to mention many reported victories over the Turks, it is certainly the case that when the armies first were brought into the promised land, it was a great success that Jerusalem was reconquered by our troops and that the Christians ruled for eighty-eight years. And they were reconquering more and more land until contentions started to arise among the Christian princes themselves, to such an extent that the Turks now occupy a great deal of land because of the disagreements in our camp rather than because of their own military valor, and the chief cause of such disagreements was Luther himself. For as is clear from Johann Cochlaeus's *De actis et scriptis Lutheri* concerning the year 1526, the Hungarians were destroyed because the Germans, whom the king of Hungary had called upon for help, preferred to obey Luther, who was then preaching against the war with the Turks, rather than to think of what the common good would require.[159] At least the war has this advantage, that the Turks are prevented from being as harmful as they would like to be, for if we had not fought them until now, they would have taken everything a long time ago.

His second reason is that tribulation and persecution are more useful to the Church than victory and peace; hence in *Sermo de matrimonio* he condemns the practice of the Church to pray for peace and quiet, when one should rather pray for tribulations. But while tribulation and persecution certainly are useful, they are dangerous and one should not so much seek them as tolerate them when it cannot be otherwise. Hence in Matthew 6 we are commanded to pray "and lead us not into temptation,"[160] and in 1 Timothy 2 the apostle orders us to pray for kings, that we may lead a quiet and peaceful life, and blessed Augustine in book 10 of the *Confessiones,* chapter 28, says that sorrows have to be tolerated, neither loved nor desired nor sought.

The third reason, and the one that seems to have been the chief one, is hatred against the Pontiff, for sometimes Luther attacked the Pontiff with so much hatred that clearly he wished to see the Turks occupy all the kingdoms of Christendom, if the name of the Pontiff could at least be wiped out in this way. And it is not guesswork that this was his wish and desire; we gather it from his own words, for in his address *An den christlichen Adel deutscher Nation,* chapter 25, he says that there is no better government anywhere than among the Turks, who are governed by the laws of

159. Bellarmine is here referring to the battle of Mohács (29 August 1526), in which the Ottoman army defeated the Hungarians and killed King Lewis of Hungary as he was escaping from the battlefield. For more information on this battle in the context of the religious conflicts in central Europe, see R. R. Betts, "Poland, Bohemia and Hungary," in Elton, *The Reformation.*

160. Matthew 6:13.

the Koran, and there is no worse government than among the Christians, who are ruled by canon and civil law. And in the *assertio* of article 34 he says that the Pontiff and his followers are much worse and more cruel than the Turks, and it is foolish to fight against the Turks alongside those who are even worse than they are, and in an epistle against two imperial mandates he says: "I beg all the pious Christians not to obey in any way, not to serve in the army and not to hold anything against the Turks, since the Turks are ten times more prudent and honest than our princes." With these words what else is he trying to suggest but that we must assist the Turks against the Christians?

But this opinion contains so much absurdity and impiety that Luther himself, once his ardor cooled somewhat, wrote the plain contrary, for this is what he says in his report on the Saxon visitation: "Some preachers cry with temerity that we must not resist the Turks. Such speech is seditious and must neither be uttered nor permitted. The authorities are then obliged to resist the Turks, who not only want to pillage the lands and violate and kill the women and children, but also to abrogate and destroy the laws of the land, the worship of God, and every good regulation. Therefore the princes must especially fight, etc."; and in the same book: "It would be far more tolerable for a good man to see his sons killed than soaked in Muslim customs, since the Turks know or regard no honesty at all." These are his words.

# It does not pertain to the magistrate
# to judge in matters of religion

The fifth question follows, concerning the duty of the political magistrate in the cause of religion. In this regard there are three errors. The first is the error of those who attribute too much to the magistrates, such as Brenz in *Prolegomena;* Melanchthon in *Loci,* chapter on the magistrate; and others, who want kings to be not only the protectors and defenders of religion, but also its judges and teachers. For they say that to judge controversies of faith, to preside over general councils, to appoint ministers and pastors, and to carry out other similar duties pertain to kings as chief members of the Church. We discussed this error a great deal in the *Controversiae,* on the judge of controversies, the Supreme Pontiff, and the councils, where we showed that kings have the first place among Christians as Christian men, that is, as citizens of the earthly city, but not as fellow citizens among the saints and servants of God, nor as members of the Church. For in this last respect the bishops have the first place, and the chief is the Supreme Pontiff, second the priests, third the deacons and the other ecclesiastical ministers, and last the laymen, among whom also kings and princes are numbered.

Hence when Chrysostom addresses the deacons in his homily 83 on Matthew, he says: "If any commander, the consul himself, he who is adorned with the crown, acts impiously, repress and punish him, for you have a greater authority than he." And Gelasius in his epistle to Emperor Anastasius says: "O my most loving son, know that even if you preside over humankind because of your excellence in earthly matters, nevertheless you lower your head devoutly in front of those who preside over divine matters and from them you await the source of your salvation, and when receiving the heavenly sacraments from those to whom this pertains, know that you must submit to, rather than command, the religious hierarchy. Know therefore that in these matters you depend on their judgment, and they cannot be reduced to your will."[161]

Finally, Christ committed the task of governing the Church to Peter and the bishops, not to Tiberius and his prefects, and for three hundred years the Church was governed most successfully by bishops and prelates alone, without any Christian king, except for a very few who either ruled for a very short time, as Philippus Caesar, or ruled only in a certain province, as Lucius king of the Britons. See more in the already mentioned passages.

---

161. This is the same epistle from which the canon "Duo sunt" on the relation between spiritual and temporal authority was taken (the text of the entire epistle can be found in PL, vol. 59, cols. 41–47). On the importance of the "Duo sunt" and on Bellarmine's use of it, see *On the Temporal Power of the Pope. Against William Barclay*, chap. 2, p. 153.

## ✂ CHAPTER 18 ✂

# The defense of religion pertains to the magistrate

The second error is made by those who go to the other extreme and teach that kings must take care of their commonwealth and the public peace, but not religion. They teach that everybody should be allowed to believe and live as they wish, provided that they do not disturb the public peace. The pagans once found themselves in this error, for they approved every religion and admitted every philosophical sect, as Augustine says in *De civitate Dei*, book 18, chapter 51. Hence the blessed Leo, in his first sermon on Peter and Paul [82], says: "When this city, while ignorant of the Author of its progress, dominated almost every people, it was a slave to every people's errors and seemed to have adopted a great religion because it did not reject any falsehood." And the philosopher Themistius, as Socrates reports in *Historia*, book 4, chapter 23, tried to persuade Emperor Valens that the variety of sects is pleasing to God because He is then worshipped in many ways, and the more difficult it is to know God the more this is the case. A certain heresiarch by the name of Rethor taught that all sects were true, as Augustine says in his *De haeresibus*, chapter 72.

Finally, the Germans wanted and obtained such freedom in 1526, when the princes of the empire were gathered at Speyer,[162] and now they are said

162. Bellarmine is referring to the Second Diet of Speyer, which culminated in the so-called Protestation of Speyer (1529), on the basis of which the Lutheran princes of the empire fought Charles V's enforcement of the edict of Worms against Luther and asked for the liberty to choose their religion and to impose it on their subjects.

to seek the same in Flanders,[163] and they have four main arguments. The first, that faith is free. The second, that it is a gift of God. The third, that experience teaches that nothing is accomplished by coercion. The fourth, that Christians have always tolerated the Jews even if they are enemies of Christ.

This error is, however, very dangerous, and without a doubt the Christian princes are obliged not to grant their subjects freedom of belief but to see to it that the faith that the Catholic bishops and especially the Supreme Pontiff teach to be the true one is preserved. This is proved, first, by Scriptures: Proverbs 20: "A king that sitteth in the throne of judgment scattereth away all evil with his eyes";[164] likewise: "A wise king scattereth the wicked,"[165] and indeed it cannot be denied that the wicked are heretics. Likewise, Psalm 2: "Be wise now therefore, O ye kings: be instructed, ye judges of the earth. Serve the Lord with fear."[166]

Augustine in his epistle 50 [185] says: "The king serves God differently as a man and as a king: as a man, he serves Him by living in faith, as a

163. Bellarmine is referring to the religious and political agreement attempted by the leaders of Holland and Brabant with the Pacification of Ghent (1576) during the revolt of the Netherlands against Spain. More specifically, starting in the 1570s, the Catholic "governor-general" Archduke Matthias of Habsburg and the Protestant Stadholder William of Orange inaugurated a (short-lived) policy of religious toleration for both the southern and the northern provinces in the Netherlands, the purpose of the policy being to strengthen their union against Spain. (Cf. Israel, *The Dutch Republic,* pp. 179ff.) Archduke Matthias had occasion to make another attempt at implementing a policy of religious pacification later on, and Bellarmine was directly involved in this affair. After his short tenure as governor of the Netherlands, Matthias went to Hungary on behalf of his brother Rudolf, the Holy Roman Emperor, to subdue a Protestant revolt. There Matthias signed the Treaty of Vienna in 1606, with which he granted religious toleration to the Hungarian Protestants (later extended to Austria). Rudolf rejected the agreement, and a controversy between the brothers arose, which ended with Matthias's becoming king of Hungary in 1608. (In 1612, at the death of Rudolf, Matthias succeeded his brother as Holy Roman Emperor.) In 1608 Bellarmine, probably at the request of the Catholic diplomats pushing Rudolf to oppose his brother's decision, composed a short text to demonstrate that the freedom of religion that the archduke was granting was not a legitimate political and religious act on the part of a Catholic sovereign. This text has been published by Le Bachelet, *Auctarium Bellarminianum,* pp. 595–99.

164. Proverbs 20:8.
165. Proverbs 20:26.
166. Psalm 2:10–11.

king, by ordering just laws and prohibiting the opposite, and by giving appropriately strong sanctions, just as Hezekiah served God by destroying the groves and temples of the idols; as King Josiah did, by similar acts; as the king of the Ninivites did, by compelling the entire city to appease the Lord; as Darius did, by giving Daniel the authority to destroy the idols; as Nebuchadnezzar did, by a terrible law forbidding everybody who dwelled in his kingdom to blaspheme against God." And in the same letter he adds: "Who in his right mind would say to kings: in your kingdom do not attend to that which either supports or opposes the Church of your Lord; and who would say to kings: it is not your concern to see who in your kingdom wants to live piously or sacrilegiously? To them it cannot be said, it is not your concern to see who in your kingdom wants to live chastely or unchastely."

Moreover, in the New Testament, Apocalypse 2, the angel of Pergamos is blamed because he had around him some men who held the doctrine of the Nicolaitanes, and the angel of Thyatira is blamed because he allowed Jezebel to seduce the servants of God. From these things it is gathered that the mixing of Catholics with heretics is harmful to the Church. In Romans 16 Christians are ordered to avoid heretics, in Galatians 5 we read: "I would they were even cut off which trouble you,"[167] and in Titus 1: "Wherefore rebuke them sharply, that they may be sound in the faith."[168] Therefore the kings, who are the nursing fathers of the Church, as it is said in Isaiah 49,[169] must not allow such mixing.

Second, it is proved with the testimonies of popes and emperors. In his epistle 75 [156] to Leo Emperor, Leo says: "O emperor, you must realize without hesitation that regal authority has been granted to you not only to govern the world, but especially to protect the Church, so that by suppressing the rash attempts of the wicked you might defend that which is well established and restore the true peace in those matters which are perturbed." Pope Anastasius II in his epistle to Emperor Anastasius says: "I urge on Your Serenity especially this, that when the reasons of the Alexandrines reach your most pious ears, you will drive them back to

167. Galatians 5:12.
168. Titus 1:13.
169. Cf. Isaiah 49:23.

the Catholic and true faith with your authority, wisdom, and sacred commands." Gregory says similar things in book 9 [11], epistle 60 [66], to the king of England, and in book 11 [13], epistle 44 [39], to Leontia Augusta, and Agatho as well in his epistle to Constantine IV.

Moreover the pious emperors thought the same, for with the law "Cunctos populos," title "De summa trinitate et fide Catholica," Theodosius eradicated completely the freedom of belief that some princes had allowed and he ordered that the teachings of the Roman Pontiff should be believed.[170] Ambrose in his *Oratio funebris* praises Valentinian the younger because he most vigorously resisted the Romans who were asking for the ancient freedom of religion so that they could worship their gods with sacrifices. Similarly Marcian, same title, law "Nemo," severely prohibits anybody from questioning the matters defined in the Councils of Bishops and from intending to discuss them in public.[171]

It is true that Constantine the Great at the beginning of his empire allowed everybody freedom of religion, as is clear from the *Historia* of Eusebius, book 10, chapter 5, but afterward he ordered that the temples of the idols be closed and that only the Christian religion be considered valid, as Optatus reports in his *Contra Parmenianum,* book 2. Constans and Constantine, his sons, followed in their father's footsteps, as Augustine reports in epistle 166 [105], and Constantine threatened exile for those who did not assent to the decrees of the Council of Nicaea (Rufinus, bk. 10, chap. 5).

---

170. Bellarmine is here quoting from the Codex Theodosianus, a collection of laws compiled under Emperor Theodosius II at the beginning of the fifth century. The law that Bellarmine is quoting (law 2, title 1, bk. 16) was issued in 380 by Emperor Theodosius I. (It can be found in vol. 6.1, p. 5, of the *Codex Theodosianus* published in 1736–43 in Leipzig.) This law, as well as many other laws of the Thedosian code, was included in the *Corpus iuris civilis,* the body of Roman law issued by Emperor Justinian in the 530s. The *Corpus iuris civilis* was composed of four parts: the *Digest* or *Pandects* (a collection of excerpts by various jurists), the *Institutiones* (a sort of introduction or textbook), the *Codex* (a collection of imperial laws that incorporated much of the Theodosian code), and the *Novellae* (a collection of "new" laws issued by Justinian after the publication of the Code). The law quoted by Bellarmine is law 1, title 1, book 1 of the Codex Justinianus (text in *Corpus iuris civilis,* vol. 2, p. 5).

171. The law quoted is in Justinian's Code, book 1, title 1, law 4, and was issued in 452 (text in *Corpus iuris civilis,* vol. 2, pp. 6–7).

There are three emperors who allowed freedom of religion: Jovian, who was sternly warned by the Council of Antioch not to mix Catholics with heretics, as Socrates writes in book 3, chapter 21. Valens, the Arian emperor, allowed all heretics and pagans the free exercise of their religion, as Theodoretus writes in book 4, chapter 22. Finally, Julian the Apostate, who allowed freedom of religion in the hope of destroying the Christian religion, as Augustine says in epistle 166 or 165 [105]: "Julian, deserter and enemy of Christ, allowed the heretics freedom to be ruined, and then handed over to them the basilicas as temples of devils, thinking that in this way Christianity would disappear from the earth if he broke the unity of the Church from which he had fallen and if he allowed sacrilegious dissensions to develop freely."

Third, it is proved by reason. First, the temporal and the spiritual authority in the Church are not disconnected and separate things, as two political kingdoms, but are connected so as to form one body; or rather they present themselves as the body and soul in a man, for the spiritual authority is like the soul, and the temporal like the body, as Gregory of Nazianzus teaches in his *Oratio ad populum timore perculsum*. Therefore the temporal authority must be servant to the spiritual authority and protect and defend it from its enemies, and (as blessed Gregory says, book 2 [3], epistle 61 [65]) the earthly kingdom must attend to the heavenly kingdom. However, the said freedom of religion is destructive for the Church, for the bond of the Church is the profession of one faith, as Paul says in the epistle to the Ephesians 4: "One Lord, one faith, one baptism, etc."[172] Dissension in faith is, therefore, the destruction of the Church. Accordingly, princes must on no account allow this freedom if they want to perform their duty.

Second, when true religion was flourishing among the Jews, the kings could not allow freedom of religion, and much less ought Christian kings to allow it, for the Church must not be arranged any worse than the synagogue was. The antecedent is clear from Deuteronomy 17 where those who do not obey the priest are ordered to be killed, according to the sentence of the civil judge. Similarly in chapter 18 the pseudo-prophets

172. Ephesians 4:5.

are commanded to be killed, and the same is clear from the examples presented by Augustine in epistle 50 [185] about Hezekiah, Jehoshaphat, Josiah, and other pious kings, who destroyed the groves and temples of the idols and punished severely the idolaters and forced the people to worship the true God. Furthermore, it is not surprising that slightly before Christ's time various heresies started to be allowed, and in particular that of the Sadducees who denied resurrection, since the synagogue was then coming near its destruction and the Jews had truly no king who could take care of such things, only Herod the Idumaean, and the High Priests could do nothing.

Third, freedom of belief is destructive even for the temporal good of kingdoms and for public peace, as is clear, first, from Gregory, book 4 [5], epistle 32 [20], where he says that the safety of the civil commonwealth depends on the peace of the Church. Second, it is clear by reason, for where faith and obedience to God are preserved, so are faith and obedience to the prince, for faith itself teaches and demands this. Likewise, dissension in faith creates dissensions of spirits and wills, and every kingdom internally divided will perish. The experience of our own times shows the same so clearly that we need not strive to prove it.

Fourth, freedom of belief is destructive for those to whom it is allowed, for it is nothing but the freedom to err, and to err in the matter where error is most dangerous. For the true faith is only one (Ephesians 4, "one Lord, one faith, etc."); therefore the freedom to move away from that one faith is the freedom to rush into the abyss of errors. Just as it is not beneficial to allow sheep the freedom to wander through the mountains, and it is not beneficial to free the ship from its steering oar and allow it to be carried freely by the wind, so also it is not beneficial to allow the peoples freedom of belief after they have joined the one true faith. The contrary arguments will be disproved in the following question.

## CHAPTER 19

## Catholics cannot be reconciled with heretics

The third error is that of George Cassander in the book *De officio pii viri,* where he teaches that princes must find a ground for peace among Catholics, Lutherans, Calvinists, etc. But as long as they have not found it, they must allow each person to profess his own faith, provided that all accept Scripture and the Apostles' Creed, for those are all members of the true Church, even though they dissent in particular doctrines.[173] Similar things were once taught by peacemakers, inspired by Emperor Zeno; see Evagrius, book 3, chapters 14 and 30.[174] Likewise also Apelles, who, according to Eusebius, book 5 of *Historia,* chapter 13, said that the reason for faith should not be discussed, but it was sufficient to believe in the crucifix. This is clearly an error, against which Jean Hessels, among Catholic teachers, and John Calvin, among the heretics, wrote.

This opinion can in fact easily be refuted. First, Catholics, Lutherans, and Calvinists cannot be reconciled in this manner, for we do not agree on the Creed itself. For example, regarding the article "He descended into hell," we mean very different things, for we believe that Christ's soul, separated from the body, in accordance with its substance, descended to

173. During the discussions in the fall of 1592 after the death of Sixtus V about the modifications to be made to the Index of 1564, Bellarmine himself proposed to remove Cassander from the second class of heretics—those whose works could be purged—and to include him in the first class, together with Henry VIII and the Protestant theologian Matthaeus Dresserus (Drescher), "because they are heretics" (see ACDF, Index, Protocolli II, folder 9, fols. 77r–78v at fol. 77r).

174. Bellarmine refers to the *Henotikon,* or "act of union," promulgated by Emperor Zeno in 482 to put an end to the controversy over the nature of Christ.

the Limbo of the Fathers. Some heretics, however, think that "Christ descended into hell" means only that he was buried; others think he suffered the pains of hell. Likewise, we interpret the article "I believe in the holy Church," and "the communion of saints" in different ways, for there are controversies also on the specific sacraments. Finally, on "the remission of sins" we disagree immensely.

Cassander says that it is sufficient that we all admit that the Creed is true and accept it.

Against this I say, first, that the Creed is indeed only one, but not in words, only in meaning and faith, and therefore we do not have the same Creed if we disagree on its interpretation. Moreover, if it were sufficient to accept the words of the Creed, almost none of the ancient heretics would have been rightfully condemned, for the Arians, the Novatians, the Nestorians, and almost all the others accepted the words of the Apostles' Creed, but because the dissension was about the meaning, they were condemned and expelled from the Catholic Church.

Second, the foundational principle of Cassander is false, for the Lutherans and Calvinists could not be called true members of the Church even if they agreed with us on the Creed. In addition to that belief it is required that one subject oneself to the legitimate head of the Church, established by Christ, and take communion with the other members, for the Church is one visible body and therefore it has a visible head and visible members, and a member that is separate from the head and the rest of the body cannot be called a member. Certainly even if Aerius agreed with the Catholics on the meaning of the Creed, Epiphanius and Augustine nevertheless put him in their catalog of heretics because he did not want to submit to the bishop and to be in communion with the other members. And Cyprian in book 4, epistle 2 [52],[175] says that Novatian was outside of the Church because he did not want to submit himself to the Pontiff Cornelius, even if he did not introduce any other heresy.

Third, Cassander discusses these matters almost as if among Catholics, Lutherans, and Calvinists there were only dissensions regarding human

175. I have followed the numbers given in the edition of Cyprian's letters found in PL, vol. 4.

rituals and ceremonies, but there are many doctrines of the greatest importance on which we disagree, and which are not expressly in the Creed, and because of which no peace can be hoped for between Catholics and Lutherans. For example, we say that the mass is the holiest form of worship of God, while they say it is a horrible idolatry; further, invocation of the saints is for us a pious act, for them an impious one, etc.

Fourth, the holy Fathers taught us to preserve untouched not only the Creed but also all the other doctrines of faith, and not to allow them to be changed in any way because of the heretics. In Galatians 2 Paul says that he did not, even for an hour, want to give pride of place to the false brethren.[176] Once the Arians asked the Catholics to omit just one word that is neither in Scripture nor in the Creed, or to change one letter, namely, not to say ὁμοούσιον but ὁμοιούσιον, and if they did that, the Arians would promise peace. But the Catholics refused and wrote to the emperor that it was impious to change anything already defined, and if anything were to be changed in the just sanctions, it should not be because of future peace, for there can be no peace with those who do not know the laws of peace. See Theodoretus, book 2 of *Historia,* chapters 18 and 19, or *Historia tripartita,* book 5, chapters 21 and 33.[177] It is clear from the Council of Rimini that this was true, for when the less prudent Catholics, deceived by the Arians, decreed that the name ὁμοούσιον had to be removed, the Arians immediately declared to the whole world that they had won. And not satisfied with having removed ὁμοούσιον and having substituted ὁμοιούσιον for it, they soon afterward transformed ὁμοιούσιον into ἑτεροούσιον, that is, "of different substance," as Theodoretus reports in book 2 of his *Historia,* chapter 21.[178]

176. Cf. Galatians 2:4–5.

177. The *Historia tripartita* was a compilation of extracts from the historical works of Theodoretus, Socrates, and Sozomen made by Epiphanius at the direction of Cassiodorus (d. ca. 583), a Roman Christian writer and translator. Although the *Historia tripartita* was far from accurate, it was widely used as a history manual throughout the Middle Ages and the early modern times.

178. Bellarmine is here referring to the fourth century controversy over the nature of Christ between the supporters of the Nicaean orthodoxy, the Arians, and the moderate Arians. The Nicaean Creed had in fact defined Christ as ὁμοούσιον, that is, "of the same substance" as the Father. The Semi-Arians, or moderate Arians, proposed the definition of Christ as ὁμοιούσιον, that is, "of a similar substance" to that of the Father. Arians,

Hence when Emperor Valens's prefect asked Basil to submit to the circumstances and not to allow so many churches to be upset because of a small detail of doctrine, Basil replied: "Those who are nourished by divine words do not allow the corruption of even a syllable regarding divine doctrines, for if this should happen, they would rather suffer any kind of death for these doctrines." See Theodoretus, book 4, chapter 17, of the *Historia Ecclesiastica.* Eustathius and Sylvanus were provided with the same constancy, for when the emperor threatened them with exile unless they abrogated the word ὁμοούσιον, they replied: "You have the authority to punish us, but nevertheless we do not destroy what was established by the Fathers" (see *Historia tripartita,* book 5, chapter 24).

Finally, in his epistle to Euphemianus, Gelasius spoke to the heretic, who asked the Pope to bend down [*condescendere*] to them, that is, to compromise on something regarding the Catholic religion for the sake of peace, and Gelasius elegantly mocked his petition: "While you say that we should bend down to you, you reveal that you meanwhile are lowering yourself further down, or that you have already done so. So I ask, what is this slippery slope [*descensio*]? Surely you see, you understand, you do not deny that you have been lowered from a superior place to an inferior one, that you have fallen from the Catholic and Apostolic communion to the heretical and condemned one, and you wish us, who remain in the superior place, to be persuaded to descend with you; you invite us from the highest to the lowest, but we ask you to ascend with us from the lowest to the highest."

Fifth, one cannot be free to believe in one doctrine without, for the same reason, having a similar freedom in all doctrines, even those contained in the Apostles' Creed, because there is one rule of faith that is undoubted and certain for everything in which one believes, that is, the word of God as explained through the Church. If, therefore, I trust that the Church is delivering the Apostles' Creed to me, because I do not know what the apostles said from any other source than what the Church says, then I must for the same reason believe that I should invoke the saints,

---

by contrast, argued that Christ was of a different substance, ἑτεροούσιον, with respect to the Father.

because the same Church says so; or, if I cannot believe this, then for the same reason I cannot believe that that Creed was indeed the Apostles' Creed.

Sixth, Cassander's opinion is a novelty, first devised by him, as he himself says at the beginning, and therefore it must be considered suspicious. For, as Vincent of Lérins teaches beautifully in his *Commonitorium adversus profanas novitates,* what is new cannot be without suspicion, since the true faith is one and is very ancient.

Seventh, this opinion makes the true Church completely hidden and invisible; indeed, it makes it composed of flatterers and feigners only, for Cassander says that two things are required by the true Church, faith in Christ and peace with men, and hence he deduces that those who persecute Catholics and Lutherans with hostility are not part of the Church, but only those are who are at peace with everybody. Therefore those who are part of the Church must be hidden and must simulate with the Catholics that they are enemies of the Lutherans, and with the Lutherans that they are enemies of the Catholics, for the Catholics do not allow in their group those who show any external sign of favor toward the Lutherans. And even if in the Lutheran provinces all sects are permitted, nevertheless no sect allows in its own group those who are friendly to the other sects, as is well known. So those pious and peaceful men are necessarily fake and feigning when they say one thing with their mouth and hide another thing in their heart, just like Herod, who was a pagan with the pagans, and a Jew with the Jews, for he built simultaneously temples for Caesar and the true God, as Josephus reports in *Antiquitates,* book 15, chapters 13 [10] and 14 [11].

Note furthermore that Cassander says that his associates are few and hidden. But hence it is clear that they cannot constitute the Church, as the Church is so manifest and visible that it is said by the Lord in Matthew 5 to be a city on a hill. Finally, the true Church cannot exist without pastors (Ephesians 4);[179] but those hidden men have no pastor, nor can they while they remain hidden, and therefore they have no Church.

179. Ephesians 4:11.

## CHAPTER 20

# The books of heretics must be abolished

There remains the question of the punishments that the political rulers can and must inflict on heretics after the Church's judgment and sentence. We will start, however, with the books of heretics, and we will briefly show that these are rightly forbidden and burned. This is proved, first, from the ancient and continuous custom not only of Christians, but also of pagans.

First, Valerius Maximus reports in book 1, chapter 1, that in Rome when books that seemed in some measure to weaken religion were found, the *praetor urbanus*[180] on the senate's authority burned them in front of the people.[181] Cicero in *De natura deorum,* book 1, reports that Protagoras of Abdera, because he wrote books harmful to religion, was expelled from the city and the land by the Athenians, and his books were burned at the public assembly.

Later, at the time of the apostles, Luke in Acts 19 reports that many men who had been converted by the apostles gathered together inappropriate and vain books and burned them in front of everybody.[182] Clement's *Constitutiones Apostolicae,* book 1, chapter 7, says that the apostles at the

180. The *praetor urbanus* was the magistrate who administered justice to Roman citizens.

181. Valerius Maximus was a Roman historian of the first century and the author of a collection of anecdotes drawn from Greek and mostly Roman history titled *Factorum et dictorum memorabilium libri IX,* which was intended as a catalog of examples of vices and virtues. The episode reported by Bellarmine can be found in book 1, chapter 1, section 12.

182. Acts 19:19.

beginning prohibited the books of the pagans and of the false prophets.[183] Also Eusebius in *Historia,* book 7, chapter 6 [7], writes that Dionysius, bishop of Alexandria, who lived around the year 250, was blamed by the faithful because he read the books of heretics.

Afterward the zeal of the faithful against the books of heretics grew, for the Council of Nicaea ordered the books of Arius to be burned, as Nicephorus attests in book 7, chapter 18, and Constantine ordered this to be executed, having proposed capital punishment for anybody who would hide Arius's books, as is clear from his epistle in Socrates, book 1, chapter 6, and Nicephorus, book 8, chapter 25. And in book 1, chapter 24, Socrates writes that Marcellus of Ancyra was condemned because he would not burn the books that contained his errors, and heretics were not accepted for penance unless they burned their books first.

Around the same time Epiphanius, in a synod gathered in Cyprus, prohibited the reading of the books of Origen, as Socrates reports in book 6, chapter 9, of the *Historia,* and the Fourth Council of Carthage, canon 16, allows only bishops to read the books of heretics, as required by circumstances.[184] Not long afterward, when the heresy of Nestorius had been condemned in the Council of Ephesus, his books were also forbidden, and Emperor Theodosius ordered them burned, as Liberatus reports in his *Breviarium,* chapter 10; and the Theodosian Code's law "Damnato," title "De haereticis," still exists.[185] Around the same time appeared a law of Honorius and Theodosius, which obliged all astrologers to burn their books if they contained anything against the Catholic religion and to do so in front of the bishops (see lex "Mathematicos," title "De episcopali

183. Bellarmine is quoting from the fourth-century multivolume *Constitutiones Apostolicae,* a collection of treatises on Christian doctrine and liturgy to be used as a manual for the clergy. The collection was falsely attributed to St. Clement of Rome, the fourth pope after Peter.

184. The canon Bellarmine quoted was issued in 398.

185. This is law 6, title 5, book 16 of the Theodosian Code (law 6, title 5, book 1 of the Justinian Code) issued by Theodosius in 453, four years after Nestorius was officially condemned at the Council of Ephesus. As well as prohibiting Nestorius's books and commanding them to be burned, it also forbids anybody from mentioning Nestorius's name in any religious discussion (text in *Codex Theodosianus,* vol. 6.1, p. 210, and *Corpus iuris civilis,* vol. 2, p. 51).

audientia"[186]). For the same reason in the Council of Chalcedon the books of Eutyches were condemned, and a severe law of the emperors Valentinian and Marcian prohibited anybody from reading or having them, and ordered all of them to be diligently searched for and burned, as is clear from the Council of Chalcedon, act 3, and from the law itself, which still exists, law "Quicumque," paragraphs "Nulli" and "Omnes," chapter "De haereticis."[187]

In the same period blessed Leo in his epistle 91 [15] to Turbius [Turribius], chapters 15 and 16, forbade reading the books of some heretics and added that bishops who allowed these books to be kept in the houses of the faithful should be considered heretics. Soon afterward Gelasius in the Council of the Seventy Bishops proposed an index of the heretics whose books the faithful should avoid, as we find in distinction 15, canon "Sancta Romana."[188]

Later, in the fifth synod after Anthimus was condemned, his books were also damned, and Emperor Justinian established a grave punishment, namely, amputation of the hands, for those who transcribed such books and ordered these books to be burned everywhere. This decree can be found in act 1 of Synod 5, and in the *Novellae*, constitutio 42.[189] Blessed Gregory in *Moralia*, book 14, chapter 32 [56], reports that a book of Eutychius, whom the same Gregory had found guilty of heresy, was burned on the order of Emperor Tiberius. Also in the seventh synod, act 5, the books of heretics were forbidden and ordered to be burned, and in

186. This law is number 10 under title 4, "De episcopali audientia," in the Code of Justinian and law 12, title 16, book 9, of the Theodosian Code. Promulgated in 409, it prescribed the punishment of exile for astrologers who were not willing to destroy their books in front of their bishops (text in *Codex Theodosianus*, vol. 3, p. 144, and *Corpus iuris civilis*, vol. 2, p. 40).

187. This is law 8, title 5, book 1, of the Justinian Code, which was promulgated in 455 (the Council of Chalcedon was held in 451) and condemns to perpetual exile those guilty of reading the books of the heretics (text in *Corpus iuris civilis*, vol. 2, p. 52).

188. Bellarmine is here referring to canon 3, distinction 15, of the first part of Gratian's *Decretum*, attributed to Pope Gelasius during the Council of Rome (495–96). Together with a list of forbidden books written by heretics, this canon also contains a list of the acceptable works of the Fathers and a list of the books of the Bible considered apocryphal. The text can be found in *Corpus iuris canonici*, vol. 1, cols. 36–41.

189. Bellarmine refers to the Fifth Ecumenical Council, held in Constantinople in 553, and the text of the *constitutio* is in *Corpus iuris civilis*, vol. 3, pp. 263–69.

canon 9 those who read books by heretics were excommunicated.[190] The
Council of Constance, session 8, confirmed the decree of the Council of
Rome, by which the reading of books by John Wyclif was forbidden.[191]
Finally, the Council of Trent ordered that an index of prohibited books be
produced so that everybody would know which books were to be avoided
and burned.[192] From all these examples it is clear that this was always the
custom in the Church.

It should also be added in support of this argument that almost no
books by ancient heretics have survived, for how else did so many volumes
of Valentinus, Marcion, Arius, Eunomius, Nestorius, Pelagius, and others
to whom the holy Fathers replied disappear?

Second, reason tells us that speaking with heretics is very dangerous
and must be carefully avoided and that the heretics' books are even more
harmful and destructive and must be avoided. And in Romans 16: "Now
I beseech you, brethren, mark them which cause divisions and offences
contrary to the doctrine which ye have learned; and avoid them. For they
that are such serve not our Lord Jesus Christ, but their own belly; and by
good words and fair speeches deceive the hearts of the simple";[193] 2 Timothy 3: "From such turn away";[194] Titus 3: "A man that is a heretick after the
first and second admonition reject";[195] the second epistle of John: "If there
come any unto you, and bring not this doctrine, receive him not into your
house, neither bid him God speed."[196]

190. The Seventh Ecumenical Council was held in Nicaea in 787. The text of the
canon quoted by Bellarmine can be found in *Conciliorum oecumenicorum decreta*,
p. 122.

191. The part of session 8 (2 May 1415) in which the books of Wyclif were condemned can be found in *Conciliorum oecumenicorum decreta*, pp. 389–90. The Council
of Rome was held in 1412.

192. Here Bellarmine is referring to the decree of 26 February 1562, session 18 (text
in *Conciliorum oecumenicorum decreta*, pp. 697–98), with which the Council of Trent
officially decided to nominate a committee to revise the 1559 Index. The result was the
Tridentine Index of 1564. For more information on the genesis of the Tridentine Index
see Frajese, *La nascita dell'Indice*, pp. 39–92.

193. Romans 16:17–18.

194. 2 Timothy 3:5.

195. Titus 3:10.

196. 2 John 1:10.

St. Irenaeus, book 3, chapter 2, says: "The apostles and their disciples had so much fear that they did not even speak with those who corrupted the truth."

St. Cyprian, book 1, epistle 3 [55] to Cornelius, says: "O most loving brethren, you should be wary of and avoid the words and speeches of those whose discourses creep in as a cancer," and later "No transactions, no feasts, no conversations should be exchanged with such people, and we should be separated from them as much as they are exiled from the Church."

St. Athanasius said of St. Anthony in his biography: "He did not even exchange friendly words with the Manichaeans and other heretics, declaring that being friendly and talking with those people was the ruin of the soul. And he detested the Arians so much that he said to everybody that one should not even come close to them." And again the same St. Anthony, on the point of death: "Avoid the poison of heretics and schismatics, and follow my hatred toward them; you know that I have never had even a peaceful conversation with them."

St. Augustine, in epistle 62 [43], says: "Just as we warn that a heretic should be avoided so that he might not deceive the weak and young, so we do not refrain from correcting him in any way possible, etc." St. Leo, sermon 18 [69] on the Passion of the Lord, says: "Avoid the poisonous conversations of heretics; you should have nothing to do with those who are Christians only by name." These are his words.

However, if conversations with heretics should be so completely avoided, how much more their books? For an argument put in writing is better prepared and more artful than that which is used in speech. Afterward it is always at one's disposal, for while discussions and conversations are rare and the words uttered orally soon disappear, the words in books remain forever and are always with us, walk with us, and dwell with us at home. Moreover, books are spread more widely, and anybody can speak with almost the entire world at once through a book. Books invade the homes and offices of many people whom the author of the book never saw and to whom he would hardly ever be introduced. Finally, experience teaches the same, for John Wyclif corrupted very few by his speech, for he taught only in England, and there he left almost no heir to his error, but through his books he corrupted the whole of Bohemia (see Cochlaeus's *Historia Hussitarum*).

But in opposition to these arguments my adversaries object, first, that since there are many good things in the books of heretics, it seems foolish to deprive oneself of the good because of some bad elements, and this is confirmed by the fact that otherwise the writings of many Fathers will have to be burned. And furthermore the Church tolerates the books of pagans, Jews, Muslims, and also of ancient heretics such as Origen, Tertullian, Eusebius, Pelagius.

I reply that while truth certainly must not be denied, it should not be read in the books of heretics, for there the truth is harmful, not beneficial. Blessed Gregory in *Moralia*, book 5, chapter 11, writes that this is the prerogative of the heretics, to mix the true and the false, the good and the evil, for if they said only false and evil things, they would be rejected by everybody, and if they said only true and good things, they would not be heretics. Therefore they mix everything, so as to corrupt the good with the evil, and to hide the evil with the good. This is also the reason why Christ and the apostles prohibited the devils from saying true things, that is, so that they would not gain people's confidence with those true things and afterward be believed even in their falsehood: Luke 4, "And devils also came out of many, crying out, and saying, Thou art Christ the Son of God. And he rebuking them suffered them not to speak: for they knew that he was Christ";[197] and in Acts 16 Paul prohibited the Devil from saying, "These men are the servants of the most high God, which shew unto us the way of salvation."[198]

Moreover, it is not even proper to receive the truth from heretics because they are the enemies of truth. As Gellius writes in book 18, chapter 3, when the Spartans were discussing very important matters of the commonwealth, a man who was certainly well spoken and erudite, but impious and impure, expressed a very good opinion. While all liked it and it seemed that a decree should be issued according to what the man said, nevertheless they could not allow very good advice to be polluted by the

197. Luke 4:41.
198. Acts 16:17.

impiety of its author, so a very wise man was chosen, and with everybody's consent he said the same thing as the other man, and without making any mention of the first speaker, the second man's opinion was put on record in the decree.

To the first issue of the writings of the Fathers, I say that the Fathers are not enemies of the Church, and whatever they wrote that is wrong is not heresy but human error. Moreover, the errors of the Fathers are extinguished and dead, and cannot do harm, for an error is harmful as long as it is defended obstinately, but the errors of the Fathers were not discovered while they were alive; otherwise either they would have amended them themselves or they would have been expelled from the Church. But those errors were discovered and noticed after the Fathers' deaths, and they were rejected by everybody just as the Fathers would reject them if they were still alive.[199]

To the issue of the pagans, I say that their books are tolerated because they are not harmful, being dead errors, for there is nobody now who would not laugh at the doctrines of the pagans, and we never hear of Christians who are corrupted by the books of pagans and fall into paganism as they fall into heresy every day. Indeed, because there were many who supported the doctrines of the pagans at the time of the apostles, Clement writes that the books of pagans were prohibited (see book 1 of the *Constitutiones*, chapter 7), and for the same reason the books of pagans were prohibited at the Fourth Council of Carthage, chapter 16.

To the issue of the books of Jews and Muslims, I say that they are better than those of heretics, for Jews and Muslims are open enemies of Christians and do not deceive under the name of Christians, as the heretics do. Therefore even the most foolish men know how to distinguish the doctrines of Jews and Muslims from the Christian ones, while only very

199. Bellarmine took a similar position on the errors contained in the works of the Fathers of the Church in his July 1592 *votum* on the corrections to be made to Sixtus V's rules for the new Index, which prohibited such works. Bellarmine said, "The sayings of the holy Fathers that are not in agreement with the doctrine of the faith are very few and they have been either noted or explained with modesty by Catholic authors." See ACDF, Index, Protocolli II, folder 9, fols. 35r–36v, at fols. 35r–v (my translation), document published also by Godman, *Saint as Censor*, pp. 269–72, and analyzed by Frajese, *La nascita dell'Indice*, pp. 141–44.

learned men can identify heresies. Moreover, the books of Jews and Muslims are also prohibited when they contain blasphemies against Christ or are judged dangerous for Christians, as is clear from the case of the Talmud.[200]

To the issue of Origen, Tertullian, Eusebius, and Pelagius, I say that their books are permitted because those heresies are dead and those books are useful because of their antiquity. *In addition, we have nothing of Pelagius under his name, but under that of St. Jerome, as the* Commentaria brevia *on all the epistles of Paul, the* Symbolum falso inscriptum a Damaso, *and the epistle to Demetriades which can be found in volume 4, where there are other things that taste of the Pelagian heresy.*[201]

The second argument is from Paul, who in 1 Thessalonians 5 says: "Despise not prophesyings. Prove all things; hold fast that which is good."[202] And this is the meaning: if anybody makes prophecies or interprets the Scriptures, either in speech or in writing, do not reject him, but listen to him or read him, accept what is consonant with the Catholic faith, and discard the rest.

I reply that the apostle speaks of prophecies and writings about which it is not yet clear whether they are good or evil, and he does not want them to be rejected without examining them first; but when a piece of

---

200. The case of the Talmud was indeed one of the most controversial in Rome at the end of the sixteenth century. The Talmud was absolutely forbidden in the Index of 1559 but was allowed in the 1564 Index, provided that it was corrected and published under a different title. At the end of the 1570s a committee was formed, with Bellarmine as head, to expurgate the Talmud and other Jewish texts that needed to be corrected. The committee encountered many difficulties, especially the issue of the translation. In order to be corrected and possibly allowed, those texts needed to be translated from Hebrew into Latin, but who was to translate? Could converted Jewish intellectuals be allowed to participate, or should the translation be left only to Christian theologians who knew Hebrew? With this and many other questions remaining unanswered, the work of expurgation was never completed, and after twenty years of conflict within the Roman Curia between those who wanted the Talmud to be corrected and allowed and those who wanted it forbidden, and between the Roman Curia and the Jewish community, the Talmud was prohibited by Pope Clement VIII. On this see F. Parente, "The Index."

201. The passage shown here in italic type was added by Bellarmine in his corrections to the 1599 Venice edition of the work (APUG 1364, col. 496).

202. 1 Thessalonians 5:20–21.

writing has already been examined and it is clear that it is evil, he wants it to be absolutely rejected, and of this kind are all the writings which we prohibit, for they are tested, that is, they have all been examined and then prohibited because they were found to be evil.

Besides, even if the apostle is writing to the whole Church, he does not want everything to be done by everybody, but only by those who are able and who have this duty. Just as when certain suspicious articles are sent to a university to be examined, this examination does not concern everybody in the university, but only the teachers or those whom the teachers designate to this purpose. So when the apostle orders that the prophecies and interpretation of Scripture are to be examined in the Church, he certainly does not want this to be done by tailors and construction workers, but by the bishops and by others whom they choose.

They draw another argument from the testimonies of four ancient Fathers: Dionysius of Alexandria, Theophilus of Alexandria, blessed Jerome, and Gelasius. As Eusebius writes in book 7 of *Historia,* chapter 6 [7], when Dionysius was reproached because he was reading books by heretics, he replied that he had a vision in which he said to himself, "Read everything which comes to your hands, for you will be able to judge and examine everything." Similarly, when Theophilus was accused of reading Origen, he replied, as Socrates reports in *Historia,* book 6, chapter 15, that he was reading it to pick out what was good and reject what was evil. Blessed Jerome in his epistle to Alexander and Minerus said that he was reading the books of heretics to select what was good from them, even though he knew that some people were complaining about him because of that. In the volume *De anathematis vinculo,* Gelasius wanted to prove that the Council of Chalcedon could be accepted in some points and rejected in others, so he brought up the example of heretical books, parts of which are accepted and parts of which are rejected, and declared: "Examine everything; keep what is good."

To this last, I reply that the point of the example of Gelasius is this: just as in the Council of Chalcedon there were certain good things and certain evil things, certain things to be accepted and others to be rejected, so also in the books of heretics. But he does not mean to say that such books of heretics can be accepted because there are some true things mixed into them in the same way that the Council of Chalcedon is accepted. In fact, the Council of holy Fathers is one thing, heretical books are another thing, as we said, even though the truth introduced in such books is good and is to be accepted, provided that the same truth is found somewhere else. Here is what he says: "Is it not the case that in the books of those heretics we can read many things which are true? And must we reject the truth because the books with much perversity in them are rejected? Or must we accept their perverse books because the truth that is introduced in them is not denied?"

To the other examples I reply, first, that from these passages it is gathered that in the Church there had always been the custom of prohibiting the reading of books of heretics; otherwise nobody would have blamed those Fathers. Second, reading books of heretics was always granted, and it is granted even now, to bishops and many others, and therefore it is not surprising if Dionysius and Theophilus, who were Patriarchs, and St. Jerome, who has always been considered most learned, could read all books in their own right. Third I say that maybe there was not then a law of the universal Church, but only the custom of not allowing the reading of heretical books, apart from the books of Arius, but now there is a law of the universal Church and that law must be obeyed.

## CHAPTER 21

## Heretics condemned by the Church
## can be punished with temporal
## punishments and even death

In article 14, read at the Council of Constance, session 15, Jan Hus declared that it was not lawful to bring an incorrigible heretic to the secular authority and to allow him to be burned.[203] In article 33 and in its *assertio* Luther says the same. And this is not a new error, for even Donatists such as Parmenianus, Petilianus, and Gaudentius once taught it, as Augustine attests in *Contra epistolam Parmeniani,* book 1, chapter 7; *Contra litteras Petiliani,* book 2, chapter 10; *Contra epistolam Gaudentii [Contra Gaudentium],* book 2 [1], chapters 17 [13] and 26 [33]; and in epistle 50 [185] to Boniface.

All Catholics and even some heretics teach the opposite. In fact, after inflicting the ultimate punishment on Michael Servetus as a heretic, Calvin was reproached by some of his associates and published a book in which he demonstrates that it is lawful to punish heretics with capital punishment. Also Benedictus Aretius in his history of the punishment of Valentino Gentile argues that Gentile was rightly killed for heresy by the magistrate of Berne. And Théodore Beza teaches it at even greater length in his book *De haereticis a magistratu puniendis.*[204]

---

203. In his article Hus called those who thought it lawful to send a heretic to the secular judge for punishment "worse murderers than Pilate." See *Conciliorum oecumenicorum decreta,* p. 406.

204. On the trials of Michael Servetus and Valentino Gentile and their significance in the context of sixteenth-century religious conflicts, see D. Cantimori, *Eretici Italiani del Cinquecento.*

We will, then, briefly show that incorrigible heretics and especially the relapsed can and must be rejected by the Church and punished by the secular authorities with temporal punishments and even with death.

First, this is proved out of Scripture. The Old Testament in Deuteronomy 13 most vigorously commands the killing without mercy of false prophets who incite the worship of other gods, and chapter 17 says that in dubious matters the High Priest should be consulted and then immediately adds: "And the man that will do presumptuously, and will not hearken unto the priest that standeth to minister there before the Lord thy God, or unto the judge, even that man shall die";[205] and again in chapter 18 a false prophet is ordered to be killed. In this matter Elias, Josiah, Jehu, and others observed the same law and killed many false prophets, as is clear in 3 Kings 18 and 4 Kings 10 and 23, and there is basically no difference between our heretics and the false prophets of that time. And not only did holy kings and prophets punish the wicked with death, but also Nebuchadnezzar (as it says in Daniel 3) issued an edict that whoever spoke against the God of Daniel, that is, the true God, should be killed, and his house should be ravaged, in which edict he performed a most just act of deference toward the true God, as Augustine says in epistle 50 [185] and elsewhere. In the New Testament we read, first of all, in Matthew 18 that the Church can expel, and have considered as heathens and publicans, those who do not want to obey,[206] and therefore the Church can send them to the secular authority as men who are no longer children of the Church. Then in Romans 13 we read that the secular authority can punish the wicked with capital punishment: "For he beareth not the sword in vain: for he is the minister of God, a revenger to execute wrath upon him that doeth evil, etc."[207] From these two passages it is clearly understood that it is lawful that heretics, who in everyone's judgment are rebels against the Church and disturb the public peace, be removed from the Church and punished with death by the secular judge.

Moreover, Christ and his apostle compared heretics to those things that without controversy are repelled by violence, for in Matthew 7 the

205. Deuteronomy 17:12.
206. Cf. Matthew 18:17.
207. Romans 13:4.

Lord says: "Beware of false prophets, which come to you in sheep's clothing, but inwardly they are ravening wolves,"[208] and in Acts 20: "For I
know this, that after my departing shall grievous wolves enter in among
you, not sparing the flock."[209] By "wolves" is certainly meant heretics, as
St. Ambrose beautifully explains in his commentary on the beginning of
Luke 10. And the ravening wolves are killed rightfully if they cannot be
driven away otherwise, for the life of the sheep must be considered more
important than the death of the wolves. Likewise in John 10 we find: "He
that entereth not by the door into the sheepfold, but climbeth up some
other way, the same is a thief and a robber,"[210] where by "thief and robber"
is meant heretics and all the seducers and inventors of sects, as Chrysostom and Augustine explain; and it is well known how thieves and robbers
are punished. Likewise in 2 Timothy 2 heresy is compared to a cancer that
is not cured with medicines but must be surgically removed; otherwise it
keeps spreading and corrupts the whole body. Finally, in John 2 Christ
forced the money changers with a scourge to leave the temple. And in
Acts 5 Peter killed Ananias and Sapphira because they dared to lie to the
Holy Spirit, while in Acts 13 Paul punished with blindness a false prophet
who tried to turn a proconsul away from faith.[211]

Second, it is proved by the sentences and laws of the emperors, which
the Church has always approved. Emperor Constantine exiled Arius and
some of his associates following the petition of the Synod of Nicaea, as
Sozomen attests in *Historia,* book 1, chapter 20. He also punished the
Donatists, as Augustine reports in *Contra epistolam Parmeniani,* book 1,
chapter 7, and in epistle 166 [105] to the Donatists, where he lists many
good emperors who issued most severe laws against heretics, while Julian
the Apostate only supported them.

Later Theodosius, Valentinian, Marcian, and other most pious emperors issued laws against heretics in which they sometimes penalized
them by depriving them of some pounds of gold, sometimes of all their
goods, sometimes with exile or lashes, and sometimes with the ultimate

208. Matthew 7:15.
209. Acts 20:29.
210. John 10:1.
211. Cf., respectively, 2 Timothy 2:16–17; John 2:15; Acts 5:1–10; Acts 13:9–11.

punishment, as is clear in title "De haereticis," laws "Manichaeos," "Ariani," "Quicumque." By this last law of Theodosius and Martianus all who attempt to teach impious doctrines are ordered to be executed, and those who listen to the teachers of impious doctrines are fined with some pounds of gold.[212] According to Paulus Diaconus [*Historia Romana*] book 16, Justinian by law expelled all heretics from the territories of the whole empire, after giving them three months to convert. Subsequently Emperor Micheles, also according to Paulus Diaconus, [*Historia Romana*] book 24, decreed capital punishment for heretics.

Third, it is proved through the laws of the Church: in the chapter "Ad abolendam"[213] and the chapter "Excommunicamus, [*Liber extra*], de haereticis,"[214] and in "Sexto, de haereticis," chapter "Super eo,"[215] the Church determines that incorrigible heretics should be sent to the secular authority to be punished in the appropriate manner. Likewise the Council of Constance, session 15, condemned the opinion of Jan Hus and sent Hus himself and Jerome of Prague to the secular authority, which burned both of them. Finally, Leo X condemned the articles of Luther.

212. Bellarmine is here quoting, respectively, law 62, title 5, book 16 of the Codex Theodosianus (text in *Codex Theodosianus*, vol. 6.1, p. 204), which punished heretics with exile; law 5, title 5, book 1 of the Justinian Code (text in *Corpus iuris civilis*, vol. 2, p. 51), which appears in a slightly different formulation in the Theodosian Code as well, namely, law 65, title 5, book 16 (text in *Codex Theodosianus*, vol. 6.1, p. 207), and was promulgated in 428 to issue a series of punishments, including death, for heretics; and finally the already cited "Quicumque" (see p. 94, n. 187).

213. Bellarmine is quoting from book 5 of Gregory's *Decretales*, title 7, chapter 9. This law was issued by Pope Lucius III and ratified at the Council of Verona in 1184. It prescribed that heretics should be excommunicated and left to the secular authority for punishment (text in *Corpus iuris canonici*, vol. 2, cols. 780–82).

214. This is chapter 13 of book 5, title 7, of Gregory's *Decretales*, issued by Innocent III and ratified at the Lateran Council in 1215. It is a fundamental canon for the question of papal authority because in it Innocent III did not simply relinquish heretics to the secular authorities but decreed that secular authorities that did not comply with the pope's request to eliminate and punish the heretics after being admonished by the bishop should also be excommunicated. If the secular ruler did not return to obedience to the pope within a year, the pope could absolve the ruler's subjects from their oath of allegiance and give the land to Catholic rulers so that they would purge it of heresy (the text of this canon is in *Corpus iuris canonici*, vol. 2, cols. 787–89).

215. This is chapter 4 of book 5 of the *Liber sextus*, title 2 (text in *Corpus iuris canonici*, vol. 2, cols. 1070–71), issued by Alexander IV. It prescribed that relapsed heretics should be sent to the secular judges without any further examination.

Fourth, it is proved by the testimonies of the Fathers. In *De exhortatione martyrii,* chapter 5, Cyprian repeats from Deuteronomy 13 that the pseudo-prophets must be killed and then adds: "If this was done in the Old Testament, with all the more reason it must be done now."

In his commentary on the passage in Galatians 5, "A little leaven leaveneth the whole lump,"[216] Jerome says: "Therefore, a spark must be extinguished immediately after it appears, and the leaven must be moved away from the near lump, the rotten flesh must be removed, and an animal with scabies must be pushed away from the sheepfold, so that the spark may not burn the whole house, the leaven may not leaven the whole lump, the rotten flesh may not corrupt the whole body, the animal may not kill the whole flock. Arius was a spark, but because the spark was not suppressed immediately, his fire devastated the whole world."

In *Retractationes,* book 2, chapter 5, and in epistles 48 [93] and 50 [185], Augustine retracts what he had said before, namely, that heretics should not be compelled to faith by force, and he proves at length that this is most useful. He still makes an exception, however, for capital punishment, not because he thinks that they did not deserve it, but because he considers such punishment not consonant with the clemency of the Church, and also because there was no imperial law yet that ordered the execution of heretics, for the law, "Quicumque," chapter "De haereticis," was issued soon after Augustine's death.[217]

However, it is clear that Augustine thought that killing heretics was just, for in *Contra epistolam Parmeniani,* book 1, chapter 7, he shows that if the Donatists were punished with death, they would be justly punished. And in his treatise 11 on John he says: "They kill the souls and are afflicted in the bodies, they cause eternal death and complain of suffering temporal death, etc." There Augustine is saying that they falsely complain of being killed by the emperors; nevertheless, even if it were true, their complaint would still be unjust. Finally, in epistle 50 [185] to Boniface he says that the Church certainly does not want to kill any heretic, but just as the household of David could not enjoy any peace until Absalom had been

216. Galatians 5:9.
217. See p. 94, n. 187.

killed, and David had been consoled for the death of his son by the peace in his kingdom, so when the laws of the emperors against heretics result in some people's death, the sorrow of the maternal heart of the Church is sweetened and healed by the liberation of so many peoples.

In epistle 91 [15] to Turbius [Turribius], chapter 1, St. Leo says: "Rightly our Fathers, in whose time such abominable heresy broke out, took vigorous action all over the world to have the impious frenzy driven out of the universal Church. Then also the princes of the world detested this sacrilegious madness so much that they used the sword of public law to strike down its author and his disciples. This severity was for a long time a helpful supplement to ecclesiastical mildness, which shies away from violent revenge and is satisfied with the sentence of the priest because it is after all supported by the severe sanctions of Christian princes, for sometimes those who fear corporeal punishment recur to spiritual remedies." When Optatus of Milevis, book 3, replied to the calumnies of heretics who were very upset that two of their own had been killed by the prefect Macharius, he said: "You see that Moses, Phinee, Elias, and Macharius have done a similar thing, because it is the revenge of the one God that proceeds from all of them."

In book 1, epistle 72 [74] to Gennadius, Exarch of Africa, St. Gregory praises Gennadius because he persecuted the heretics with great zeal and St. Gregory exhorts him to keep going.

In sermon 66 on the Song of Songs, St. Bernard says: "It is better without a doubt that they be punished by the sword—the sword, that is, of him who does not bear it in vain—than to allow many people to be drawn into error. For he is the minister of God, an avenger to execute wrath upon whoever does evil. Some people find it surprising that the heretics being taken to their execution seem to be not only patient, but also cheerful, but they do not quite appreciate how much power the Devil has, not only over the bodies of men, but also over their hearts, once God has allowed him to take possession of them. For is it not more surprising to see a man killing himself rather than willingly being killed by another?"

Finally, it is proved by natural reason. First, heretics can be rightfully excommunicated, as everybody says, and therefore also killed. This conclusion is proved because excommunication is a heavier punishment than temporal death. Augustine, in *Contra adversarium legis et prophetarum,* book 1, chapter 17, says that it is more horrible to be sent to Satan through excommunication than to be hit by the sword, to be burned in flames, or to be thrown to the beasts to be devoured.

Second, experience teaches that there is no other remedy, for as the Church progressed it tried out all remedies. First, it used only excommunication, then it added pecuniary sanctions, next it used exile, and, finally, it was obliged to implement the death penalty, for heretics despise excommunication, and they say it is cold lightning. If you threaten a pecuniary sanction, they neither fear God nor show reverence toward men, knowing that there will be no lack of fools who will believe in them and will support them. If you lock them in prison or send them into exile, they corrupt with speech those who are near them and with books those who are far. Therefore the only remedy is to send them quickly to the place where they belong.

Third, forgers by everybody's judgment deserve death, and heretics are forgers of the word of God.

Fourth, according to Augustine's argument in epistle 50 [185], it is more serious for a man not to keep his word to God than for a wife to be false to her husband, but the latter is punished with death, so why not also the former?

Fifth, there are three grounds on which reason teaches that those men must be killed, and Galen describes them beautifully in the book titled *Quod mores animi corporis temperamenta sequantur,* toward the end of the book.[218]

The first is so that the wicked may not harm the good, or the innocent may not be crushed by the guilty. For this reason it is in everybody's judgment very just that murderers, adulterers, and thieves are killed.

The second is so that many people may be reformed through the punishment of a few, and those who did not want to be helpful to the com-

218. Bellarmine's reference to Galen is an indication of the influence that the Greek physician and natural philosopher enjoyed in early modern Europe and in particular in humanistic circles—his *editio princeps* was published in Venice by Aldo Manuzio in 1525. For an introduction to early modern medicine and its relationship to ancient medicine and natural philosophy, see Siraisi, *Medieval and Early Renaissance Medicine.*

monwealth while alive may be so in death. For this reason we also see that everybody finds it very just that certain horribly shameful acts are punished, even though they do not harm those who are close except by example. Thus necromancy and certain impious acts against nature are most severely punished so that other people may understand that those are immense crimes and not dare to commit similar ones.

The third is that it is often a benefit for the people themselves to be killed, when it is clear that they are becoming worse and worse and it is not likely that they will ever return to a sane mind.

All these reasons, then, suggest that heretics must be killed. First of all, heretics are more harmful to their neighbors than any pirate or thief, since they destroy the souls and indeed the foundation of everything that is good and fill the commonwealth with riots, acts that necessarily follow differences in religion.

Furthermore, their punishment benefits many others who, without such punishment, would do nothing, but who would be prompted by the punishment to realize the gravity of the heresy that they are following, and to consider that perhaps they might end their present life in misery and not reach the future beatitude. Therefore also the blessed Augustine attests, in epistle 48 [93], that many people converted after the imperial laws forbade heretics from going unpunished, and we see this happening every day in places where the Inquisition flourishes.

Finally, it is beneficial for obstinate heretics to be removed from this life, for the longer they live, the more errors they come up with, the more people they corrupt, and the more damnation they acquire for themselves.

## The objections are refuted

The arguments of Luther and other heretics remain to be taken care of. The first argument, from the experience of the whole Church, is the following. Luther says that the Church from the beginning until now burned no heretic; therefore, it does not seem to be the will of the spirit that they be burned.

I reply that this argument proves very well not Luther's opinion, but Luther's ignorance and impudence, for either Luther ignored that virtually an infinite number of heretics were either burned or otherwise killed, in which case he is ignorant, or he did not ignore it, in which case he is guilty of being impudent and a liar. For it can be shown that heretics were often burned by the Church if we just present a few examples out of many. The heresiarch Priscillian with his associates was killed by the Christian emperor Maximus, as St. Jerome attests in his *De viris illustribus,* and Optatus remembered the killed Donatists in book 3 of *Contra Parmenianum.*

A certain Basilius, a sorcerer and therefore a heretic, for truly there are hardly any sorcerers who are not heretics, was burned by a Christian and Catholic people, as blessed Gregory attests in book 1 of the *Dialogi,* chapter 4.

Again, another Basilius, initiator of Bogomilism, was publicly burned by Emperor Alexius Comnenus, as Zonaras writes in his *Vita Alexii.*[219]

---

219. Bogomilism was a dualist heretical sect which spread in central Europe in the tenth century.

In sermon 66 on the Song of Songs, Bernard attests that the ultimate punishment was inflicted on heretics also in his own time. Once during the time of Innocent III, 180 Albigensian heretics were burned together after St. Dominic had confuted them with words and miracles and had converted many of their associates. Blessed Antonino of Florence, in his *Chronicon,* third part, title 19, chapter 1, paragraph 4, narrates the whole episode.

Not to mention infinitely many other cases, Jan Hus and Jerome of Prague were burned at the Council of Constance by Emperor Sigismund.

Luther replies to this last example that he was talking about heretics, and Hus and Jerome of Prague were not heretics. But nevertheless at least Priscillianus, the followers of Bogomilism, and the Albigensians were heretics. Besides, Jan Hus was a heretic both for us Catholics and Luther himself. It is well known that he was a heretic for us, and as for Luther, he himself proves this in his book *Contra Henricum regem Angliae.* Here he affirms that it is impious and blasphemous to deny that in the Eucharist there is true bread together with the body of the Lord, and that it is pious and Catholic to deny the conversion of the bread into the body. But Jan Hus remained of the opposite opinion until his death and asserted publicly that he died holding this opinion, believing most firmly in the conversion of the bread into the body of Christ, as John Cochlaeus reports in *Historia Hussitarum,* book 2, p. 76.

The second argument is that experience proves that nothing is accomplished with fear. I reply that experience tells the contrary, for Donatists, Manichaeans, and Albigensians were overthrown and destroyed with weapons. Likewise, (in his epistle 48 [93]) Augustine attests that, for fear of punishment, many people converted in his own time.

The third argument is that the Church tolerates Jews, so why not heretics? I reply, first, that the Jews never accepted the Christian faith, while the heretics did. Second, the Jews worship the religion that God established, even though temporarily, while heretics worship a religion invented by the Devil. Third, the Judaic sect is useful for the Church, for their books are prophecies of our matters, and their ceremonies prefigure our rituals; from this we prove to the pagans that we did not invent these prophecies, since they are preserved by our enemies. Finally, the Jews do

not try to corrupt the Christians, in general, as heretics do. See the Fourth
Council of Toledo, canons 55 and 56,[220] Augustine on Psalm 59, and also
Bernard in epistle 322 [363] to the people of Speyer and 323 [365] to the
Bishop of Mainz.

The fourth argument is drawn from Isaiah 2: "They shall beat their
swords into plowshares, and their spears into pruning hooks."[221] But this
is not to the point, for, as blessed Jerome explains, the prophet describes
the time of the coming of the Messiah, and says that it will be the time
of the greatest peace, so that men will change their tools of war into
tools of agriculture, and they will not use them any longer for battle,
at least not for a long time. But this time was fulfilled in the nativity of
Christ, for there was never such a general and continuous peace in the
whole world as in the time of Augustus. Then, if it is true that there will be
no war in the Church, as Luther deduces from this passage, it will be clear
that there is no Church among the Lutherans, for they waged most serious
wars among themselves and against the Catholics, as for example the war
against Charles V in which the Elector of Saxony was captured.[222]

The fifth argument is drawn from Isaiah 11: "They shall not hurt nor destroy in all my holy mountain."[223] I reply that this is an argument against
Luther himself, for the prophet does not say that the Catholics shall not
kill the heretics, but rather the opposite, that the heretics shall not kill and
harm the Catholics, as the prophet speaks of lions, bears, snakes, and bees
and other poisonous animals, of which he had said: "And the sucking child
shall play on the hole of the asp, and the weaned child shall put his hand
on the cockatrice's den."[224] But by these beasts are meant the Devil and
the heretics, his ministers, as Jerome and Cyril explain; and the prophet
says that they shall neither kill nor harm the whole Church, and even

220. The Fourth Council of Toledo was held in 633.
221. Isaiah 2:4.
222. Bellarmine is referring to John Frederick, prince elector of Saxony and leader
of the Protestant faction during the Schmalkaldic War between the Protestant princes
and Emperor Charles V. The war lasted from 1546 to 1547 and ended with the battle of
Mühlberg, in which the Protestants were defeated and John Frederick captured.
223. Isaiah 11:9.
224. Isaiah 11:8.

though the heretics seem to harm the Church, nevertheless in truth they do not, but they enforce it and make it progress in wisdom and patience.

The sixth argument comes from Matthew 18, where the Lord established that heretics should be considered heathens and publicans, not that they should be burned. And Paul in his epistle to Titus, chapter 3, orders that heretics should be avoided, not killed, and therefore it is not lawful to kill them. I reply that it is certainly true that Christ and Paul in this passage did not order the heretics to be burned, but they did not prohibit it either, and therefore nothing can be deduced from this passage. And Luther himself used this argument, for in book 2 of his dispute with Karlstadt, who was attacking Luther for designating as sacraments what Christ did not prescribe as such, Luther replied: And why do you prohibit the designation as sacraments of what Christ did not prohibit as such?[225]

Moreover, Christ and Paul never order us to kill adulterers and forgers, to hang robbers, to burn thieves; and nevertheless this happens and it happens rightly, and Luther would not dare to deny it.

The seventh argument arises from the following facts. According to Sulpicius, *Historia Sacra,* toward the end of book 2, blessed Martin of Tours vigorously reproached the bishops Hydatius and Ithacius who were lobbying the emperor for the death of the heretic Priscillian, and in the same passage Sulpicius accuses them of being guilty of a great crime because of this.

I reply that those bishops are deservedly accused for two reasons. First, because they deferred a matter of the Church to the emperor, for Priscillian, who was accused at the council, appealed his case from the council to the emperor, and the two bishops allowed that. Martin says about this issue that it is a new and unheard-of sin that a Church matter should be judged by a secular judge. Second, those bishops assumed the role of accusers in a case involving capital punishment, but even if it is the prerogative of bishops to excommunicate heretics and to leave them to the secular judge and even to exhort the judges to fulfill their duty, nevertheless it is

225. Bellarmine is here referring to the theological dispute between Luther and Karlstadt in Jena in 1524, which was recorded and published in the same year as *Weß sich Doctor Andreas Bodenstein von Karlstadt mit Doctor Martino Luther.*

not appropriate for the bishop to act as accuser. However, it is clear that Sulpicius thought that Priscillian and his associates were justly killed from his words: "In this way these men, who because of an appalling example were completely unworthy of the light of the day, were killed."

The eighth argument is drawn from 1 Corinthians 11: "For there must be also heresies among you, that they which are approved may be made manifest among you";[226] therefore heresies must not be destroyed. I reply that the meaning of this sentence is that given the wickedness of the Devil, who always plants heresies, given human nature, corrupt and prone to evil, and, last, given the divine permission, heresies are necessarily found in the world, just as we say that there must be some bad grass in the garden, and just as the Lord says in Matthew 18: "For it must needs be that offences come."[227] Therefore the apostle does not order us to plant heresies nor to destroy them according to our strength, but he only predicts that which will always exist in the world, just as we try most justly to remove scandals and to extirpate the bad grass from the garden even if we know that all scandals will never be removed.

The ninth argument comes from Luke 11 [9], where the Lord says to the disciples who wanted to burn the Samaritans: "Ye know not what manner of spirit ye are of."[228] I reply, first, that there is a very great difference between those Samaritans and the heretics, for the former never promised that they would keep the religion of Christ, which was presented to them then for the first time, and therefore they were not obliged to. But the heretics promised and declared that they would, and therefore they are rightly obliged to. Then, Jacob and John wanted to burn the Samaritans not so much out of zeal for the salvation of souls, but out of lust for revenge, and therefore they are deservedly blamed. The Church, indeed, persecutes heretics out of zeal for the salvation of those souls that they pervert, out of the same zeal with which Christ twice with a scourge expelled those from the temple who were selling sheep and oxen "and overthrew the tables"[229] (John 2 and Matthew 21). Peter killed Ananias and Sapphira

226. 1 Corinthians 11:19.
227. Matthew 18:7.
228. Luke 9:55.
229. John 2:15, Matthew 21:12.

(Acts 5). Paul delivered the man who committed fornication "unto Satan for the destruction of the flesh"[230] (1 Corinthians 5), not to mention Moses, Phinehas, Eliah, Mattithiah, and others who killed many people out of zeal for God.

The tenth argument comes from Matthew 13: "Let both grow together until the harvest,"[231] where the Lord openly speaks of heretics and prohibits that they be killed, as Chrysostom says explaining this passage, and likewise Cyprian in book 3, epistle 3 [51] to Maximus and Urbanus, where, speaking of this parable, he says that it is granted only to God to destroy the vessels of earth[232] and to root up the tares.

I reply, by "tares" is meant not only heretics, but all evil men, as is clear from the explanation of the Lord when he says: "The good seed are the children of the kingdom; but the tares are the children of the wicked one"[233] and later: "As therefore the tares are gathered and burned in the fire; so shall it be in the end of this world. The Son of man shall send forth his angels, and they shall gather out of his kingdom all things that offend, and them which do iniquity; And shall cast them into a furnace of fire."[234] And when the Lord prohibits the extirpation of the wicked, he does not prohibit the killing of this or that person but prohibits that good men try to eliminate the wicked everywhere and to leave no wicked man at all, for this could not happen without a great calamity for the good, and this is what the Lord says: "Lest while ye gather up the tares, ye root up also the wheat with them."[235] Therefore this is a general parable, and it teaches only that it will never happen that all the wicked would be eliminated before the end of the world.[236]

Regarding the particular question whether heretics, robbers, or other wicked men should be extirpated, it must always be considered whether,

---

230. 1 Corinthians 5:5.
231. Matthew 13:30.
232. 2 Timothy 2:20.
233. Matthew 13:38.
234. Matthew 13:40–42.
235. Matthew 13:29.
236. Bellarmine also comments on those verses from Matthew 13 in his treatise against Barclay, chapter 9, defending the legitimacy of the papal deposition of a secular ruler, in particular Gregory VII's sentence against Henry IV (cf. pp. 221–24).

according to the reasoning of the Lord, this could be done without damage to good people, and if this can be done, then without a doubt those must be extirpated. If, however, they cannot be extirpated, either because we do not know them enough, or because there is a danger of punishing the innocent instead of the guilty, or because they are stronger than we are and there is a danger that if we fight them in battle more of our people may die than their people, then we must keep quiet. This is what Augustine replies in *Contra epistolam Parmeniani,* book 3, chapter 2, explaining the same passage [Matthew 13:29–30] that was brought up against him by the Donatists. And Chrysostom teaches the same, as is clear from these words: "The Lord prohibits the extirpation of the tares lest while they are gathered the wheat is also rooted up with them, for if we killed the heretics now, a cruel and unstoppable war would be caused." Moreover, Cyprian in book 3, epistle 3 [51] to Maximus and Urbanus, interprets this parable as referring not to heretics, but to evil Christians, and he does not so much prohibit the killing of the wicked but says that it pertains to the Lord alone to distinguish the wicked from the good and to clean up completely the wheat from the tares.

The eleventh argument comes from John 6, where, when many of the disciples were walking away, the Lord says: "Will ye also go away?";[237] therefore the Church must do likewise.

I deny the conclusion, first, because the disciples did not oblige themselves to stay as the heretics did through baptism. Second, because it was appropriate that Christ, Who had come to be judged and not to judge, would not Himself take revenge for the injuries He suffered, but would leave them to be vindicated by His spiritual children, and we have the symbol of this in the figure of David, who, as long as he lived, never wanted to kill Shimei, who had cursed him, but ordered Solomon to commit the murder so as not to leave that sin unpunished (3 Kings 2).[238]

The twelfth argument is that faith is a gift of God; therefore, nobody can force anybody into it. I reply, faith is a gift of God as much as an act of free will; otherwise, in fact, even chastity and the other virtues are

237. John 6:67.
238. 1 Kings 2 in the King James Version.

gifts of God, but nevertheless adulterers, murderers, and robbers are justly punished and obliged to live chastely and honestly. Also, wisdom is a gift of God, but nevertheless in Proverbs 29 it is written: "The rod and reproof give wisdom."[239] Finally, faith is a gift of God, but God preserves such a gift in various ways, one of which is correction.

The thirteenth argument is that the Lord gave to the Church the sword of the spirit, which is the word of God, but not a sword of iron. Indeed, He said to Peter who wanted to defend Him with the sword of iron in John 18: "Put up thy sword into the sheath."[240]

I reply that just as the Church has ecclesiastical and secular princes, who are almost two arms of the Church, so it has two swords, the spiritual and the material, and therefore when the right hand cannot convert the heretic with the spiritual sword, it asks the left hand to help and to convert the heretics with the sword of iron, and maybe the Lord meant this when he forbade Peter, who was the future prince of the clergy, from using the sword of iron.

In *De consideratione,* book 4, St. Bernard says: "Why do you try again to seize the sword which you have been ordered once to put back in its sheath? For if anybody denies that it is yours, they do not seem to me to pay enough attention to the words of the Lord when He says: 'Put up thy sword into its sheath.'[241] It is therefore really yours, perhaps subject to your nod, but if it need not be unsheathed by your hand, [it must be unsheathed in some other way]. Besides, if indeed this did not pertain to you in any way, then the Lord would not have replied 'It is enough' but 'It is too much,' when the apostles said 'Here are two swords.'[242] Therefore the Church has both swords, the spiritual and the material. But while the latter has to be taken out for the Church, the former has to be taken out by the Church. While the former is in the hand of the priest, the latter is in the hand of the soldier but clearly subject to the nod of the priest and at the command of the emperor." These are his words, and in any case it could be said more briefly that the Lord prohibited the use of

239. Proverbs 29:15.
240. John 18:11.
241. Ibid.
242. Luke 22:38.

the sword only by a private authority, for Peter was not yet pontiff, but a disciple.[243]

The fourteenth argument is that the Church spares heretics only once, but the apostle in his epistle to Titus, chapter 3, orders that they be forgiven at least twice.

I reply that even if all Latin and Greek manuscripts now constantly have: "A man that is an heretick after the first and second admonition reject,"[244] nevertheless in some of the Greek and Latin ones there was not this version, but "after the first admonition reject," as is clear from Irenaeus, book 3, chapter 3; Tertullian in *De praescriptione;* Cyprian in *Ad Quirinum,* book 3, chapter 78; and Ambrose and Jerome in their commentary on this passage of the apostle. Therefore it is not certain which version is the true one. Moreover, in this passage of the apostle—*which St. Jerome approves more in our version, as did St. Athanasius, according to him*—[245]the apostle does not talk about the pardon to be given to a converted heretic but of the admonition that is given before the heretic is excommunicated through the sentence of a judge. The Church, indeed, observes this procedure not only in the case of heretics, but also in the case of every other person whom it excommunicates, for it always gives at least two admonitions beforehand.

The fifteenth argument is that heretics are outside of the Church, and in 1 Corinthians 5 it is said: "But them that are without God judgeth."[246] I reply that they are outside of the Church, but with the duty and obligation of remaining inside, and therefore they can be forced to come back as we force sheep when they leave the flock.

The sixteenth argument is that wishing the death of heretics is against

243. Bellarmine devotes the entire chapter 19 of his treatise against Barclay to explain this passage from Bernard's *De consideratione,* which is a *locus classicus* for the question of papal authority in temporal matters. See I. S. Robinson, "Church and Papacy," in Burns, ed., *Cambridge History of Medieval Political Thought,* pp. 252–305 at pp. 300ff., and J. A. Watt, "Spiritual and Temporal Power," in ibid., pp. 367–423, at pp. 368–74.

244. Titus 3:10.

245. This italic phrase was added by Bellarmine himself to the 1599 Venice edition of this work (APUG 1364, col. 504).

246. 1 Corinthians 5:13.

the mildness of the Church. But it is not against the mildness of the Church, because the Church is held to show compassion toward its children, and it would certainly be harsh and cruel if it showed compassion toward the wolves rather than the sheep. Second, the Church tried all other methods before it could be persuaded to inflict the ultimate punishment. For, as we said above, initially it only excommunicated them, but seeing that this alone was not sufficient, it added pecuniary sanctions, then the loss of all goods, then exile, and in the end it came to this, as is sufficiently clear from various laws of ancient emperors under the title "De haereticis." [247]

The seventeenth argument is that faith is free. Yes, but "free" is understood in two ways. In one sense it means free from obligation, as when we say that one is free to make a vow of chastity or to enter a religious order; but he is not free to break the vow or leave his order. In this sense faith for those who never accepted it is free from the obligation of human law, but not of divine law, and therefore men do not force them, but God will punish them. But for those who professed it with baptism, faith is not free from the obligation of either divine or human law, and therefore men force them to keep it. In the second sense "free" is taken as opposed to "compulsory," and in this sense one is free not to believe, as he is free to commit other sins, but such freedom does not prevent men who act badly from being punished. Indeed, it rather demands that they be punished, for if a person is free to believe or not believe, he could believe and remain in the Church as he should have, and because he did not do so, he is deservedly punished: this is the reply of St. Augustine in epistle 50 [185] to Boniface, and Contra epistolam Gaudentii [Contra Gaudentium], book 2 [1], chapter 11 [19], where he says: "Free will has been given to man, but if man has done evil, he should suffer the punishment."

The eighteenth argument is that the apostles never called upon the secular arm against the heretics. St. Augustine in epistle 50 [185] and in other places replies that the apostles did not do so because there was no

247. This is title 5, book 16, of the Theodosian Code and title 5, book 1, of the Justinian Code (text in Corpus iuris civilis, vol. 2, pp. 50–60).

Christian prince then to call upon. Then, in fact, that prophecy of Psalm 2 was fulfilled: "The kings of the earth set themselves, and the rulers take counsel together, against the Lord, and against his anointed";[248] and afterward, in the time of Constantine, that other prophecy that follows in the same Psalm started to be fulfilled: "Be wise now therefore, O ye kings: be instructed, ye judges of the earth. Serve the Lord with fear,"[249] and soon the Church invoked the help of the secular arm.

248. Psalm 2:2.
249. Psalm 2:10–11.

*On the Temporal Power of the Pope.*
*Against William Barclay*

# Preface

Whoever brought recently to light the book by William Barclay titled *De potestate Papae* has not dared to declare his name, nor the name of the printer or the place of publication. Indeed, even if in certain copies this book is said to be published in Pont à Mousson, I have found out that this is false.[1] Evidently the person was afraid of punishment and blame (and rightly so), rather than expecting approval and praise. He openly disclosed only the name of the author, which, if the author were still alive, perhaps he would have gladly concealed, because the publisher knew that the author was summoned and brought before the Supreme Judge and that he does not dwell among the mortals anymore. This indeed is not evidence of a good work, "For every one that doeth evil hateth the light, neither cometh to the light, lest his deeds should be reproved. But he that doeth truth cometh to the light, that his deeds may be made manifest, that they are wrought in God."[2]

Perhaps Barclay himself was afraid to be blamed for an incredible arrogance and rashness, as if, almost as another Goliath, he were moving alone against the battle lines of all Catholic writers. In fact, ignoring the multitude of his adversaries, he on purpose took upon himself to oppose only my own works. But I am not so important as to think that the cause of the Catholic Church depends on myself only; I know my imperfections and I know I am one of many, and I do not engage in battle if the common cause will be put in jeopardy, whether I succeed or fail in my discussion.

On this matter I will report, first of all, the opinions of the most illustrious writers from every nation of the Christian world, so that everybody

---

1. The editions of Barclay's *De potestate Papae* to which Bellarmine refers here are STC 1408.3 (s.l., *vere* London) and STC 1408 (Mussiponti, *vere* London).

2. John 3:20–21.

may understand that Barclay's opinion is unique and contrary to all Catholic authors, both theologians and professors of canon and civil law. And it would be indeed surprising—if Barclay were alive and were introduced to the presence of so many very learned men from Italy, France, Spain, Germany—if he dared to look at so many opposite lights and to open his mouth or even mutter.

Second, and so that nobody could have any doubt on the opinion of the Catholic Church, I will collect the Fathers from several councils into one supercouncil, as it were, in which several Popes, more than a few Patriarchs, numerous archbishops, bishops, abbots, and other most learned men who once gathered in different places and times now congregate again all together, and overwhelm Barclay with their judgments, summoned alone in their midst.

Finally, once it is sufficiently asserted from both individual authors and general councils what the Pope's authority in temporal matters means for the Catholic Church, then I will respond to Barclay's objections and examine his arguments. And whereas Barclay denies in general terms the Pope's authority in temporal matters, I will affirm it in general terms, not taking too much effort to establish whether that authority is absolute or whether it extends only to spiritual matters.[3] Therefore, as I am about to report the opinions of the most illustrious authors of the Western Church on the Pope's authority in temporal matters, it seems appropriate to start from Italy, since I see that the same observation has been made at the Council of Constance, session 41.[4]

---

3. Bellarmine's strategy in this text is twofold. On the one hand, and especially in this introductory part of the treatise, Bellarmine indeed quotes from a number of theologians and canonists who hold very different views on the nature and extent of the pontifical authority, from the ultrapapalist Agostino Trionfo to the Dominican theologians Vitoria and Soto. Afterward and starting with chapter 2, however, Bellarmine concentrates specifically on the doctrine of *indirecta potestas* against the position of both those who, like Barclay, denied the pope any authority in temporal matters and those who granted the pope the plenitude of power in the temporal sphere as well as in the spiritual sphere.

4. Bellarmine is referring to the order in which the cardinals entered the conclave to vote for Oddo Colonna, elected as Pope Martin V in the above-mentioned session of the Council of Constance, 8 November 1417.

## Opinions of illustrious authors from Italy

From Italy the first author who would come forth is Pope Gregory VII, who in book 8 of his *Registrum,* epistle 2 [21] to the Bishop of Metz, abundantly points out that Christian princes can be excommunicated and deprived of their dominion, and their subjects can be absolved from their allegiance by the Roman Pontiff: "Regarding your request to be supported by our writings and fortified against the infamy of those who jabber with their impious mouth that the authority of the Holy and Apostolic See could not excommunicate King Henry and could not absolve anybody from their oath of allegiance, etc."

St. Thomas Aquinas, who not only flourished for his excellent doctrine, but also shone in such glory of sanctity that it would be impossible to doubt that he was exceedingly far from any adulation toward the Pope, in his 2a 2ae, question 10, article 10, says: "We need to consider that dominion or primacy is introduced by human law, but the distinction between faithful and infidels is of divine law. However the divine law, which comes from grace, does not remove the human law, which comes from natural reason; therefore the distinction between faithful and infidels, considered in itself, does not remove the dominion and the primacy of the infidels over the faithful. Nevertheless, this right of dominion or primacy can justly be removed through the decision and order of the Church which has the authority of God, for the infidels because of their impiety deserve to forfeit their authority over the faithful, who are converted into God's children. However, the Church sometimes does that, and sometimes not." These are the words of St. Thomas, who makes two points against Barclay. The first is that dominion and primacy are introduced by human law, and they are not of divine law, as Barclay frequently affirms. Second, infidel princes can be deprived of the dominion they have over the faithful by the authority of the Church, which without a doubt most fully resides in the Pope. And by infidels Thomas does not mean only heathens, as Barclay seems to think, but all the infidels, whether they are pagans, Jews, or heretics. In fact, in article 6 of the same question he lists and compares with each other the different kinds of infidelity and says: "Heretics are infidels absolutely and completely worse than pagans and Jews"; and later, in article 10, he says clearly of all the infidels, "They can be deprived of the dominion they have over the faithful if the Church thinks it is expedient." In question 12, article 2, he reiterates this and adds: "Even because of other crimes the Church can deprive the rulers of the dominion they have over others." The same author in the same part, question 60, article 6, says: "In response to the third [objection], secular authority is subordinated to the spiritual as the body is subordinated to the soul, and therefore the judgment is not usurped if a spiritual leader interferes in a temporal affair." The same St. Thomas, in his commentary on the second book of the *Sententiae,* distinction 44, at the end, says that in the Pope resides the highest form of both spiritual and temporal authority. Likewise in his book 3 of *De regimine principum,* chapter 10, he says again the same thing: "If one says that (the plenitude of power of the Pope) applies only to the spiritual authority, this cannot be possible, for the corporeal and temporal depend on the spiritual and eternal." And at chapter 19: "The same applies to the case of a prince of a whole kingdom, since, in order to maintain his government, he may extend his authority over his subjects by imposing taxes, destroying cities and towns for the protection of the whole kingdom. It is much more fitting, then, to apply this to the supreme prince, that is the Pope, that would do the same for the good of the whole of Christianity." That is what he said. And even though there is some doubt whether the author of this be St. Thomas or not, since in chapters 20 and following he mentions Emperor Albert, who lived after St. Thomas died, and because in the above-mentioned chapter 10 more than once he calls Peter "Christ's successor [*successor*]"; and those authors who speak properly, and St. Thomas *in primis,* do not usually use that word, "successor"; nevertheless this author is ancient and learned, and Barclay cannot spurn him.[5]

St. Bonaventure, a most learned man and most holy cardinal bishop

5. The authorship of *De regimine principum* is indeed a disputed issue. Dedicated to "the king of Cyprus," probably Hugh II of Lusignan, the treatise appeared to have been started by Aquinas, who then abandoned it after the death of its dedicatee. The treatise was later completed by Tolomeo of Lucca. For more information on this, see Dyson's introduction in *Aquinas: Political Writings,* pp. xix–xxi.

of Albano, was so far from flattering the Pope that not even the slightest suspicion of such a crime was ever attached to him, and yet, in his book *De ecclesiastica hierarchia,* part 2, chapter 1, he speaks thus: "Indeed priests and bishops can remove kings and depose emperors for cause, which happened oftentimes and has been seen, for instance, when their malice requires it and the need of the commonwealth demands it. By contrast, the Supreme Pontiff, in whom the highest authority on earth resides, is not judged by a king, or a secular prince, or any other man, but is left to the judgment of God alone."

Giles of Rome, an Augustinian friar and archbishop of Bourges, in his treatise *De potestate ecclesiastica,* part 1, chapter 30 [4], says: "Some might say, however, that kings and princes are subjected spiritually, and not temporally, to the Church. But those who say so do not grasp the force of the argument. For if kings and princes were subjected to the Church only spiritually, one sword would not be subject to the other, temporal matters would not be subjected to the spiritual, there would be no order in authorities, and the lowest would not be led back to the highest through the intermediate." Here are the words of this author, who in that whole treatise demonstrates that the authority of the Church, which in the Supreme Pastor is at its fullest, extends not only to spiritual matters, but also to temporal.

Blessed Agostino Trionfo, also known as Agostino from Ancona, who was a man so pious and learned that on his tomb we can see inscribed the title of "Blessed," in his book *De potestate Ecclesiae,* question 22, article 3, says: "Who will go on to deny that the emperor can be deposed by the Pope? Whoever is in charge of putting him on the throne is in charge of deposing him, as those very examples demonstrate."

Blessed John of Capistrano, who gave prestige to the Catholic Church with his teaching and his miracles, in his book *De potestate [auctoritate] Papae,* in the second part of the second principal section, in the eighteenth argument, at p. 56 of the edition printed in Venice in 1588, says: "The Pope must be superior to the princes in both spiritual and temporal affairs, so that he may be considered worthier for his preeminence and supreme in everything."

St. Antonino, bishop of Florence, a man equally holy and learned and completely alien from any form of flattery, in his *Summa,* part 3, title 22, chapter 3, section 7, says: "The authority of emperors, kings, and princes is such that it has to be instituted, regulated, and confirmed by the Pope if it is legitimate; and by the Pope it must be judged and condemned if it is not." Also in chapter 5, section 7, he says: "[the Pope] can depose kings for a reasonable cause."

The Dominican Isidoro from Milan in his *De imperii militantis Ecclesiae dignitate,* book 2, title 8, conclusion 3, says: "The Pope can depose emperors and kings because of their pressing defects."

Gabriel Biel, a famous theologian, in section 23 of his *Canonis Missae expositio* says: "(God), Who has appointed only one (namely the Pope) over everybody for the government of His Church, rules and protects so that everybody is governed by only one, as the body is governed by the head." And toward the end: "The Pope transfers the supreme secular authority from people to people, and he can depose the emperor," etc.

Tommaso Cajetan, a Dominican cardinal famous for both his knowledge and the integrity of his life, in *Apologia de comparata auctoritate Papae et Concilii,* part 2, chapter 13, to the eighth [objection], teaches the same thing. To the eighth objection of his adversary, posed with these words: "Eighth: we found only a few Popes who declared they have the supreme authority in temporal matters, while the rest of the Popes have declared the opposite," he responds: "To the eighth point it is replied that since the authority of the Pope is directed in spiritual matters to the absolutely supreme end of mankind, then two areas compete for his authority: first, what is not directly related to temporal matters; and second, what in temporal matters is related to spiritual matters. The Pope has the latter because of the fact that everything, including temporal matters, needs to be ordered for that supreme end, and without a doubt by the person whose concern it is to direct everything to that end, such as Christ's Vicar. The former springs from the very nature of his authority. From this it follows, then, that the Pope as Pope can truly make determinations in both areas and can do this because he both has and does not have the supreme authority in temporal matters. Both these statements are true for a sensible mind. The affirmative, in fact, is true regarding spiritual matters, and the negative is true directly, that is, insofar as temporal matters as such are concerned. Therefore no error can occur from the Pope's decision in either."

Alexander of St. Elpidio, of the Order of the Hermits of St. Augustine, in his book *De auctoritate Summi Pontificis et iurisdictione imperii,* chapter 9, says: "Whoever does not subject himself to the Vicar of God and to the authority of the Church does not subject himself to God: therefore, no king, no temporal prince, in whatever condition, can ever be lifted from this obligation if he wants to be called a Christian both in name and in deed, because they must be subjected to the supreme spiritual authority even in temporal matters."

Pietro del Monte, bishop of Brescia, in his *Monarchia,* part 2, question 4, at the end says: "The Pope has a great authority over the emperor, since he deposes him in case of a crime."

Petrus de Ancharano in his commentary on chapter 6, title "De constitutionibus,"[6] says: "The Pope has both swords, and he has authority over the empire, and it is for this reason that he crowns, anoints, and sometimes deposes the emperor."

Silvestro Mazzolini da Prierio, a Dominican theologian and a very learned canonist, in his *Summa Sylvestrina,* at the entry "Pope," n. 10, says: "The Pope can choose the emperor by himself immediately when it is expedient because of a just and reasonable cause, since whoever is in charge of directing all the faithful to peace and the spiritual end is also in charge of choosing the attendants," and later: "The Pope can excommunicate the emperor who is worthy of being excommunicated, and he can depose the emperor who is worthy of being deposed." And n. 11: "The Pope has the universal jurisdiction in spiritual and temporal matters over all kings and Christian princes." And later: "[The Pope] can depose [the emperor] for a reasonable cause."

Astesanus in his *Summa Astensis,* part 1, book 2, title 64, article 4,

---

6. This is chapter 6, title 2, "De constitutionibus," of the first book of Gregory IX's *Decretales,* which forbids the members of a chapter, that is, a body of clerics serving a cathedral, to change the constitution of their order without a reason, and which begins with "Since we all are one body in Christ, and as individuals we are each the other's limbs, the higher must not envy the lower, and the older must not envy the younger" (text in *Corpus iuris canonici,* vol. 2, cols. 8–9).

p. 201, says: "From what has been said before, you should gather that secular princes and temporal sovereigns must be excommunicated and deposed by the Church and expelled from their land, and the lands that they occupy can be transferred to other Catholics, not only because of their own heretical beliefs, but also because of their negligence in extirpating others' heretical beliefs. The same applies even if the prince is found negligent, ineffective, and inept regarding his kingdom and the administration of justice, and this is why Zachary deposed Childeric and Innocent deposed Otto."

Nicholas de Tudeschis, abbot of Palermo, in his commentary on the chapter "Solitae," title "De majoritate et obedientia," section 7, says: "The Pope can reasonably reproach the emperor and the other secular princes, and this is not surprising, since indeed he can also depose them for cause."[7] The abbot illustrates the same in his commentary on the chapter "Per venerabilem," title "Qui filii sint legitimi."[8]

Giovanni of Anagni, archdeacon of Bologna, in his discussion of the chapter "Licet," title "De voto," section 10, says: "The Pope deprives a layman from his rank of birth, because he has authority over kings and kingdoms. Hence he deposes the emperor."[9]

Bartolus of Sassoferrato in his commentary on the law "Si imperialis,"

7. The chapter "Solitae" is the sixth of the first book of Gregory IX's *Decretales,* title 33, "De majoritate et obedientia," and is one of the most important decretals in the debate over the pope's authority. This chapter is the letter of Innocent III to Emperor Alexius of Constantinople (1201), in which the pope reminded the emperor that the secular rulers were subject to the spiritual ruler (text in *Corpus iuris canonici,* vol. 2, cols. 196–98). Section 7, quoted here by Bellarmine, was the end of the letter, in which the pope invited the emperor to follow his suggestions for the benefit of the Church.

8. The chapter "Per venerabilem" is the thirteenth chapter of title 17, "Qui filii sint legitimi," of the fourth book of Gregory IX's *Decretales,* and it is the letter of Innocent III to Count William of Montpellier (1202), in which the pope required the nobleman to legitimize his bastard sons on the basis of the *plenitudo potestatis* of the pope, which extended to temporal matters also (text in *Corpus iuris canonici,* vol. 2, cols. 714–16). This canon, like the previous one, became a classic reference in the debates over the papal authority.

9. The chapter "Licet" is the sixth chapter of the third book, title 34, "De voto et voti redemptione," of the third book of Gregory's *Decretales,* and it is the 1198 letter of Pope Innocent III to Andreas, son of the king of Hungary, in which the pope obliged Andreas to keep his dead father's vow under pain of excommunication and of the forfeiture of his right to inherit the kingdom (text in *Corpus iuris canonici,* vol. 2, cols. 590–91).

chapter "De legibus," section 4, says: "The princes of Germany have the right to choose the emperor, but only you, the Pope, have the right to depose him."[10]

Baldus de Ubaldis, in his *In prooemio lecturae feudorum veteris,* says: "Only the Pope deposes the emperor."

Pietro Andrea Gambari, in his treatise *De officio et potestate legati,* book 2, title "De variis ordinariorum nominibus," section 220, says: "Only the Pope deposes the emperor and the kings if their crimes persuade him to."

Ristoro Castaldi, in his book *De imperatore,* question 81, says: "The Pope alone, without the council, deposes the emperor, for the tribunal of the Pope and the tribunal of Christ are the same thing." And later: "If it is expedient, the Pope punishes and deposes a prince, no matter to what extent he is exempted."

Domenico Toschi, a cardinal and a very learned man who is still alive and a few years ago completed a great work, in his sixth volume of *Practicae conclusiones,* at the entry "Pope," quotes many authors on this issue and I refer the reader who wants more references to him.

## Opinion of illustrious authors from France

St. Bernard of Clairvaux, in *De consideratione,* book 4, chapter 4 [3], says: "Why do you try again to seize the sword which you have been ordered once to put back in its sheath? For if anybody denies that it is yours, they do not seem to me to pay enough attention to the words of the Lord when he says: 'Put up thy sword into its sheath.'[11] It is therefore really yours, perhaps subject to your nod, but if it need not be unsheathed by your hand, it must be unsheathed in some other way. Besides, if indeed this did not pertain to you in any way, then the Lord would not have replied 'It is enough' but 'It is too much,' when the apostles said 'Here are two swords.'[12] Therefore the Church has both swords, the spiritual and the material. But while the latter has to be taken out for the Church, the former

---

10. This is law 12 of chapter 14, "De legibus et constitutionibus principum et edictis," of the first book of Justinian's Code (text in *Corpus iuris civilis,* vol. 2, p. 68).

11. John 18:11.

12. Luke 22:38.

has to be taken out by the Church; while the former is in the hand of the priest, the latter is in the hand of the soldier but clearly subject to the nod of the priest and at the command of the emperor." This is what was said by St. Bernard, who certainly would not say that the Church has the material sword and that it has to be taken not only for the Church but also at the nod of the priest, if he thought, like Barclay, that the authority in temporal matters did not pertain in any way to the Church and to its Head. But we will say more on this point in the appropriate passages.[13]

Pierre de la Palude, Patriarch of Jerusalem, a very learned man, in his treatise *De causa immediata ecclesiasticae potestatis,* article 4, which deals with the Pope's authority, speaks as such: "Even if the Pope does not have the authority to confirm any king who initially acquired the kingdom with the people's consent, nevertheless he can depose any such king not only because of heresy or schism or any other intolerable crime amid his population, but also because of his incompetence, that is, if he felt that an inexperienced man or a man with insufficient strength ruled the kingdom, and because of this man's incompetence the realm of the faithful was in danger." And later justifying this proposition he says: "Because the Pope is superior in spiritual matters and consequently also in temporal matters insofar as it is necessary for the spiritual good."

Durandus of St. Pourçain, a famous theologian, in his book *De origine iurisdictionum,* question 3, says: "Since both authorities, temporal and spiritual, are necessary, therefore (Christ) conferred both authorities on Peter." And later: "These are the real limits of the temporal and spiritual jurisdictions since the foundation of the Church, and those limits cannot be transgressed. For the temporal jurisdiction does not extend in any way to spiritual matters, of which it knows nothing at all. The spiritual jurisdiction, by contrast, extends in the first place and chiefly to spiritual matters, but in the second place and by a certain consequence it extends also to men's actions in temporal matters that are for the sake of the spiritual end."

Hervé de Nedellec, master-general of the Dominicans and a very astute theologian, in his treatise *De potestate Papae,* section "Ad evidentiam secundi,"

---

13. Cf. pp. 280–85.

speaks thus: "It pertains to the Pope to correct every abuse of both the ecclesi-astical authority and the earthly authority within the Christian people."

Jacques Almain in his treatise *De suprema potestate ecclesiastica et tempo-rali,* second principal question, which is about the supreme lay authority, in chapter 5, responds to the third allegation: "The Pope can depose the emperor in two cases: first, for a purely spiritual crime, such as heresy, and second, when those who are in charge of deposing him by normal pro-ceedings [*iure ordinario*] are negligent in doing it." In the same passage, to the fourth allegation he says: "If the population of the empire becomes heretical, or moves to another religion, thus abandoning the Christian religion, the Pope could deprive that population of the imperial dignity and transfer it to another population."

Hostiensis in his *Summa,* in the entry on heretics, in the section "Qua poena puniantur," n. 11, says: "Consider that the temporal sovereigns can be excommunicated and their lands can be given to Catholics to occupy, not only because of their heretical beliefs, but also if, after being admon-ished, they neglect to extirpate others' heretical beliefs that they have the possibility to exterminate. The same applies for a prince who might be found negligent in ruling and administering justice, which is why Pope Zachary deposed Childeric, king of the Franks."

Petrus Bertrandus, cardinal and bishop of Autun, in his treatise *De origine iurisdictionis,* question 4, n. 5, says: "The spiritual authority must dominate every human creature; and as Jesus Christ when He was in this world and even from the eternal world was Lord of nature, and on the basis of natural law could have carried out any sentence of condemnation and deposition against emperors and anybody else, so also His Vicar for the same reason."

Jean de Selve, in his treatise *De beneficio,* part 3, question 8, says: "The Pope can depose the king."

Etienne Aufreri, in his treatise *De potestate saecularium,* nn. 5 and 6, says: "The Pope deposes the emperor himself as his inferior if there are reasons that require it; and in every delicate affair, and in the most difficult circumstances which generate scandal in Christendom, the Pope, because of such superiority, can interfere even among the laity and can exercise such authority as God has granted to him."

Guillaume Durand, bishop of Mende, commonly called "speculator," in *Speculum,* book 1, title "De legato," section "Nunc ostendendum," n. 17, says: "The Pope deposes the emperor because of his impiety and gives guardians to princes if they are inept for ruling."

Johannes Faber, in his commentary over the first law of the title "De summa trinitate et fide Catholica,"[14] section 10, says: "However, there is no doubt that the Pope is superior to every Christian, both in temporal and in spiritual matters." And later: "When it is a matter of danger for the soul or for the people, the Pope can, and must, make provisions and, if need be, can depose any king."

Aegidius Bellamera, bishop of Avignon, in his commentary to the canon "Alius," section 2, speaks thus: "The Pope can depose the emperor who owes his temporal goods to him."[15] And later: "and [he can depose] also other kings, even if they do not hold their lands as fief, do not owe him their temporal goods, and do not swear him any oath of allegiance, for example, because of crimes or neglects." And later: "But this deposition of kings that must be carried out by the Pope does not spring from ordinary authority, but from a certain supreme and absolute authority; and it seems very just and most propitious for the commonwealth that the Pope holds that certain absolute authority, that there should be an absolute monarch who could correct such excesses of kings and administer justice over them." See the same author, in his discussion of the chapter "Novit," title "De iudicis," and of the chapter "Solitae."[16]

14. This is the first law of the first book of Justinian's Code, title 1 "De summa trinitate." The law, issued by Theodosius in 380, instituted Christianity as the official religion of Rome (text in *Corpus iuris civilis,* vol. 2, p. 5). See also p. 84, n. 170.

15. This is canon 3, causa 15, question 6, of the second part of Gratian's *Decretum.* This law was supposed to be composed of part of the letter written by Pope Gelasius I to Emperor Anastasius, but since the law concerned the legitimacy of Pope Zachary's deposition of Childeric and his appointment of Pippin to the throne of the Franks, the attribution to Gelasius is evidently false. For the text of the law and a discussion of its attribution, see *Corpus iuris canonici,* vol. 1, col. 756.

16. The canon "Novit" is the thirteenth chapter of the second book of Gregory's *Decretales,* title 1 "De iudicis." It was issued by Innocent III and concerned the right of the pope to intervene in a dispute between King Philip of France and King John of England, not because the pope wanted to "upset or diminish the jurisdiction and authority of the king of France" but because the dispute in question concerned sinful acts (text in *Corpus iuris canonici,* vol. 2, cols. 242–44).

Jean Quintin, called "Haeduus," in his discussion of the canon "No-vit," section 64, says: "Therefore we argue that both swords are given to the Church; that is, the Pontiff of the Church has the right and the authority both in spiritual and in all temporal matters, and he can make decisions and determinations on both for cause, and his decrees must be obeyed; for although as a man he is mortal, nevertheless he is empowered from the heavenly authority." And later, section 127, he says: "With this right, Pope Zachary in the year of our Lord 753 dispossessed Childeric, the legitimate king of France, successor of a long series of ancestors, and ruler of his ancestors' kingdom, and substituted in his place the Belgian Pippin; and his reason was that it was a sin for a man so inferior in authority and incompetent to control the steering oars of the state." And later: "Hence also Leo, as the Roman Pontiff, supported by the same authority, appointed Charles king and Roman emperor."

Raymond Le Roux, in his *Contra [In] Molinaeum*, chapter 6, p. 106, says: "We do not ignore that Pope Leo III conferred on Charlemagne the empire that had been taken away from the Greeks, for this is attested in both our Annals and the Greeks' books; and both Charlemagne and his French and German successors believed that this was rightfully obtained. I gloss over Pippin, appointed king by Stephen II, or, as some say, Zachary, after Childeric, who was an inept, stupid, and bastard king, had been forced into a monastery."

## Opinion of illustrious authors from Spain

St. Raymond of Peñafort, in his *Summa Raymundina,* book 1, title "De haereticis," section 7, says: "From these premises you should gather especially among other things that the judge, that is, the secular authority, can be not only excommunicated by the Church but also deposed, and this not only because of his own heretical beliefs, but also because of his negligence in extirpating others' heretical beliefs; and you should extend such punishment and the Church's authority whenever a secular prince might be inept, dissolute, and negligent regarding his government and the observance of justice." See also question 17, section 4, "Si quis princeps."

Alvarus Pelagius, bishop of Silves, from the Franciscan Order, in his treatise *De planctu Ecclesiae,* book 1, article 21, says: "The Pope transfers the empire and confirms the emperor, anoints him who has been elected according to the procedure of the Church and crowns him, and deprives him of the kingdom if he is insolent or if he persecutes the Church."

Juan de Torquemada, a very learned cardinal of the Holy Roman Church, in his *Summa de Ecclesia,* book 2, chapter 113, proposition 4, teaches that the Pope by the right of the Papacy does not have any authority directly in temporal matters outside of his ecclesiastical realm; but at chapter 114 he teaches in sixteen conclusions that the Pope has the most ample authority in temporal matters insofar as they relate to spiritual matters. At this point I will refer to only one of these conclusions. In the fourth proposition, the Roman Pontiff appears to have jurisdiction even in temporal matters, since he not only can punish with an ecclesiastical censure secular princes who fail in the use of their jurisdiction but also can depose from office those who are evidently negligent. The reader should see the whole chapter and the commentary of the same author on the chapter "Alius," section 15, question 6.

Cyprianus Benetus from Aragon, a Dominican, in his book *De prima orbis sede,* in response to the sixth point before the second part of the first conclusion, says: "The handing over of the keys includes the conferring of earthly powers for the preservation of spiritual goods."

Francisco de Vitoria, a Dominican, in his *De potestate Ecclesiae, relectio* 1, question 5, proposition 8, says: "Concerning the spiritual end, the Pope has the most ample temporal authority over all the princes and kings and the emperor," and below: "When it is necessary for the spiritual end, he can do not only what the secular princes can do but can also institute new princes and remove others and divide empires."

Domingo de Soto, a Dominican, in his commentary on the fourth book of the *Sententiae,* distinction 25, question 2, article 1, conclusion 5, says: "Any civil authority is subject to the ecclesiastical authority in what concerns spiritual matters, so that the Pope, through his spiritual authority, as often as the concern for the faith and religion urges it, not only can move against the kings with the thunderbolts of ecclesiastical censures and punish them but also can deprive every Christian prince of his temporal goods, and even proceed to the actual deprivation of those things."

Alfonso de Castro, a Franciscan, book 2, chapter 7, of his *De iusta haereticorum punitione,* speaks thus: "And it must not surprise anybody that the Pope can depose a king from his regal office and deprive him of his kingdom because of the crime of heresy, since in matters of faith even kings are subject to the Supreme Pontiff, just like the other inferiors."

Jacobus Simancas, bishop of Badajoz, in his book *De Catholicis institutionibus,* title 45, n. 25, says: "Even though the ecclesiastical authority is distinct from the secular, and the Pope does not have civil jurisdiction in the kingdoms of secular princes, nevertheless whenever the spiritual end is concerned, the Supreme Pontiff still has the most ample authority over all the orthodox princes. Therefore if a prince was inept, or issued unjust laws against religion or against morality, or if he did something of this kind to the detriment of spiritual matters, the Pope could, in the right conditions, apply a suitable remedy depriving such a prince of his government and jurisdiction."

Domingo Bañez, in his commentary on 2a 2ae, question 10, article 10, at the end of the commentary, in the section on the fourth conclusion, says: "Therefore this authority that the Pope has to remove the power and jurisdiction from the infidels to the faithful comes from the positive divine law; as to when he should make use of this authority, that is left to his power and judgment"; and at question 12, article 2, in his commentary to the section on the last conclusion he says: "The Church deprives not only princes who are completely apostate of the right to govern over their subjects but also those who have fallen into heresy in some manner."

Martin Ledesma in his commentary *Secunda quartae,* question 20, article 4, conclusion 8, says: "Insofar as the spiritual end is concerned, the Pope has the most ample temporal authority over all the princes, kings, and emperors."

Gregory of Valencia, in his commentary on 2a 2ae, disputation 1, question 12, point 2, assertion 2, says: "By ecclesiastical law anyone can be deprived completely of his power and superiority over his subjects through the authority and judgment of the Supreme Pontiff because of the sin of apostasy from the faith, and there is no doubt about this assertion among those truly orthodox."

Guillem Montserrat, a Catalan, in his treatise *De successione regum,* section 40, says: "The Pope, Vicar of Christ, can remove any Christian prince for cause; just as he removed and deposed Childeric, king of France, and appointed Pippin in his place, and transferred the Roman empire from the Greeks to the Germans."

Alfonso Alvarez Guerrero, in his *Speculum,* chapter 16, says: "Hence is it that the Pope can transfer the empire from a certain people to another with the greatest reason," and later: "and [the Pope] deposes the emperor himself as his inferior, if most serious and delicate reasons require it."

Antonius Cordubensis, a Franciscan, in book 1 of his *Quaestionarium,* question 57, doubt 3, says: "The civil authority is subject not to the temporal authority of the Pope, but to his spiritual authority, in a certain way, in case of necessity or great advantage for spiritual matters. And the Church and the Pope in the greatest degree have power and authority, or a form of temporal jurisdiction, for the sake of the spiritual end over all men and princes and kings of the kingdoms of the whole world."

Luis de Molina, book 1 of *De iustitia et iure,* treatise 2, disputation 29, conclusion 3, says: "The spiritual authority of the Supreme Pontiff includes a supreme and most ample temporal power over all kings and over every other member of the Church. This temporal power is a sort of consequence of the Pontiff's spiritual authority, and therefore it can be exercised only insofar as the spiritual end requires. Thus, the Supreme Pontiff can depose kings and deprive them of their kingdoms if the spiritual end requires it."

Diego Covarrubias, in his treatise *De resurrectione* [*restitutione*] *super Regulam,* "Peccatum," part 2, section 9, n. 7, says: "This opinion is true in this sense, that is, the Pope truly has temporal authority even over emperors, insofar as this authority is useful and necessary for the government of the Catholic Church and the exercise of spiritual authority."

Fernando Vázquez de Menchaca, in book 1 of *Illustres controversiae,* chapter 21, says: "Besides, the Pope has also jurisdiction in temporal affairs, insofar as those are necessary for the spiritual enterprise." And below: "The partisans of both factions generally grant this."

Miguel de Aninyon, in his treatise *De unitate ovilis et pastoris,* n. 12, says: "In the Pope there are both supreme authorities, even if he cannot make use of the temporal sword, and since the Pope's authority came directly from God, he is subject only to God; by contrast the emperor's authority came from Christ's Vicar, to whom it is subordinate, and therefore the Pope can transfer the empire from a certain people to another, and he anoints and crowns and confirms and endorses and reproaches the emperor and he also deposes him if there are reasons that require it."

Martin de Azpilcueta Navarrus, in his commentary on the canon "Novit," notation 3, section 41, says: "The ecclesiastical authority is a form of authority that is different from the civil and far more noble than it, just as gold is a form of metal different from lead and more noble than it. The ecclesiastical authority embraces fully only spiritual matters, but indirectly it embraces also temporal matters, insofar as these are necessary for obtaining the spiritual end"; and below, section 99: "It is gathered that the reason why the Pope can depose kings even if they are negligent in governing their realms is that because of such negligence the people of God, subject to those kings, are diverted from obtaining eternal life." Moreover, this author quotes many other authors of the same opinion.

## *Opinion of illustrious authors from German-speaking lands*

Stephen, bishop of Halberstadt, in the letter which can be found in the appendix of Marianus Scotus's *Chronicon,* speaking of Emperor Henry IV, says: "Lord Henry is a heretic, excommunicated by the Apostolic See because of his abominable evils, and he can hold neither power nor any authority over us because we are Catholic."

Hugh of St. Victor, from the Saxon nation, a man most illustrious both for his learning and for his sanctity, in *De sacramentis,* book 1 [2], part 2, chapter 41 [4], says: "The spiritual authority has the power to instruct the earthly authority to be good, and it has the power to judge it if it is not. The former, however, is established in the first place by God and, if it strays, can be judged only by Him."

Henry of Ghent, in *Quodlibeta* 6, question 33, says: "Peter was, after

Christ, hierarchically first over the universal Church, and he handed down both keys and entrusted both swords; so that the government of the universal Church, both spiritual and in temporal matters, should pertain to him."

Ulrich of Strasbourg, in his *Summa,* speaks as such: "If the king was manifestly a heretic, or if, prompted by the Church, he nevertheless neglected the administration of his kingdom insofar as matters of faith are concerned, for instance, if he did not make an effort to eliminate the heretics, he could be deprived of his regal dignity by the Church." Juan de Torquemada in the above-mentioned passage quotes this author.

Dionysius the Carthusian, in his book *De regimine politiae,* article 19, says: "In the Church of God there is one supreme bishop, that is, the Pope, the ruler, in whom there are both authorities and the plenitude of power, and the apex, that is, of both spiritual and secular authority. Therefore, he has jurisdiction over, and the right to dispose of, all the kingdoms and principalities of the faithful not only in spiritual matters but also in temporal matters, as long as a reasonable motive requires it. In fact, he can also depose emperors and deprive kings of their kingdoms, if their way of life makes them worthy of being deposed and deprived of their kingdoms."

John Driedo in *De libertate Christiana,* book 1, chapter 14, says: "In truth this should not be passed over in silence, that the Pope, on the basis of the plenitude of power over all the Christian princes, can deprive kings and princes of their kingdoms and empires because of the crime of heresy, and he can exempt completely the Christian people from obedience and subjection to them in temporal matters." See also chapter 9, in which the author demonstrates that the temporal authority is subject to the spiritual for the sake of the spiritual end.

Albert Pighius in *De ecclesiastica hierarchia,* book 5, chapter 2, says: "Since all these (kings and princes, that is, the Christian ones) are like parts and members of the Church, necessarily they are also subject to the head of the ecclesiastical hierarchy, so that he may control them with the whip of his power, keep them all working together for their mutual advantage and the advantage of the whole body, hold them to their duty, correct those who transgress, and, if the necessity of the whole requires it, remove them from their administration and their office and appoint others in their place, or order that these must be appointed through those to whom this pertains by law or custom." See the same author, chapter 14, where he repeats this point and demonstrates it with the examples he offers.

Jacobus Latomus, in his book *De Ecclesia,* chapter 14, says: "From such principles it is gathered that a king, or any other earthly Christian prince, can rightly be deprived of his kingdom and realm by the Church; since the kingdom and the realm with its inhabitants, as we said above, passed into the body and the right of the Church through holy baptism and through free acceptance of the Christian religion, the kingdom and realm were dedicated, consecrated, and donated with an irrevocable gift to Christ and to his Spouse." These are the arguments of this author, who proved in another book, titled *De primatu Romani Pontificis,* that the authority of the Church resides at its fullest in the Supreme Pontiff.

Conradus Brunus, in *De legationibus,* book 3, chapter 6, says: "This jurisdiction encompasses civil and criminal sentences, summons, investigations, accusations, and also punishments and ecclesiastical censures over ecclesiastical people and matters, but also, in many cases, it is exercised over lay persons and temporal affairs. In all these the Supreme Pontiff has the most ample jurisdiction, while the jurisdiction of archbishops and bishops is bound and enclosed within certain limits, etc."

## Opinion of illustrious authors
## from England and Scotland

Alexander of Hales, an English Franciscan, a man very learned and the teacher of St. Thomas and St. Bonaventure, in part 4, question 10, of his explanation of the canon of the Mass, on the passage "et pro rege," writes: "The spiritual authority has the power to instruct the earthly authority and judge if it is good: the former, by contrast, is instituted by God in the first place, and when it strays it can be judged by God alone." The same Alexander, part 4, question 79, clauses 5 and 6, says: "God wanted some to have power over the remaining majority, and then some fewer to have power over those, and so on until we get to only one, that is, the Pope, who is immediately below God." In this passage Alexander teaches that the Pope is superior to all the other authorities in such a way that he alone is immediately below God.

The Englishman Robert Holcot in his commentary on the Book of Wisdom, section 200, says: "He is the king of kings, to whom all the nations and peoples who receive temporal goods from him are subjected; nevertheless he has to submit to the priesthood and to the Supreme Pontiff." And later: "Samuel anointed David as king, in the form in which the Vicar of Christ and head of the Church confers the realm and the regal authority for the advantage of the Church; hence, the right and the authority to examine the person elected to be king and to promote him to sovereignty belong to the Pope."

Francis Mayron, a Scot,[17] in his commentary on the fourth book of the *Sententiae,* distinction 19, question 4, says: "The plenitude of power in both jurisdictions concurs in the same person: this is clear by the authority of Christ who said 'whatsoever thou shalt bind, etc.'"[18]

The Englishman John Baconthorpe, a Carmelite, in his prologue to the fourth book of the *Sententiae,* question 11, article 4, says: "The Pope has power to make judgments on kingdoms and kings in war and peace; in fact he can oblige temporal princes to preserve peace and justice with each other." And below: "[The Pope] has power to depose a king, so that the kingdom can be entrusted to another, for reason of impiety or incompetence. Likewise he has power to depose the emperor and to entrust the empire to another if that emperor does not defend the Church."

Thomas Netter of the same religious order, in *Doctrinalis fidei antiquae,* book 2, article 3, chapter 75, explaining in which sense St. Gregory had defined himself as the servant of the emperor, says: "Certainly, blessed Gregory did not prejudice in any way the eminency of his status over that of the emperor when he put the king before himself nominally, and this is apparent once we consider attentively the matter that they were then discussing, which we will properly see if we examine his later actions and writings. Consider whether he did not deem himself the master of emperors and kings when, after giving certain privileges to a Senator Presbyter

17. Mayron was not Scottish but French. Bellarmine had probably mistaken his place of birth for that of his master, Duns Scotus.
18. Matthew 16:19.

and Abbot of the Hospital of the French, under threat to the dignity and office of every violator of such privilege, he concluded, etc." These are the words of this author, who immediately adds these two privileges of St. Gregory, by which kings are threatened with the deprivations of their kingdoms if they should presume to violate those privileges.

Reginald Pole, cardinal of the Holy Roman Church, in his book *De Summo Pontifice,* chapter 8, says: "From what we said earlier it can be concluded that the Vicar of Christ, to whom a special office and the highest office of all is entrusted, namely, that which concerns the final end of man, on earth and in the government of the Church possesses the highest and special authority among all the other servants of God, or emperors, kings, princes, or by whatever name they are called."

Nicholas Sander in *De visibili Monarchia Ecclesiae,* book 2, chapter 4, says: "From that which both divine law and the light of natural reason reveal, it is abundantly clear how far from the truth are those who think that Christian kings in their kingdoms always have supreme power and that they are never subject to the bishops, so that when they sin obstinately in matters of faith they cannot be removed from their kingdom." He also said in an earlier passage: "The Pope therefore will carry out the removal from government over the people of a king who has imbued the Christian people with a false doctrine in the same way that a shepherd carries out the removal of an ill-tempered ram."

Thus we have the doctrine that flourished in the Church before Barclay and I started our contest. St. Augustine, in *Adversus [Contra] Julianum,* book 2, last chapter, after adducing the testimonies of eleven authors, some of whom had lived two hundred years before him, some one hundred, and some in his own time, declares that in no ecclesiastical council have that many illustrious authors and masters ever gathered all together; and he wonders whether Julian, once called in that assembly, would have dared to open his mouth and to oppose those very dignified and learned men. With how much greater reason can we then declare that in no synod, no matter how large, have more than seventy illustrious authors ever gathered, some of whom lived five hundred years ago and gave glory to the Church not only for their doctrine but also for their sanctity and miracles, in different centuries and different parts of the Christian world!

And while we cannot say whether Barclay, called in this circle of so many illustrious authors, if he were alive, would realize that he should surrender rather than retain his own opinion, I can surely affirm that either those books by all these people, which the Church has been using for so many centuries already, have to be destroyed, or Barclay's booklet has to be consigned to the avenging flames as scandalous, reckless, seditious, and erroneous.

## Opinion of the councils regarding the Supreme Pontiff's authority in temporal matters

But if perhaps individual witnesses, though numerous and distinguished beyond all exception, fail to convince somebody, I will now present groups of co-witnesses, almost innumerable, who will testify against Barclay. The Greek historians Glycas, Theophanes, Cedrenus, and Zonaras writing on Leo the Isaurian, and the Latin historians including Sigebert writing around the year 727, Paulus Diaconus writing in his book 21, and Platina in his biography of Gregory III attest that nine hundred years ago Emperor Leo the Isaurian was excommunicated by Pope Gregory II for the crime of heresy and was deprived of the revenues from Italy and therefore from a part of his empire (although the Latin historians attribute this act to Gregory III, for he confirmed the sentence of Gregory II). The Greek author Joannes Zonaras in his biography of Leo the Isaurian attests further that Gregory II's sentence was declared in the bishops' synod, and these are his words in vol. 3 of the *Annales:* "Gregory, who then was in charge of the Church of ancient Rome, bound the emperor and his associates with an anathema by the synod, and stopped the revenues that were paid to the empire up to that time through a pact made with the Franks." Therefore, that entire synod agreed with Pope Gregory, and there are as many testimonies for this as there were bishops gathered in that synod.

Later, after about three hundred years, when Pope Gregory VII excommunicated Emperor Henry IV and deprived him of his empire and kingdom after having warned him several times, he did this not secretly and with his own decision only, but in a synod in Rome, in which many bishops gathered from everywhere, with their unanimous agreement and praise, publicly and with a solemn ritual and ceremony. Of this synod it is written in book 7 of Gregory VII's *Registrum* that it was held in the year 1080, the seventh year of Gregory's pontificate, and that it included archbishops and bishops, as well as abbots and a countless number of clergymen from different religious orders and laymen.

To this we should add five other councils called by Gregory VII's successors, that is, the Council of Benevento called by Victor III; the Council of Piacenza called by Urban II; the Council of Rome called by Paschal II; the Council of Cologne called by Gelasius II; and the Council of Reims called by Callistus II, in which Gregory VII's sentence was confirmed.[19] On these councils see chapter 9 of my treatise.

Besides, when Pope Urban II excommunicated and deprived of the crown Philip I, king of the Franks, because, after being warned for repudiating his legitimate wife and marrying an adulterous woman, Philip refused to obey, the Pope did this in the very large Council of Claremont, as Sigebert testifies in his chronicle of the year 1095 and even more clearly Matthew Paris reports on William II for the year 1095. Also, together with excommunicating Philip, the Pope deprived him of the regal dignity, as can be gathered from Ivo, bishop of Chartres, who in his letter 28 [46] to Pope Urban II speaks in this manner: "Those who are coming to you with the craftiness of their small intelligence and with gracious words have promised that they would obtain from the apostolic See impunity for the scandal on behalf of the king. They will make this argument also: that the king and the kingdom will depart from obedience to you if you do not give him back the crown and absolve him from the anathema." This can also be gathered from the historians who attest that Pope Urban forbade that the excommunicated Philip wear the regal crown (see Johannes Nauclerus's *Chronicle,* generation 37; Paulus Aemilius in book 3 on the thirty-eighth king; Jean Papire Masson,[20] *Annales,* book 3). Add also what

19. The councils mentioned by Bellarmine were celebrated between 1087 and 1119.

20. Bellarmine's mention of Jean Papire Masson in this context is very interesting, for Bellarmine in 1592 had produced two very sharp censures of another of the French historian and ex-Jesuit's works, *De vitis episcoporum urbis.* For Bellarmine, Masson's biographies of the popes were doctrinally and historically faulty: Masson often quoted heretical and forbidden works in his text, and he questioned the pope's authority over the Church in general. (Bellarmine wrote that already the title, *On the Lives of the*

is written in *Sommaire de l'histoire des François* of Nicolas Vignier; that is, for the whole time in which Philip lived under anathema, in the public records it was not written, as was customary, "under Philip's reign," but "under Christ's reign," since evidently the people did not consider an excommunicated king to be a king.

Also, Pope Innocent III in 1215 called the Lateran General Council, which rightly is usually called the greatest: in fact along with the Pope himself were present two Patriarchs of the Eastern Church, the one of Constantinople and the one of Jerusalem, in person; two Patriarchs, the Patriarch of Alexandria and that of Antioch, through their legates; seventy archbishops; four hundred and twelve bishops; eight hundred abbots and priors of convent; the legates of the emperors of the West and the East, and also those of the kings of Jerusalem, France, Spain, England, and Cyprus. Thus, in this most illustrious gathering of the Christian world, a canon against the heretics was issued—the third in order—in these words: "We excommunicate and declare anathema against every heresy raised against this holy orthodox Catholic faith, which before we have set forth, etc." And below: "If then a temporal ruler, after being admonished by the Church, neglects to purge his land of the infamy of heresy, he is to be bound with the chain of excommunication by the Metropolitan bishop and the bishops of his province. And if he does not comply within a year, this will be brought to the notice of the Supreme Pontiff, who from then on may declare his vassals absolved from their loyalty toward him and may declare his land free to be occupied by Catholics who may possess it with no objection once they have exterminated the heretics, and who may keep it in the purity of faith with the right of the princely lord un-

---

*Bishops of Rome*, "in this historical moment is offensive and not without a reason, since the Lutheran heresies which argue that the Roman Pontiffs are not Pontiffs of the whole Church are strong.") Masson also calumniated the popes without historical proofs. In sum, as Bellarmine wrote, Masson was so inaccurate that "he does not deserve the name of historian." (Bellarmine's censures of Masson can be found in ACDF, Index, Protocolli I, fols. 606r–609v—my translation—and they have been published by Godman, *Saint as Censor*, pp. 279–83, and discussed in ibid., pp. 163–64). The relationship between historical accuracy and doctrinal orthodoxy in works of history was an issue to which Bellarmine paid much attention in his role as censor, even when dealing with Catholic authors. See p. 397, n. 253.

touched, provided that he presents no obstruction on this and opposes no impediment. The same law applies also to those who do not have princely lords."[21]

What would Barclay say to this? If this is not the voice of the Catholic Church, where, I pray, will we find it? And if it is (as it most truly is), will whoever refuses to be obedient to it, as Barclay did, not have to be considered a heretic, a publican, and not at all Catholic and pious?[22] If the Pope does not have the authority on earth to dispose of temporal affairs to the point of deposing those princes who are either heretic themselves, or support in any way other heretics, why in issuing that canon did no one out of so many complain? Why did not even one of so many speakers for emperors and kings dare to mutter against it? Certainly parasites of temporal princes had not yet arisen, who, in order to seem to make temporal kingdoms firm, snatch away the eternal kingdom from those whom they flatter.

But let us add the Council of Lyon. Thus, Pope Innocent IV in 1245 celebrated a General Council in Lyon, in which, besides archbishops called from everywhere, even Balduinus, the emperor of the Eastern Roman Empire, along with many other princes, took part. Paulus Aemilius and Nauclerus attest that even St. Louis, king of the French, was in Lyon at that time and assisted the Pope. And in that gathering, which without a doubt represented the universal Church, the sentence against Emperor Frederick II was declared with these words: "We therefore, after careful discussion with our brothers and the holy council about his impious excesses which we have before mentioned and many others, since we hold the place of Christ on earth (although unworthy) and since it has been told to us through the person of Peter, 'Whatsoever thou shalt bind on earth shall be bound in heaven,'[23] we declare and announce that the above-mentioned prince, who has rendered himself unworthy of his sovereignty, his kingdom, and every office and dignity, and who, because of his faults, has been debased by God so that he may not rule an empire or a kingdom, is bound to his sins, and that he is debased and deprived

21. On this canon see p. 105, n. 214.
22. Cf. Matthew 18:15–17.
23. Matthew 16:19.

of every office and dignity. Furthermore, we deprive him by sentence, absolving perpetually all who are bound to him by an oath of allegiance from such an oath; forbidding strictly, by the apostolic authority, anyone from obeying and devoting himself to him as to his emperor; declaring that whoever hereafter will offer him advice, help, or support as emperor or king is subject immediately to the sentence of excommunication. Those to whom electing the emperor pertains should freely elect a successor. We will arrange to provide for the above-mentioned kingdom of Sicily, with the advice of our brothers, as we will see fit."

This is the Pope's sentence, with the approbation of the entire council, that is, with the universal consent and praise of the prelates of the Church; and nevertheless one, I do not know who, dares to disagree, to publish his book and to bewitch the eyes of the unlearned. But if every single council of the Catholic Church by itself, and especially when the Supreme Pontiff presides over them, gives the most ample evidence, so that no one is allowed to dissent, how great a temerity would it be if one dared to contradict ten most numerous councils joined together at the same time? Indeed, even if those councils were held in different places and times, nevertheless they can easily all be brought together in front of the eyes of the mind, and out of them one, the greatest and the most numerous one, can be created, when at the same time we can see Gregory VII, Victor III, Urban II, Paschal II, Gelasius II, Callistus II, Innocent III, and Innocent IV, all most holy and most learned Popes, excommunicating by their apostolic authority kings who are heretics or heretics' protectors and deposing them from the throne of the realm; and at the same time all prelates of the Church with the legates of almost all the princes approving and commending as most rightful the sentences of so many Popes. Certainly if Barclay, or anybody like him, were introduced in such a gathering, it would be surprising if he dared to speak, or indeed if he did not at once lose his speech. St. Augustine in book 1 of his treatise *Adversus* [*Contra*] *Julianum,* chapter 2 [5], considered the Synod of Diospolis of fourteen bishops of Palestine to have had an authority great enough to suppress the audacity of a Julian; why then should not more than a thousand bishops who gathered in ten councils have a much greater authority to condemn the temerity of a Barclay? Therefore I, an old man, am now obliged to defend against Barclay this opinion of the Catholic Church, which I briefly touched upon when I was young in my disputation *De Summo Pontifice,* and indeed I would have never suspected that a man who calls himself Catholic would have caused me to undertake such labor, as I do not pay the slightest attention to those who are without[24] and who continuously write against me.

---

24. Here Bellarmine is making reference to 1 Corinthians 5:12–13: "For what have I to do to judge them also that are without? do not ye judge them that are within? But them that are without God judgeth."

# Barclay's justification

Thus, having said these things as a sort of prolegomena, I come to Barclay's book. In the first chapter he is completely absorbed in justifying and excusing himself for writing what he wrote on this issue of the Pope's authority, and the first thing he proves is that he was entitled to state his opinion because many other Catholics did so.

He says: "If many theologians and jurists, one after the other, have applied themselves to examining this same question, and if the judgment of earlier authors on it has not prejudiced the opinion of later authors, why should not I by my own right in a certain way claim for myself some space to investigate this truth (since I spent my life in this intellectual pursuit)?"

But how relevant this reason may be can be seen from the fact that he did not persuade even his own son or a single friend. Why, in fact, did Barclay's heir or whoever it was who published his book, who certainly was a great friend of his, decide that his name and the name of the printer and the place of publication should be passed over in silence, unless he believed, not without reason, that the author was not allowed to write what he wrote without punishment? For otherwise the errors of all the heretics could be excused. Thus it was granted to Catholic authors who agreed on the issue to dispute on the manner, but it was not permitted to Barclay to deny completely the authority of the Supreme Pontiff in temporal matters, against all the other authors and against the opinion of even all the general councils. In the same manner it was and it is allowed to teachers at schools, who acknowledge in God the unity of His essence together with the Trinity of the Persons, to discuss several aspects of the attributes of the divine essence and the constitution of the Persons, but it was not allowed to old and new Arians to multiply in their writings the essences of God or to mix up the Trinity. By the same token, it was and it is allowed to Catholic scholars who agree on the substance of the seven sacraments to discuss several aspects that do not pertain to the foundations of the faith; but it is not and was not allowed to the members of the Lutheran and Calvinist sects to write so much against the substance and the number of the sacraments; and the same can be said for other doctrines of faith.

Barclay adds: "First of all, the reader should be advised that I honor that See with every reverence and benevolence, and that neither here nor anywhere else do I do anything to take away any of the authority and dignity of the Vicar of Christ and successor of the holy apostles Peter and Paul." But this seems similar to what St. Mark writes in chapter 15: "And they smote him on the head with a reed . . . and bowing their knees worshipped him,"[25] and to what St. John writes in chapter 19: "And they came to him and said, Hail, King of the Jews! and they smote him with their hands."[26] That is how Barclay honors with every reverence and benevolence the Apostolic See, but in the meanwhile he almost cuts in half its authority. Later he adds: "Therefore I pray those who before me have written with good disposition (as I think), not to be indignant or enraged if I will depart from their opinion; for in fact (as St. Augustine says in his epistle 3 [148]) we must not consider the opinions of any author, be he Catholic and highly praised, as canonical Scripture, etc."

I am neither indignant nor enraged because Barclay or any other has departed from my opinion, but I cannot accept calmly that anyone should depart from the unanimous opinion of the authors in such an important matter, and indeed even from the sense and agreement of the universal councils. And even if we do not owe to the books of the scholars, however Catholic and highly praised, that reverence which we owe to the sacred Scripture, nevertheless it cannot be denied that much honor has to be given in any case to the unanimous opinion of the authors; so that whoever attempts to write against this torrent of scholars, so to speak, cannot be excused from the accusation of temerity. Indeed, St. Augustine, that

25. Mark 15:19.
26. John 19:3.

very same who had written that the opinions of any man should not be in any way put on the same level as the authority of the divine Scripture, attacked Julian's temerity, because he dared to oppose eleven Catholic authors, whose words and opinions he explains accurately in *Adversus [Contra] Julianum,* book 1, chapter 2 [7], and book 2 in the last chapter.

Then Barclay, coming closer to the matter, reports two opinions of Catholic authors. The first, which very many canonists follow, is that in the Supreme Pontiff there are both spiritual and temporal authorities, as he is the Vicar of Christ. The second, which is almost unanimous among theologians, is that the authority of the Supreme Pontiff as Vicar of Christ is properly and in itself spiritual, but nevertheless through this authority he can dispose of temporal matters as they refer to spiritual matters. And then he proposes his own opinion, in support of which he quotes no Catholic author:

"Neither one of these opinions, as far as temporal authority is concerned, appears to be strong enough," and a little below: "These theologians then confute very strongly the canonists' opinion, but *pace* their arguments, I will say that they do not have a better understanding." These are his words, and he rather openly betrays himself to be like another Ishmael, to have dwelled in the presence of all his brethren so that his hand could be against every man (Genesis 16).[27]

He occupies the last part of the first chapter in refuting, or rather mocking, Bozio, who, though considering himself a theologian, nevertheless preferred to adhere to the canonists' opinion. On this point I have nothing to say, for I have chosen neither to refute nor to defend Bozio's opinion, and I have decided to dispute only that on which all Catholics agree and on which we all disagree with Barclay, and to defend myself from his objections.[28]

27. This is Bellarmine's paraphrase of Genesis 16:11–12.

28. Here Bellarmine is referring to the treatise *De temporali ecclesiae monarchia,* published in 1602 under the name of Francesco Bozio, an Italian Oratorian. The treatise, which represented one of the most vigorous assertions of the universal authority of the pope in both temporal and spiritual matters, was not truly Francesco's work but was written mostly by Francesco's brother, Tommaso, another Oratorian and political theorist. On Tommaso's and Francesco's political and ecclesiological views, see Mastellone, "Tommaso Bozio, teorico dell'ordine ecclesiastico." Bellarmine's explicit refusal to engage with Bozio's theories has to be placed within the context of the vivid opposition in Rome with which Bellarmine's theory of *potestas indirecta* met on the part of those who, like Bozio, thought that the Jesuit had not defended the pope's plenitude of power strongly enough. See the introduction, pp. ix–x.

---

# Examination of the principle or
# foundation of Barclay's doctrine

In the second chapter Barclay attempts to lay out the principles of his doctrine. Of these principles one, and perhaps the central, is that ecclesiastical and political authority are by divine law distinct and separate, so that, even if they both come from God, each one, limited in its own boundaries, cannot invade the other's boundaries by its own right, and neither one has power [*imperium*] over the other.[29] In order to prove this principle he adduces the canons "Duo sunt,"[30] "Cum ad verum,"[31] "Novit," "Per venerabilem"; the first book of St. Bernard's *De consideratione,* the second chapter of the second book of John Driedo's *De libertate Christiana;* and

29. The issue of the relationship between political commonwealth and spiritual commonwealth is indeed not only the central theme of Barclay's treatise but also the key point of Bellarmine's own theory. It is a point that the Jesuit had to return to several times over the course of his intellectual career from the 1580s to the 1610s: see the introduction.

30. This canon, the tenth canon of distinction 96 of the first part of Gratian's *Decretum,* was one of the fundamental references for the debates over papal authority. Drawn from the letter of Pope Gelasius I to Emperor Anastasius, it distinguished the function of the "auctoritas sacra Pontificum" from that of the "regalis potestas" of the emperor (text in *Corpus iuris canonici,* vol. 1, cols. 340–41). On the issues raised by this canon and on the debates that followed, see I. S. Robinson, "Church and Papacy," in Burns, ed., *Cambridge History of Medieval Political Thought,* pp. 252–305 at pp. 288–300.

31. The canon "Cum ad verum" is no. 6, distinction 96 of the first part of Gratian's *Decretum,* and it is taken from the letter written by Pope Nicholas I to Emperor Michael III in 865 (full text of this letter in PL, vol. 119, cols. 926–73). The canon states that the duties and obligations of the temporal and spiritual authorities are distinct, and it affirms that the emperors need the popes "for eternal life," but that the popes make use of the emperors' laws "only for the course of temporal matters" (text in *Corpus iuris canonici,* vol. 1, col. 339).

the words of Hosius, bishop of Cordova, reported in Athanasius's epistle *Ad solitariam vitam agentes.*

But we argue that this principle or foundation is completely false in its last clause, that is, in those last words: "Neither one has power over the other." In fact, we affirm that the ecclesiastical authority is indeed distinct from the political, but it is not only far more noble but also superior to it, since it can direct and correct the political authority and in certain cases, that is, for the sake of the spiritual end and eternal life, it can rule over it.

And that last clause, that is, "Neither one has power over the other," cannot be found in the testimonies alleged from the canons or from the scholars. In the canon "Duo sunt," which is taken from the letter of Pope Gelasius I to Emperor Anastasius, these words are found: "Certainly, august emperor, there are two authorities by which this world is chiefly ruled: the sacred authority of the Popes and the regal authority. In those authorities the weight of the clergy is that much heavier since they will render account in divine judgment for the governing of mankind," and later: "You should know that you depend on their judgment, and they cannot be reduced to your will."

In this passage not only can we not find what Barclay says, that is, "Neither one has power," but indeed what we do find is the exact opposite. In fact, if the Pope will have to render account in front of God for governing mankind, certainly he must rule over those governments, and if perchance they may stray, he has to correct them and lead them back to the right track. How then can he rule and correct human governments if he has no power over them?

Likewise in the canon "Cum ad verum," which is taken from the letter of Pope Nicholas I to Emperor Michael, we cannot find those words: "Neither one authority has power." These are, indeed, Pope Nicholas's words: "When we get to the truth, neither did the emperor overstep the rights of the pontificate, nor did the Pope usurp the title of the emperors, since the mediator between God and men, Jesus Christ, a man, separated the duties of both authorities, each with its own acts and dignities, distinct from the other."

Here also with no word is it shown that "Neither one authority has power over the other," but only that the acts, dignities, and duties are distinct. And seeing that the same Nicholas a little further on adds that the Christian emperors need the ministry of the Popes for eternal life and, by contrast, that the Popes use imperial laws only for the duration of the earthly life, it is most clearly demonstrated that the end of pontifical authority is superior to that of political authority, and that the Pope's authority has power over the political authority to the extent to which it is necessary that the political authority does not constitute an impediment to eternal life, to which it has to be directed by the pontifical authority.

Likewise also in the canons "Novit" and "Per venerabilem" of Pope Innocent III, there is absolutely nothing from which one can infer that the political authority is not subject to the spiritual, or ecclesiastical. Otherwise the same Pope would have not established in the Lateran General Council, decree 3, that the secular princes could be deprived of their political authority by the Apostolic See, if they were negligent in purifying their lands from the stain of heresy and if, after being admonished by the bishops, they failed to obey.[32] Neither would the same Pope have deposed Emperor Otto IV if he had thought that the ecclesiastical authority had no power over the political authority.

Even St. Bernard, in the first book of *De consideratione*, certainly says that the Pope's authority is exercised against sins and it is spiritual, but the same St. Bernard, in the fourth book of the same work, chapter 4 [3], says that the Church has both swords, the spiritual and the material, but he would not say if he did not believe that the material sword is subject to the spiritual.

Furthermore, of John Driedo's opinion there cannot be any doubt; in fact he says that the political authority must be subject to the spiritual, so that the Pope, in certain cases concerning eternal life, may deprive kings and princes of their kingdoms and dominions, as we have indicated while reporting his words.

Last, the words of Hosius, bishop of Cordoba, as reported by St. Atha-

---

32. The text of this decree can be found in *Conciliorum oecumenicorum decreta*, pp. 209–11.

nasius, demonstrate that there is a distinction between the duties of each authority but do not demonstrate that they are at the same level, as he says: "To you God entrusted the empire, and to us He committed matters of the Church; and just as whoever steals the empire from you goes against the divine order, so beware of rendering yourself guilty of a great crime by allocating for yourself what is the Church's. It is written: 'Render to Caesar the things that are Caesar's and to God the things that are God's.'[33] Therefore it is not lawful for us to hold the empire on earth and for you, as emperor, to hold the authority of burning incense and performing sacred rites." These words were said by this author, who does not disagree with St. Gregory of Nazianzus, who in his oration *Ad populum timore perculsum* most clearly says that the ecclesiastical authority is related to the political in the same way the soul is related to the body: but nobody has called in question that the soul is superior to the body and rules and governs it.

Then Barclay proceeds and attacks Bozio and rebukes his responses and disputations, but I will leave all of these to Bozio himself, for I did not take up cudgels to defend anything but that which concerns our common cause or my own specific cause, such as what Barclay says in the last part: that one authority cannot be subordinated and subject to the other unless the dignity and duty which are in the subordinated are also included in the subordinating. For all of us Catholics teach the subordination and subjection of the political authority to the ecclesiastical, but not all of us grant what Barclay infers from it. In fact, such subordination can be understood in two manners. First, that the authority which is in the subordinate derives from the subordinating, such as the authority of the vicar which derives from the person whose vicar this is, and the authority of the ambassador, which derives from the prince who sent him, and the authority of the judge or the governor, which derives from the king. In this case, without a doubt, the authority of the subordinating includes that of the subordinate. The other way is not that one derives from the other, but that it is subject and subordinate only because the end of the first is subject and subordinate to the end of the second, as are the subordination and subjections of the

33. Matthew 22:21 but compare Mark 12:17 and Luke 20:25.

different arts with respect to the art of governing peoples, which can be called regal.[34] Truly in fact the poet said:

> Let others better mold the running mass
> Of metals, and inform the breathing brass,
> And soften into flesh a marble face;
> Plead better at the bar; describe the skies,
> And when the stars descend, and when they rise.
> But, Rome, 'tis thine alone, with awful sway,
> To rule mankind, and make the world obey,
>
> .   .   .   .   .   .   .   .   .   .   .   .   .   .   .   .
>
> These are imperial arts, and worthy thee.[35]

Indeed the art of governing peoples is distinct from arts such as sculpture, rhetoric, astronomy, and similar ones, and it is not that one derives from the other or that one properly includes the other, and yet all are subordinated and subject to the art of governing peoples, so that the king could rule all for the common advantage of the people and, if they do not obey, he could eliminate them from his kingdom, or remove any artisan and substitute others for him, since the ends of the other arts are subjected and subordinated to the end of the regal art.

Now, then, if the subjection and subordination of the political authority to the ecclesiastical are understood in the first way, so that it follows that the political authority is conjoined with the ecclesiastical, I do not see how this would agree with the words of Supreme Pontiffs Gelasius, Nicholas, and Innocent III, and also Hosius, Bernard, Driedo. But if it is understood in the second way, which is how we understand it, then Barclay's reasoning and examples imply absolutely nothing. In fact, just as the art of ruling people does not include sculpture, and sculpture does not derive from the art of ruling people, but still the art of ruling people commands sculpture, and it holds it as subject and subordinate, and the king can and must command the sculptor not to sculpt obscene statues, not to corrupt the young, not to make sculptures from gold or silver so that those metals

---

34. This line of argument is the same as the opening of Aristotle's *Nichomachean Ethics*, book 1, chapters 1 and 2: cf. chapter 13 of this book.

35. Virgil, *Aeneid*, book 6, vv. 847–52. Dryden's translation.

can be used for a more necessary use, not to sell his statues at too high a price so as to curb greed; so the ecclesiastical art of governing souls, which is the art of arts and resides chiefly in the Pope, does not necessarily include the art of ruling people, and it is not necessary that all the kingdoms derive from the Church. But nevertheless, since its end is eternal life, to which all the other ends are subordinated, the political art of governing people is subject and subordinate to it, and the Supreme Pontiff can and must command kings not to abuse their regal authority to destroy the Church, to foster heresies and schisms, and ultimately to the eternal ruin of their soul and of the souls of the peoples subject to them; and if they do not obey after being admonished, he can expel them from the Church through excommunication, and absolve the peoples from their oath of allegiance, and finally even strip them of their kingdom and deprive them of their regal authority.

# The authority of the Supreme Pontiff in temporal matters is not a dubious question and it does not depend only on the opinions of the scholars

In the third chapter Barclay argues that there is nothing certain on the authority of the Supreme Pontiff in temporal matters, but that the whole question is freely discussed among theologians and canonists.

He says: "The great disagreement on this issue between theologians and canonists and within each group—while the latter argue for a direct authority, the former for an indirect—makes this question of the temporal authority of the Pope appear dubious and uncertain, and grounded entirely in men's opinion. Therefore the truth of this question must be investigated with the light of reason and the sharpness of the discussion." These are his words.

But there is a great difference in an investigation between whether something is and what or how something is. Not even the pagans used to question that God existed, but there were many opinions among philosophers regarding the nature of the gods. No Catholic denies that God is triune and one, but all believe it with the most secure faith; nevertheless how many opinions are there among the Scholastic theologians regarding the constitution of the Persons, their relationships, the concepts? In the same way, regarding authority in temporal matters, it is not an opinion, but a certainty among Catholics that it exists, even if there is no lack of debate over what this authority is and what kind of authority this is, that is, whether it is in itself and properly temporal, or rather indeed spiritual but it may dispose of temporal matters through a certain necessary consequence and for the sake of spiritual matters. Hence when Barclay reasons as such he does not infer correctly: "There is a disagreement between theologians and canonists: the former argue for a direct authority, the latter for an indirect. Therefore the question of the Pope's temporal authority is dubious and uncertain and it is entirely grounded in men's opinion."

In fact, we demonstrate it is a certain and well-studied issue that the Supreme Pontiff can dispose of temporal affairs for just reasons and he can also sometimes depose temporal princes themselves in this way:

First, from the unanimous consent of the authors whose words we have reported at the beginning of this dispute. What these scholars teach with unanimous consent in different times and places is reputed as the understanding and teaching of the universal Church. In fact, God instituted pastors and teachers in the Church, as it is said in Ephesians 4,[36] so that the people may follow them as their leaders and may not withdraw from them unless perhaps they should see one bringing something new against the common doctrine, as in our time Barclay did.

Second, we demonstrate it through "Unam sanctam," title "De maioritate et obedientia," *Extravagantes,*[37] where we are taught that sword is under sword, that the temporal authority is subjected to the spiritual, and that if the earthly authority strays it will be judged by the spiritual authority; if a minor spiritual authority strays it will be judged by its superior, but if the supreme authority strays, it will be judged by God alone. And it is not a hurdle that the deliberation of that decretal seems to have been revoked by Clement V, in "Meruit," title "De privilegiis," *Extravagantes,* for Clement V did not revoke Boniface's canon; he rather seems to have declared the ancient obligation which men hold to obey and subject themselves to the Apostolic See.[38]

36. Cf. Ephesians 4:11–16.

37. This is chapter 1, title 8, of the first book of the *Extravagantes,* and it is the bull promulgated by Boniface VIII in 1302 (text in *Corpus iuris canonici,* vol. 2, cols. 1245–46). It is one of the strongest affirmations of the pope's plenitude of power, a *locus classicus* in the debate over papal prerogatives and authority.

38. Bellarmine is here referring to chapter 2, title 7, of the fifth book of *Extravagantes,* promulgated by Pope Clement V in 1306 (text in *Corpus iuris canonici,* vol. 2,

Third, we demonstrate it from the above-mentioned councils, the last two of which were general. For how can what general, Catholic, and lawful councils prove be called into question and depend only on the opinion of men? Indeed those ten councils, and especially the last two, the Lateran and the one of Lyon, most clearly teach that temporal princes can be deposed by the Supreme Pontiff when the necessity of the Church requires it, and on this account the temporal authority of the princes is subject and subordinate to the spiritual authority of the Popes.

Fourth, we prove it from the sacred Scriptures, as Gregory VII proves it in his epistle 21 of the eighth book. For in Scriptures and tradition we find the ecclesiastical primacy of the Roman Pontiff most clearly established, and in this primacy the most ample authority to rule, bind, loose, and absolve anybody, even kings and emperors, is contained. And this is something that neither Barclay nor any other Catholic denies. From this principle, therefore, it follows clearly enough that the Pope has authority to dispose of temporal matters, to the point of deposing kings and emperors themselves; indeed, through this spiritual authority the Supreme Pontiff can bind secular princes with the bond of excommunication, he can absolve peoples from their oath of allegiance and obedience, he can oblige those peoples under pain of excommunication not to obey an excommunicated king and to choose for themselves another king. Moreover, since the end of the spiritual government is the attaining of eternal life, which is the supreme and ultimate end to which all the other ends are subordinated, it is certainly necessary that every temporal authority be subjected and subordinated to the spiritual authority of the supreme ecclesiastical bishop, who must rule it and judge and correct it if it strays, and finally dispose it so that it does not prevent the salvation of the Christian people. And this is the reason why Gregory VII and Innocent IV, in deposing emperors, to show that they were doing it lawfully, have alleged the words of God: "Whatsoever thou shalt bind on earth shall be bound in heaven: and whatsoever thou shalt loose on earth shall be loosed in heaven" (Matthew

---

col. 1300). It declared that the "Unam sanctam" was not intended to cause "prejudice" to the king and kingdom of France, since they were not to be considered "more subjected to the Roman Church than before" the promulgation of the bull.

16),[39] and "Feed my sheep" (John 16 [21]),[40] evidently to indicate that their authority to dispose of temporal matters, when the salvation of the souls, the safety of religion, and the preservation of the Church require it, does not depend on the uncertain opinions of men but on the divine order of Christ, eternal King and Supreme Pontiff, who is God, above everything, and to whom is glory forever, as the apostle says in Romans 11.[41]

But let us see what Barclay opposes to these:

1. The first of his arguments is this: "It is absurd and unjust to say that pagan princes have been received into the Church in a harsher and worse manner than private individuals, or that the Pope now has more authority over secular Christian princes than once the Blessed Peter and the rest of the apostles had over any one child of the Church: they had no right and temporal authority then over Christian laymen; therefore, the Pope today has no temporal authority over secular princes."

The assumption of the argument, "Of whom do the kings of the earth take custom,"[42] is false and absolutely contrary to the sacred Scriptures. First, the apostles had the right to receive laymen's temporal goods, which the apostle in his first epistle to the Corinthians, chapter 9, proves, when he says: "If we have sown unto you spiritual things, is it a great thing if we shall reap your carnal things? If others be partakers of this power over you, are not we rather? Nevertheless, we have not used this power, but suffer all things, lest we should hinder the gospel of Christ. Do ye not know that they which minister about holy things live of the things of the temple? and they which wait at the altar are partakers with the altar?"[43] Thus the Lord also ordained to those who announce the Gospel to live of the Gospel. Then the apostles could order Christians to appoint Christian judges in civil trials, so as not to go to the courts of pagan magistrates, as the apostle commands in the first epistle to the Corinthians, chapter 6, saying: "Dare any of you, having a matter against another, go to law before the unjust and not before the saints? Do ye not know that the saints shall

39. Matthew 16:19.
40. John 21:17.
41. This is Bellarmine's paraphrase of Romans 11:36.
42. Matthew 17:25.
43. 1 Corinthians 9:11–13.

judge the world? and if the world shall be judged by you, are ye unworthy to judge the smallest matters? Know ye not that we shall judge angels? how much more things that pertain to this life? If then ye have judgments of things pertaining to this life, set them to judge who are least esteemed in the church."[44] Therefore, if the apostles could establish courts in civil trials and command the laymen to support with their means the ministers of the Gospel, how could they have no right over the temporal goods of laymen?

2. But Barclay says: "It is more than certain that in the times of the apostles the ecclesiastical authority was completely separate from the political authority and that this was entirely outside of the Church, in the hands of the pagan princes, so much so that the apostles themselves were under the temporal authority of the pagans, which also Albert Pighius and Robert Bellarmine and other illustrious theologians frankly acknowledge." And I reply that even now the ecclesiastical authority is separate from the political: in fact, the authorities of Popes and kings are not the same, but they are different. Yet because, as we said before, the ecclesiastical authority, which is spiritual, is superior to the political and temporal authority and must direct temporal authority toward the supreme end of eternal life, thus it can dispose of temporal goods insofar as they concern spiritual matters. It is true, however, that in the times of the apostles the pagans had all the political authority, that is to say, not any authority, but the regal or imperial authority, because then there was no Christian king or emperor. But from this nothing follows but that the ecclesiastical authority at that time did not have an administration set up, especially in temporal matters, as it does in our time. Indeed I, together with Albert Pighius and some others, wrote that the apostles themselves were under the temporal authority of the pagan princes, but afterward, recollecting and considering my books more diligently, I determined that the apostles were subject to those princes *de facto*, not *de iure*, as I put it in the *Recognitio* of my works.[45]

44. 1 Corinthians 6:1–4.
45. Bellarmine is here referring to a work he published in 1608 at Ingolstadt, the *Recognitio librorum omnium,* in which he corrected a number of points from his *Controversiae.* The passage being discussed by Bellarmine and Barclay refers to the *Controversia*

3. But Barclay says: "Christ did not come to destroy the law but to fulfill it,[46] not to eliminate the laws of nature and the laws of nations nor to deprive anybody of his temporal right over his own things. Therefore, as before Him the kings ruled over their subjects by their temporal authority, so even after He came and withdrew from us into heaven, the kings kept that same authority, confirmed by the apostolic doctrine and weakened in no part. If, therefore, Peter and the rest of the apostles, before following Christ, were subjected to the temporal sovereignty and jurisdiction of pagan princes, which cannot be denied, and the Lord never freed them clearly and expressly from their obligation to the law, it necessarily follows that they have remained under the same yoke, even after they became apostles."

I reply that Christ did not come to destroy the law but to fulfill it; therefore, He did not remove the laws of nations and the laws of nature but completed them; He did not deprive kings and princes of their power or jurisdiction but regulated their power and jurisdiction. In fact, even in the Church itself kings and princes are no less endowed with political authority than the pagans were. This only was added, that He put above them a great Pastor, who acts as His Vicar on earth, by whom they should be directed if they perhaps happen to stray from the path that leads to the kingdom of heaven. This blessing of God must be acknowledged as one of the most important by all the faithful, but by nobody more so than kings

---

de Summo Pontifice, book 2, chapter 19, in which Bellarmine writes that Paul had appealed to Caesar as his legitimate prince, and therefore the apostles were subject both de iure and de facto to the pagan emperors. In the Recognitio Bellarmine retracted this position, writing, "If the reason for the exemption of the clergy is that they are ministers of Christ who is prince of the kings of the earth, certainly they are exempted de iure not only from the authority of the Christian princes but also from that of pagan princes" (see Recognitio, in Opera omnia, vol. 1, p. 11). The issue of the exemption of the clergy from the authority of pagan rulers was a very crucial one for Bellarmine's theory and was one on which the Jesuit had changed his mind often since the publication of Controversia de clericis. In that work Bellarmine denied that clergymen were exempted iure divino from the authority of the political sovereign (see p. xviii, n. 22). Behind this issue, as is clear from Barclay's passages and Bellarmine's discussion in this chapter, lay the crucial question of the nature and autonomy of the Christian commonwealth with respect to the non-Christian or pre-Christian one. On this see Höpfl, Jesuit Political Thought, pp. 339ff.

46. This reference is to Matthew 5:17.

and princes, who are liable to more serious falls the higher the place they occupy, and so much more do they need the bishop and pastor of their souls, as Cardinal Reginald Pole advised elegantly and abundantly in his *Dialogus de Pontifice Maximo* [*De Summo Pontifice*].

Moreover, it seems absolutely contrary to the Gospel to say that Christ had not expressly and clearly freed Peter and the apostles from the obligation they had toward the pagan princes. In Matthew 17 Christ paid the double drachma for himself and Peter to avoid causing offence. Moreover, He demonstrated that neither He nor Peter was obliged to pay that tribute with these words: "Of whom do the kings of the earth take custom or tribute? of their own children or of strangers? Peter saith unto Him, Of strangers. Jesus saith unto him, Then are the children free."[47] And with these words He declared that since He was the Son of the King of all kings, He was exempt from any custom or tribute, and since the Son of the King is exempt, also His household is considered exempt; and therefore Peter and the apostles, who were part of the household of Christ, by His favor, must have been exempt also, but we have more abundantly written on this issue elsewhere.[48]

4. But Barclay does not rest and in fact adds: "But from their doctrine and deeds it is clear that they were subjects of the princes just like the other citizens: obviously they cannot be reproached for the same thing that Christ reproached the Scribes and the Pharisees for, that is, that they did one thing and taught another. In fact, they taught that Christians ought to show subjection and obedience to kings and princes, as we said before, and for this reason Paul himself appealed to Caesar and established that all Christians were subject to the temporal authority not only for fear of wrath but for conscience."[49]

Without a doubt the apostles were not like the Pharisees, who taught one thing and did another; in fact they were not subject *de iure* to the temporal authorities like the other citizens, since they were appointed by God as princes of all the earth, as we read in Psalm 44 [45], and even

47. Matthew 17:25–26.
48. The issue of clerical exemption was treated in the controversy *De clericis*—see especially chapter 28.
49. This is Barclay's paraphrase of Romans 13:5.

though their authority was spiritual, not temporal, nevertheless it was a true authority and far more noble than the temporal one. Furthermore, St. Paul appealed to Caesar as to the judge of the governor of Judea and of the Israelites, who were oppressing him unlawfully, for otherwise that issue, which is spiritual, that is, the one concerning the resurrection of Christ and the ceremonies of the Mosaic law, could not legally pertain to a pagan ruler. See the Acts of the Apostles, chapters 21, 22, 23, 24, 25, and 26. Also, the same Paul in his epistle to the Romans, chapter 13, delivered a universal doctrine of obedience on the part of inferiors toward superiors when he said: "Let every soul be subject unto the higher powers."[50] Afterward he applied such doctrine specifically to the obedience that subjects owe to their temporal sovereigns and concluded, "Render therefore to all their dues: tribute to whom tribute is due; custom to whom custom; fear to whom fear; honour to whom honour."[51] Therefore, if somebody proves himself not to be subject to any authority, he will not be bound by this sentence of the apostle, even if it might be necessary that he be subject *de facto,* or to avoid offence.

5. Barclay adds: "In fact, regarding what some say, that Blessed Paul was not talking there about the temporal authority of the secular princes but about authority in general, that is, that everybody should be obedient to his own superior, the layman to a layman, the clergyman to a clergyman, this is a mere sophistry and a response that is unworthy of learned men and theologians. In fact, at that time men commonly meant as 'authority' nothing but the political and temporal authority."

I reply that in the apostle's words, as we said earlier, there are certain general sentences and certain specific ones. Who indeed can deny that "let every soul be subject unto the higher powers" is a general sentence? Likewise this, "There is no power but of God" and "Whosoever therefore resisteth the power, resisteth the ordinance of God." But when the apostle added, "for rulers are not a terror to good works but to the evil" and later, "But if thou do that which is evil, be afraid, for he beareth not the sword in vain,"[52] it is obvious that by "higher powers" he meant to indicate "politi-

---

50. Romans 13:1.
51. Romans 13:7.
52. These are all Romans 13:1–4.

cal princes." Thus it is, then, that by "higher powers" he meant to indicate "political princes" but not only them, for in fact the apostle preferred to conceive and express his doctrine in general terms so that it would profit more people; hence he also advises, in other places, that sons be obedient to their parents, wives to their husbands, servants to their masters, and peoples to their ecclesiastical rulers. Indeed Barclay says, at that time by "authority" people commonly recognized nothing but political and temporal authority, which is an opinion entirely unworthy of a learned man and jurist. In fact, paternal authority, proprietary authority, spousal authority, the kind of authority of the master over the disciple, and indeed ecclesiastical authority have always been very well known, and all these authorities (if we want to speak properly) are most clearly distinguished from political authority.[53] And concerning ecclesiastical authority, does not the apostle talk about that very frequently? Certainly he does so when he says: "For though I should boast somewhat more of our authority, which the Lord hath given us for edification, and not for your destruction, I should not be ashamed" in the second epistle to the Corinthians, chapter 10;[54] or "Therefore I write these things being absent, lest being present I should use sharpness, according to the power which the Lord hath given me," ibid., chapter 13;[55] and "Obey them that have the rule over you, and submit yourselves," in his epistle to the Hebrews, chapter 13.[56]

6. Barclay invokes the testimony of St. Augustine in his commentary on some propositions of the epistle to the Romans. From this testimony Barclay gathers first, that the profession of the Christian religion does not exempt anybody from being subject to the temporal authority. Second, that the apostles, and St. Peter himself, were subject to the pagan magistrate.

---

53. Bellarmine's passing reference to the intrinsic difference between paternal and political authority—a point that he will mention several times during the course of his treatise—introduces a very important theme in the history of political thought in early modern Europe, especially in the English context. For the implications of this debate see Skinner, *Foundations*, vol. 2, pp. 156ff.; Sommerville, "From Suarez to Filmer"; Sommerville, "Absolutism and Royalism," in Burns and Goldie, eds., *Cambridge History of Political Thought*, pp. 347–73, at pp. 358–61.

54. 2 Corinthians 10:8.

55. 2 Corinthians 13:10.

56. Hebrews 13:17.

Third, that those first Christians were not allowed to forsake the authority of pagan princes and to institute other princes for themselves, even if their strengths were sufficient to do so. Fourth, that Augustine understood the words of the apostle to indicate temporal authority only. Fifth, that Augustine included himself in the number of those whom the apostle commands to be subject to the temporal authorities; from this it follows that even bishops and all clergymen must be subject to those same temporal authorities. Sixth, that the duty of subjects is twofold: one, to be obedient to the king when he does not command anything against God; and two, not to be obedient to the king when God commands the opposite.

I reply that St. Augustine truly teaches that the profession of the Christian religion does not exempt anybody from being subject to temporal authority, which he deduces most correctly from the words of the apostle and against which we do not contend. However, from this it does not follow that St. Peter and the rest of the apostles were subject *de iure* to the temporal authorities, and neither does St. Augustine say so. In fact, even though the profession of the Christian religion did not exempt the apostles from that subjection, the apostolic sovereignty, which is far more noble than any temporal sovereignty, did.

We will deal later in the appropriate place with the question of whether the Christians were allowed to forsake the pagan emperors. For now we say only that this is not inferred from St. Augustine's or the apostle's words. In fact, St. Augustine, from the apostle, teaches that Christians owe obedience to temporal princes as long as, obviously, they rule with authority, but not if they lose their sovereignty. Neither the apostle nor St. Augustine in this passage settles the issue of whether Christians were allowed to deprive pagans of their authority.

However, it is false that St. Augustine in that passage meant temporal authority only: in fact, never in Augustine or in Paul do we find the word *only*, and we have St. John Chrysostom together with Theodoretus and Theophylactus, who discuss authority in general, and St. Anselm who discusses the ecclesiastical and temporal authorities, and St. Bernard in his letters 42 and 183 who also discusses both.

Regarding the fact that Augustine numbered himself among those who were ordered to be obedient to temporal authorities, that does not force us to infer that bishops and clergymen are not exempt from the temporal authority. For when he says: "Since we are made of body and soul and since, as long as we are in this life, we make use also of temporal things for support in living this life, and insofar as this life is concerned it is necessary for us to be subject to the authorities, that is, to the men who administer human affairs in some official capacity," he shows that all men need laws and political magistrates, without which this life cannot be lived in peace. Likewise also Pope Nicholas in his letter to Emperor Michael writes that even the Pontiffs themselves make use of imperial laws for the course of temporal affairs; all, in fact, must observe such laws, but not all because of the force of such laws, but some because of the force of the laws [*vi legum*], some because of the force of reason [*vi rationis*].

7. Barclay goes on and says: "What can be considered more unworthy and unjust than that the princes who profess Christ's faith will be oppressed by a heavier yoke than private individuals from the people? For private men, when they surrendered to the spiritual authority of the Church, did not lose any good or temporal right except for those things that they willingly offered, as is clear from the Acts of the Apostles. Similarly, therefore, even princes, when they joined Christ, kept their temporal rights, I say, and their power and political authority complete and intact."

I reply that private men who are admitted into the Church certainly do not forfeit their goods and other temporal rights, and yet they can be obliged by the Church to support their parish priests and, as the apostle says, let those who sow spiritual things reap carnal things,[57] and they were hardly bound to do these things before accepting the faith. Also, they can, as a punishment for different sins, not only be obliged by their confessors in the internal forum to atone for their sins by giving alms, but also be fined by the bishops in the external forum with pecuniary sanctions and also be put in prison, as is clear from the Council of Trent, session 25, chapter 3.[58] By the same token, temporal princes who join Christ's household lose neither their power nor their jurisdiction but subject themselves

57. This is a paraphrase of 1 Corinthians 9:11.
58. Bellarmine is referring to the third chapter of the "Decretum de reformatione generali," issued at Trent on 3–4 December 1563 (text in *Conciliorum oecumenicorum decreta*, pp. 761–62).

to him whom Christ has put in charge of His household, to be ruled and led by him in the path that leads to life.

8. Barclay adds: "It does not help our adversaries' cause to say that the apostles therefore had no temporal authority over the princes of their time because they had not yet converted to Christianity, on the basis of the following: 'For what have I to do to judge them also that are without?' (1 Corinthians 5),[59] but now the Pope has that authority, for they became Christians and sons of the Church, whose supreme Prince and head on earth and Father of all Christians is he, and the right order of nature and reason demands that the son be subject to the father, and not the father to the son. This, I say, is such an insignificant reason that it is surprising that learned men are giving any space to it. In fact, that spiritual subjection by which the princes became the sons of the Pope is thoroughly distinct and separate from the temporal subjection, so much so that one does not follow the other. Rather, it is just like a guardian or consul, who, while he is in office, can give himself to adoption to another and therefore transfer the paternal authority into the family of the adoptive father. Yet he does not transfer to the adopting father through that legal action the consular fasces or anything else that by the right of his office pertains to him."

It is surprising how easily Barclay gives judgments over the works of learned men. Since they can be twisted back against him with the best right, his responses and comparisons are so insignificant that it is hardly credible that they could have satisfied their author. Indeed, that comparison of the adopted son, on which his entire response depends, does not fit the argument. The authority of the guardian and that of the consul are not only distinct and separate, but the former is also inferior to the latter; and if a father abuses his paternal authority he can be corrected by the guardian and by the consul, and much more so by the king and prince, and in certain cases he can be deprived of his paternal authority. On the contrary, if a guardian or consul or prince abuses his political authority, by virtue of his power he could not be corrected by an adoptive father or even his natural father, and even less could he be deprived of his authority. Now, however, the authority of the Supreme Pontiff, spiritual and supernatural,

---

59. 1 Corinthians 5:12.

is more sublime than the regal, which is temporal and earthly; and this greater authority should not be compared with the human authority of an adoptive father toward a son who is a guardian or consul, that is, with an inferior authority with respect to a superior, but with the authority of a prince or guardian toward the paternal authority of private persons, that is, with a superior authority with respect to an inferior. From this it follows that even though the authority of the Pope and that of the king are distinct and separate, and one does not necessarily follow the other, nevertheless when they are found in the same body of the Church, the authority of the Pope is so preeminent that it can and should rule and correct the regal authority, and not be ruled and corrected by it. Therefore, Barclay's entire deceit is based on the fact that he thought that the spiritual and supernatural paternity of the Supreme Pontiff toward the Christian kings and princes is not at all more sublime than the human and civil paternity of a private person toward an adoptive child, which is an obvious and childish illusion.

9. Barclay says: "To these add the fact that when the Christian commonwealth was greatly prosperous for the number of the faithful, for the sanctity of the Pontiffs, for the erudition and the examples of the teachers, and also when it was plagued and shaken by evil Christian princes, not only, I will say, was there no direct and clear claim but also not even the slightest claim was made to this sovereignty and temporal jurisdiction over secular princes."[60]

I could ask Barclay why it is that in the Old Testament so many centuries went by before the Pope commanded that a king be deposed and another substituted for him, which happened when the Pontiff Jehoiada not only deposed the queen Athaliah but also ordered that she be killed,

---

60. The question of the historical reasons why the popes did not depose pagan emperors (that is, whether they did not depose them because they had no authority to do so or whether they did not have the strength to do so) is a question to which Barclay and Bellarmine return often in their works. It is a central theme of the debate, as it was linked with the question of the relationship between a spiritual and a secular commonwealth and the question of how such a relationship changed after the birth of Christ. For the implications of this line of argument from the point of view of the process of state formation in early modern Europe, see Prodi, *The Papal Prince*, pp. 62ff.

and substituted for her King Joash (4 Kings 11).[61] Then, after the separation of the kingdom of Solomon into the kingdoms of Israel and of Judah,
when there was no one among the kings of Israel who was pious but all
were impious and idolatrous, why did the Prophet of God, after having
tolerated many others, anoint Jehu as king and order him to kill the king
Joram, to whom he had sworn allegiance? And this Jehu did at once, and
he was praised by God for that, as we see from 4 Kings 9 and 10.[62] Barclay
would reply, I suppose, that this was the will of God, whose judgments are
inscrutable. Therefore in the same way does the Church, which is guided
by the Spirit of God, not always put forth its authority but according to
the place and time, as the Spirit of Christ suggests and commands. And
certainly in its first three hundred years the Christian Church had but
very few Christian kings (such as Lucius in Britain and Donaldus in Scotland) who, since they were pious, did not give a reason to the Church to
enforce its authority over them. The kings that succeeded afterward were
either very pious and religious, such as Constantine the Great, Constans
his son, Jovian, Valentinian, Gratian, Theodosius, Honorius, and others;
or very impious and blasphemous, such as Constantine II, Julian, Valens,
Theodoricus, Totila, Gensericus, Hunericus, and others. The Church had
to display benevolence, not severity, toward the former; but toward the
latter, since they were very powerful, it would not have been useful to
display severity, and therefore patience rather than authority had to be
employed. However, when during the time of Pope Gregory II the Italian people suffered under the empire of Leo the Isaurian, a heretic and a
persecutor, and were ready to cast off the yoke of the impious prince if the
Pontiff had ordered or approved it, at that time indeed it seemed fit to the
Apostolic See to exercise its authority, obviously when it would have not
been in vain. Thus also did Pope Zachary not consider deposing the king
Childeric and raising Pippin to the kingdom until the Frankish people
and noblemen demanded it, and the Pope's intention would not have
been prudent if he had tried to dismiss the king, no matter how inept and
idle, against the will of the Frankish people and noblemen.

61. 2 Kings 11.
62. 2 Kings 9–10.

And if Barclay makes so much of seven hundred years of silence, why can we not make even more of the words and deeds of nine hundred years? In fact, while the Pontiffs and the authors of the Church of earlier times did not affirm that the Apostolic See had a certain authority to dispose of temporal matters insofar as they concern spiritual matters, they did not deny it either, whereas Pontiffs and authors of later times clearly stated that the Church did not lack such an authority. Certainly the Church is the same, and the gates of Hell shall not prevail against it, and the Church of later times does not lack men who are illustrious for doctrine and sanctity. Therefore, whoever thinks that whatever was not expressly said or done in the ancient Church is not to be admitted, thinks harshly about the Church of Christ, for it would be as if the more recent Church ceased to be the Church, or lacked the prerogative of explaining, declaring, and even instituting and regulating what pertains to the faith and to Christian morality.

10. Barclay introduces St. Gregory who, in his epistle 61 [65], book 2 [3], calls himself an "unworthy servant of the emperor" and says that authority over all men was given to the emperor from heaven. There he notes that the word *all* comprehends even the Pope, if the Pope is a man. And lest somebody reply that St. Gregory spoke in this way out of humility, Barclay quotes sermon 29 [181] by Augustine on the words of the apostle [1 John 1:8–9]: "If you lie on account of humility, if you were not a sinner before lying, by lying you have become what you had avoided." Then he adds St. Gregory's words at the end of that epistle: "I did what I had to do on both accounts: I have demonstrated my obedience to the emperor, and for God I did not conceal what I felt."

But St. Gregory called himself a servant not only of the emperor but of all the faithful, since at the beginning of his letters he wrote: "Gregory, servant of the servants of God." And John the Deacon, in book 4 of his *Vita Sancti Gregorii,* chapter 58, attests that St. Gregory used to call all the priests "brothers," and all clerics "sons." He used to call all laymen "lords," but I think Barclay would not concede that St. Gregory was subject to all laymen. Furthermore, regarding what St. Gregory wrote, that the authority was given to the emperor from heaven, this does not mean that imperial authority comes immediately from God, but it comes from

God in that sense in which Paul in the epistle to the Romans, chapter 13, says: "There is no power but of God." Every authority, in fact, comes from God, but one immediately, as the kind of authority that Moses, Peter, and Paul had, and the other by means of men's consent, as is the kind of authority of kings, consuls, tribunes. In fact, as St. Thomas demonstrates in 2a 2ae, question 10, article 10, and question 12, article 2, human dominion and sovereignty are of human law, not of divine law. Regarding what St. Gregory adds, "over all men," this signifies over all men who are subjects of the Roman Empire; otherwise the authority of Emperor Mauritius would have reached even over the inhabitants of the Antipodes, the Galamantes, and the Indians, and yet it did not reach over the neighboring Persians, or Scythians, or the Germans and the Franks, or the Hispanics, or innumerable others. Therefore Barclay could have avoided that deduction: "Therefore also over the Pope, if the Pope is a man."

Neither did St. Gregory lie out of humility, when he called himself servant of those to whom he was not subject. We call *servant,* in fact, him who is at the "service" of the interest of others, whether he does that by obeying or by commanding: indeed, even Paul wrote that he was the servant of the Corinthians, over whom, however, he says he received authority from Christ (2 Corinthians 4 and 13).[63] Furthermore, and regarding the obedience St. Gregory wrote that he showed toward the emperor, I say that obedience was forced upon him and offered *de facto,* not *de iure.* The same St. Gregory, in his commentary on Psalm 101, writes regarding Emperor Mauritius: "His madness reaches such a degree of temerity that he attributes to himself, as head of all churches, the Roman Church, and usurps the right of earthly authority over the dominions of the nations."

Barclay proceeds and exclaims: "O divine high priest and sentence enforced by some of the Pontiffs of later times! Alas, O Goodness, from which that benign and humble confession has been forced out from our time, which little by little was overgrown by that threatening and proud language against kings and emperors! 'We, sitting on the supreme throne of justice, and holding supreme power over all kings and princes of the entire earth, and every people, tribe, and nation, declare, command, order,

63. These are verses 5 and 10, respectively.

etc., that that authority has been given to us not by human but by divine institution!' And that these words are false and foolish is clear from the fact that the Pope has neither temporal nor spiritual authority over infidel princes and peoples, who are more numerous than the Christians, as Bellarmine in his book *De Romano* [*Summo*] *Pontifice* shows with very solid reasons."

St. Gregory himself refuted the foolish exclamation and praise of that humble confession in the privilege he conceded to the monastery of St. Medard, which was subscribed by Gregory himself and many bishops as we can read in book 22 [14] of the Epistles after epistle 31 [32],[64] where it is said about that privilege: "If then a king, nobleman, judge, or any secular person violates or contradicts the decrees of this apostolic authority and our injunction, or orders something contrary to it, no matter his office or high position, he should, as someone who perverts the Catholic faith and destroys the sacred Church of God, be deprived of his office and should be removed from the Christian community and excluded from partaking of the body and blood of Jesus Christ our Lord." And previously he had said that he established it with divine authority in the place of Blessed Peter, prince of the apostles. St. Gregory uses the same words in another, similar privilege, which is found in book 11 [13], epistle 10 [8], and is addressed to a Senator Abbot. Therefore that humble servant of the servants of God did not ignore the eminence of his dignity. For he, by divine authority in the place of the prince of the apostles, was not afraid to rule over all kings, threatening to deprive them of their dignity, no matter their office and high position, so that they would not dare to violate the decrees of his order. What is there, then, in the bulls of Pius V and Sixtus V (quoted by Barclay in the margin), which Barclay calls threatening and proud, that is not in that privilege given by the humble Gregory?[65] Pius and Sixtus say that they have received their authority by divine institution, while

64. The text of this privilege can be found in PL, vol. 77, cols. 1330–34.

65. Bellarmine is referring to Pius V's bull against Elizabeth I (1570), in which the pope excommunicated the queen and exonerated her Catholic subjects from allegiance to their sovereign, who had been declared illegitimate on the ground of her heresy. Bellarmine also refers to Sixtus V's 1585 bull against Henri of Navarre and the prince of Condé in which the pope declared them heretics and as such unfitting candidates for the throne of France and exonerated their vassals from their obedience.

Gregory says that he gives orders by divine authority. The first ones say that they have authority over all kings, while the latter says, if a king or any secular person . . . etc. The first ones say: "We declare, command," etc., while the latter: "If any king . . . violates the decrees of this apostolic authority and of our order." But, Barclay says, it is clear from the fact that the Pope has neither temporal nor spiritual authority over infidel princes that those words of Pius V and Sixtus V are false and foolish. If the words are false and foolish, much more so will be St. Gregory's words in letter 61 [65], book 2 [3], above quoted and praised by Barclay, when St. Gregory says that God gave to Emperor Mauritius authority over all men, for it is agreed that Emperor Mauritius's authority was not over all men, for it reached only the men who were subject to the Roman Empire, which at that time did not include even a third of mankind. As, then, the words of St. Gregory on Mauritius's authority over all men must be understood as all men who were subject to the Roman Empire, in the same way the words of the Pontiffs on their authority over all kings and peoples must be understood as all kings and peoples who are in the Catholic Church, which is spread over the entire earth. The former words, in fact, teach us that the latter ones must be understood as such. Indeed Pius V at the beginning of his bull writes that there is one true Church of God, and it is entirely entrusted to St. Peter and to his successors, and hence it follows that the Supreme Pontiff has authority over all kings and peoples, that is, who are part of the Church, which is the whole world.

Sixtus V indeed says that he has the care of all churches, peoples, and nations; and he does not say he has authority over all peoples and nations, but over the churches that are among all peoples and nations. A similar expression can be found in St. Bernard, book 3 of *De consideratione*, chapter 1, where he says that the entire world pertains to the care of the Supreme Pontiff: "So you are the heir and the world is your inheritance," and "Those who might want to search out the things that are not in your care have to go outside of the world"; nevertheless he himself says that the Pope is not the lord of the world, but the whole world pertains to him, because he has to support the faithful and rule over them with his authority and apply himself with care and diligence to convert the infidels, as the apostles did.

Also St. Thomas in 2a 2ae, question 12, article 2, says that the Pope has authority over the faithful and the infidels who have at any time embraced the faith, and not over those who never embraced the faith, which is consistent with that passage of Paul in 1 Corinthians 5: "For what have I to do to judge them also that are without?"[66] In the passage that Barclay noted I have followed those authors and many others, as one may see in book 5 of my work *De Summo Pontifice,* chapter 2. And what we demonstrated before with St. Thomas does not contradict these things; that is, any infidel can be deprived by the Supreme Pontiff of the power he has over the faithful. For even if judging them that are without does not pertain absolutely to the Pontiff, and he does not have any ordinary authority over them, because they are part of the flock that has been entrusted to him only *in potentia,* nevertheless, in order to preserve the faithful, he has from God the authority to deprive infidel princes of the power they have over the faithful, as St. Thomas himself shows in 2a 2ae, question 10, article 10.

Finally I add that the words of Pius V are not as proud and threatening as Barclay says. These are his words in the bull of excommunication of Elizabeth, alleged queen of England: "He Whose kingdom is in heaven, to Whom every authority has been given on earth and in heaven, has handed over one, holy Catholic and Apostolic Church, outside of which there is no salvation, to only one person on earth, that is Peter, prince of the apostles, and his successor, the Roman Pontiff, to be governed in the plenitude of power. He established him alone as prince over all peoples and all kingdoms, so that he may root out, pull down, destroy, throw down, and plant, and build, so that he may preserve in unity of spirit the Christian people, bound with the bond of mutual charity, and present the Christian people safe and sound to its Savior: and performing this duty we, called by God's benignity to the steering oars of this Church, do not spare any effort, etc." And later: "We, sustained by the authority of Him Who wanted to place us in this supreme throne of justice (albeit unfit for such charge), out of the plenitude of the apostolic authority declare that the said Elizabeth is a heretic and a patroness of heretics, and that those who support her have incurred the sentence of the above-mentioned

66. 1 Corinthians 5:12.

anathema and are cut off from the unity of the body of Christ; moreover that she is deprived of the alleged right to that aforementioned kingdom, and also any dominion, dignity, and privilege, etc."

Also, Sixtus V's bull begins in this way: "The authority given by the immense power of the eternal King to Blessed Peter and his successors is superior to all the authorities of the earthly kings and princes, and being firm on a solid rock, it proffers judgments over all, unshaken and unbent from virtue by no adversity or even favorable winds." And later: "Therefore on this most high throne, and in the plenitude of power which the King of kings himself and Lord of lords has given us, albeit unworthy, established by the authority of Omnipotent God and of the blessed apostles Peter and Paul, and by our own authority, in consultation with our venerable brothers the cardinals of the Holy Roman Church, we announce and declare, etc." Therefore the exact phrase that Barclay quotes cannot be found either in the bull of Pius V or in that of Sixtus V, but Barclay builds it from various passages in the way that he thought most effective to inflame hatred. I pass over other statements that are in this third chapter, for they are neither arguments nor reasoning, but slanders and insults against the Pontiffs; and we want to imitate Him who, when He was reviled, reviled not again, and when He suffered, He threatened not (1 Peter 2).[67]

67. Bellarmine is paraphrasing verse 23.

# On the false cause attributed by Barclay to the origin of the temporal authority of the Pope

In the fourth chapter Barclay discusses the origin of the temporal authority of the Pope, as if it had already been established that by divine law only spiritual matters pertain to the Supreme Pontiff. But since this is neither established nor true, we could easily have avoided talking about this whole chapter, since it is not to the point and it certainly lacks a solid foundation. But let us see what it is that Barclay here alleges.

He says: "I see two principal issues that have provided the opportunity to the Pontiffs to arrogate to themselves such an authority. The first is that great honor which, as it was fair to do, was bestowed upon the Supreme Pastor of souls by Christian princes and peoples, and it still must be bestowed, as well as the previously held opinion of the sanctity of the See of the Blessed Apostles Peter and Paul." And later: "The sword of excommunication offered the second opportunity to seize so much temporal jurisdiction."

Barclay seeks in vain whence such an authority came to the Supreme Pontiffs, for the reason is clear, and the scholars with universal consent and the general councils themselves have reported it, that is, the supreme spiritual authority received from God by the apostle Peter and his successors over the whole Church, out of which it clearly follows that for the sake of spiritual matters and eternal life, the Supreme Pontiff could dispose also of temporal matters, as has been explained in the previous chapter. But what Barclay says, that the Pontiffs seized the occasion to arrogate to themselves the temporal authority over kings and princes from the highest honor that was bestowed upon the Supreme Pontiff, and the previously held sanctity of that Apostolic See, appears to be false on the basis of the things that Barclay himself wrote. Indeed, the highest honor and the previously held sanctity were not lacking in the first thousand years; for then it shone at its greatest. Nevertheless Barclay contends that Gregory VII was the first to usurp for himself temporal authority over kings and princes, one thousand seventy years after our Savior's arrival. Perhaps he will say that in those first years the Pontiffs were most worthy, and later worse Pontiffs started to aspire to the glory of empire. But Gregory VII was a most holy man and illustrious not only because of the integrity of his life but also for his miracles, of which there are as many witnesses as there are authors from that time, except for the schismatics and the heretics. Likewise, even Innocent III and Innocent IV, who seem to have made use of this authority more than the others, were considered most praiseworthy Pontiffs. Besides, it is not true that Gregory VII was the first to hold temporal authority; in fact, even Gregory I, Gregory II, and other most worthy and most praised Pontiffs before Gregory VII were reported to hold that authority, as we will explain shortly after.

Moreover, excommunication is certainly an instrument that the Pontiffs commonly use to curb the authorities of this world, but even without this instrument Supreme Pontiffs have more than once disposed of temporal offices for the advantage of the Church and for the salvation of souls, as when Zachary ordered that Childeric, king of the Franks, be deposed and commanded that Pippin be anointed and raised to the throne, and he exonerated the people from offering obedience and allegiance to Childeric; and when Adrian I conferred on Charlemagne, king of the Franks, the title *Patricius Romanus;* and when Leo III declared the same Charles the emperor of the West. Therefore, it is not true that excommunication gave to the Popes the opportunity to arrogate for themselves the temporal authority.

But I wish to note some things that in this chapter Barclay blurts out not without great temerity.

1. The first is this: "But here the reader should be warned that the opinion, celebrated by everybody's voice, that any excommunication must be feared, has to be understood with this exception: excommunication which

clearly appears to be unjust. Then such an excommunication must not be taken into account or feared, provided that the excommunicated person is free from contempt and presumption." All the good authors who distinguish between an unjust and an invalid excommunication condemn this doctrine of Barclay's. Indeed they teach, with St. Gregory, that an unjust excommunication must be feared, but an invalid one must not, unless, sometimes, because of scandal, that is, when the invalidity of the excommunication is not known. And lest it be necessary to report individual scholars, let us listen to Navarrus, who attests that this is the general doctrine. In *Enchiridion,* chapter 27, section 3, Navarrus speaks thus: "The sentence of excommunication, however unjust, is regularly valid, and because of this Gregory in chapter 1, part 2, question 3, said that excommunication must be feared whether it be just or unjust," and later the gloss and the scholars clearly say that an unjust excommunication is valid and binding, and it is different from an invalid one.[68]

2. The other is in these words: "Of this kind of excommunication seems to be that which is put forth against subjects because they obey their excommunicated king or prince in matters which are of temporal jurisdiction and do not disagree with God's orders." We can demonstrate the temerity of this doctrine from the fact that on the basis of it the sentence of Innocent IV, given in the Council of Lyon, is condemned. What temerity can be greater than to brand as a manifest injustice a sentence of the Supreme Pontiff, given in a general council and approved by the consent of everybody?

3. The third is in these words: "And indeed Gregory VII, motivated in part by Emperor Henry IV's public crime and in part by the personal affront, was the first to openly claim for himself the right to give and to take away kingdoms." But that Gregory VII was the first to have claimed for himself the right to give and to take away kingdoms is completely false!

68. This discussion on the validity of an unjust excommunication should be traced back to Gregory the Great's pronouncement in his homily 26 on the Gospel: "The sentence of the pastor must be feared, whether it be just or unjust." This statement was incorporated into canon law as chapter 1 of question 3, causa 11, of the second part of Gratian's *Decretum* (text in *Corpus iuris canonici,* vol. 1, col. 642). By *Gloss* Bellarmine means the *Glossa ordinaria in Decretum,* which was the standard gloss on Gratian's work compiled and revised in the first half of the thirteenth century.

In fact, already above we counted six Popes who before Gregory VII did the same, that is, Gregory I, Gregory II, Zachary, Leo III, Gregory IV, and Adrian II. Indeed, Gregory I added to the above-mentioned privilege these words: "But if any king, superior, etc. . . . let him be deprived of his office." Gregory II deprived Emperor Leo the Isaurian of the revenues of Italy, as Zonaras, Cedrenus, and others attest. Zachary deposed Childeric from his kingdom and raised Pippin to the throne, as the very ancient Frankish annals attest, in which we read: "Given his authority [Zachary] ordered that Pippin be appointed king." And later: "According to the decree of the Roman Pontiff, Pippin is called king of the Franks." Aimoinus, Einhard, Lambert of Hersfeld, Regino of Prüm, Sigebert, Hermann Contractus, Marianus Scotus, Burchard of Ursperg, Otto of Freising, and Albert Krantz, whose words we quoted before, say the same.[69] Leo III transferred the empire of the West from the Greeks to the Franks, which we have proved with the testimonies of historians, Pontiffs, emperors, and the prince electors themselves in book 1 of *De translatione imperii*.[70] Gregory IV with his authority rescinded the decree of the Franks by which

69. Bellarmine had to review many of these authors when he was involved with drafting the new Index of Prohibited Books in 1592. See Godman, *Saint as Censor,* pp. 160–67.

70. Bellarmine is referring to his treatise *De translatione imperii,* in three volumes, which he had written as a rebuttal to a 1566 work similarly titled *De translatione imperii* and composed by Matthias Flacius Illyricus, the leader of the Centuriators of Magdeburg and one of the most important Protestant historians of his time. The history of the composition and publication of Bellarmine's *De translatione imperii* was somewhat troubled. Published for the first time in the 1586 Ingolstadt edition of the *Controversiae,* the work had been completed by 1583. In a 1584 letter addressed to Alfonso Salmerón, a celebrated Jesuit theologian, Bellarmine wrote about a "treatise composed last year" against Flacius's book which "was doing great damage at the court of the German princes, because they, persuaded by that book, thought it false that the pope was the author of the transfer of the empire from the Greeks to the Germans in the person of Charlemagne." However, Cardinal Sirleto, who was the prefect of the Congregation of the Index from 1571 to 1585, halted the publication of Bellarmine's work because it was contrary to the interests of the Apostolic See; specifically it could have contributed to a controversy over the role of the pope in Germany, where the situation was relatively smooth. (Bellarmine's letter can be found in ARSI, Opp. Nn. 243, volume 1, fols. 57r–58v, my translation.) Such contrasts within the Congregation of the Index should be taken as instances of the complicated and fragile equilibrium within the Roman Curia over the question of the pope's political prerogatives.

Louis the Pious was deprived of his empire and restored the empire to Louis, as Marianus Scotus reports in book 3 of his *Chronicum,* and these are his words: "Louis in Aquis received the queen who was coming to meet him by order of Pope Gregory; and even if Louis's sons had not only deprived their father of the empire but also taken away from him his wife Judith, nevertheless he got both back at the order of Gregory." And Paulus Aemilius, in his book 2 of *De rebus gestis Francorum,* said: "The Council of Bishops was held in Lyon, where the sons of Emperor Louis had gathered, and the empire was taken away from the father, which order was presently annulled by Gregory the Supreme Pontiff." Last, Adrian II, more than two hundred years before Gregory VII, after learning that the empire of Louis the Younger was being attacked by King Charles the Bald, wrote to Charles a threatening letter, as Aimoinus in book 5, chapter 24, attests with these words: "The Pope's letters said that no mortal should invade, disturb, or attempt to conquer the people and kingdom that had been Lothar's, which were due to Emperor Louis, his spiritual son, by hereditary law, and which came to him after Lothar's death. If anybody should presume to do so, he would not only be disqualified from performing his office, but he would also be placed entirely in the hands of the Devil, bound by the chains of anathema, and deprived of the name of Christian."

4. The fourth is in the following words: "Truthfully, Gregory did not accomplish anything from that fact but bloody and wild tragedies, and he failed miserably because he was stopped by obstinate force of arms." That this is false is very well known, for not Gregory's decree but Henry's disobedience gave birth to bloody and wild tragedies. What Gregory especially desired, that is, to snatch from the hands of the laity the investitures of bishops, he accomplished entirely, partly by himself and partly through his successors, since all his successors, Victor III, Urban II, Paschal II, Gelasius II, and Callistus II, in whose time peace between the clergy and the kingdom was achieved when the emperors submitted, confirmed Gregory's sentence and decree. In fact, Burchard of Ursperg in his chronicle for the year 1122 writes thus: "He, in whose hands is the heart of the king, bent every animosity of the emperor under obedience to apostolic reverence for the sake of Mother Church and beyond the hopes of many, etc." See the whole passage.

5. The fifth and last is in these words, where he praises lavishly Hosius, bishop of Cordoba, whom he calls a great man and most noble confessor, and he says that from his opinion it follows that the Church of early times did not have any temporal authority over princes, and it did not believe that it did, not even in the case of heresy, which is the most serious and destructive crime. But while we know that Hosius was once a great man, we do not ignore that later he fell most shamefully into the Arian heresy. Athanasius in his epistle *Ad solitariam vitam agentes* and in *Apologia secunda;* Hilary in his book *De synodis;* Epiphanius at the entry "Heresy," section 73; Sebadius in his book *Contra Arianos;* Sulpicius in book 2 of *Sacra historia;* Socrates in book 2, chapter 26; Sozomen in book 4, chapter 5; Vigilius Martyr in book 5 *Adversus Eutychem;* and, finally, Isidore of Seville in *De viris illustribus* on Gregory Boeticus all report it. Also, even if Hosius had never fallen into heresy, nevertheless he should not be regarded so highly by Catholic men as to be placed before general councils, and not one, but many, and before all the scholars that we mentioned at the beginning, who teach with universal consent that princes can be deposed and deprived of their realm by the Supreme Pontiff because of heresy. Finally I add that Hosius's words do not oppose at all the general opinion. What did he say, in fact? That it was not allowed to the Pontiff to govern the empire, as it was not allowed to the emperors to govern the pontificate. But even if the Pontiff does not govern the empire, nevertheless he can, by virtue of that very pontifical authority, keep a heretical emperor away from the Church and remove the empire from him so that he should not harm the Church. Zachary also was not a king, and yet he was able to depose the king; Leo III was not an emperor, and yet he was able to transfer the empire from one people to another. Indeed, if the Pope were king or emperor, he could not depose the emperor or king by virtue of his imperial or regal authority, for an equal does not have authority over an equal; so then what the Pope does, he does by virtue of the apostolic authority, that is, the supreme spiritual authority, as Christ's Vicar, not as an earthly prince. From these things it is clear how much the perverse love of one's own opinion impedes the light of reason; in fact Barclay, captured by love for his opinion, thought he saw clearly in the words of Hosius something that we do not see even a trace of.

On the authority in temporal matters
which the theologians attribute
indirectly to the Supreme Pontiff

In the fifth chapter Barclay, after having blown up (as he says himself) the
opinion of the canonists and of Bozio, attempts to refute the opinion of
the theologians who say that the Pope has authority in temporal matters
indirectly. But before I refute his arguments, I will briefly explain what we
mean by the expressions "directly" and "indirectly," and who is the author
of those expressions. Thus, by the expressions "directly" and "indirectly"
we do not mean, as some say sarcastically, that the Pontiff has the spiritual
authority directly, that is, justly and legitimately, while he has the temporal authority indirectly, that is, unjustly and by usurpation. Rather,
the pontifical authority is properly and in itself a spiritual authority, and
therefore it directly deals with spiritual matters as its primary object. But
indirectly, that is, whenever spiritual matters are concerned, by inference
and by necessary consequence, as we say, it deals with temporal matters as
its secondary object, to which the spiritual authority does not turn unless
in the case about which Innocent III speaks in his chapter "Per venerabilem," where he says: "In other regions, having examined certain causes,
we exercise temporal jurisdiction for cause." In the same way St. Bernard
speaks in book 1 of *De consideratione,* chapter 5 [7]: "But it is one thing to
extend into those temporal matters incidentally and for an urgent cause,
and another thing to apply oneself further into these, as great and worthy
matters." Also, as author of these expressions we have Innocent IV, a most
learned Pontiff, who, explaining chapter "Novit," section "De feudo," says

that the Pontiff does not judge directly on fiefs, but only indirectly and for reason of sin. Juan de Torquemada, Tommaso Cajetan, Pierre de la Palude, Durandus, Francisco de Vitoria, Domingo de Soto, Martin Ledesma, Jacobus Simancas, Antonius Cordubensis, Navarrus, Luis de Molina, and others use the same distinction.

I come, therefore, to Barclay's arguments. He brings as the first argument the one that I had used against those who wanted the Pope's authority to be both pontifical and regal, that is, spiritual and temporal, and who argued also that temporal kings are not so much kings as executors of the pontifical authority and will. This was my argument: the authority of earthly kings comes from God, as these Popes themselves acknowledge, that is, St. Leo, epistle 38 [78] to Martianus; St. Gelasius in his epistle to Anastasius; St. Gregory in book 2 [3], epistle 61 [65]; Nicholas in his epistle to Michael. Therefore, either the Supreme Pontiff can take away the capacity to govern from kings and emperors as the supreme king and emperor, or he cannot. If he can, then he is a greater king than Christ, since he can take away what Christ gave. If he cannot, then he does not truly have regal authority over those kings and emperors. Barclay then twists this argument against my own opinion and that of the other theologians:

1. "Either the Supreme Pontiff can deprive kings and emperors of their kingdoms and empires and give them to others in a certain way, that is, either directly or indirectly, or he cannot. If he can, then he is in some way greater than God, for he takes away what God gave, for an inferior or equal cannot take away what has been given from a superior or equal, not even the Vicar of Him Who gave those things, without an express order of God (lest somebody reply that the Pope does that as the Vicar of Christ, given that he received no express or tacit order in this respect). If he cannot, then it is false what they say, that he has the supreme authority to dispose indirectly of all temporal matters of the Christians and to depose kings and emperors from their throne and to put others in their place."

But when we said that from the sentence of the Popes the authority of earthly kings comes from God, we do not mean that it comes from God immediately, as indeed the authority of the Supreme Pontiff does, but that it comes from God in the sense that God wanted a political government among humans, and therefore He gave men some natural instinct to elect for themselves a magistrate by whom to be governed.[71] Besides, God wanted the political government to be distinct from the ecclesiastical, as clearly Pope Nicholas showed in his epistle to Michael, and after him Innocent in chapter "Solitae," and, before both, Gelasius, in his epistle to Anastasius. From this it is evident that my argument is solid, and Barclay's argument is entirely weak. In fact, if the Supreme Pontiff had spiritual and temporal authority directly, and if the Pontiff were the king of the world as he is Pontiff of the universal Church, and if the rest of the kings were mere executors of the temporal jurisdiction, certainly the Pontiff could of his own will deprive any king of the administration and government of the temporal jurisdiction. In this way he could remove the political government or merge it with the ecclesiastical one and he would be greater than Christ, because he could remove or merge authorities that Christ wanted to exist, and to exist distinct from one another. But if we attribute to the Supreme Pontiff only the spiritual authority directly, and the temporal one indirectly, that is, only whenever spiritual matters are concerned, it does not follow that the Pontiff can remove or merge the political government, but it follows only that the Pontiff can direct and correct the political authority through his most eminent spiritual and apostolic authority, and that he can take away political government from one prince and give it to another if that is necessary to the spiritual end. And, to reply to the argument in the proper structure, when he says, "Either the Supreme Pontiff can in a certain way, that is either directly or indirectly, deprive kings and emperors of their kingdoms and empires and give those empires to others, or he cannot," I reply: "He can." When he infers: "If he can, then he is in some way greater than God, since he takes away what God gave," I deny the deduction; in fact God did not give a kingdom immediately to this or that king, but we say that the authority of kings comes from God because God wanted a political government among men, and He wanted this to be distinct from the ecclesiastical. Therefore, when the Supreme Pontiff transfers a kingdom from one king to another he does not take away what

71. The argument of the civil government as originating indirectly from God through men's consent is a key point of the neo-Thomist theories regarding the origin of temporal government and the relationship between temporal and spiritual rulers. See Skinner, *Foundations*, vol. 2, pp. 161ff.

God gave, but he orders and directs it. And just as God gives kingdoms to men through men's consent and deliberation, and He can, indeed usually does, change them and transfer them from one people to another through those men's consent and deliberation, He can also change and transfer them with a greater reason for the spiritual end through His general Vicar, whom He appointed in charge of His entire household. But, Barclay says, this Vicar does not have God's mandate, neither express nor tacit. But indeed he has the express mandate, even though such mandate is expressed in general terms: precisely because he is appointed as the shepherd of the whole flock and as the overseer of the entire household and as the head of the whole body of the Church in place of Christ, he is understood to have the mandate to rule and direct and correct all the sheep of the entire flock, all the servants who are in the household, and all the parts which are in the body. The emperors and kings are not excluded, unless they want to be excluded from the number of Christ's flock and Christ's servants and the parts of Christ's body.

2. Then Barclay alleges another argument, which I proposed against the opinion of those who attribute to the Supreme Pontiff temporal authority directly in all the kingdoms of the world, and he tries to twist this argument against my own and the other theologians' opinion on the indirect temporal authority, that is, for the sake of spiritual matters. Here is how he speaks: "But here we will adapt to our purpose by very good right another argument, by far the most effective, from the same book and chapter by Bellarmine which we reported before. If it is true that the Pope has the authority to dispose indirectly of all temporal matters of all Christians, either he has it by divine law or by human law. If he has it by divine law, it should be evident from Scriptures, or certainly from the apostles' tradition. But we have nothing from Scriptures, only that the keys of the heavenly kingdom were given to the Pontiff, and there is no mention of the keys of the kingdom on earth, and our adversaries find no apostles' tradition."

I say that the Supreme Pontiff has by divine law the authority to dispose of the temporal matters of Christians for the sake of the spiritual end. This is indeed evident from Scriptures. In fact, on the issue of the keys of the heavenly kingdom handed over to the apostle Peter and his successors

(Matthew 16), the keys of the earthly kingdom are indeed not meant and no mention is made of them in the Gospel, for it was not necessary that the supreme Prince of the Church be at the same time the temporal monarch of this world. What is meant is the authority to dispose of temporal matters to the extent to which those matters assist in opening the heavenly kingdom for the faithful, or they impede and hinder the opening of the heavenly kingdom for the faithful.

3. "But," says Barclay, "if they say that there is no need to confirm this authority by either God's express word or the apostles' tradition, since only indirectly and from a sort of connection this authority belongs to the Pope, as a kind of inseparable addition and appendix of his spiritual authority by which he is placed as the supreme shepherd of souls over all the sheep of the Christian flock, we still beg from them some proof of this addition and connection from Scriptures or apostolic tradition."

I have said already that the authority of which we speak is found expressly in Scriptures, but in general and not specifically, for example, in Matthew 16, "And I will give unto thee the keys";[72] and John 21, "Feed my sheep."[73] And from these divine testimonies is gathered, as has been explained more than once, that specific addition and connection of the authority to dispose of temporal matters for the sake of spiritual matters. And it is not true what Barclay adds, that such great authority has been passed over in the Church for so many centuries in deep silence both by Christ and by the apostles and their successors. In fact, it is clearly shown by Christ in the above-mentioned passages, and it is also indicated by the apostle in 1 Corinthians 6, when he says: "Know ye not that we shall judge angels? how much more things that pertain to this life?"[74] and this matter is demonstrated by the successors of the apostles Peter and Paul, that is, the Roman Pontiffs, in their deposing kings and emperors from the year of our Lord 700, for before then either necessity or opportunity was lacking.

4. Barclay again objects: "If either authority can be separated from the other, that is, both the spiritual from the temporal and conversely, we will

72. Matthew 16:19.
73. John 21:15–17.
74. 1 Corinthians 6:3.

have to consider the sentence that establishes that what cannot be done directly cannot be done indirectly either. In fact, prudent men establish that when an action is prohibited directly, that action cannot be done even indirectly or consequently, unless the prohibited action follows necessarily something else that is by right permitted, so that the permitted action cannot be effected without the prohibited action, and unless (to speak with Jacques Cujas, book 5, section 'generaliter de donatione inter virum et uxorem') the case of both actions is so mixed that it would be impossible to separate the two. Hence it is concluded that he who cannot alienate something by himself cannot even give credit to a suit that has come over that thing—according to Nicholas de Tudeschis in his commentary on chapter 54 'Dudum,' title 'De electione,'[75] and chapter 'Cum pridem,' title 'De pactis'[76]—because certainly in this way he would alienate that thing obliquely and indirectly. Therefore, if the Pope, insofar as he is Pope, has no temporal jurisdiction directly over Christians, which they grant, by the above-mentioned sentence of the law, it appears to follow that he certainly cannot have it indirectly either. Thus, in order to persuade men of their opinion they must offer some testimony from Scripture or from apostolic tradition, or at least demonstrate that the temporal authority of which they speak is so conjoined with the spiritual one that it is impossible in any way to extract and separate one from the other, so that, I say, the spiritual cannot exist without the temporal. Since they could not do it, they have followed nothing but uncertain opinions and reasoning which do not seem to demonstrate satisfactorily what they assume."

I reply that on the issue of the conjunction and separation of ecclesias-

75. This is canon 54, title 6 "De electione," of the first book of Gregory's *Decretales*. This law was issued by Gregory IX, and it refers to the vacancy of the Church of Rouen, whose occupant already had other ecclesiastical benefices. The law reiterated that anyone having an ecclesiastical office involving pastoral care was prohibited from acquiring another such office without the pope's dispensation (text in *Corpus iuris canonici*, vol. 2, cols. 93–94).

76. This is canon 4, title 35 "De pactis," of the first book of Gregory IX's *Decretales*. The law was taken from a letter by Pope Alexander III to the bishops of Exeter and Worcester in which the pope took issue with their accepting money to solve a dispute in their churches. The pope decreed that when a disputed ecclesiastical benefice was settled by means of a financial agreement, the agreement was invalid (text in *Corpus iuris canonici*, vol. 2, cols. 204–5).

tical and political authority, there can be a double question: one, whether the ecclesiastical authority could exist without the temporal to the degree that there would not be any political prince in the Church and, conversely, whether we could find a political authority in some people where there would be no ecclesiastical prelate. In this sense we grant that those authorities can be found entirely separate. In fact, in the early times of the Church, the Church was on earth without any Christian temporal prince, and in those times there were and even now there are kingdoms of infidels where there is no ecclesiastical prelate.

The other question can be whether an ecclesiastical or spiritual authority could exist that does not have attached in any way the authority to dispose of temporal matters for the sake of spiritual matters. In this sense we deny that a supreme ecclesiastical or spiritual authority that has no temporal authority attached in some way, that is, for the sake of spiritual matters, can exist. In fact even in times in which there were no temporal princes in the Church, the ecclesiastical Prince was able to command the faithful to support with temporal goods those who administered sacraments and also to command the faithful to sort out among themselves their civil suits and not to visit the tribunals of the infidels for these matters. Both of these the apostle teaches in 1 Corinthians 6 and 9. Also, the Church was able to oppose an infidel prince if he tried to divert the faithful from the worship of the true God, as St. Thomas teaches in 2a 2ae, question 10, article 10. Last, in those times the use of that authority over princes was lacking because there was no prince, but the authority itself was not lacking: the authority, in fact, is one thing; the use of that authority quite another. Therefore, Barclay's foundation of the separation of those authorities completely collapses, and as this falls, the entire edifice of his arguments falls. In fact, what he presents from civil and canon law does not hinder the argument, for we do not grant that the spiritual power can be entirely separated from the temporal, and we know for a fact the opposite, both from the testimony of Scripture and from the praxis of the Church. Barclay, however, assumes as a certain and granted proposition that we lack the testimony of Scripture and that those authorities cannot be joined in any way, which none of us grant; indeed we even contend it is false. Besides, it happens that when in the Church there are temporal princes, as after the first two or three hundred years there always were, then the ecclesiastical and political authorities are conjoined with a yet stricter bond, since the political prince is subject to the spiritual prince as the son is to the father and the limb to the body. Indeed the political and spiritual commonwealths form one Church, not two; and the head of that one Church is the Vicar of Christ and the successor of Peter. Therefore, if Barclay's arguments could have some value for the princes who never accepted the Christian faith, which nevertheless we do not admit, certainly they have absolutely no value for Christian princes or for those who have become Christian at some point. But on this issue more must be said at the appropriate place.

# Why in the first seven hundred years the Supreme Pontiffs did not depose heretical or apostate kings

In his sixth chapter Barclay produces an argument that supposedly cannot be refuted: there was neither use, nor example, nor any mention of such a papal authority in the Church for around a thousand years, when many Christian princes were abusing their kingdoms and empires impiously, cruelly, perversely, and with great detriment to the Church. Then he presents a reply to this argument, one which Franciscus Romulus gave to the same argument twenty years ago in his *Responsio ad Apologiam quae falso Catholica inscribitur*.[77] Barclay struggles to rebut that reply in the whole chapter and the following ones until the twelfth, in an extremely verbose and most distasteful manner and with much clamor, so that in these six chapters he chose to behave not like a jurist or a disputing theologian, but as an orator in a tragedy. Therefore, now I will insert Franciscus Romulus's entire response as Barclay reports it, and then I will respond to the individual points of Barclay's confutation. This is how Franciscus Romulus speaks in chapter 8: "But now regarding what our adversary objects to in

77. This pamphlet, whose complete title was *Responsio ad praecipua capita Apologiae quae falso Catholica inscribitur pro successione Henrici Navarreni in Francorum regno*, was actually written by Bellarmine under the pseudonym Franciscus Romulus. Bellarmine was rebutting Pierre de Belloy's *Apologie Catholique* (1585), in which Belloy had attacked the excommunication of Henri of Navarre on the basis of a Gallican-based theory of the divine right of kings. See J. H. M. Salmon, "Catholic Resistance Theory, Ultramontanism and the Royalist Response, 1580–1620," Burns and Goldie, eds., *Cambridge History of Political Thought*, pp. 219–53, at pp. 233–41.

the fourth place on the custom of our ancestors, who tolerated many heretical princes such as Constantius II, Valens, and the Arians Anastasius, Eutychianus, Heraclius Monothelitha, and others, it does not help the argument, for the Church must not use its authority in a temerarious and inappropriate manner. Indeed, it often happens that certain kings have such a great strength mixed with impiety and cruelty that an ecclesiastical censure is not useful for restraining them and greatly hurts the Catholic peoples, against whom the princes who have been angered rage even more. What advantage could have come to the Church, I ask, if it had attempted to excommunicate and deprive of their throne the Ostrogoth kings in Italy, or the Visigoth kings in Spain, or the Vandals in Africa, even if the Church could have done it by the best right? The same has to be understood about Constantius, Valens, and the others whom we mentioned earlier. Such were those times that bishops had to be prepared to undergo martyrdom rather than to restrain those princes. And when the Church saw that some room for maneuver for its authority opened up either with spiritual advantage for those princes or at least without any harm and disaster for the peoples, it did not desert this task, as the examples named earlier demonstrate. In this way the Church ordered that Leo the Isaurian be deprived of part of his empire, and Henry IV of the whole empire, and Childeric of the kingdom of France; and in fact one after the other Leo lost part of his empire, Henry IV the entirety of his, and Childeric the kingdom of France. Likewise the Church did not tolerate those old emperors Constantius, Valens, and the rest (as our adversary imagines) because they had succeeded legitimately to the empire—otherwise it would have tolerated also Leo and Henry and Childeric, who had succeeded to the empire no less legitimately—but because it could not restrain them without detriment to the people, while it could do so with the others."

This response by Franciscus Romulus must be protected from Barclay's attacks, both because it is immensely useful to our argument and because it is the response of a Catholic and erudite man, whose book I have seen long ago printed not in Rome, as Barclay makes up, but in France, and I do not remember which city.[78] Thus, Barclay first of all chose to censure

---

78. The first edition of the work was indeed published in Rome in 1586, then reprinted in Paris in 1587, and once again reprinted in Fani in 1591.

that part where it says: "Such were those times that bishops had to be prepared to undergo martyrdom rather than to restrain princes." Which words Barclay, in his modesty, says are false and founded in mere and extraordinary falsehoods, and then he adds that they seem to him unworthy of a Catholic, not to mention a theologian, to bring forth. Last he interprets those words in such an unfavorable light as to cry out: "What then? Do we happen to live in times in which bishops must be soldiers rather than martyrs? And defend the law of God and the Church with battles rather than preaching?" and then, after seizing the opportunity, in that whole chapter he raves madly with the most furious rage against the morality of bishops and cardinals.

As for us, we will briefly respond, leaving aside insults and slanders and overlooking his whole snarling eloquence. First, I say that what he assumes at the beginning of the chapter, that for around a thousand years neither use nor example nor any mention of such papal authority existed in the Church, is false. For certainly the examples of Gregory I, Gregory II, and Gregory IV, and also Zachary and Leo III, above mentioned, evidently show the contrary. Then I add that Franciscus Romulus did not divide his response into two parts, as Barclay makes up. His response is one and is simple; that is, in those times the Church was not able to use its authority: therefore it had to undergo martyrdom rather than reject the faith. Likewise even in these times, when either pagans, as in the islands of Japan, or heretics, as in Britain, prevail, many are drawn to martyrdom and in fact they accept martyrdom with the strongest will rather than allowing themselves to be brought to deny the faith. Finally I add that the appropriate time for martyrdom is when denying the faith can be avoided by neither escape nor just defense but by suffering only. Indeed, the Lord in the Gospel did not prohibit response to force with force on all occasions, and He not only allowed escape, but also in certain cases such as when either the need of the Church or a greater advantage required it, He ordered it by saying: "But when they persecute you in this city, flee ye into another" (Matthew 10),[79] and He ordered not to rush onto the swords of persecutors but to suffer with patience death inflicted for the profession of faith. Also, regarding the issue of escaping, the mandate of God and

79. Matthew 10:23.

the testimonies and examples of the holy prophets and apostles, which St. Athanasius brings forward in abundance in his *Apologia pro fuga sua,* are so clear that there is no doubt left for Catholics on this topic. Moreover, the wars of the Maccabees against Antiochus who strove to force the people of God to idolatry; the wars of the Catholics against the heretics in Africa in the time of St. Gregory, of which St. Gregory himself speaks in book 1, epistle 77 [75] to the Exarch Gennadius, where he praises Gennadius because he persecuted with arms the heretics with great zeal and incites and urges him to proceed with manly vigor; the wars of the Catholics against the Albigensian heretics and against Raymond of Toulouse, their patron, when with the help of divine grace Simon de Montfort, with a small band of soldiers, killed more than one hundred thousand in one battle, as Paulus Aemilius writes in book 6 of *Historiae Francorum;* the wars of our times of the Swiss Catholics against the Swiss Zwinglian heretics, all these show that the Church is allowed to respond to force with force and to repel by the law of war the persecutions of pagans and heretics, if there is strength. In fact, regarding the last case, as Johann Cochlaeus writes in *De actis Lutheri* of the year 1531, even if the Swiss who were fighting for the Catholic faith were inferior in number and strength, and superior only in the justice of their cause, they defeated the heretics gloriously in five battles. Moreover, when the Catholics started to be vexed by the Arian emperor Constantius, St. Athanasius and other Catholic bishops, fleeing to the orthodox Prince Constans, the emperor in the West, had threatening letters sent to Constantius, as we can see in *Historia tripartita,* book 4, chapter 25. Because of those letters the persecution stopped for a while, but soon after Constans's death and after Constantius II became emperor of the whole Roman world, since no one dared to resist him, there came a time when the bishops were obliged to get ready for martyrdom and not think about excommunicating and deposing the emperor. And this is the opinion of Franciscus Romulus, not that which Barclay attributes to him, as he would have it that once the bishops had to be martyrs, whereas now they have to be soldiers.

# Why the Church did not depose the heretic emperor Constantius and the apostate emperor Julian

In the seventh chapter Barclay attacks the last words of Franciscus Romulus: "Likewise the Church did not tolerate those old emperors Constantius II, Valens, and the rest (as our adversary imagines) because they had succeeded legitimately to the empire—otherwise it would have tolerated also Leo and Henry and Childeric, who had succeeded to the empire not less legitimately—but because it could not restrain them without detriment to the people, while it could do so with the others." And he marvels that Bellarmine in book 1 of *De Summo Pontifice*, chapter 7, wrote the very same thing. And so that he might marvel more, he should know that St. Thomas in 2a 2ae, question 12, article 2, to the first [objection], argued the same, where he says that the Church tolerated the faithful's obedience to Julian the Apostate because, being still new, it did not yet have the strength to restrain earthly princes. Therefore, Barclay thinks that the Church could have easily removed from their respective thrones both the Arian emperor Constantius II and the emperor Julian the Apostate if it had wanted to, but the Church did not do so because it knew that they had succeeded to the empire legitimately. These are his arguments. First, because in the time of Constantius II the whole world was Christian and the greater part of it orthodox: "I say it is absolutely false that the Church could not restrain the ancient rulers as easily as the more recent ones, not to say more easily, and without detriment for the people, whether the Church had wanted to try by force of arms or to use some trick and the work of a devout person. In fact, the entire world under Constantius II was already Christian (as is apparent from the letters of Constantine the Great to the Church, reported by Eusebius and Nicephorus), and the largest part of it was orthodox, so that the strength to overcome the emperor was not lacking in any way if they had thought that struggling by arms with a legitimate prince was right and pious."

I reply, first, it is not true that at the time of Constantius II the whole world was Christian, and in those epistles Constantine does not say this. If this were true, why would Symmachus, the prefect of Rome, have tried to persuade Emperor Valentinian to restore the sacred rites to the Roman tribes with a long oration (which can be found in St. Ambrose's epistles 29 [17] and 31 [18])? Why would St. John Chrysostom in his oration *De sancto Babyla* and Theodoretus in his books *De curandis Graecorum affectionibus* [*Graecarum affectionum curatio*] have disputed so much against the pagans of their time? Why would St. Augustine and Paulus Orosius have written against the accusations of the pagans, the former in the books *De civitate Dei,* the latter in a history of the slaughters that the Romans suffered before Christ's advent? Finally, there were the barbarians, with whom after Constantine's time the Romans were fighting continually in the east and the north: the Parthians, the Persians, the Sarmatians, the Goths—were they not for the most part pagan?

Then, even if this were true, nevertheless it cannot be rightly inferred that it was easy for the Church to restrain Constantius II or Julian. Those emperors were extremely powerful and commanded many armed legions, against which the unarmed multitude of the faithful could do nothing, especially since they did not have a Christian prince who was willing and able to arm them and lead them armed against these emperors. Certainly in our own time there are many Christians in the empire of the Turks, and maybe they number more than the Turks themselves; nevertheless, since they have neither commander nor weapons ready, they cannot do anything against the king of the Turks. This was the reason why neither the Italians nor the Africans nor the Gauls could shake off the yoke of the Goths, the Vandals, and the Franks, respectively. But it was easy for Pope Gregory to exclude Leo, the Greek emperor, from the empire of Italy, because his forces in Italy were weakened, and the noblemen in Italy desired especially this, that is, that the Pope would give them the opportunity to revolt against the impious emperor. For the same reason Pope Zachary was able to deprive Childeric, king of the Franks, of his kingdom without problems, because the Frankish noblemen wanted that and because the king, having transferred the authority of governing to the Magister of the Palace, was wallowing in laziness and idleness. Last, Pope Gregory did not declare that Emperor Henry had to be deposed until his most serious crimes, reported to the Pope by the voices of the people, demanded justice, as Marianus Scotus and other historians of his time show.

Barclay adds that in the time of Constantius II there were many monks, in Egypt, Libya, and other places in Asia and Europe, who were not less zealous than that monk who stabbed Henri III, king of the French,[80] and those monks could have easily removed Constantius II if it had been permitted.

I reply that it does not pertain to the monks or other clergymen to commit bloody acts, as we can see in causa 23, question 8, canons 1ff.;[81] and even less to kill kings by treacherous acts. Besides, the Supreme Pontiffs are not accustomed to restrain kings in this way. Their custom is first to reproach them in a fatherly way, then to deprive them of the sacraments through an ecclesiastical censure, and finally to absolve their subjects from their oath of allegiance and deprive them of their regal office and authority, if the matter requires it. The execution pertains to others. Wherefore Pope Innocent is reported to have said in the Council of Lyon, when he deprived Frederick II of the empire: "I have done what I had to; may God do and pursue this matter as He wishes." Matthew Paris reports this episode when talking about Henry III and relating the events of the year of our Lord 1245.

Then Barclay proceeds and contends that it was easy for the Church to remove Julian the Apostate and the Arian Valens, since their army was

80. Bellarmine is referring to Jacques Clément, a Dominican friar who in 1589 stabbed and killed Henri III, king of France.

81. Bellarmine is referring to the canons included in question 8, causa 23, of the second part of Gratian's *Decretum*. This question comprises a series of laws concerning the use of weapons and punishment, and many of those laws concerned the prohibition of clergymen from taking arms against their enemies (text in *Corpus iuris canonici*, vol. 1, cols. 953–65).

in large part composed of Catholics obedient to the bishops. Since the Church did not do this, it follows that either the Pontiffs of that time did not perform their duty or they believed that they were not permitted to depose princes, however heretical or apostate they might be.

My answer is that it was extremely difficult to depose Julian the Apostate, because he alone was the ruler of the empire, and it is not true that his whole army was Christian; in fact, Rufinus, book 2, chapter 1, writes that the whole army was infected with sacrileges and with idolatrous sacrifices. For example, as is written in *Historia tripartita,* book 7, chapter 1, Julian issued a law according to which all the soldiers should make sacrifices to idols or else they would be expelled from the army. The army was therefore full of pagans or of men who had deserted Christ. And this does not contradict what my adversary quotes from Ruffinus, Socrates, and Theodoretus, that when Jovian refused to accept the empire because, being a Christian, he did not want to be the emperor of pagans, the army had cried out with one voice, "We too are Christians." For that exclamation signified that many of them were Christian in their heart and vow, but not by manifest profession; otherwise Jovian would not have hurled the charge of paganism against them, nor would he have said that he did not want to be the emperor of pagans. Therefore, if there were Christians in Julian's army, they were hidden and were considered pagans because they were stained by their relationship with the impious. Regarding Valens, we could say exactly the same: that even though there were a few in his army who were Catholic, the majority, nevertheless, followed the errors of the prince. And there is no other reason why Valentinian, the Catholic emperor, tolerated his brother, the heretic Valens, but that it was not easy to remove him from the imperial throne without danger and a war with an uncertain outcome.

Finally, Barclay adds two testimonies from the Fathers, one from St. Gregory of Nazianzus, his first oration *In Julianum* [4], whose words are: "He was restrained by God's clemency and the Christians' tears, which were already abundant and were shed by many, since they had only this remedy against their persecutor." The other, from St. Augustine, in his treatise on Psalm 124, who speaks thus: "Julian was an infidel emperor; was he not an apostate, impious and idolatrous? The Christian soldiers served the infidel emperor, but when they came to the cause of Christ, they did not recognize any other emperor but the One Who was in heaven. When Julian wanted them to worship idols and to burn incense, they put God before the emperor; but when he ordered them to form a battle-line and to go against the enemies, they immediately complied: in fact they were distinguishing between the eternal Lord and the temporal lord, and yet they were subject to the temporal lord also on account of the eternal Lord."

I reply that St. Gregory says that no other remedy against Julian's persecution existed besides tears, since the Church had no strength with which it could oppose his tyranny. Indeed, for this reason they had to implore God's mercy with tears, because they could not expect any help from anything else. And Gregory did not deny that the political authority must be subject to the spiritual authority of the Pontiffs, since he left written in clear terms precisely this, in his oration *Ad populum pertimescentem,* for in that passage he speaks about a subjection *de facto,* not *de iure.* St. Augustine rightly says that the Christian soldiers served Julian, an infidel emperor, because at the beginning of his empire he tolerated Christians, and not only did he tolerate soldiers being Christians but also allowed the Catholic bishops, whom the Arian Constantius II had banished, to return to their sees, as Rufinus says in book 1, chapter 27. Afterward, though, as we quoted from the *Historia tripartita,* he obliged everybody either to offer sacrifices to the idols or to withdraw from the army. At that time Jovian and Valentinian preferred to cast away the sword belt rather than to offer sacrifices to idols, and for this reason God, who compensates a hundred-fold in this life, soon after in exchange for their sword belt gave both of them a regal crown. Therefore, Barclay interprets wrongly those words "when they came to the cause of Christ": he says in fact that the cause of the Church is the cause of Christ, and therefore if it was permitted to depose an apostate emperor, the Christian soldiers should have turned their weapons back against Julian himself, at the order of the Church. But St. Augustine shows how his previous words should be interpreted when he writes: "When Julian wanted them to worship idols, they put God before him," and thus St. Augustine calls this the cause of Christ; even if the cause of the Church is also the cause of Christ, nevertheless Christian soldiers were not bound to turn their weapons against their emperor, even if he was an apostate and a persecutor, before he was judged an enemy. The Church, on its part, thought that he should rather be tolerated than provoked, since it did not have enough strength to depose him, as St. Thomas responds to this very argument in 2a 2ae, question 12, article 2.

## CHAPTER 8

# Why the Church did not depose the Arian Valentinian the Younger

In chapter 8 Barclay demonstrates that the Church did not lack the strength with which to depose from the empire the heretical emperor Valentinian the Younger, but Franciscus Romulus, whose disputation Barclay took up in order to rebut it, made no mention whatsoever of this Valentinian because he knew that it was easy for St. Ambrose to overthrow him, especially because a most powerful Christian prince was already armed to restrain the heretical Valentinian and the entire city of Milan, and the soldiers themselves stood by Ambrose. Why then, you would ask, did St. Ambrose tolerate the heretical Valentinian? The reason is clear: because Valentinian was young, and he began to persecute the Church not by his own judgment but following his mother's authority. St. Ambrose in fact hoped that Valentinian could be easily persuaded to follow the faith and piety of his father Valentinian the Elder and his brother Gratian and his colleague Theodosius also, all Christian emperors, which shortly happened. Valentinian in fact came to his senses, and he started to honor St. Ambrose so much that there was no one he confided in or trusted more than Ambrose. Thereafter, in the end, the emperor considered Ambrose as a father, and whoever wants to read the oration of St. Ambrose himself that was pronounced at the funeral of Emperor Valentinian will realize that all these things are true. From this, then, we reply to Barclay's objection regarding Emperor Theodosius, who embraced Valentinian when he was fleeing to him and, after having banished Maximus, restored him to the empire.

Barclay says: "It is noteworthy that a heretic banished by a Catholic flees to another Catholic for help, and from him he is both reproached on account of his heresy and received kindly and reinstated in the empire out of respect for majesty; and because the Church did not praise rebellion for religion against the legitimate prince, Maximus is called neither the reformer of the empire nor the restorer of the Church, but a rebel and a tyrant."

I reply that Theodosius agreed to help Valentinian against Maximus for very good reasons, first because he guessed that once separated from his mother, it was easy to lead him to the Catholic faith, which, as we said, was done immediately; then because Theodosius had been called by Gratian, Valentinian's brother, to share the empire, therefore it was right not to abandon in so great danger the brother of his benefactor and a colleague in ruling the empire; and last because Maximus had usurped the empire and killed Gratian, the legitimate ruler, not so much because of religion, but because of his lust for power. Therefore Theodosius took arms not against a defender of the Catholic faith, but against a murderer of the emperor and an illegitimate usurper of the empire.

After having explained this, Barclay, jumping about as if he had gained the victory, says: "Since things are thus, I would wish now that our adversaries cease to impose their fiction on us, or at least I would wish that they say what they have based their argument on."

But what all the scholars and also the general councils have reported cannot be called "fiction." As to what we based our argument on, we have shown it more than once, and later we will show it more clearly.

Barclay adds: "It is certain that everybody in that time thought that no temporal authority in any way and for any reason belonged to either the bishop of Rome or the universal Church, but that regarding temporal punishments, those should be left to the judgment of God alone." And slightly later: "As a testimony of this I first bring Tertullian, who speaking of emperors in *Apologeticus* says that they realize that God is the only one in whose power alone they are, to whom alone they are inferiors, and after whom they are the first before all gods and all men. In the book *Ad Scapulam* Tertullian says that we honor the emperor in the way in which we are permitted to do and which is expedient for him, regarding him as the man next to God who from God has received all his power, and is inferior to God alone. This the emperor wants also; in fact, he is superior to everybody insofar as he is inferior to the true God alone."

It is false that it is certain that all the scholars of that time thought that no temporal authority over Christian princes in any way and for any reason belonged to either the bishop of Rome or the universal Church. In fact, the authors whom Barclay presents are very few and do not say what he affirms. Tertullian, who is quoted in the first place, speaks about pagan princes, who ruled the whole Roman Empire and had not yet placed their scepters under Christ. Therefore they could be said to be *de facto* inferior to God in the administration of temporal affairs. "But," Barclay says, "the law of Christ does not deprive anybody of his right, and therefore kings and emperors who become members of the Church do not lose anything of their temporal right." This is true; they do not lose anything and rather they gain many things, since even temporal kings become what before they were not. But they must not be offended if in order to gain the heavenly kingdom they need to submit to the Vicar of Christ, meaning that now they are not permitted to abuse their temporal authority for their own ends and other people's destruction.

In the second place Barclay brings up Ambrose, who in *Apologia David* speaks thus: "As long as David was king he was not restrained by any law, for kings are free from the bonds of crimes and they are not called to punishment by any law, for they are protected by their supreme authority [*imperii potestate*]."

Kings are exempt from political laws, both their own and those of their predecessors, because an equal does not have authority over an equal. However, they are not exempt from the laws of God and of the Church, and we see that this was the case from the examples of the kings from the Old Testament, as, for instance, David. For this reason, in fact, when King Uzziah wanted to burn incense in God's temple, which was a duty of the high priest, and did not desist after being reproached by the priests, immediately he was struck by leprosy and was obliged by the judgment of the priests to live separately and to relinquish the administration of the kingdom, as is said in book 2 of Paralipomena, chapter 26. Joseph, in *Antiquitates,* book 9, chapter 11 [10], adds that from that time Uzziah lived as an ordinary man and was consumed by a profound grief. In a very similar vein, when the Supreme Pontiff determines that a Christian prince is infected with the leprosy of heresy, he segregates the prince from his relations with other excellent men by the sentence of excommunication. Moreover, so that the prince may not infect others, the Pontiff absolves his subjects from their oath of allegiance and, if it is necessary, he orders them under the same pain of excommunication not to consider him as king and not to submit themselves to him as to their king.

Third, Barclay presents as a witness Gregory of Tours, who in book 5 of his *Historia Francorum,* chapter 18, addresses the king with these words: "If any one of us, O King, wants to transgress the limits of justice, he can be reproached by you, but if you do it, who will reproach you? We speak to you, but you listen only if you wish to, and if you do not listen, who will condemn you but He Who declared to be justice Himself?"

But Gregory speaks of the authority that kings have to reproach individual men but that individual men do not have to reproach kings. In fact, King Childeric had accused Praetextatus of Rouen of *laesa majestas*[82] at the Synod of Paris, in which Gregory was sitting, along with many others, and since Gregory knew that Praetextatus was innocent and was incriminated by false witnesses who had been set up, he did not want in any way to consent to Praetextatus's condemnation. Therefore the king, knowing that Gregory alone was resisting him, said to him: "O Bishop, you are bound to render justice to all, and behold, I cannot obtain justice from you! By contrast, I see that you are an accomplice to iniquity, and in you that proverb is fulfilled, that ravens do not peck out other ravens' eyes." Thus Gregory wanted to show that nobody can refuse to render justice to the king, since the king can oblige anybody to do so. By contrast, the king can refuse to render justice, since nobody can oblige him to do so. In order to demonstrate these points, Gregory then replied with the words above mentioned: "If any of us, O King, wants to transgress the limits, he can be reproached by you, but if you do it, who will reproach you?" And that this is the sense of these words is clear not only by the pre-

---

82. *Laesa majestas,* in French *lèse majesté* and in English literally "injured majesty," indicates a crime that violates the majesty of the sovereign.

ceding words but also from the result of that case: after the king had tried with various ways and treacheries to extort from the synod a sentence of condemnation against Praetextatus, and he had not succeeded, acting by force he threw Praetextatus in prison. When Praetextatus tried to escape, he was heavily beaten and sent into exile, as Gregory narrates in the same passage, and also Aimoinus in *Historia Francorum,* book 2 [3], chapter 26. And this was not the end of Queen Frédégonde's furor, for whose grace the king undertook all this. In fact, after Pretextatus had been reinstated in his see through King Gutrannus, he was killed by an assassin before the sacred altar in a plot by the queen, as the same Gregory testifies in book 8, chapter 31, and this Pretextatus started to be included among the holy martyrs. This is, thus, that authority that the kings have over bishops, that is, the authority, acting by force, to punish them unjustly, if they wish, and which the bishops do not have over kings, that is, the authority to force them to obey once they have been justly condemned, unless they be aided by another superior temporal authority.

In the fourth place Barclay offers the testimony of St. Gregory the Pope, who called himself servant of the emperor and said that the authority over all men had been given to the emperor from heaven. Of this testimony we have said enough in the third chapter, and it is not necessary to repeat those things.

Last he presents Otto of Freising in his epistle to Emperor Frederick, whose words are these: "The kings only, as they are above the laws and held to divine judgment, are not constrained by the laws of the world; hence this pertains to kings and prophets alike, 'Against thee only have I sinned,'"[83] and also: "While, according to the apostle, it is terrible for a mortal man to fall into the hands of the living God, for kings, however, who have nobody above them to be afraid of, it is even more terrible, for they can sin with less restraint than the rest."

I reply that Otto of Freising clearly speaks of the laws of the world, to which without a doubt kings are not subject by coactive subjection. Indeed, not only in the quoted words do we find "not constrained by the laws of the world," but also slightly before Otto speaks thus: "Besides,

83. Psalm 51:4.

since we cannot find any mortal person who is not subject to the laws of the world and who, being subject of the laws, is not constrained by them, kings only, as they are above the laws . . . etc." But, Barclay adds, "In Otto's opinion kings have nobody to be afraid of above them but God; therefore they are free not only from the laws of the world but also from the laws of the Church, at least insofar as temporal punishment is concerned; otherwise they would have the Supreme Pontiff above them to be afraid of, and not God alone. Besides, in the opinion of the same Otto, kings are held to God's judgment only and therefore they are not subject to the Pope at least in temporal matters."

My answer is that Otto, a Catholic and pious bishop, did not mean to say that kings are not bound by the laws of the Pontiff or that they do not have the Vicar of Christ above them to be afraid of, or that they are not subject to the judgment of the Supreme Pontiff at least in spiritual matters and insofar as spiritual punishments are concerned. Indeed, if that were what he wanted to say, he would be a heretic. Therefore, when he says that the kings are held to God's judgment only and that they do not have anybody above them to fear but God and are absolved from the laws since they are above the laws, it is necessary to add a qualification, either on the part of the laws or in regard to the punishment. Barclay gladly admits the qualification in regard to the punishment, but we say that this qualification must be understood in regard to the laws. We demonstrate this because, in Otto's words, that qualification in regard to the laws can be found when he says that the kings are not subject to the laws of the world and again that they are not restrained by the laws of the world; the qualification on the part of the punishment, that is, insofar as temporal punishment is concerned, cannot be read anywhere in his words.

Besides, Otto knew that King Childeric had been deposed by the Supreme Pontiff, and later Emperor Henry IV had been dismissed by Pope Gregory VII, and in fact he recalls both issues in his *Historia*, book 5, chapter 23, and book 6, chapters 34, 35, and 36, and he does not complain about what was done; rather he seems to approve it when he praises Gregory VII with these words (bk. 6, chap. 34): "Cast as a model for his flock, he demonstrated by example what he taught by word, and as a strong champion through everything he did not fear to set himself up as a bulwark for the House of God," and at chapter 36: "The Church, deprived of such a great Pastor who was especially zealous and influential among all priests and Roman Pontiffs, suffered not a small sorrow." Therefore the sense of Otto's words will be this, that kings are not restrained by the laws of the world, and, insofar as those laws are concerned, they are held to God's judgment only, and, insofar as those same laws are concerned, they have no one above them to be afraid of, but God only.

Because of these testimonies Barclay exults and says: "If those who support the opposite opinion could produce the testimonies of so many ancient Fathers, or even just one testimony, in which it is distinctly written that the Church or its head, the Supreme Pontiff, has that authority over secular kings and princes and can restrain them with temporal punishment in any way, that is, either directly or indirectly, and punish them by depriving them of their kingdom or of part of their kingdom, truly I will not refrain from admitting that this whole quarrel should be resolved in their favor without a challenge."

The authors quoted by Barclay did not write distinctly that Christian kings and princes cannot be restrained by temporal punishment by either the Church or its head, the Supreme Pontiff, either directly or indirectly, or punished by being deprived of their kingdom or part of their kingdom. If they had distinctly written this, we could oppose to Tertullian St. Cyprian (who refers to Tertullian), who in book 1, epistle 3 [55], commands that no commerce be held with heretics, which before St. Irenaeus, older than Tertullian, had taught in *Adversus haereses,* book 3, chapter 3, by saying: "The apostles and their disciples had so much fear that they did not nominally communicate with any of those who defiled the truth; just as Paul says, reject a heretic man after the first admonition." And the testimonies of all the Fathers can be adduced in support of this opinion. From those it clearly follows that a heretical king should not be tolerated by the Church, if possible, but should be excommunicated and that faithful people should be exempted from being obedient to him, meaning they should neither be compelled to serve the person whom they are ordered to reject, nor to have commerce with the person to whom they should not even speak.

We could oppose to St. Ambrose St. Gregory of Nazianzus, his equal, who in his oration *Ad populum timore perculsum et praesidem irascentem* compared the spiritual authority to the soul, and the temporal to the flesh, and taught that the temporal authority must be subject to the spiritual as the flesh is subject to the soul. And this is precisely the foundation of our opinion. To St. Gregory of Tours we could oppose St. Gregory of Rome, his contemporary, who, as we said before, in two privileges set down those words: "If any king or nobleman or judge or any secular person violates the decree of this apostolic authority or our orders, they should be deprived of their office." Finally to Otto of Freising we could oppose Gregory VII, who lived about a hundred years before, who openly writes that a king of the world can be deprived of his kingdom for certain reasons by the Apostolic See; see his epistle to the Bishop of Metz. We would also oppose St. Bernard and Hugh of St. Victor, who were highly reputed in Otto's time, whose testimonies we offered in the preface; besides, St. Thomas and St. Bonaventure, not much later than Otto, but far superior in doctrine and sanctity, who teach most clearly what Barclay demands; see their testimonies above-mentioned. Moreover, to five testimonies of ancient writers we would oppose more than seventy testimonies of authors from different times.

And finally, to five men called as witnesses by Barclay we would oppose ten councils out of which two were without a doubt general councils. And it is not that we should believe less in councils, especially general ones, because they were more recent. The Church is the same, and the authority of the councils is the same, no matter how old they are; and just as in the Council of Nicaea, three hundred years after our Lord's advent, the Church was allowed to officially interpret the Scriptures regarding the consubstantiality of the son, especially this: "I and the Father are one," in the same way the same Church after seven hundred years was allowed to interpret the Scriptures regarding the authority of the Supreme Pontiff, such as this: "Whatsoever thou shalt bind on earth shall be bound in heaven: and whatsoever thou shalt loose on earth shall be loosed in heaven." And if Barclay wanted to keep his promise on this, the whole quarrel would be finished without a challenge.

# Whether or not later princes could be deprived of their kingdom by the Church's authority without damage to the people; and also whether or not Gregory VII's sentence against the emperor Henry was lawful

In chapter 9 Barclay attempts to demonstrate that the other part of Franciscus Romulus's opinion, that the Church was able to deprive Childeric, Leo, and Henry of their kingdom or of part of their kingdom without damaging the people, is false. He proves that it is false because Pope Gregory VII deposed Henry IV not without damage to the people, since, as Otto of Freising attests, from that act wars, schisms, and many other things of this kind originated. But Franciscus Romulus did not talk only about Henry but also about Leo and Childeric. It is evident, in fact, that Emperor Leo the Isaurian was deprived of part of his kingdom without any damage to his people; and the same thing is most evident in the case of the deposition of King Childeric and of the elevation to the throne of Pippin. To these two examples Barclay has nothing to oppose and, therefore, covering these up in silence, he lingers on Henry's case only. And if we add the transferring of the empire from the Greeks to the Franks completed by Pope Leo III without damage to the people, the three examples that Franciscus Romulus wanted to offer are complete. However, because Barclay decided to reproach Franciscus Romulus for Henry's deposition only, as if either he did not know the history, or because he decided to lie for another reason, I reply that the Christian people received some damage from Henry's excommunication and deposition, but the advantages were greater than the damage, so that it can justly be said that the act was completed without damage to the people, for, indeed, he who wastes the grain that he scatters while sowing the furrows cannot be said to be suffering damage if at the time of the harvest he joyfully reports to have increased it. The holy and wise Pope Gregory saw that the provinces were full of concubines and simony, and he noticed that the emperors sold for their own gain the investitures of bishoprics and monasteries against the sacred canons and especially those of the eighth general synod. He put his mind to cleansing and liberating the Church, and notwithstanding the many difficulties and dangers, partly by himself and partly through his successors, he brought to a successful ending what he wanted. For he removed the concubines from the priests and succeeded in having the ecclesiastical benefices given and taken for free, and, in what was the most difficult thing of all, he regained the investitures of the churches when Henry V, the son of Henry IV, gave them back freely to Pope Callistus II. And Burchard of Ursperg in his chronicle reports that this was done not without manifest signs and prodigies from heaven.

But now I wish to discuss section by section what Barclay extracted from Otto of Freising and other authors against Gregory VII. First then, he mentions Otto's words in book 6, chapter 35: "I read and re-read the deeds of the Roman kings and emperors, and I cannot find any of them before him (Henry IV) who was excommunicated or deprived of his kingdom by the Pontiff; unless perhaps one thinks that it should be considered an anathema that Philip was placed for a brief period of time among the penitents by the bishop of Rome, or that Theodosius was excluded from the portals of the Church by Ambrose because of the cruel massacre he committed."

Certainly Otto was a man famous for his doctrine, morality, and nobility, but nevertheless reading and re-reading he did not find everything. In fact, Nicephorus in book 13, chapter 34, attests that Emperor Archadius was excommunicated by Pope Innocent I for having banished John Chrysostom; Nicephorus even reports the sentence of that excommunication word by word, and Gregory VII in his letter to the bishop of Metz reports the same excommunication. Greek and Latin historians attest that

Emperor Leo the Isaurian also was excommunicated and deprived of the revenues of Italy for his iconoclastic heresy by Gregory II and again by Gregory III, as we have shown before.

Then Barclay recalls, from the same Otto, the evils that befell the Church for the excommunication of Emperor Henry, that is, the wars, schism, the Pope's exile, the murder of King Rudolf, elected by Gregory, and other things of this kind, and after having listed those he cries out: "Is this restraining the prince without damaging the people?"

But when the apostles began to preach the Gospel of Christ in Jerusalem, a great persecution broke out in the Church: Stephen was stoned, Jacob was beheaded, Peter was thrown in prison, and the faithful were dispersed in various regions. When the same Gospel began to be preached among the pagans, the entire Roman Empire was stirred, grave persecutions began, temporal goods were pillaged, churches were set on fire, incredible massacres of saints were perpetrated over the world. So I ask: was the Gospel preached for the people's damage or for the people's salvation? If we consider the issue with the eyes of the flesh, it will appear that the Gospel produced not the salvation but the ruin of the people; but if we look at the same issue with the eye of the mind, cleansed by the light of faith, then it will clearly appear that idolatry was driven out of the world, the Church spread, the martyrs were crowned, and, finally, all that is good came to us through the Gospel. That is what the Church accomplished (as we said slightly earlier) when Pope Gregory punished Emperor Henry with excommunication.

Barclay proceeds, and he blames what Gregory did with these words: "It is possible that Gregory did it with good intentions (let God judge intentions), but it is not possible that he did it rightly, prudently, and according to the duties of his office; and in fact he even made a great mistake in terms of human custom and decision, for he attributed to himself what truly was not his, that is, the duty of deposing and removing the emperor and the authority of substituting another in his place," and later: "Then Pope Gregory appears to me gravely guilty in this matter."

Barclay voices bluntly enough his opinion on the Lord's Anointed and his and every Christian's Judge: he says, without even a tone of doubt or supposition or opinion, but in certain and absolute terms, as if he were speaking of a well-established and certain issue, that it is not possible that Gregory behaved rightly and prudently in that matter. But I demonstrate with these arguments that Barclay's opinion is false and reckless, not to say sacrilegious and blasphemous.

First, it is well known that Gregory's sentence was approved by all the bishops who sat with him in the Council of Rome. And who would believe that the Pontiff together with the whole Council produced a sentence as unjust and imprudent as Barclay says? Then, all Gregory's successors confirmed his decision: Victor III, Urban II, Paschal II, Gelasius II, and Callistus II, in whose time peace was made between the clergy and the kingdom, and nevertheless they all saw the wars and schisms occasioned by Pope Gregory's sentence. This is a most certain argument, that the sentence produced by Gregory was just and prudent, since so many most prudent and just Pontiffs, with the collaboration of the bishops' councils and despite the persecution of the schismatics, undertook to defend and confirm that sentence.

Regarding Victor III, who was Pope very soon after Gregory, there is the testimony of Leo Ostiensis in *Chronicum Cassinense,* book 3, chapter 71, who says that Victor had called the Council of Benevento and there he confirmed Gregory's sentence on the investiture with this conclusion: "If any emperor, king, duke, prince, nobleman, or any other secular ruler dares to confer a bishopric or any other ecclesiastical office, he should know that he is bound by the bond of this sentence."

Regarding Urban II, the immediate successor of Victor III, Bernold of Constance, a historian of that time, writes that in the Synod of Benevento, in the year of our Lord 1091, Urban confirmed the sentence of excommunication against the Anti-Pope Wibert of Ravenna and all his accomplices—among whom the leader was Emperor Henry. Also in the year 1095 the same sentence was confirmed by Urban in the Synod of Piacenza, in front of an innumerable multitude, and in the same year the same sentence was confirmed in the General Council of Claremont.

Regarding Paschal II, Urban II's immediate successor, Burchard of Ursperg attests that in 1102, at the General Council of Rome, Gregory VII's sentence was confirmed by Paschal, and Henry and all his followers were excommunicated. The same abbot Burchard of Ursperg adds that he was present in Rome and he heard on Maundy Thursday from the mouth of the Pope himself when Henry was declared excommunicated.

On Gelasius II, the immediate successor of Paschal, the same Burchard attests that in the year 1118 he confirmed Paschal's decree on Emperor Henry's excommunication through Conon, bishop cardinal of Praenestina, his legate in the Council of Cologne and in the Second Council of Fritzlar.

On Callistus II, Gelasius's immediate successor, Burchard of Ursperg in *Chronicum*, also the Abbot Suger in *Vita Ludovici Regis Francorum*, and also Roger of Hoveden in *Annales Anglicani* attest that Callistus in the Council of Reims, composed of four hundred Fathers, confirmed the decrees issued in the councils by his predecessors, that is, by Gregory, Victor, Urban, Paschal, and Gelasius.

Third, Gregory VII's judgment was approved by all the good people who lived then and who could know much better the justice or injustice of that cause than Barclay, who lived more than five hundred years after that. Marianus Scotus, who was Gregory's contemporary, in his *Chronicon* for the year 1075 says: "Gregory, having heard the just laments and cries of the Catholics against Henry and the enormity of his crimes, inflamed by the zeal of God, declared the above-mentioned king excommunicated, chiefly because of simony, and this act pleased the Catholic men and without a doubt displeased the simonists and the king's followers." Here Marianus does not talk about one or two people but in general about the Catholic multitude approving what the Pontiff had done.

Lambert of Hersfeld, who lived in the same period, in *Historia rerum Germanicarum* [*Germanorum res praeclare . . . olim gestae*] says: "Hildebrand's constancy and his invincible will against greed ruled out any indication of human deceit," and below: "The signs and prodigies that rather frequently happened through the prayers of Pope Gregory and his very fervent zeal for God and for the laws of the Church strengthened him against the poisonous tongues of his detractors." This was said by Lambert, who disconcerted not only the detractors of his own time but also the detractor Barclay. And Gregory would not have been so dear to God, and through him God would not have accomplished so many miracles, if he had issued a sentence so unjust and imprudent and if he had been the cause of so many evils as Barclay says. The same Lambert reports there of the horrible death of William, bishop of Utrecht, who opposed Gregory as Barclay later did: "Suddenly seized by a most grave sickness, with a miserable wail in front of everybody, he said that by the just judgment of God he had lost the present and the eternal life, since he had made much effort for the king for all the things that wrongly he wanted, and for hope of gaining his favor knowingly and on purpose he piled grave insults on an innocent man, a most holy Roman Pontiff and a man full of apostolic virtues." St. Anselm of Canterbury, who lived in the same time, at the beginning of his book *De fermentato et azymo ad Waleramum* said: "I say few words to a wise man. If I were certain that Your Prudence did not support the successor of Julius Caesar, Nero, and Julian, against the Successor and Vicar of the Apostle Peter, very gladly I would address you as a dear friend and as a reverend bishop." This is what was written by St. Anselm, who compares Emperor Henry with Julius Caesar, the oppressor of the commonwealth; with Nero, persecutor of the Church; and with Julian the Apostate and the persecutor; and he did not even dare to salute Bishop Walram, who he thought supported Henry against Gregory, which certainly he would not do if he believed that Gregory's sentence against the emperor was unjust. The same Anselm, in his epistle 8 [56] to William, defends Gregory's sentence and openly declares that it was just. St. Anselm, bishop of Lucca, an author of the same period and a most holy man famous for his miracles, wrote an epistle to the Anti-Pope Wibert of Ravenna, whom Henry the emperor had opposed to Pope Gregory, in which he praised Gregory magnificently. He also wrote an *Apologeticus* [*Contra Guibertum*] for Gregory against that Wibert, in which, among other things, he refutes the argument that Barclay now uses and then the Anti-Pope and his accomplices used, that is, that Gregory was the cause of turmoil and bloodshed especially in Saxony, whose blood he said was crying against Gregory and his supporters. One of those supporters was St. Anselm of Lucca, who then speaks thus in book 1 of his *Apologeticus* [*Contra Guibertum*]: "The blood of Saxony does not cry against us but against you along with the entire world, which shuddered at the filth of your crime. The heaven cries; the earth cries; every Church of the just, both the one that is still in this earthly pilgrimage and the one that already reigns with Christ, cries; Christ cries; the Father cries for the spouse of His Son; the Holy Spirit cries Who every day prays for her with inenarrable laments, etc." Here he says most correctly that the turmoil and wars must not be attributed to Gregory, who for his pastoral duty tried to protect his flock from the wolves, but to the disobedience and the obstinacy of those who raged as ferociously against the shepherd and the flock as they should have humbly obeyed God and His Vicar who were admonishing and advising them for their salvation.

Indeed, how horrendous and intolerable were Henry's crimes is seen from the following witnesses. St. Gebhard of Constance, who died three years after Gregory VII's death, that is, in the year 1088, while discussing with Wezilo, the archbishop of Mainz, declared openly that the emperor had been deprived both of his kingdom and of communion by a not unjust judgment with the apostolic sentence, and his opinion was so much approved by a certain council that Wezilo's contrary opinion was declared a heresy (see Burchard of Ursperg in *Chronicum* for the year 1085). Stephen of Halberstadt, from the same period, in his letter to Walram which Dodechinus, the continuator of Marianus Scotus, reports for the year of our Lord 1090, says: "Lord Henry, whom they call king, sells bishoprics and abbeys: indeed, he sold Constance, Bamberg, Mainz, and several others for money; Ratisbon, Augsburg, Strasburg, for military support; the Abbey of Fulda for adultery; the bishopric of Muenster (which is impious to mention and to hear mention of) for filthy acts of sodomy"; and below: "Excommunicated for those impious evils by the Apostolic See, he could not hold either the kingdom or any authority over us who are Catholics." Leo, bishop of Ostia, an author of the same time, in *Chronicum Cassinense* writes much on Gregory's justice, wisdom, zeal, and other virtues. But in book 3, chapter 53, he reports also a celestial vision by which God Himself is testified to have approved of what Gregory did and what now Barclay together with the old schismatics has dared to reproach. Somebody saw, then, a very white dove over Gregory who was celebrating Mass, and even if he who saw it was hesitant to reveal the vision, he was ordered from heaven to disclose it with these words: "Go quickly and announce this to the ears of the Pope, that he may finish what he began with the constancy and the strength of the Holy Spirit."

Bernold, an author of the same time, presbyter of Constance, in his *Chronicum* writes many things in support of the justice of Gregory's cause, but among other things he reports this on Imbricus, bishop of Augsburg: "Imbricus, bishop of Augsburg, who on the previous Easter day swore allegiance to King Rudolf, not worrying at all about committing perjury, supported Henry once he came to the throne. While celebrating mass for him on a certain day, the wretch imposed on himself this condition, that the sacred partaking of the sacrifice would turn against him if his lord Henry had usurped the kingdom for himself unjustly. After this reckless partaking of the sacrifice, for the short time in which he lived he never got out of bed healthy, and around the first of July he died deprived of the ecclesiastical communion."

These are seven authors who lived in the same period as Gregory, to whom I would add four more who lived not long after. William, bishop of Tyre, in book 1 of *De bello sacro,* chapter 13, speaking of the perverse morals of Emperor Henry said: "Our Lord the Pope, considering that this was done against any form of integrity, and carefully assessing that the laws of the Church were being disregarded for this reason, warned that emperor once, twice, and three times to desist from such a detestable obstinacy, and since he could not change him with his salutary precepts, he bound him with the chain of anathema."

Otto of Freising, as we noted before, acknowledged that Gregory was a most holy man, in book 6, chapters 34 and 36, and in book 7, chapter 1, and it is not possible that a man so holy pronounced publicly an unjust sentence and never withdrew it, which in fact he never did, as it is clear from those words which Otto reports in book 6, chapter 36, that Gregory, about to die, had pronounced: "I loved justice and hated iniquity, and for this reason I am dying in exile."

Dodechinus, Marianus Scotus's continuator, in his chronicle for the year 1106 says: "It is clearly evident that Henry was a perverse man and was ejected from the Church by a right judgment. In fact he sold everything spiritual." Also, for the years 1090 and 1093 he reports so many and such horrible crimes committed by Henry that it is surprising that anyone should affirm that he was condemned unjustly, which nevertheless Barclay boldly does.

Burchard of Ursperg in his chronicle for the year 1106 narrates the sudden death of Henry, as miserable for him as cheerful for all others, and he says: "It is a miserable thing to say that a man of such a great name, such a great dignity, and such a great courage, who had acquired so firmly the world under the profession of the Christian faith, like any poor dead man, did not deserve the pious and compassionate mourning of anybody among so many Christians, but rather with the news of his death he filled the hearts and mouths of all true Christians both here and everywhere simultaneously with an infinite joy, even excessive. Israel did not sing louder to God after the drowning of the pharaoh, and Rome did not salute with a more solemn celebration Augustus or any other emperor. The bit that was in the people's jaw was turned into a song, just like the voice of blessed solemnity." And this is Burchard, who certainly should be enough to silence Barclay's unjust talk. How is it, in fact, that Henry was oppressed by the unjust sentence of Gregory and no one was found in the entire Christian world who mourned his death? Indeed, no one was found who did not rejoice completely as Israel once did after the drowning of the pharaoh or as the Roman people did for their prince in triumph? No person was found in the whole world who perceived Henry's justice? No person who saw Gregory's injustice? But let us hear what the same writer says soon after: "This is the end, this is the ruin, this the final fate of Henry, called by his followers the fourth of the Roman emperors, but called correctly by the Catholics, that is, by all that keep by Christian law their faith and obedience to Peter and his successors, the arch-pirate as well as the arch-heretic as well as the apostate and the persecutor more of souls than of bodies, as somebody who, not satisfied with natural and usual crimes, was accused of having devised and put in practice new crimes, never heard of in previous centuries, and some of those incredible." But enough of those, for if I wanted to adduce later authors in support of Gregory's justice and sanctity, there would be no end. And the reader might see what we wrote in *De Summo Pontifice*, book 4, chapter 13.

Barclay proceeds, and he strives to prove that Henry should not have been excommunicated by Gregory, for a great number of people had participated in Henry's crime. As a proof he adduces the opinion of St. Augustine from book 3 of his *Contra epistolam Parmeniani*, chapter 2, which is reported in Gratian's decree 23, question 4, canon "Non potest."[84] The words of St. Augustine are these: "The reproach of one by many cannot be salutary unless the one reproached does not have a multitude associated with him. In fact, once the sickness infects many, there is nothing left to the good but sorrow and lament, so that the innocent ones should deserve to escape from ruin by the mark that was revealed to St. Ezekiel.[85] Otherwise, when they want to eradicate the tares, they will eradicate the wheat as well, and they will not clean the Lord's crop through diligence, but through temerity they will rather be numbered among those who need to be purged. For that reason the apostle, even if he had found many who were stained by lust and were filthy from their fornication, writing to the Corinthians in the second epistle, did not order the Corinthians to refrain from eating with the lustful and the fornicators. For they were many and he could not have said about them: 'If any man that is called a brother be a fornicator, or covetous, or an idolator, or a railer, or a drunkard, or an extortioner; with such an one no not to eat.'[86] Rather he said: 'And lest, when I come again, my God will humble me among you, and that I shall bewail many which have sinned already, and have not repented of the uncleanness and fornication and lasciviousness which they have committed.'[87] Therefore, he threatened that they should be punished by a divine punishment through his mourning rather than through the recommendation that the others abstain from association with them," and slightly below: "Truly if the contagion of sin invades the multitude, the severe mercy of divine discipline is necessary: in fact, suggestions of separations (that is, of [ex]communication)[88] are both vain and dangerous, and even sacrilegious, for they become both impious and arrogant, and they upset more the good, weak men than correct the evil, bold ones." Barclay adds: "Since this is the case, anybody, I think, out of the doctrine

84. This is canon 32, question 4, causa 23, of the second part of Gratian's *Decretum*, and it comes from book 3 of Augustine's *Contra epistolam Parmeniani* (text in *Corpus iuris canonici*, vol. 1, col. 914).

85. Cf. Ezekiel 9:4.

86. 1 Corinthians 5:11.

87. 2 Corinthians 12:21.

88. The words in parentheses are Barclay's addition, and they cannot be found in Augustine's text.

of St. Augustine, which is the doctrine of the Church, will see clearly that regarding the actions of Gregory against Henry, the Pope made a grave mistake, etc."

Barclay's temerity has no limits! In fact, on the basis of one passage from Augustine, which Barclay did not even understand correctly, Barclay presumes to say that the Pope made a grave mistake, and he dares to condemn a sentence issued in a council by the Supreme Pontiff and confirmed by many other Popes and councils. We, however, will show that it was not the Pope who made a mistake in his judgment, but rather Barclay who made a mistake in his understanding of this issue.

First, St. Augustine speaks of punishment, or excommunication, of one who has many accomplices in his crime, as is obvious from these words "when truly that sickness infects many, etc.," and from these: "therefore the apostle, even if he had found many who were stained by lust and were filthy from their fornication, etc." But Gregory excommunicated Henry for the crimes that he alone had committed, that is, because he sold bishoprics and abbeys and he did not want to come to his senses once he was admonished. Therefore that passage quoted from St. Augustine or from Gratian does not help the argument.

Second, St. Augustine speaks against Parmenianus and other Donatists, who had separated themselves from the universal Church and were saying that they alone were the Church without stains and spots. Therefore, St. Augustine teaches that because of the multitude of the sinners, a separation should not be made, since a mixture of good and evil people will always exist until the end of the world. Then, in fact (as Matthew 13 says) "The angels shall come forth and sever the wicked from among the just."[89] And this is the reason why St. Augustine said that suggestions of such separation are not only vain and dangerous but also sacrilegious and arrogant, for whoever makes such a separation takes on himself the duty of God, Who alone can separate all the good from all the wicked, which will happen in the last day. And in the meantime it is necessary that the good fishes are in the same net as the bad fishes, and the grain in the same place as the chaff, and the tares in the same field as the wheat. Again, Gregory

89. Matthew 13:49.

did not undertake anything like that; he wanted only to punish with an ecclesiastical censure a man who was publicly guilty of many and intolerable crimes.

Third, what the Lord says in Matthew 13, "Let both grow together until the harvest,"[90] does not mean that one should not clean out the tares by excommunicating those who cannot be corrected, nor does it prohibit killing evildoers, burning heretics, and prosecuting thieves and other people destructive to the Church or the commonwealth. If the Lord had wanted to issue such a prohibition, in fact, David would have gravely sinned when he says in Psalm 100: "I will early destroy all the wicked of the land."[91] Also, all the princes who every day hang bandits and thieves and highway robbers, with the intention of eliminating as many as possible with more and more diligence and with more and more painful punishments, would sin. Moreover, Pope Innocent III, who, along with the Lateran Council, excommunicated all the heretics fully knowing how many there were, would have also sinned. Indeed, the Catholic princes who overcame and exterminated almost completely countless Albigensian heretics would also have sinned. Therefore, when God says, "Let them both grow together until the harvest," He is not so much giving an order as anticipating what the future will be. He meant, in fact, that good men would always be with wicked men, and no matter how much effort they put forth, men would never be able to separate all the good from all the wicked, which is also the meaning of Isaiah 6: "Hear ye indeed, but understand not; and see ye indeed, but perceive not. Make the heart of this people fat, and make their ears heavy, and shut their eyes,"[92] which the Lord explains in Matthew 13: "By hearing ye shall hear and shall not understand; and seeing ye shall see and shall not perceive: for this people's heart is waxed gross."[93] And also the apostle, quoting that passage from Isaiah, says in Acts 28: "Hearing ye shall hear and shall not understand; and seeing ye shall see and not perceive: for the heart of this people is waxed gross."[94] Therefore, those

---

90. Matthew 13:30.
91. In the King James Bible this is Psalm 101:8.
92. Isaiah 6:9–10.
93. Matthew 13:14–15.
94. Acts 28:26–27.

words of Isaiah "Hear ye indeed, but understand not" mean this, "You will hear, but you will not understand," and those words "The heart of this people is waxed gross" mean "The heart of this people will be waxed gross," or, as St. John explains at chapter 12, "He hath blinded their eyes and hardened their heart."[95] In this manner St. Augustine in his explanation of the Psalms teaches that all the evil imprecations that are expressed as an imperative, as "Pour out thy wrath upon the heathen,"[96] and others like this, are predictions rather than imprecations. Similar expressions are found in the Gospel, such as John 2: "Destroy this temple,"[97] that is, "You will destroy," or "I will permit you to destroy"; or Matthew 23: "Fill ye up then the measure of your fathers,"[98] that is, "You will fill," or "I will permit you to fill"; or John 13: "That thou doest, do quickly,"[99] that is, "What is going through your mind, to betray me, you will do it sooner than you think, with my permission." Likewise, then, "Let both grow together until the harvest" seems to mean this: you will let, or permit, whether you want it or not, both to grow until the harvest; in fact, with all your diligence you will never be able to accomplish separating the many wicked from the good until the day of judgment, for at that time I will send my angels who will separate the wicked from among the just.

Fourth, I say that I approve the opinion of those who say that in this parable the separation of the wicked, that is the heretics or other evildoers, is not prohibited absolutely, except when there is the danger that together with the tares the wheat also may be eradicated, that is, that the pious may be involved with the impious. In any other case it is allowed to eradicate the tares when there is no danger that the wheat may be eradicated; but there is still the risk that the wheat may be corrupted by being mixed with tares. This judgment, however, does not pertain to everybody, but only to the father of the household, or to him whom Christ appointed over His household. Therefore, it did not pertain to Barclay to judge whether Gregory VII had acted justly when he eradicated part of the tares by ex-

95. John 12:40.
96. Psalm 79:6.
97. John 2:19.
98. Matthew 23:32.
99. John 13:27.

communicating Henry; but it would pertain to the Supreme Pontiff to punish Barclay if he were still alive.

Last, Barclay adds some arguments from the history of Sigebert in order to prove that Pope Gregory made a grave mistake in what he did against Emperor Henry. "Pope Hildebrand, that is Gregory VII, Sigebert says in his chronicle for the year 1085, is dying while being exiled in Salerno, and about this I found it written: 'We want you, who are solicitous in the care of the Church, to know that our apostolic lord, Hildebrand, who is also known as Gregory, now about to die, called one of twelve cardinals, the one whom he liked much beyond the others, and confessed to God, and St. Peter and the whole Church, that he had sinned much in carrying out his pastoral duties, which had been entrusted to him as to the ruler of the Church, and with the Devil's temptation he had stirred up wrath and hatred among men. Then finally he sent this above-mentioned confessor to the emperor and to the whole Church to ask for indulgence for himself, because he was seeing the end of his life and he was quickly putting on the angelic garment [*angelica vestis*], and he dismissed and freed the emperor and all the Christian people, the living and the dead, the clergymen and the laymen, from the bond of all his bans and ordered his friends to leave the house of Deodoricus and the emperor's friends to enter.'"

But Sigebert, as John Trithemius testifies in his *Catalogus scriptorum,* was one of the followers of Emperor Henry and therefore he deserves no credit, and what he writes in this passage is without a doubt false, since he does not have and does not dare to indicate an authoritative source. We, on the other hand, have a very authoritative and most credible author who writes that Gregory, soon before dying, said: "I loved justice and I hated iniquity, and that is why I am dying in exile." These words are completely the opposite to those which Sigebert writes; in fact, in these words he says he acted justly, in the other words he says he sinned gravely. The words above-mentioned are in Otto of Freising, book 6, chapter 36. Bernold in his chronicle for the year 1085, and Leo Ostiensis in *Chronicum Cassinense,* book 3, chapter 64, both describe Gregory's death and show that he remained in that same constancy until his last breath and that he was famous for great miracles, both while he was alive and after he died. Besides, the confirmation of Gregory's sentence against Henry, which we have demonstrated above to have been issued by five of his successors, Victor III, Urban II, Paschal II, Gelasius II, and Callistus II, most clearly shows that what Sigebert wrote on Gregory's repentance is an invention. Finally, Sigebert's narrative contradicts and opposes itself. In fact, if Gregory had acknowledged that he had sinned gravely in his pastoral duties and had done what he did with the Devil's temptation, how is it that he affirmed so boldly that he should put on quickly the angelic garment? Certainly for a sin so grave he should have expected not the garment of the angels, but the heavy punishment of Purgatory and Hell.

# The opinion of Otto of Freising on Pope Gregory VII's sentence is discussed

In the tenth chapter Barclay carries on to no purpose. In fact, he returns to prove on the basis of Otto of Freising's authority that Pope Gregory was not allowed to deprive Emperor Henry from communion or the kingdom. And first, he repeats the parts from Otto, book 4 [6], chapter 35, that he had quoted before: "I read and re-read the deeds of the Roman kings and emperors, and I cannot find any of them before Emperor Henry who was excommunicated or deprived of his kingdom by the Pontiff." Then he adds, from *De gestis Friderici imperatoris,* book 1, chapter 1, that it seems a novelty to Otto of Freising that Emperor Henry had been struck with the sword of anathema by the Roman Pontiff. But we have replied to these points in the previous chapter, and we have shown clearly that they are not a novelty.

He adds, that Gregory's sentence had been unjust can be understood from what Otto of Freising writes in the same passage, that is, book 6, chapter 17, from Gregory's decree: "Among other evils it followed that a Pope was placed over a Pope, and a king over a king"; "By which words," Barclay says, "Otto shows that both actions were taken with the same right, or rather with the same injustice, because just as a Pope was placed over a Pope unjustly, so was a king set unjustly over a king."

Otto, however, while he indeed writes that the fact that a Pope was placed over a Pope, and a king over a king, was occasioned by Gregory's decree, does not say that both actions were taken with the same right or with the same injustice. In fact, he could not say it, for the legitimate authority of the head of the Church placed a king over a king, while the disobedience of a schismatic king placed a Pope over a Pope, and I do not know whether Barclay would be able to find one Catholic man who said or wrote that an emperor could lawfully depose a Pope and impose another. Very many Catholic authors, on the other hand, wrote that the Pope could excommunicate an emperor and depose him for right reasons, and many general councils, whose testimonies we referred to in the prolegomena of this book and some of which we have mentioned in the previous chapter, decreed it.

Then Otto details the evils born out of Henry's excommunication and disobedience, but he does not determine whether they were just or unjust, for there can be some evils that are just, as the evils coming from punishment, and such was Henry's deposition; and there can also be evils that are unjust, as the evils coming from guilt, and such was the creation of the Anti-Pope Wibert of Ravenna, managed and accomplished by the emperor.

Barclay proceeds, and he considers those words of Otto of Freising from the same book, chapter 36: "Since, therefore, the kingdom, separated from the Church in the person of its prince, was gravely hit, also the Church, deprived of such a great pastor, who was of peculiar zeal and authority among all the priests and the Roman Pontiffs, suffered not a small sorrow." "This," Barclay says, "does not sound like anything but a statement that because the empire was violated in the person of the prince, the Church was violated in the person of the Pontiff, or that because the kingdom was hit in the person of the prince, the Church was hit in the person of the Pontiff. Since in those issues he does not posit a distinction of justice or injustice, and since they cannot be both done justly, it follows that he thinks that both were done unjustly."

I answer: Barclay did not understand Otto's words. For Otto does not talk about Gregory's deposition from his pontificate in the same manner in which he talks about Henry's deposition from his empire. Rather, he says that the empire was hit in the person of the prince, for the prince was excommunicated and deposed, and that the Church was hit in the person of the Pontiff, because, having been taken away from mankind by death, he left a great sorrow in the Church. Therefore, Barclay does not reason correctly in writing that an injustice had occurred both by the empire being hit in the person of the prince and by the Church being hit in the person of the Pontiff. In fact, Henry was deposed from his empire by a sentence of the Church; and in this sentence justice and injustice could not both be present, and it is sufficiently clear that that sentence was most just. On the other hand, Gregory died of natural causes, and if injustice has a place in this, then we will have to call God unjust, which is a grave blasphemy. Gregory was not killed by Henry in the way in which Henry was deposed by Gregory, but, as we said, he died piously and religiously of natural causes. And natural death comes from God after Original Sin, and He himself gave that most just sentence: "Dust thou art, and unto dust shalt thou return" in Genesis 3,[100] and about God it is said that "The Lord killeth, and maketh alive" in 2 [1] Kings 2,[101] and in the Book of Wisdom 16: "You are the Lord who has power of life and death,"[102] and in Ecclesiasticus 11: "Life and death are from God."[103] And it cannot be said that Pope Gregory, from Otto's opinion, was killed by God as a punishment for the sin committed in deposing the emperor, for the same Otto says that Gregory was a man of peculiar zeal. But even if Gregory was killed by God as a punishment for the sin committed, nevertheless his death could not be defined as unjust, unless the injustice would be attributed to God.

Barclay goes on, and from book 1 of Otto's *De gestis Friderici,* chapter 6, strives to prove that the deposition of the emperor carried out by Gregory had been unjust, since Otto calls the desertion of the emperor by Rudolf, duke of Swabia, a "rebellion." However, Barclay says, we call it "rebellion" when an inferior abandons a superior, but the emperor would not have been a superior if he had been lawfully deposed. Therefore, in Otto's opinion he was not deposed lawfully. He proves the same from book 7 of *Historia,* chapter 8, where Otto calls Henry IV "emperor" even after his deposition.

I reply that not only he who abandons his legitimate prince, but also

100. Genesis 3:19.
101. 1 Samuel 2:6.
102. Book of Wisdom 16:13. This is one of the deutero-canonical books of the Old Testament in the Vulgate. It is not included in Protestant Bibles. The translation is mine.
103. Ecclesiasticus 11:14. This is another of the deutero-canonical books not included in the King James Bible. The translation is mine.

he who abandons a prince who reigns *de facto* and not *de iure,* is said to be rebelling. In the same manner not only whoever reigns *de iure* but also whoever reigns *de facto* is called a king. For even the sacred authors do not observe that specificity of the words, namely, that they should call somebody a king only if he reigns legitimately, and that they should say that somebody rebels only if he abandons a legitimate prince. For in 4 Kings 18[104] it is set down as praise of the most excellent King Hezekiah that he had rebelled against the king of the Assyrians, and there "rebellion" is used for the desertion of an illegitimate king. Also in the same book, chapter 9, Jehu, appointed king by order of God while King Joram was still alive, is said to have conspired against his lord and to have killed him, together with his progeny; and in this case "conspiracy," which is something greater than simple rebellion, is used in a positive sense, for he conspired against a king dethroned and condemned by God. Therefore, the Lord said to Jehu in 4 Kings 10: "Because thou hast done well in executing that which is right in mine eyes, and hast done unto the house of Ahab according to all that was in mine heart, thy children of the fourth generation shall sit on the throne of Israel."[105] So we do not consider it surprising that Otto calls a "rebellion" a defection from a king already removed, since we have the very same manner of speech in the divine Scriptures. We can say the same regarding the name of "king." In 2 Kings 15, when Absalom, David's son, after having expelled the father, started to reign in Jerusalem, he was not the legitimate king but truly a tyrant, and nevertheless David himself called him king when he said to Ittai the Gittite: "Wherefore goest thou also with us? Return to thy place, and abide with the king."[106] Likewise in 3 Kings 15, Zimri, after having killed the legitimate king, most unjustly usurped the title for himself, and yet Scripture says: "And Zimri went in and smote him, and killed him, in the twenty and seventh year of Asa king of Judah, and reigned in his stead. And it came to pass, when he began to reign, as soon as he sat on his throne, that he slew all the house of Baasha, etc."[107] And so that it may not seem like a great thing to Barclay that Otto

104. 2 Kings 18 in the King James Bible.
105. 2 Kings 10:30.
106. 2 Samuel 15:19.
107. These references come from 1 Kings 16:10–11.

should call Henry emperor even after his excommunication and deposition, he should know that the same name can be found in Burchard of Ursperg and other authors, indeed even in Leo Ostiensis himself, who was much devoted to Gregory VII. In fact, in his book 3 of *Chronicum Cassinense,* chapter 49, Henry is called "emperor" by Leo more than ten times, and as Leo relates, very often the abbot Desiderius, who succeeded to Gregory in the pontificate [as Pope Victor III], called Henry "emperor" after his removal from the throne, for no other reason than as a matter of fact, even if he did not rule legitimately.

Barclay proceeds and says: "There is another passage from the same author, *De gestis Friderici,* book 1, chapter 8, in which he more openly declares the same, that is, that the Pope with that excommunication and dethroning did not deprive Henry of any right to the kingdom. In fact, he narrated afterward that Berthold, Rudolf's son-in-law (whom, as it was said, the Pope appointed as king), after having killed his father-in-law usurped the dukedom of Swabia as if it had been given to him by his father-in-law. And on the other side Henry, deposed by the Pope's sentence, gave the same dukedom to a nobleman from Swabia by the name of Frederick, who forced Berthold to sign a peace treaty and to surrender the dukedom. He adds that this Berthold, even though in this matter he surrendered at the same time to imperial authority and to justice, nevertheless is reported to have been very powerful and strong. And behold how he, although not speaking directly, affirms that imperial authority and justice stand on the side of Henry, against whom the Pontiff had issued the sentence of deposition long before."

In this passage Barclay presents a suspicious witness, for Emperor Frederick I, who was Otto of Freising's nephew, was a descendant of this Frederick. Indeed, Otto was not only Emperor Frederick's uncle, but also Emperor Henry IV's grandson. Therefore Otto, in order not to hurt his maternal grandfather, Emperor Henry IV, and the son of his uterine brother, Emperor Frederick I, wrote that Berthold surrendered to imperial authority and to justice in the matter of the dukedom of Swabia. And this is the reason why Otto in his *Historia* makes a compromise: on the one hand, he magnificently praises Gregory VII in book 6, chapter 34, and indeed he could not have reproached a man of very famous sanctity with a clean conscience. On the other hand, he does not portray Henry, as other historians do, as the author of most impious and numerous crimes, but very mildly he notes his excesses and his lascivious life in book 7, chapter 11. What he says in this passage, that Berthold surrendered to imperial authority and justice, does not compel us to determine that Otto thought that Henry was unjustly deposed by Gregory, for, as Otto himself narrates, after a long controversy Frederick, with the help of the emperor, forced Berthold to sign a peace treaty according to which Berthold would keep Turgetum, a most noble city in Swabia, and Berthold would then leave the rest of Swabia to Frederick. Therefore, Berthold surrendered to imperial authority as to a superior to which he could not be equal, and he surrendered to justice because in a dubious situation he thought that it was just, having kept the title of duke and the most noble city, to leave the rest to the stronger. Indeed, if Berthold had thought that Swabia had been unjustly in his possession, he should have surrendered the whole dukedom without keeping either a specific part of it or the title of duke, but he indeed kept it and transferred it to his successors, as the same Otto testifies. And if Barclay wants to say that Otto thought that Henry was unjustly condemned by Gregory, then Otto will contradict himself, for in book 6 of *Historia,* chapter 34, he says that Gregory was a strong champion through everything, and he was not afraid to set himself up as a bulwark for the House of God, and at chapter 36 he says that it was appropriate for the emperor to be struck with the sword of anathema. Also, the same Otto mentions that Gregory before his death said: "I loved justice and I hated injustice," and that the Church suffered not a small sorrow in the death of such a pastor, who had a peculiar zeal and authority among all the Roman Pontiffs, and in book 7, chapter 1, he says that after Gregory, the Supreme Pontiff, of blessed memory, died in Salerno, etc. Those things, indeed, do not in any way fit in with the opinion of a most grave injustice, which the deposition of the emperor would have been if Gregory indeed had not been able to depose him justly, for this injustice alone would have stained without a doubt all the praises of Gregory.

Finally Barclay, since he had nothing else to present from Otto and since he could not remain silent, repeats what he said before, that kings, according to Otto's opinion, have no one to fear but God above them. He also repeats what he had complained of before in a most verbose way, the many evils that had invaded the world and especially the Church because of the excommunication of Emperor Henry. We have replied to all these before, and we do not enjoy repeating the same things in vain.

In the last section Barclay, in the middle of the argument, presents the words that Gregory VII, after deposing Henry, used to pray for the apostles Peter and Paul to confirm his sentence, issued by their authority, so that everybody would understand that the son of iniquity had lost the empire not accidentally, but by the apostles' action. Barclay says that that prayer was not heard by the apostles, "since nothing happened that was favorable to the Pontiff and to the pontifical authority and its supporters, while in the meantime Henry triumphed and kept his empire."

But that Gregory's prayer was indeed fully heard is proved by the most heavy afflictions from heaven that oppressed Henry. First, forsaken by a great part of Germany, he was forced to throw himself at the Pontiff's feet to ask for mercy with most humble prayers. Then, Henry fought a long and uncertain battle with two rivals, Rudolf and Hermann. Later, after being imprisoned by his own son, he was forced to relinquish the crown, the scepter, and all the imperial emblems. After escaping from prison he settled in Laeodium, from which place he spoke of his incredible suffering in the letters that can be found in the work of Burchard of Ursperg. Finally, seized by sudden death, he found nobody to mourn him, whereas, on the contrary, the whole world exulted most gladly because of his unhappy end, as we have reported above from Burchard of Ursperg. This is, then, Henry's triumph, which Barclay fabricates! Moreover, that the Pope's side proceeded to a better and better position with the help of God, which manifested itself through signs and miracles, and eventually prevailed, is well known from what all the historians narrate about Callistus II and Henry V, and especially Burchard of Ursperg in his chronicle for the year 1120 and those following.

# On the comparison between
# Julius II and Clement VIII[108]

In chapter 11 Barclay repeats many of the things he had already said, and he does not add anything that it seems to me should be refuted with a new response but one thing, that is, when he exalts with real praise Pope Clement VIII, but not so much to praise him as to attack Julius II through a comparison with the other. He says: "Who would not judge Clement VIII's paternal piety joined with very great prudence, with which he labors to bring back to, and keep in, harmony Christian kings and princes, more useful to the infinite parts of the Church than the armored Julius's martial furors with which he struggled impiously and inhumanely to set Italy, France, Germany, Spain, and the other Christian peoples one against the other with hostile intentions?"

In order to respond to this, I want to warn the reader that the Roman Pontiffs, who are at the same time also temporal princes of a not negligible empire, by their office are no less obliged than the other princes to conserve what the Apostolic See or the Roman Church has. The other supreme kings and princes can and should wage wars for the protection of their kingdoms or other possessions, and if they have to enter into a

108. Julius II, Giuliano della Rovere (1443–1513), was an active pope both politically and militarily, participating both in the League of Cambrai against the Republic of Venice in 1509 and in the Holy League against France in 1511, as well as actually fighting in some of the battles. Clement VIII, Ippolito Aldobrandini (1536–1605), is mentioned by Barclay in this context as the pope who in 1595 absolved Henri IV of France from the excommunication pronounced against him by Sixtus V, thus legitimizing his accession to the throne of France.

league with other princes to defend them, they can justly undertake an agreement with the princes their allies and push back the enemy with joint forces when they have a just cause to wage war. In the same manner, also the Roman Pontiffs, who are temporal princes, with every right can and should protect with arms the peoples entrusted to them, and if the situation requires, wage war against the enemies and call other princes for help or to form a coalition in the war.[109] And Julius II was not the first to have waged war to reclaim the provinces of the Roman Church or to have undertaken an agreement with great princes. In fact, Pius II long before had an army and waged a glorious war against his enemies, as Nauclerus and Platina report. Before the time of Pius II, Innocent VI, a man famous for his prudence and the integrity of his life, most successfully recovered militarily the ecclesiastical dominion occupied by different tyrants through his legate Cardinal Albornoz, as the same Nauclerus and Platina and many other historians write. Clement IV, who was Pope many years before Innocent VI and was considered a holy Pontiff, called from France Charles d'Anjou, brother of St. Louis, king of the French, to eject, with arms, the tyrant Manfred from the kingdom of Naples, which was a fief of the Roman Church, and he appointed Charles himself as king after having imposed an annual payment of forty thousand golden *nummi*[110] in recognition of the fief. Those same authors and others whom they quote testify to this.

But before these times Pope Leo IX, famous not only for the integrity of his life but also for his divine miracles, and indeed also numbered among the saints, fought in person in the army against the Normans to recover the city of Benevento, as Hermann Contractus in his chronicle, and Leo Ostiensis in *Chronicum Cassinense*, book 2, chapter 88, attest. There happened that memorable event, that when the Pope was defeated and made captive by the Normans, the victors behaved with such a sub-

---

109. On the implications of the double status of the pope as both universal spiritual leader of Christianity and temporal ruler "of a not negligible empire" (as Bellarmine puts it), see Prodi, *The Papal Prince*.

110. The *nummus* was technically the name of a coin issued in late antiquity, but by the early Middle Ages the term was used as a synonym of "coin." The approximate value of the payment imposed by the Pope on Charles was ten thousand ounces of gold.

mission and a reverence toward the defeated man that the captive seemed to rule and dominate the victors. Further on, Leo IV, who was Pope more than two hundred years before Leo IX, a man most holy and famous for his miracles, as Anastasius attests in his biography, led an army against the Saracens who, having landed in Ostia Tiberina with a great fleet, wanted to seize and plunder the city of Rome. After starting with a prayer to God and bestowing the apostolic benediction on the army, Leo IV obtained a memorable victory. I omit the alliance of Zachary, Stephen II, Adrian, Leo III, and other Pontiffs with the kings of the Franks for the recovery and the protection of provinces and cities that belonged to the Roman Church against the Lombards and the Greeks. I also omit the very strong Maccabees, who were both high priests and princes and who waged great wars to defend their homeland. Last, I omit Moses, a most wise pontiff and prince, who did not hesitate to fight in arms against the Amorites and other agitators of his people.

Julius II, therefore, imitating those most famous and holy men, and emulating their virtue and diligence, partly with his own army and partly with the help of the kings, his allies, recovered with great effort the possessions of the Church, which were almost all lost. And whoever wants to blame this effort will necessarily have to blame also the effort and the virtue of the other holy Pontiffs, and also the military virtue of the Maccabees and of Moses himself. And Clement VIII cannot be excluded from this number, for just as he strove to bring back peace among the Christian princes, as Barclay says, in the same way he did not neglect to prepare an army when he had to recover Ferrara.[111] In fact, he lacked the occasion, not the will, to wage war for the Church's possession, since God, in Whose hands the hearts of the princes are, wished for that most noble city to go back to the Church before the soldiers' swords were drawn. But Barclay did not ignore the praise received by Clement for this: he wanted to conceal it so as to reproach Julius more freely.

---

111. Ferrara was recovered by Pope Clement VIII through the intercession of Henri IV, king of France, in 1598.

## CHAPTER 12

The arguments against the theologians'
opinion on the authority of the Supreme
Pontiff in temporal matters are refuted

In chapter 12 Barclay tries to affirm and demonstrate further his thesis that
the Supreme Pontiff has no authority in temporal matters over kings and
other Christian princes.

His first argument is that the entire Christian antiquity always thought
that kings were inferior to God alone. This argument was advanced before,
in chapter 8, where also we abundantly replied. It is one of this author's
habits that he repeats and imposes the same arguments very often. I do
not know whether he does this to enlarge his book or to obtain by relentlessness the approval that he cannot obtain by the force of his reasoning.
Leaving aside this first argument, then, let us hear the second.

2. He says: "What about this: the Popes themselves say that the kings
have no superior in temporal matters, as for example in the chapter 'Per
venerabilem.' It cannot be true at the same time that they have and do not
have a superior. Therefore, it is false that they have no superior in temporal matters, if another can legitimately take away from them their
temporal rights and give them to somebody else."

I reply that the Pope's sentence in that chapter is that kings are supreme
temporal princes, and thus they have no temporal prince above them, in
the same manner in which the dukes and other inferior princes in the
same kingdom have the king as their superior in temporal matters. On
this, Ecclesiastes, chapter 5, speaks such: "For he that is higher than the

highest regardeth; and there be higher than they,"[112] and St. Peter in the first epistle, chapter 2, says: "Submit yourselves to every ordinance of man for the Lord's sake: whether it be to the king, as supreme, or unto governors, as unto them that are sent by him."[113] Thus likewise it is that the king has no other king or temporal prince over him; otherwise he would not be the supreme king in regard to temporal or political sovereignty. And perhaps this is the same reason why Innocent himself in that chapter "Per venerabilem," slightly above, said: "Several princes do not recognize as their superior anybody but the Roman Pontiff," and later he added that exception, as he said: "The king of Franks does not recognize anybody superior in temporal matters," by which we understand that the discussion regarded temporal superiors. In fact, the king does not recognize any temporal prince above him, but he recognizes as such the Supreme Pontiff, a spiritual prince, who can judge of temporal matters insofar as they relate to spiritual matters. Barclay says: "It cannot be true at the same time that they have and do not have a superior." I reply: that they have and that they do not have a superior in the same matter cannot both be true at the same time, but when the matter is different, nothing prevents them both from being true. To have a red cloak and not to have a red cloak cannot both be true, but to have a red cloak and not to have a black cloak can both be simultaneously true. Likewise, therefore, that the king has a temporal superior in temporal matters and that the king does not have a temporal superior in temporal matters cannot both be true, but that the king has a spiritual superior in temporal matters, and that he does not have a temporal superior in temporal matters, can be simultaneously, and indeed are, most true.

3. But Barclay keeps pushing: "Regarding the distinction that they make in the expressions 'directly' and 'indirectly,' such distinction does not pertain to the faculty of making judgments and to the effect of the judgment, but only to the manner and origin of the acquisition of such an authority. In fact, the canonists say that the Pope received temporal authority over the whole world directly from Christ. Those others, however, deny that he

112. Ecclesiastes 5:8.
113. 1 Peter 2:13–14.

received such authority directly, in itself, so to speak, simply and without any other consideration, but only indirectly, that is, as a consequence and by reason of his spiritual authority, which he directly received from God. But this distinction in these definitions must be referred to the origin and the manner of acquisition of the temporal authority, not to its strength and effect." This is Barclay, who is willing to admit that the Pontiff in the theologians' opinion has temporal authority over kings indirectly and is their judge in temporal matters, which seems to contradict Innocent, when he, in the above-mentioned chapter, says that kings have no superior in temporal matters.

But a distinction is needed to understand whether Barclay infers rightly or wrongly that the Pontiff has temporal authority over kings and is their judge in temporal matters. The authority to dispose of temporal matters, whether the authority itself is spiritual or temporal, rightly implies that the Pontiff has temporal authority over kings. But if by temporal authority one understands an authority that is in itself of a temporal nature, like the authority of the kings and of other political princes, then it does not rightly follow from the theologians' opinion that the Pontiff has temporal authority over kings, as the theologians attribute to the Supreme Pontiff temporal and spiritual authority only in the realm of the Church, and this authority Innocent in the chapter "Per venerabilem" calls plenitude of authority in St. Peter's patrimony. On the other hand, they attribute to the Pope in the other Christian territories and over kings only a spiritual authority, which properly and in itself involves spiritual matters and involves temporal ones as they are subordinated to the spiritual. Therefore, when we speak properly we say that the Pontiff has authority in temporal matters, but that he has no temporal authority insofar as he is Pope. From this it follows that the verbal distinction between "directly" and "indirectly" does not refer, properly speaking, to the manner of acquisition of the authority, as Barclay falsely affirms, but to the explanation of the secondary and consequent object of the supreme spiritual authority, which, as we said before, concerns primarily and directly spiritual matters and secondarily and indirectly, that is, insofar as they concern spiritual matters, the temporal matters. This opinion of the theologians in no way contradicts Innocent's words in the chapter "Per venerabilem," as is clear from what we said.

4. Thereafter, Barclay adds this argument: "But if the opinion of my adversaries is correct, not only will Christian kings and princes be vassals and clients of the Pope in temporal matters, but also (which is baser) they will hold their kingdoms and sovereignty almost as a favor from him. I show that this is the case easily from the principles of my adversaries: the Supreme Pontiff can take away the kingdom from one king and give it to another, if this is necessary for the salvation of souls. Judging and deciding whether this is in fact necessary pertains to the Pontiff himself, and nobody can judge whether his judgment be right or wrong. Therefore, whenever he likes he will be able to deprive anybody of his kingdom and give it to another."

But Christian kings and other princes, apart from those who are vassals of the Church, should not be called clients of the Supreme Pontiff as Barclay wanted to do in order to ignite hatred against the Church, and even less do they hold their kingdoms and sovereignty as a favor from him. Rather, they are true kings and true princes, so much more noble and successful than the pagan kings and princes because not only do they reign on earth during their life, but they also move on to the eternal and heavenly kingdom, if they reign justly and piously. Indeed, Barclay's argument is defective in all its parts, for that proposition, that the Supreme Pontiff can take away a kingdom from somebody and give it to somebody else if it is necessary for the salvation of souls, needs an explication, for it can be both correctly and incorrectly understood and both true and false. Certainly the Pontiff can, if it is necessary for the salvation of souls, take away the kingdom from somebody but only if he has admonished that person before, if he has given the person the time to come back to his senses, if he has seen that the person was dangerous and incorrigible. He can also give the kingdom to somebody else, but not to anyone he arbitrarily decides on, for in this way, truly, kings would reign as by a favor, but he must give it to the person who is rightly entitled to it, because of succession or of election. And if perhaps nobody is entitled to the kingdom, this must be given to the one whom reason should indicate. In this way, in fact, Innocent IV at the Council of Lyon, after having deposed the emperor Frederick, left the free election of the successor to the princes-electors, to whom it pertained by law. In this way also Gregory VII, after Henry's deposition, confirmed Rudolf, who was elected by the princes. Also in this way Zachary assigned the kingdom of the Franks to Pippin, because he was actually the administrator of the kingdom and the noblemen demanded him. Also Leo III transferred the Western Empire from the Greeks to the Franks because they were the strongest in the West, and they alone could perform that office and the Roman people favored them very much. In the same way also in the Old Testament the Pontiff Jehoiada, after he ordered the killing of Queen Athaliah, who had usurped the kingdom, conferred it on the son of the dead king, who was entitled to it by hereditary law (see 4 Kings 11),[114] and the Pontiff Azariah, when King Uzziah was removed from the community because of leprosy that had stricken him from heaven, did not leave the administration of the kingdom to whomever he wanted, but to him who was entitled to it, that is, the son of the king (2 Paralipomena 26).[115] Therefore, that proposition by Barclay, if it is incorrectly understood, is false, and if it is correctly understood does not prove that kings reign by favor. Indeed, that assumption, "Judging and deciding whether this is in fact necessary pertains to the Pontiff himself, as no one can judge whether his judgment be right or wrong," is similar to Barclay's other proposition; that is, incorrectly explained it is false, and correctly explained it is certainly true, but from this we cannot infer that the kingdoms given by the Supreme Pontiff are held by favor, which is Barclay's conclusion. Certainly, judging whether depriving a king of his kingdom is necessary for the salvation of souls pertains to the Pope, but it does not pertain to him to make up necessities to cover up his wishes or to follow his greed under pretext of necessity. And because this is a most serious issue and the necessity must be manifest and certain, the Pontiffs ordinarily do this in episcopal synods or in consistories of the cardinals of the Holy Roman Church, after having explained their reasons and with the consent of the Fathers, as we showed before.

114. 2 Kings 11.
115. 2 Chronicles 26.

5. Barclay continues, and after elaborating on and repeating the previous argument with many words, as is his habit, adds these words: "But every authority and every power and jurisdiction is acquired by human or divine law, and whoever acquires or holds something, if he does not have it by either human or divine law, he holds it unjustly, as most clearly Augustine discusses against the Donatists in treatise 6 *Ad capitulum I Joannis,* canon 'Quo iure,' distinction 8.[116] Therefore, it cannot be that the Pope exercises justly any temporal authority over secular kings and princes unless it is clear that such an authority is attributed to him either by natural law or by divine law."

I reply that the authority over Christian princes and kings, not properly a temporal authority, but one that extends to temporal matters, is attributed to the Supreme Pontiff as the Vicar of Christ by divine law. From that which Barclay himself deduces, that the most ample spiritual authority by divine law pertains to the Roman Pontiff over all kings and princes, we gather that by the same divine law an authority that extends to temporal matters belongs to the Roman Pontiff, because the order of a superior over an inferior authority, that is, spiritual and temporal authority, requires it. But, our adversary says, we cannot find any passage in either divine or human laws granting him this authority. I reply: indeed, passages can be found in divine law that attribute to him this authority, and passages can be found in human law that explain the passages of divine law. This is what is written in Matthew 16: "And I will give unto thee the keys,"[117] and in John 21: "Feed my sheep";[118] and we find this explained in many councils, especially in the Council of Rome under Gregory VII, the Lateran Council under Innocent III, and the Council of Lyon under Innocent IV, in the sense that the power to bind and to loose and to feed and to rule the universal Church extends not only to spiritual matters but also to temporal ones for the sake of spiritual matters, which

116. This is canon 1, distinction 8, of the first part of Gratian's *Decretum,* which declares that "*iure divino* everything is common to everybody, but *iure constitutionis* one thing is mine, another is yours" (text in *Corpus iuris canonici,* vol. 1, cols. 12–13).

117. Matthew 16:19.

118. John 21:17.

also the common opinion of Catholic scholars and praxis and experience confirm.

6. "But," Barclay says, "The kings' power and authority is openly commended and approved by many testimonies of the sacred Scriptures, when it is said, 'By me kings reign,' 'Power is given by the Lord to you,' 'The kings of the Gentiles exercise lordship over them,' 'The king's heart is in the hand of the Lord,' 'I gave thee a king in mine anger,' 'My son, fear thou the Lord and the king,' 'Honour the king,'[119] and many other passages similar to these."

My reply is that the first passage does not demonstrate that authority is given by God to the kings, but that wisdom is necessary for kings to rule as they should. Those are words of wisdom, which exhort kings to the pursuit of wisdom if they want to reign truly and judge correctly when issuing laws. The second passage certainly says that the regal authority comes from God, but it says this so that the kings do not become arrogant but understand that they have God above them by whom they will be severely punished if they abuse their authority. The third passage does not attribute authority but reproach for the abuse of authority; for pagan kings, who lack true knowledge of God, unsatisfied by the regal administration, very often try to dominate their peoples as if these were slaves, and they transform a legitimate power into a tyrannical one, and from kings they become tyrants, the abuse of which authority the Greek word κατακυριεύσιν, meaning "violent dominion," more clearly shows. The fourth passage shows the authority of God over kings, not the authority given by God to kings, for such is God's omnipotence that it holds not only the bodies but also the hearts of kings and moves them back and forth as it wishes. The fifth passage does not commend regal authority but warns that God will permit his people, because of their sins, to fall under an unjust and cruel king who will not so much rule as devour them. The sixth and seventh passages teach the fear of the people toward the king, not the authority of the king over the people. But whatever these passages may be about, as we do not deny that regal power comes from God, so

119. Proverbs 8:15, Wisdom 6:4 (my translation), Luke 22:25, Proverbs 21:1, Hosea 13:11, Proverbs 24:21, 1 Peter 2:17.

it must not be denied that apostolic authority comes from God; indeed, every authority comes from God, as the apostle says in Romans 13: "There is no power but of God."[120] About the question of whether regal authority is subject to apostolic authority, or whether it is subject to this only in spiritual matters and not also in temporal, there is nothing in these passages, either open or hidden, and this issue is not explored.

Last, Barclay brings forth an argument that more than once he has brought forth before: "Finally, seeing that this temporal authority and jurisdiction of the Pope of which we speak is not included in Scripture with explicit words of God; is not received from apostolic tradition by hand, as it were; is not observed in the custom and habit of the Church or held by any Pontiff for all these thousand years and more; is not praised by the ancient Fathers of the Church and indeed we cannot find any of them who approved or even mentioned it, what necessity, for heaven's sake, obliges us to accept it or by what authority can they persuade us?"

I answer that many are the things from the word of God which we believe as explained by the Church, even if they are not explicitly contained in the word of God. We do not read explicitly in Scripture that the Son is consubstantial with the Father, but we believe it because the Church teaches that the words of God in John 10, "I and my Father are one,"[121] have to be understood in such a way. We do not read explicitly in Scripture that the Spirit proceeds from the Son, but we believe it because the Church teaches that the words of God in John 16: "He shall glorify me: for he shall receive of mine, and shall shew it unto you. All things that the Father hath are mine: therefore said I, that he shall take of mine and shall shew it unto you,"[122] have to be understood in such a way. We do not read explicitly in Scripture about infant baptism, but we believe in it because the Church teaches that those words in John 3, "Except a man be born of water and of the Spirit, etc.,"[123] and Matthew 19, "Suffer little children and forbid them not, to come unto me,"[124] have to be understood in such

120. Romans 13:1.
121. John 10:30.
122. John 16:14–15.
123. John 3:5.
124. Matthew 19:14.

a way. Likewise we do not read explicitly in Scripture that the authority of the Supreme Pontiff extends to temporal matters and especially to kingdoms and empires, but we believe it because the Church in general councils teaches that those words of God in Matthew 16, "And I will give unto thee the keys,"[125] have to be understood in such a way. Indeed, it is false that this authority was not used in the Church for all these thousand years and more. We have, in fact, already shown above that it was used after the year 700 during the times of Popes Gregory II and Zachary, and again after the year 800 during the times of Leo III and Gregory IV. It is also false that it was not praised or mentioned by the ancient Fathers, since it was mentioned rather obscurely by Gregory of Nazianzus and openly by Gregory of Rome, and afterward in later centuries it has been very openly praised and celebrated by all the authors, several of whom are included among the saints. What Barclay says in the last point, that our reasons are not demonstrations but dialectic syllogisms and therefore they do not constitute certain faith, we will in the following chapter explain what kind of argument this is and how much weight and significance it has.

125. Matthew 16:19.

# The first of Bellarmine's arguments in support of the authority of the Pontiff in temporal matters is defended

In chapter 13 Barclay attempts to refute the arguments that I adduced in book 5 of *De Summo Pontifice*, chapter 7, to prove the Supreme Pontiff's authority in temporal matters. And he says at the beginning that no one has gathered the reasons for this authority more diligently than Bellarmine and has proposed them more acutely than Bellarmine and has drawn his conclusions in a pithier and more precise manner than Bellarmine—evidently saying so in order to persuade readers that once he refutes Bellarmine, the whole discussion will be over. I must also mention at the beginning that I do not agree with what Barclay says about my diligence, acuteness, and precision. For I know that there are many who have dealt with this topic before me who are more learned and diligent and precise than I am, and I have tried to imitate their diligence and zeal in proportion to the weakness of my own mind, and therefore the peak of victory is not in refuting me, as Barclay tries to persuade his readers. Also, I thought that the reader should be warned that in demonstrating this issue I have adduced only reasons and examples, not Scriptures, councils, and Fathers, for I have dealt with those most abundantly in my former books, when I confirmed the spiritual primacy of the Supreme Pontiff. Because once this was confirmed and firmed up, I thought that it would be very easy to deduce from this, as from a spring, the rivers of reasons to demonstrate the authority in temporal matters.

My first argument, which Barclay reports verbatim, was this: civil authority is subject to spiritual authority when they are both part of the same Christian commonwealth, and therefore the spiritual prince can rule over the temporal princes and he can dispose of temporal matters for the sake of the spiritual good, as every superior can rule over his inferior. The fact that political authority, not only insofar as it is Christian but also insofar as it is political, is subject to ecclesiastical authority as such, is demonstrated first on the basis of their ends. In fact, the temporal end is subordinated to the spiritual, as is clear from the fact that temporal happiness is not absolutely the ultimate end, and therefore it has to be referred to spiritual happiness. Indeed, that the faculties are subordinated in the same way the ends are is clear from Aristotle's *Nicomachean Ethics,* book 1, chapter 1.[126] Second, kings and popes, clergymen and laymen, do not constitute two commonwealths but one, that is, one Church, as we are all one body, as we can see in Romans 12 and 1 Corinthians 12. In every body the parts are connected and dependent upon each other. Since it is not correct to claim that the spiritual parts depend on the temporal, then the temporal parts depend on and are subject to the spiritual. Third, if a temporal government hinders a spiritual good, by universal judgment the temporal prince is required to change that manner of government even at the expense of some temporal good, and therefore this is an indication that the temporal authority is subject to the spiritual.

This is my first argument, reported by Barclay accurately enough. And to this he replies that what I assumed, that civil authority is subject to spiritual authority when they are both part of the same Christian commonwealth, is false. And he tries to prove that it is false with these words: "These two authorities are parts of the Christian commonwealth in such a way that neither one rules over the other, and both fit together with mutual love since they both exist freely and in their own right. Each, then, recognizes and respects the other in its role and duty, and each exercises its own function at its own will, so there is indeed much harmony and agreement between them for the preservation of the Christian commonwealth."

126. On these arguments see chap. 2 of this book.

But in these words I see an affirmation, not a demonstration, that the political and the ecclesiastical authorities are joined in the same Christian Church by the bond of benevolence and not by the bond of subjection of the one to the other, which would be correctly affirmed if the political and the ecclesiastical authority were of the same order and almost constituted two separate commonwealths like the Swiss cantons. But on the basis of the divine Scriptures, Pontiffs and kings, clergymen and laymen reborn in Christ, form one commonwealth, indeed one city, indeed one household, indeed one body. And spiritual and temporal authority do not converge in the Church as two commonwealths converge in a federation, but as the spirit and the flesh converge in one man, as Gregory of Nazianzus taught clearly in his oration *Ad populum timore perculsum*. And it is certain that the spirit must rule over the flesh, not the other way around, and in the Church of Christ Pontiffs and kings are not like the chief rams in the sheepfold but rather like the shepherds and the sheep, and whether the shepherds should rule over the sheep or the sheep over the shepherds is not something that can be called into doubt.

Barclay adds: "The Church is sustained, strengthened, and thrives because of both authorities or, as Gilbert Génebrard put it, both magistracies; and in order to protect it and preserve it in good state 'each needs the other's friendly assistance,'[127] so that as long as they keep their unity, the Catholic commonwealth blossoms with innumerable gifts of harmony and peace. But when they dissolve their unity, the spiritual authority, despite being supported by divine virtue, since it is nevertheless weaker in the eyes of men and is deprived of corporal resources, is generally neglected; and the temporal authority, despite being powerful and strong, quickly falls to its own ruin through every crime and folly because it is deprived of the heavenly grace which it enjoyed because of its conjunction with the spiritual authority."

All these arguments, I say, contradict their author, not Bellarmine, for Bellarmine says that it is the optimal state when those two authorities concur and it is extremely dangerous when they fight with each other.

127. Horace, *Ars poetica*, v. 411 (my translation).

But from this it does not follow that one is not legitimately subject to the other. In fact, the optimal state in a man is when spirit and flesh concur, and it is dangerous if they do not, and often they do not when the flesh is reluctant to accept the dominion [*imperium*] of the spirit and the spirit tries to bring the flesh back to servitude. But nevertheless no wise man gathers from this discord that there should be no dominion of the spirit over the flesh, for most clearly the opposite is gathered. In fact, in the same way, from this discord of the two authorities, the spiritual and the political, many disadvantages arise in the same Christian commonwealth, and because the concord between the two is necessary, so it must be gathered that it was devised by the wisdom of Christ, the Founder of the Christian commonwealth, to subject one authority to the other, so that they might keep and foster peace and concord with one another more easily.

Barclay adds the testimony of Hosius of Cordova and of St. Bernard, but since we have replied more than once to Hosius's testimony, let us hear St. Bernard's words in *De consideratione,* book 1, chapter 5 [6]: "These most base and earthly things have their own judges, the kings and princes of the earth; why do you invade the boundaries of others? Why do you reach with your sickle into the crop of others?"

But St. Bernard himself makes his position clear when in the same passage he adds: "Not because you are unworthy, but because it is unworthy of you to insist on such matters, as you are busy with more important things. Finally, when necessity requires it, hear not what I think but what the apostle thinks. 'If the world shall be judged by you, are ye unworthy to judge the smallest matters?'"[128] However, it is one thing to deal with such matters occasionally and when there is an urgent reason, but it is another thing to deal with these matters as if they were great and worthy of such attention by such people." Here he demonstrates that the Supreme Pontiffs should be chiefly occupied with more important things and should leave these most base and earthly things to minor judges, that is, to the kings and princes of the earth. Just as the apostle said in 1 Corinthians 6: "If then ye have judgments of things pertaining to this life,

128. Here Bernard is referring to 1 Corinthians 6:2.

set them to judge who are least esteemed in the church,"[129] so St. Bernard in this passage called earthly matters "boundaries of others" and "crop of others," not because the Pontiff cannot involve himself in these earthly and base affairs but because he should not neglect more important matters. But Barclay does not quote these words prudently enough (not to say in a fraudulent way), because these words, if the passage is reported in its entirety, carry with them their own explanation.

He uses the same trick when adducing John Driedo from book 2 of *De libertate Christiana,* chapter 2: "Christ distinguished the duties of both authorities, so that one would preside over divine and spiritual matters and people, and the other over secular and lay," and below: "Look, you see clearly that Christ distinguished the duties of both authorities, and therefore the distinction between the ecclesiastical authority of the Pope and the secular and imperial authority is made by divine law."

I reply that John Driedo writes that those two authorities are distin guished, but he does not deny in this passage that one is subject to the other, that is, that the temporal authority is subject to the spiritual authority; indeed, he openly affirms this slightly below in the same passage, when he says: "Therefore the Pope and the emperor are in the Church not like two supreme governors, divided among themselves, so that neither one recognizes and respects the other as his superior, since in this way the kingdom so divided will go to ruin." These are Driedo's words, and that gloss by Barclay, that the emperor must recognize and respect the Pope as his superior in spiritual matters, and the Pope must do the same with the emperor in temporal matters, is not valid. In fact, John Driedo explained his opinion in book 1 of the same work, chapter 9, when he taught that insofar as the spiritual end is concerned, the temporal authority is subject to the spiritual, and in chapter 14 he taught that the Pope has the plenitude of power over all Christian kings and princes, and he can deprive them of their kingdom and he can completely exempt the Christian people from their obedience and subjection to them. Nowhere did he teach that the spiritual authority is subject to the temporal, or that the Pontiff can be deprived of the Papacy by the kings or that the people can be freed

129. 1 Corinthians 6:4.

from obedience and subjection to him. Barclay alleges an ancient gloss in canon "Adrianus," distinction 63,[130] that says "Just as one is the father of the other in spiritual matters, so the other is the father of the former in temporal matters." However, I was unable to find this gloss either in new or in old editions. Perhaps it was rejected like a crazy old lady, or it has long since left the world of the living because of very old age.

Finally Barclay adds Bellarmine's testimony, so as to pit Bellarmine against Bellarmine and to strike him down with a blow of his own sword. "Bellarmine in book 5 of *De Summo Pontifice,* chapter 3, says: 'Note that just as the sun and the moon are not the same star, and as the moon did not create the sun but God did, so the pontificate and the empire are not the same thing and one does not absolutely depend on the other.'" After having said these words, Barclay adds: "Certainly the sun and the moon are two great stars, which Pope Innocent in chapter 'Solitae' interprets allegorically as the two dignities, that is, the pontifical and the regal authorities, and compares the former to the sun and the latter to the moon. Hence in this way I argue that the moon is no less the moon or does not the less exist in itself when it gives way to the sun and, by turning, loses the light it borrowed from the sun, than when it is illuminated by the full circle and glow of its rays, and in neither case does the one depend on the other but both, holding the order and manner of their institution, serve God and the world; in this way also the regal or political authority, relying on its own strength, always exists in itself. Even if political authority receives a great source of light to live well and piously from the pontifical and spiritual authority, it is not changed, diminished, or augmented in any part of its οὐσία, or essence, by either its presence or its absence, and much less is the temporal authority subjected to the spiritual authority when the latter is present."

Comparisons, I reply, are not appropriate in all cases, but only in the matter for whose explanation they are introduced. Therefore, trying to make everything fit is to no purpose. Christ is called the Lamb of God because of His gentleness, and He is called a lion because of His strength,

---

130. This is canon 22, distinction 63, of the first part of Gratian's *Decretum,* and it concerns Pope Adrian's granting to Charlemagne the right and authority to elect the pontiff (text in *Corpus iuris canonici,* vol. 1, col. 241).

and He is called a stone because of His firmness, and a grapevine because of His fruitfulness. But one cannot attribute to Christ the stupidity of a sheep, or the cruelty of a lion, or the hardness of a stone, or the fragility of the grapevine. Therefore, Innocent III correctly compared the pontifical authority to the sun and the regal authority to the moon, because the former presides over spiritual matters, and the latter over temporal; the former is superior, the latter is inferior. And I noted not incorrectly that the Pontificate and the empire are as distinct as the sun and the moon, and both come from God, and that the empire does not absolutely depend on the Pontificate, since in fact the Roman Empire existed before the Christian Pontificate, and therefore it was not instituted by the Pontiff, and the Pontiff never took away the empire but only transferred it from one man to another, or from one people to another. We also grant to Barclay that the pontifical and regal authorities, like the sun and the moon, do not depend on one another as far as their essence is concerned. But we do not grant what Barclay declares in conclusion, that the moon is not subject to the sun. Indeed, the moon is subject to the sun because it receives its light from it; and the sun is not subject to the moon because it does not receive anything from it. And it is not just the moon that is subject to the sun, but all the other stars are too, because they receive light from the sun, and Cicero speaks correctly about the sun in his *Somnium Scipionis,* where he calls it the leader and the prince and the master of the other stars.[131] Therefore, just as the moon is subject to the sun, but the sun is not subject to the moon, so the king is subject to the Pope, but the Pope is not subject to the king.

---

131. Cicero's *Somnium Scipionis,* or *The Dream of Scipio,* is part of book 6 of Cicero's *De republica,* in which Scipio Africanus appears in a dream to his grandson, Publius Cornelius Scipio Aemilianus. The text was widely known and commented on from late antiquity through the Renaissance (among the numerous commentaries I will mention only the long one by Macrobius in the early fifth century and the influential commentary by the humanist scholar Luis Vives in the sixteenth century), and it was considered a philosophical reflection on the immortality of the soul, on the relation between microcosm and macrocosm, and on the nature of the divine; see Zetzel's edition of Cicero's *On the Commonwealth.*

# Bellarmine's confirmation of the
# first argument is defended

In chapter 14 Barclay examines the three arguments with which I demonstrated the assumption of the first argument, or the antecedent of the first enthymeme, to use the terminology of the Schools.[132] This was the first argument: the temporal end is subordinate to the spiritual end, but since faculties have to be subordinate as ends are, therefore the temporal faculty or authority is subordinate to the spiritual faculty or authority. Barclay replies to this argument with these words:

"I deny firmly that there is such an order or subordination of the ends of these authorities insofar as these authorities are as such. In fact, the end of the political or civil authority, insofar as it is a political authority, does not imply absolutely anything but temporal happiness, that is, the common good and an orderly tranquillity of life, as Bellarmine himself says in another place. The political authority, he says, has its princes, laws, courts, etc., and likewise the ecclesiastical one has its bishops, canons, courts. The former has temporal peace as its end, the latter eternal salvation." These are the words of Barclay, who later confirms the same thing from the apostle, 1 Timothy 2, who orders us to pray for the kings that we might lead a peaceful life in all godliness and honesty. He says the same out of Navarrus, who in his commentary on chapter "Novit," section 90, says that the end of the lay authority is a good, blessed, and peaceful life

132. The *enthymeme* is one of the two technical proofs, together with the example, of rhetoric, and as such it is the rhetorical counterpart to dialectic syllogism. Aristotle discusses it in his *Prior Analytics*, 2, sections 23–27, and throughout his *Rhetoric*.

for mortals, and this is the end of the laws emanated by it; but the end of the ecclesiastical authority is eternal and supernatural life, and this is the end of the laws emanated by it.

Barclay denies something most certain from the consent of all the scholars, and he cannot defend his paradoxes in any other manner but by denying boldly all the counterarguments. Nothing is better known among theologians and philosophers than that there is an order among efficient and final causes, and that the inferior are subordinate to the superior. Of course God is the first efficient cause of everything, and to Him the secondary or universal causes are subordinate, such as these inferior things are, and any one of these produces its own effects not without the action of Heaven and the cooperation of God, that is, of the first and highest cause. Therefore, in the same manner the absolutely ultimate end is God, and to Him all the other ends are referred and subordinated in order. The immediate end of political authority is the peace of the temporal commonwealth, but this peace is subordinate to the supernatural peace of man with God, and this is subordinate to the blessed peace in the heavenly Jerusalem, which is finally subordinate to the glory of God the Creator Who is the first principle and the last end of everything. And this is what the authors whom Barclay quotes teach. Bellarmine, who is mentioned in the first place, in book 5 of *De Summo Pontifice,* chapter 6, when he says that the end of political authority is temporal peace and the end of ecclesiastical authority is eternal salvation, slightly afterward adds these words: "When those authorities are conjoined, they form one body and therefore they must be connected, and the inferior must be subject and subordinate to the superior," and he justifies this argument in chapter 7: "since the end of temporal authority is subordinate to the end of spiritual authority." Also the holy apostle in 1 Timothy 2, whom Barclay quoted in the second place when he ordered prayers for the kings that we may lead a peaceful life, added, "in all godliness and honesty,"[133] in order to show that a tranquil life, which is the end of political authority, is subordinate to the godliness and honesty that is the end of spiritual authority, through which we reach the ultimate end, that is, eternal happiness.

133. 1 Timothy 2:2.

Finally Navarrus, whom Barclay brought up in the third place, in his commentary on chapter "Novit," section 90, writes that the end of temporal authority is a good and blessed life for mortals, while the end of spiritual authority is eternal life in Heaven. But the same author in the same place, section 97, demonstrates that the end of temporal authority is subordinate to the end of spiritual authority, when he teaches from St. Thomas's *De regimine principum,* book 3, chapter 12, that Christ's dominion is directed toward the salvation of the soul and to spiritual goods, but does not exclude temporal matters in the sense in which they refer to the spiritual. Consider, Navarrus says, those words, "in the sense in which they refer to the spiritual": in fact, this supreme paternal authority of the Pope is extended to those matters, that is, to temporal matters, just in this sense and not in any other. In the same passage Navarrus brings up another passage from St. Thomas, 2a 2ae, question 40, article 2, to the third [objection]: "All persons and arts and virtues to which an end pertains have to dispose of the things that exist for that end, but physical wars among the faithful people have to be referred to the spiritual divine good, of which clergymen are in charge, and therefore it pertains to the clergymen to carry on and to induce the others to fight just wars." Here St. Thomas teaches that physical wars refer to a spiritual good, as not an immediate but as a mediate end. In fact, the immediate end of a physical war is temporal victory and peace, but since this refers to a spiritual good, like all other temporal matters, therefore it is said that a physical war has a spiritual good as its end, that is, its mediate end. And for this reason carrying on just wars pertains in a certain way to clergymen, that is, to the ecclesiastical authority, whose immediate end is the spiritual good. The same St. Thomas has many similar passages on the subordination of the ends, as in 1a 2ae, question 1, article 4, and in book 3 of his *Summa contra Gentiles,* chapters 17ff.

Afterward Barclay attacks my second argument, which was the following: kings and Pontiffs, clergymen and laymen, do not form two commonwealths, but one, that is, one Church; we are indeed one body (Romans 12 and 1 Corinthians 12). And in every body the parts are connected and dependent upon one another. Since it is not correct to affirm that spiritual matters are dependent on the temporal, therefore temporal matters depend on and are subject to the spiritual.

Of this second argument Barclay speaks thus: "The second argument is so useless and misleading that nothing more absurd can be said, or nothing more false can be gathered, than that which is concluded: is there any old woman so silly as not to know that this deduction, that they are parts of the same body and therefore one depends on the other, has no value? In fact, a foot does not depend on the other foot, and an arm does not depend on the other arm, and a shoulder does not depend on the other shoulder, but on a third element."

Barclay forgot, when he wrote this, the things he had said slightly before, that nobody proposed argument more acutely than Bellarmine, and nobody made conclusions in a pithier and more precise manner than Bellarmine, since these statements do not fit well with the arguments most acutely proposed and most precisely concluded, which can be disproved with no effort by any silly old woman. But I pass over the lack of coherence of Barclay, who now raises Bellarmine up to the skies with praises, now brings him down to the abyss with insults. In fact, Bellarmine is not content with being judged by Barclay or by others like him, who are not legitimate judges, since we all will stand in front of the tribunal of Christ, and by Him we will be judged justly and truly and without any passion. Regarding what I said, that the parts of the body are connected and one depends on the other, I meant it regarding the parts of a different kind, such as the fingers, the hand, the arm, the shoulder, and the head; and not regarding parts of the same kind such as the two hands, the two feet, the two eyes, the two ears. For the political and ecclesiastical authority of which we were speaking are of a different kind, as is well known. Moreover, those words must be understood after considering the nature of the thing; otherwise there would not be a demonstration so certain as to be able to withstand objections. Therefore, the regal authority, which in its own kind is supreme, if it coexists in the same body with the pontifical authority, which also in its own kind is supreme, necessarily must be either below or above, lest in the same body there be two heads. And since it is sufficiently evident that the Pontiff is the head of the Church in the place of

Christ, clearly it follows that the king either must not be a part of the same body, or must be below the Pontiff. Likewise the political authority, which chiefly resides in the king, must be either subject to the spiritual, which chiefly resides in the Pontiff, or remain outside the Church, just as a finger that does not depend on a hand cannot be in a body, or a hand that does not depend on an arm, or an arm that does not depend on a shoulder, or a shoulder that does not depend on a head. What Barclay says slightly afterward—that the spiritual and political authority are like two shoulders in a body, and neither one is subjected to the other but both are subjected to Christ, the one head—not only is false, since those authorities are not of the same kind so that they might be compared with two shoulders in the same way in which two regal authorities would be rightly compared with two shoulders; but also borders on a heresy which is very strong in this time. In fact, the heretics of this time strive to proclaim nothing more eagerly than the fact that the Supreme Pontiff is not the head of the visible body of the Church, to whom all Christians, no matter how important, necessarily must be subject if they want to attain salvation. And this point Barclay, who throughout his entire book professes himself a Catholic, concedes to those heretics of his own accord. Therefore, the spiritual and political authority cannot be correctly compared with two shoulders but must be compared with the spirit and the flesh, as St. Gregory of Nazianzus does in his oration, often quoted, *Ad populum timore perculsum;* or with an arm and the head, that is, with the most important parts, among which, however, one, even if it is in itself very strong and robust, must be directed and governed by the other, which is superior.

But Barclay pushes on and presents my own writing against me in book 3 of *De Summo Pontifice,* chapter 19, where I admit that the kings of the earth do not have judges on earth as far as political matters are concerned, and he contends that I contradict myself, for in one passage I teach that kings have no judges on earth insofar as political matters are concerned, and in another passage I declare that the Pontiff is the judge of the kings, so that he can even deprive them of their kingdom by his sentence.

I reply that Innocent III in the chapter "Per venerabilem" writes that kings have no superior in temporal matters; nevertheless the same Innocent deposed Emperor Otto IV. Let Barclay dare to argue that Innocent contradicts himself, and I will not be sad to be reproached together with such a Pontiff. But my defense is ready: kings do not have judges on earth insofar as political or temporal matters are concerned, as long as their government is limited to political and temporal matters and it does not impede spiritual matters. Besides, kings are said not to have judges in political and temporal matters because they have no political or temporal judge above them, even though they have a spiritual judge by whom they can be directed and judged even in temporal matters insofar as these concern spiritual matters.

What Barclay adds, that the distinction of those expressions "directly" and "indirectly" involves the form and the manner, and not the strength and the effect of the judgment, has already been refuted above, in chapter 12, where we specifically discussed those expressions.

My third argument remains, and it was the following: if a temporal government hinders a spiritual good, by universal judgment the temporal prince is required to change that manner of government even at the expense of some temporal good, and therefore this is an indication that the temporal authority is subject to the spiritual.

Barclay opposes this argument in two ways. First, he notes that even if I had undertaken to offer a demonstration, nevertheless I have offered only indirect evidence. Second, he denies the deduction of the argument, for Barclay says that from the fact that a temporal prince is required to change the manner of government if through that he hinders a spiritual good, it follows that spiritual matters are worthier than temporal, not that the temporal authority is subject to the spiritual.

But it is neither new nor unusual, after having produced demonstrations, to produce arguments from indirect evidence also. And concerning the deduction, Barclay is mistaken, since from his antecedent, "A political prince is required to change his government if it opposes a spiritual good," it does not follow absolutely that the spiritual good is more noble and worthy than the temporal, but it follows that the temporal good is subject to the spiritual good as to its end. On this basis the temporal authority is subject to the spiritual authority, for the necessity of changing the manner of government in this case does not originate from the dignity or nobility of the spiritual good in absolute terms, but from the subordination of the one to the other, which I have shown clearly in book 5 of my *De Summo Pontifice*, chapter 7, while explaining this third argument, and in response to this explanation Barclay says nothing.

## CHAPTER 15

# Barclay's digression is refuted

In chapter 15 Barclay, not satisfied with what he said in response to my first argument, before moving to examine and refute the second, repeats again his opinion on the ecclesiastical and political authority, which is: temporal princes must be subject to the bishops insofar as spiritual matters are concerned, and by contrast bishops must be subject to the princes insofar as temporal matters are concerned; and in the same way in which the bishops can oblige the temporal princes with spiritual punishment to be obedient in matters of the soul, so the temporal princes can oblige the bishops with corporal punishment to be obedient in temporal matters, provided that those are not contrary to the Catholic faith and morality. However, he makes an exception for the Supreme Pontiff, who he says is not subject to any temporal prince, because he is also a supreme temporal prince in the territories under the Church's jurisdiction. In sum, Barclay deprives the clergy of every exemption from the authority of secular princes. And in the first place, to firm up this opinion, he produces the testimony of Franciscus Romulus in *Responsio ad certa capita Apologiae,* who clearly affirms that the bishops must be subject to the kings in temporal matters, and the kings to the bishops in spiritual matters. But the reply is easy, for Franciscus Romulus in that passage talks about the obligation that bishops and other clergymen have to observe political laws and not to upset the political order constituted by the kings, as also Pope Gelasius and Pope Nicholas teach, the former in the epistle to Emperor Anastasius, the latter in the epistle to Emperor Michael, and in that passage Franciscus Romulus adduced both. But from this it does not follow that a bishop can be obliged by a king to be obedient or that he can be punished if he is not, since the king has no authority over bishops or clergymen, which is stated most clearly in the Council of Constance, session 31.[134]

Second, he produces the testimony of Bellarmine himself, from the book *De clericis,* chapter 28, where he teaches that clergymen as citizens are parts and members of the political commonwealth, and for this they are obliged to observe the political laws. But since Bellarmine himself in that passage makes an exception for the coactive authority, from which he says clergymen are free, Barclay protests and says: "It is true rather that clergymen can be obliged by a temporal judge to obey the laws, when a reason requires it, so that in this case they do not enjoy the benefice of their clerical exemption, which benefice, as is sufficiently clear, they have received from the laws of the emperors and of the princes. In fact, whoever goes against the laws, invokes their help in vain."

And here Barclay, as is his habit, speaks against the opinion of all the Catholics: no matter how much theologians and canonists dispute over the law of exemption, they all teach that the clergy are by a certain law exempt from, and cannot be coerced by, the lay authority. Whether what one man only teaches is more true than what everybody teaches I leave to others to judge, but we will say more on this issue later and we have said much also in the book *De clericis.*

Third, Barclay produces the testimony of St. Gregory in his epistle 15 [40], book 4 [5], where St. Gregory, writing to Mauritius, speaks thus: "Our Lord [Mauritius] should not be displeased too quickly with the clergy on the basis of his earthly authority but should rule over them with a most thoughtful consideration for Him Whom they serve, so as to show due reverence." Barclay adds: "Evidently he should rule over them insofar as they are citizens and parts of the commonwealth, and he should show due reverence, insofar as they are priests and spiritual fathers, to whom the emperor himself, as a son of the Church, is subject."

I reply that St. Gregory's words could be explained in this sense, that he meant that the emperor can rule over the priests by issuing political laws,

---

134. In the session mentioned by Bellarmine, held on 31 March 1417, the Fathers issued a warning against Philip, Count of Vertus, at the request of the bishop of Asti (see *Conciliorum oecumenicorum decreta,* p. 412).

which the priests also are obliged to observe by force of reason [*vi rationis*] but not by force of law [*vi legis*]; but that the emperor must show reverence toward them by not punishing them himself if they do not observe the laws, but by letting them be punished by their prelates. But since from St. Gregory himself in his commentary on Psalm 101 we learned that Mauritius ruled in a tyrannical way in the last years of his empire and that he began to rage against the priests especially, it is not surprising that St. Gregory spoke like that in order to try to mitigate and moderate the yoke of the tyrant, if he was not able to remove it.

Fourth, Barclay produces the testimony of Scripture, 3 Kings 2, where King Solomon condemned the priest Abiathar to death because the priest had supported Adonijah's plot, and the King removed him from the priesthood.[135] I reply: it is not improbable that in the Old Testament the king was absolutely superior to the Pontiff, both because St. Thomas teaches this in book 1 of *De regimine principum*, chapter 12, and because in the Old Testament the promises were temporal and the sacrifices were carnal. But because it is more probable that also in the Old Testament the Pontiff was superior to the king, as we showed in *De Summo Pontifice*, book 2, chapter 29, indeed we persist in the same reply that we wrote in that passage, that Solomon condemned Abiathar to death and removed him from the priesthood and substituted another for him not as king, but as a prophet with divine inspiration. In fact, what we read in the Scriptures, 3 Kings 2, "that he might fulfill the word of the Lord, which he spake concerning the house of Eli in Shiloh,"[136] is the reason why Solomon did it. But Barclay says that the expression "that he might fulfill the word of the Lord" means nothing but that what the Lord had predicted was going to happen had then happened, just as when it is said in Matthew 27 that the impious soldiers had parted Christ's garments among themselves, so that the passage of the Psalms, "They part my garments among them," might be fulfilled.[137]

I reply, "so that the word of the Lord might be fulfilled" sometimes means only that something was predicted and later fulfilled, as in the

135. 1 Kings 2:23–27.
136. 1 Kings 2:27.
137. Matthew 27:35 and Psalm 22:18.

passage mentioned by my adversary. Sometimes it means that something was done with the wish and intention that obedience may be shown to God, Who wanted that to be done through a certain man, as in 4 Kings 9 when Jehu ordered that King Joram, after being killed, be thrown off a chariot into the field of the Jezreelites, so that the word of the Lord which had been spoken by the prophet Elijah, "Take him and cast him from the chariot in the field according to the word of the Lord," might be fulfilled.[138] But that what is reported from 3 Kings 2 should be understood in this second manner can be proved by the Hebrew word: in fact, where we, in our Latin text, have "So Solomon thrust out Abiathar from being priest unto the Lord; that the word of the Lord might be fulfilled,[139] which he spake concerning the house of Eli in Shiloh," in Hebrew the word *fulfill* [140] is of an active meaning, "to fulfill," or "so that he might fulfill the word of the Lord." Therefore the words of the Latin text have to be understood in this way, that is, that the word of the Lord might be fulfilled (add: by Solomon himself, etc.). You should add that from Barclay's opinion the king cannot punish a priest with a spiritual punishment and cannot interfere in spiritual affairs but only in temporal ones. But Solomon deprived Abiathar of the sacerdotal office and substituted another in his place; therefore, either he went beyond the limit of his authority, or he did this not as king but as a prophet and by a special divine inspiration, as we said before. Finally, if the reader is not satisfied by these arguments, we can say that in the sacred Scripture Solomon's action is narrated, but it is not specified whether he acted rightly or wrongly. Likewise, even in that passage it is narrated that the murder of Adonijah, Solomon's brother, was accomplished by order of Solomon himself because Adonijah had asked to be given Abishag the Shunammite as his wife, but it can be disputed whether this was done rightly or wrongly. Therefore, whoever would say that King Solomon deprived a priest of his office and killed his own brother because

---

138. 2 Kings 9.

139. This is again 1 Kings 2:27. Bellarmine is quoting from the Vulgate, in which the form of the verb used is the passive. In the King James version it is active, but in this passage I have modified the King James Version in order to make Bellarmine's argument clearer.

140. In Hebrew in the text.

he had asked that the woman who had been his father's maid be given to him as his wife, and therefore kings can deprive priests of their office and substitute others in their places and they can kill their own brothers if they ask that some beautiful woman whom the king himself may love be given to them as their wife, would not reason correctly. He who would say this, I say, would not reason correctly, since kings do many things often because of their authority, not because of justice, and we must see not what they can do but rather what they should do or what they could do by right, for it is not true what was said to the emperor Caracalla, that kings are permitted to do whatever they please.[141]

Barclay adds: "That man, albeit very learned, is equally deceived, when he says in that same book 2 of *De Summo Pontifice,* chapter 29, that it is not surprising if in the Old Testament the supreme authority was the temporal, and in the New Testament it was the spiritual, since in the Old Testament there were only temporal promises and in the New Testament there were spiritual and eternal promises."

I posed that opinion as probable, according to the authority of St. Thomas in book 1 of *De regimine principum* (or to the authority of the author of that book, whoever he might have been) and according to the reasoning advanced by that author, which is of no small value. Barclay, however, says that indeed the regal authority in both Testaments was only temporal, and the pontifical authority only spiritual, but he proves it without any authority or reasoning. Therefore, no one should be surprised if we value an ancient author speaking with reason above Barclay, a recent author who uses ancient authors with no reason.

Having dispensed with these arguments, Barclay surveys and lists in order the privileges of exemptions that have been given by kings or emperors to the clergy, from which he gathers that clergymen in their person are subject to the political authority in temporal matters, for if they were

141. Bellarmine is referring to the anecdote about Emperor Caracalla, which is narrated in the *Historia Augusta* but also in Aurelius Victor's *De Caesaribus,* and which concerns Caracalla's incestuous relationship with his mother, Julia Domna. According to the story, the emperor had once seen his mother naked and had said, "I would, if it were allowed"; to which she replied, "If you want, it is allowed: don't you know that you are the emperor and you give laws, not receive them?" (See *Historia Augusta,* "Caracalla," 10, 1–2, and Aurelius Victor, *Liber de Caesaribus,* 21, 1–3.)

not subject they would not need privileges and they would not have asked for them and they would not have accepted them when offered. I reply briefly to this that we at this point have not undertaken to dispute the authority of the kings over clergymen, but the authority of the Supreme Pontiff in temporal matters, and it is not fair to move from one discussion to another. Therefore, we refer the reader back to the arguments that we advanced in the *Controversiae* on clerical exemption and especially in the editions after 1598, in which we explained our opinion slightly more clearly and fully than in the previous editions.[142] It also happens that Barclay speaks again and more broadly of this issue in chapters 32 and 33, where he boasts of having found a new doctrine, against all authors, in the matter of exemption.

142. See p. xviii, n. 22.

## CHAPTER 16

# ᨠᨠ CHAPTER 16 ᨠᨠ

## The other digression of Barclay is refuted

In chapter 16 Barclay, after interrupting his response to my arguments in support of the authority of the Pontiff in temporal matters, makes another digression on the authority of kings over Pontiffs. And since in book 2 of *De Summo Pontifice*, chapter 29, I had said that a distinction between pagan and Christian kings must be recognized, since the former had not subjected themselves through baptism to the Supreme Pontiff as Vicar of Christ, while the latter had, and therefore it could be said as a probability that the Supreme Pontiffs once were subject to the pagan emperors with respect to temporal matters but that they were never *de iure* subject to the Christian emperors, Barclay attempts to attack this distinction and promises to demonstrate that the Supreme Pontiffs are no less subject *de iure* to Christian princes than to pagan princes insofar as temporal matters are concerned. He makes an exception, however, for those Pontiffs who after gaining temporal jurisdiction in certain provinces became supreme political princes; as such they became absolute rulers just like other kings and princes. However, he uses this reasoning: temporal princes through baptism have subjected themselves to the spiritual authority of the Supreme Pontiff as Vicar of Christ. From this subjection it does not follow that the Supreme Pontiff is not subject to the temporal authority of the Christian princes. Therefore, Bellarmine's argument is faulty.

What I had said in the passage quoted on the temporal subjection of the Supreme Pontiffs to the pagan emperors I changed in the *Recognitio* of my works, published two years ago, for I had followed the authority of Albert Pighius but afterward I realized that the reason of his opinion was not firm enough.[143] But this has nothing to do with Barclay: indeed, whether the Pontiffs were subject to the temporal authority of the pagan emperors or not, Barclay's reasoning is faulty and Bellarmine's argument has no fault. In fact, since kings through baptism have subjected themselves to the spiritual authority of the Pontiff, they are considered to have subjected also their kingdoms and their political authority to the same spiritual authority; that is, they wanted to be directed and corrected by the Pontiff if they have strayed in any way from the path to salvation in temporal matters. Besides, all the things that Barclay adds regarding Emperor Constantine and kings Clodoveus and Donaldus, who did not lose their empire and kingdoms through baptism, are meaningless, since we do not say that kings lose their kingdoms through baptism or that they lose any of their rights. On the contrary, we affirm that kings reign more truly and more successfully after baptism. Moreover, the Vicar of Christ does not lay claims on the kingdoms of his spiritual children and he does not desire to diminish or disturb their temporal jurisdiction, as Innocent III wrote clearly in the chapter above-mentioned, "Per venerabilem." Rather, he strives to act so that they may reign on earth in a way that allows them not to lose the heavenly kingdom, and in a way that allows the earthly kingdoms to be at the service of the heavenly one, as St. Gregory in book 2 [3], epistle 61 [65], writes very clearly.

Afterward Barclay adds a comparison by which he thinks his opinion is very aptly explained and very effectively confirmed. This is the comparison: "If a son holds a public magistracy while his father is still alive, he will have to obey his father in those issues pertaining to domestic matters, and if he behaves badly toward his father he will be in the position of being punished by him with disinheritance or other punishments to which the paternal authority extends. However, the son will not have to obey the father in those issues pertaining to public administration, and his father will not be able to deprive him of the magistracy or to punish him with the other punishments that are usually inflicted by a public magistrate. By contrast, the father will have to rise up in front of his son who holds

143. See pp. 163–64 and n. 45.

a magistracy and will have to obey him in public and political matters but not in domestic matters, and the son will be able to punish the father and to proceed legally against him just as against other private men if he should commit a crime against the public laws. Likewise, then, the Pontiff, who is the father of all Christians, even kings and princes, will be able to rule over kings in those issues that pertain to domestic, that is to say ecclesiastical, matters and to punish them with the most grave sentence of disinheritance, that is to say, excommunication, but he will not be able to give them any orders concerning political government, nor will he be able to deprive them of their kingdoms. Conversely, kings will be able to rule over the Pontiff in those issues that pertain to political government but not in ecclesiastical and spiritual matters."

I have already suggested before that Barclay enlarges his book by repeating often the same things, so that from a small booklet a book of regular size may be produced. In fact, he had already proposed the same comparison before, in chapter 3, with the difference that in the earlier passage he had compared the Pontiff to an adoptive father, and in this passage he compares him simply to a father. But as far as the present matter is concerned, the comparison is the same. And as we have suggested in chapter 3, that comparison was so inappropriate and infantile that it is surprising that Barclay did not notice the faults of the comparison that he himself adduced. In fact, the authority of a public magistrate is greater than the paternal authority of private citizens, and if justice requires it, it can deprive a father of his paternal authority. By contrast, however, the father, being a private citizen, cannot direct or correct a public magistrate and much less can he deprive him of his authority. However, the authority of the Supreme Pontiff is indeed a paternal authority but hardly similar to the paternal authority of private citizens. Rather, it is similar to the authority of God, Whose Vicar on earth the Pontiff is, and therefore it is a supernatural, spiritual, public authority, much more sublime than any political or human authority. Therefore, there are two faults in Barclay's comparison: one is that he equates the political authority of the magistrate with the authority of private citizens even if the former, the superior, is subjected to the latter, the inferior. The second is that he made the pontifi-

cal authority similar to the human and private paternal authority, even if
this is a public and divine authority and no greater or equal authority can
be found on earth. See what we said on this point in chapter 3.

Finally Barclay adds the testimony of Nicholas of Cusa, who in *De concordia Catholica,* book 3, chapter 3, writes that there was an ancient gloss
to the canon "Adrianus," distinction 63, saying that "The Pope is the father
of [Charlemagne as] *Patricius*[144] in spiritual matters, and [Charlemagne as]
*Patricius* is the father of the Pope in temporal matters," and in chapter 4
Cusa writes, "It is not in the power of the Roman Pontiff to appoint a king
or emperor for any province throughout the world without that province's
consent." I have replied already above to the first testimony, that the ancient gloss was rightly outdated and eliminated. I reply to the second that
the Roman Pontiff can, especially in case of heresy, excommunicate and
depose kings and emperors, and he can free their subjects from their obedience, but he lets those to whom this pertains by law free to decide who
should succeed in their places. Therefore, he does not oppose emperors
and kings out of his own will and against the will of the people, and he
does not take away the rights of succession and of election, and this is the
only thing that Cardinal [Cusa] seeks to prove.

144. See p. 180 for a similar use of the term *Patricius.*

# The second argument in support of the authority of the Supreme Pontiff in temporal matters is defended

In chapter 17 Barclay, once he was done with digressions, returns to examine and refute Bellarmine's arguments, and since on the first argument enough has been said in chapter 14, he now attacks the second, which he accurately transcribed. He says, then, that the second argument is that the ecclesiastical commonwealth must be perfect and self-sufficient for attaining its end, as all well-instituted commonwealths are; therefore, it must have every authority necessary to attain its end. The authority of using and disposing of temporal matters is necessary to the spiritual end, for otherwise impious princes could without restraint support heretics and destroy religion. Therefore, the ecclesiastical commonwealth also has this authority. Any commonwealth, because it must be perfect and self-sufficient, can rule over another sovereign commonwealth and oblige it to change its government, and it can even depose the other commonwealth's prince and appoint another, when it cannot otherwise defend itself from the harm inflicted by that other commonwealth. Likewise how much more will the spiritual commonwealth be able to rule over the temporal commonwealth, which is subject to it, and oblige it to change its government and depose the princes and appoint others, when it cannot otherwise protect its own spiritual good.[145]

145. Bellarmine's argument about the need for the commonwealth to be "self-sufficient" and "perfect" comes from Aristotle and Aquinas (see *Politics,* bk. 1, chap. 2, and *Summa theologiae,* 1a 2ae, question 90, articles 2 and 3).

Barclay attacks this argument, reported accurately enough, in two points. First, he denies that in the Church there are two commonwealths, one composed of clergymen and one composed of laymen, one spiritual and one temporal, one sacred and one political. He proves this from my first argument, in which I said that the political and the spiritual authorities are part of the same Christian commonwealth and that clergymen and laymen do not constitute two commonwealths in the Church but one.

Second, he denies that the authority to dispose of temporal matters is necessary to the spiritual end, which he proves from what the Apostle Peter affirms in Acts [5:]4, that he did not have the authority to dispose of the temporal goods of Ananias, to whom he said: "Whiles it remained, was it not thine own? and after it was sold, was it not in thine own power?"[146]

To the first point there is a very easy reply. The spiritual or ecclesiastical commonwealth and the temporal or political commonwealth are both two and one: two parts, one total, just as the spirit and the flesh joined together at the same time constitute one man; indeed, they are one man, as is said in the Athanasian Creed and as is gathered from Genesis [2:]7, where we read: "And the Lord God formed man of the dust of the ground, and breathed into his nostrils the breath of life; and man became a living soul."[147] Nevertheless, they are so distinct in their powers, laws, and acts that the apostle says in Romans 7: "But I see another law in my members, warring against the law of my mind,"[148] and in Galatians [5:]17: "For the flesh lusteth against the Spirit, and the Spirit against the flesh,"[149] and, which is more remarkable, in 2 Corinthians 4 the spirit is called the inward man and the flesh is called the outward man when it is said: "For which cause we faint not; but though our outward man perish, yet the inward man is renewed day by day,"[150] and in Romans [7]: "For I delight in the law of God after the inward man."[151] Thus, the spirit and the flesh are one man, and two men; and the Holy Spirit, who says that they are

146. Acts 5:4.
147. Genesis 2:7.
148. Romans 7:23.
149. Galatians 5:17.
150. 2 Corinthians 4:16.
151. Romans 7:22.

both, does not contradict Itself. Therefore, Bellarmine does not contradict himself when he considers the ecclesiastical and political commonwealth in the Church now as parts of one Christian commonwealth, now as two commonwealths distinct from each other. For Bellarmine is neither the only nor the first one to say that the ecclesiastical commonwealth is very similar to the spirit and the political commonwealth to the flesh, but before him also Thomas Netter, and before him St. Thomas, and before him Alexander of Hales, and before him Hugh of St. Victor, and before him St. Gregory of Nazianzus, as we have reported before more than once.

To the second point I reply that St. Peter's words to Ananias do not mean that the Prince of the Apostles did not have the authority of disposing of Ananias's temporal goods if they had been necessary to the spiritual end, but they indicate only that St. Peter did not exercise that authority and did not want to exercise it, because there was no necessity. Of course, if Barclay's argument had any value, it would also imply that no king can dispose of the temporal goods of his subjects in case they prove necessary to the salvation of the commonwealth. In fact, every king can say to his subjects: "Whiles it remained, was it not thine own? and after it was sold, was it not in thine own power?"[152] Who obliged you to give it to the commonwealth? And if you claim to have donated it whole, why do you lie, saying that you donated it all when you kept a part of it? Therefore, just as kings have the right to dispose of the temporal goods of the citizens not so that they can despoil the citizens of their own possessions at their will, but so that they can oblige the citizens to offer their goods for the preservation of the common good; so also the apostle Peter's authority over the temporal goods of the Christians was not (as Barclay imagines us to say) so that the apostle could deprive all Christians of their own possessions without a reason, and not leave them anything as their own, but only so that he could see to it that the Christians did not abuse the temporal goods against God's law but instead used them rightly to attain eternal life. But that the apostles had some authority to dispose of temporal matters whenever spiritual matters are concerned is evident from the fact that they determined that the Christian people should provide for those who

152. This is a reference to Acts 5:4.

preached the Gospel with their own resources, and this according to God's order, as is clear from the apostle in 1 Corinthians 9.

"But," Barclay says, "for the first three hundred years the Church had no authority to dispose of temporal matters of the Christians against the will of the owners, and so either the Christian commonwealth was imperfect then or that authority is not necessary to attain the spiritual end." And here Barclay wastes many words to show that it pertained to God's providence that the primitive Church should have been equipped with all the things that were necessary to its preservation.

My answer is that the primitive Church was equipped with every authority and with all the resources that were necessary to establish a perfect commonwealth, but in the first three hundred years there were not many political princes in the church, although there were some, like Emperor Philip and King Lucius and King Donaldus. But let us pretend there were none: not because of this did the Church lack the authority to dispose of the temporal goods of the princes and to direct their political authority when they wished to become members or children of the Church. Moreover, as I just said, in that very beginning of the Church, even if there were no Christian princes and the apostles themselves were ruling the Church, there were nevertheless many rich men whose wealth the apostles disposed of by determining that the ministers of the Gospel should be provided for out of such wealth.

Then Barclay introduces the words of St. Bernard, from book 4 of *De consideratione,* chapter 3, "This is Peter, who is not known to have walked adorned with gems or silk, or covered in gold, or carried by a white horse, or escorted by a soldier or surrounded by screaming attendants, and yet without these he thought that his mandate for salvation, if you love me feed my sheep, could be sufficiently accomplished; and so in those matters you have not succeeded Peter but Constantine." Bernard says these words, to which Barclay adds: "Therefore even if the temporal authority of which we speak could seem to men necessary to the Church, nevertheless it did not seem to God either necessary or useful."

Maybe on this passage it could be said to Barclay what God Himself says in the book of Job, chapter 38: "Who is this that darkeneth counsel by words without knowledge?"[153] St. Bernard writes that the apostle Peter was poor in the riches of this world, and without owning gold and silver, without a white horse and without escort, he was able to accomplish his mandate for salvation of feeding the sheep. Bernard, however, does not say that the apostle Peter did not have the authority to dispose of the temporal goods of the Christians and of kingdoms and even empires, if a spiritual necessity demanded it. Indeed, he says the contrary, when he applies to the Pontiff as Pontiff and Christ's Vicar and Peter's successor those words from Jeremiah 1: "See, I have this day set thee over the nations and over the kingdoms, to root out, and to pull down, and to destroy, and to throw down, to build, and to plant."[154] In fact, one's personal poverty is not inconsistent with one's authority to dispose of wealth and to judge earthly kings and princes. Likewise, in fact, the superiors of religious orders, even if they are personally bound by their vow of poverty, have the authority to dispose of the very ample resources of their order. And among the ancient Romans many poor citizens, such as Fabricius, Curius, Cincinnatus, and others, after becoming consuls or dictators, disposed of kingdoms and of the resources of kings, even if they personally remained in their original poverty. Therefore, Barclay should not have confused wealth with authority, as if the same man could not be both poor in wealth and rich in authority. Then St. Bernard says that the Pontiff did not succeed Peter but succeeded Constantine in wealth and temporal possessions, and from this what does Barclay gather? That the Pontiff could fulfill his apostolic duty without his temporal realm. What then? Our question is not on the temporal realm of the Supreme Pontiff but on his spiritual and apostolic authority, which we say is extended to the disposing of temporal matters and even kingdoms and empires for the sake of the spiritual end. Barclay, however, in order to rebut this, moves the dispute to the temporal realm, which the apostles in practice lacked, so as to seem to have said something, by confusing and mixing everything. Finally Barclay, as if he had been transported to the third heaven in front of God, declares in absolute

153. Job 38:2.
154. Jeremiah 1:10.

terms that the temporal authority of which we speak did not seem to God either necessary or useful. But I ask Barclay, what temporal authority will you speak of? For if you will speak of that authority which, even if it is spiritual in itself, is extended to temporal matters, you clearly attribute to God falsehoods. God, in fact, thought that such authority was necessary to the ecclesiastical prince and for this reason he granted it to him, by saying, "Whatsoever thou shalt bind on earth shall be bound in heaven: and whatsoever thou shalt loose on earth shall be loosed in heaven."[155] The general councils that we quoted above and that could most truly say, "It seemed fit to the Holy Spirit and to us," taught that these words have to be understood in this way.

If, however, you will speak of the temporal authority over the realm which the Church has now and which it had eight hundred years ago, with absolute temerity you affirm that this authority seemed to God neither necessary nor useful. In fact (not to mention other things), if it had seemed to God that this realm was not useful to the Church, certainly the Supreme Pontiffs Zachary, Adrian, Nicholas I and Nicholas II, Leo III, Leo IV, and Leo IX, and others who by the common opinion of all the authors were excellent, most holy, and most pleasing to God, would not have maintained it and much less would they have fought to preserve it. Whether, however, one should give more credit regarding the divine judgment to so many holy Pontiffs rather than give it to Barclay alone cannot certainly be called into doubt.

But Barclay pushes again, and he twists the argument against us with these words: "I pass over the fact that, if their reasoning were good, it would follow, on the contrary, that the temporal commonwealth has the authority of disposing of spiritual matters and of deposing the supreme prince of the ecclesiastical commonwealth because it must be perfect and self-sufficient for attaining its end, and thus it must have every authority necessary to attain that end. The authority of disposing of spiritual matters and of deposing the ecclesiastical prince is necessary to the temporal end, because otherwise impious ecclesiastical princes could upset the order and peace of the temporal commonwealth and hinder the end of

155. Matthew 16:19.

the civil government, as in fact sometimes some Pontiffs did. Therefore the temporal commonwealth has this authority. The deduction is clearly false and absurd (in fact a temporal prince as such has no spiritual authority) and the premise is also false."

But between the argument that we made and that which Barclay by twisting now makes, there is as much difference as there is between truth and falsehood and between good and evil. For our proposition, that the authority of disposing of temporal matters is necessary to the spiritual end, is most true, because temporal matters are arranged for the sake of the spiritual, and the deduction that therefore the spiritual authority can dispose of temporal matters insofar as they relate to spiritual matters is good, because whoever can attain an end can also dispose of the means to that end. But Barclay's proposition, that the authority of disposing of spiritual matters is necessary to the temporal end, is false because spiritual matters are not arranged for the sake of the temporal and the authority to dispose of spiritual matters for the sake of the temporal is not a true authority but an abuse of authority and a perverting of the order, and it cannot be possible that abuse of authority or perverting of the order is necessary to any commonwealth. Since the authority of disposing of spiritual matters is not necessary to attain the temporal end, then the deduction that therefore the temporal commonwealth can dispose of spiritual matters for the sake of the temporal cannot be good. This whole point can easily be understood from the comparison, already often repeated, of the spirit and the flesh in man. In fact, the spirit can dispose of the senses and of the parts of the body for the sake of eternal life by imposing on them continence, abstinence, flagellations, fasting, vigils, works, and, what is the greatest, ordering the flesh to suffer death instead of renouncing the faith. However, the flesh cannot dispose of the intelligence and the will, and it cannot prohibit the action of praying and praising God, and much less can it order the spirit to suffer spiritual death in exchange for any temporal good, and if perhaps the spirit by indiscreet suffering of the mind, as by too much prayer or meditation, harms the health of the flesh, certainly the spirit will sin, but nevertheless because of this the flesh will not be able to rule over the spirit, but by suffering and getting weaker it will make the spirit abandon a little of its fervor. Likewise, even if perhaps the spiritual prince abuses his authority unjustly by excommunicating the temporal prince or by absolving his subjects from their obedience to him without a just cause, thus upsetting the order of the temporal commonwealth, the spiritual prince will sin, but nevertheless the temporal prince will not be able to judge over spiritual matters, or to judge the spiritual prince, and much less depose him from his spiritual See.

Barclay notices the weakness of his argument, and because of this he comes back to his earlier solution by saying: "But, as we are accustomed to say, arguing *per absurdum* is not disproving an argument. Thus I reply in a different manner to the first part of this second reason; that is, there are not two commonwealths as he thinks, but only one, in which there are two authorities, or two magistrates, the political and the ecclesiastical. Both of them have what they necessarily need to obtain their end; that is, one has the spiritual, the other the temporal jurisdiction, and the jurisdiction of one is not necessary for the other and vice versa; otherwise one would have to say that both authorities were deprived of the necessary means when they were separated, as once they were."

This is not another solution but the previous one repeated. I refuted it slightly earlier, when I showed that the ecclesiastical and political commonwealths can be said to be two and one, because they are distinct and can be found separate; but when they convene in the one body of the Church, one is subordinated to the other so that they are two parts, one total. And it does not follow that at the time in which they were separated, at the beginning of the nascent Church, they were deprived of the necessary means. In fact the political commonwealth could not fear any damage from the spiritual authority, since it was not capable of ecclesiastical censures, which are valid only over Christians, and the spiritual commonwealth had the authority of actually disposing of the temporal matters of those who were to come to it. Last, it is not true that the spiritual and political authorities are similar to two magistrates, neither one of which needs the other's jurisdiction. In fact, two magistrates depend on a king, whose authority is superior to both magistrates and who can see to it that neither one harms the other. But the spiritual and political authorities do not have a third authority in the Church to which they are subordinate and which holds each to its duty. Therefore, it is necessary that one be subordinate to the other, that is, the inferior to the superior, the temporal to the spiritual. And from this response all the arguments that Barclay presents through the end of the chapter, on the duty of the chancellor and the constable, very powerful magistrates whom only the king commands, are answered. Regarding what Barclay adds, that the spiritual and the political princes are subject to God alone in the same way in which the chancellor and the constable are subject to the king, this cannot be admitted without violating the Catholic faith, since the Church, which is the kingdom of Christ, not only recognizes Christ as its Lord and King but also knows from the sacred Scriptures and from the apostolic tradition and from the universal consent of the Fathers and scholars that there is one general Vicar of Christ on earth, who is the visible head of the visible Church. Barclay in his whole book admits that this Vicar of Christ is the Roman Pontiff; therefore (if he wants to be called a Catholic) he also must admit that the Pontiff and the king are not two magistrates immediately below Christ, but that the king must be subject to Christ and to the Pontiff, and the Pontiff to Christ alone.

# The second part of the second argument in support of the authority of the Supreme Pontiff in temporal matters is defended

In chapter 18 Barclay tries to rebut the second part of the second argument, which was proposed at the beginning of the previous chapter. This is the summary of the argument: a commonwealth can, if it is wronged by another commonwealth, and if it is upset and damaged by this other commonwealth's bad government, force with arms that commonwealth, even if it is not subject to it, to change the manner of its government, and, if necessary, it can depose its prince. Therefore, with all the more reason the spiritual commonwealth will be able to order the temporal commonwealth, subject to it, to change the manner of its government and, if necessary, to depose its prince if it is wronged by that temporal commonwealth and is upset and damaged by it.

To this argument Barclay replies what he had already replied before, that the spiritual and temporal commonwealths are not two, but one commonwealth with two authorities, neither one of which depends on the other. But since he saw that this solution was not firm, he admitted that the clergy, whose prince is the Pope, and the laity, whose prince is the king, can be considered two commonwealths constituted in the bosom of the same Church. And after admitting this he replies that the former commonwealth, that is, the clergy, has only spiritual weapons, while the latter, that is, the laity, has only corporeal, and therefore they are not similar to two commonwealths that defend themselves with arms and one constrains and submits the other.

But this solution is not any firmer than the previous one. Even if the weapons of the spiritual commonwealth, which it uses itself, are indeed spiritual, corporeal weapons are also in its power, since one sword is subject to the other, and the Church can call upon the secular arm and use through it the corporeal sword. Moreover, those very spiritual weapons can punish the temporal commonwealth and its prince, because the spiritual prince can excommunicate the temporal prince and free his subjects from their subjection and command them under pain of excommunication not to recognize the excommunicated prince as prince, but to elect another for themselves or to adhere to the legitimate successor.

Finally Barclay adds: "What more? Even if we concede to them their comparison and their conclusion, nothing can be made out of it but that the Pope has the same kind of authority to dispose of the temporal matters of the Christians and to depose their princes that the king of France is recognized to have over the English, or the Spanish, or other neighboring peoples that might wrong him, or that every one of them is recognized to have over the matters and kings of the French who might molest them. What kind or how strong this authority is can be assessed only by sword."

I reply that the comparison and reasoning that we used in proving the authority of the Pontiff does not proceed from a condition of equality but from a condition of superiority. This is in fact what we said, that if a commonwealth can punish and depose the prince of another commonwealth that is not subject to it by reason of a wrong only, with how much greater reason will the spiritual commonwealth be able to punish the temporal commonwealth, subject to it, and depose its prince, if it receives from it such a harm that it cannot protect itself otherwise than by removing that prince and substituting another? Therefore, the authority that the spiritual commonwealth has over the temporal is not similar to the authority of the French over the English or of the English over the French, but to the authority that the spirit has over the flesh which is conjoined to it, or that the head has over the limbs attached to it.[156]

---

156. Vitoria uses a similar argument in his *relectio* 1 "On the Power of the Church," question 5, article 8.

# On St. Bernard's opinion about the authority of the Supreme Pontiff in temporal matters[157]

In chapter 19 Barclay attempts to reply to the testimony of St. Bernard from his *De consideratione,* book 4, chapter 4 [3], which testimony I had adduced to confirm my second reason. Now, since St. Bernard writes in the quoted passage: "The material sword has to be taken out by the hand of the soldier at the command of the emperor but subject to the nod [*nutus*] of the supreme priest," Barclay affirms that "nod" must not be understood as "command" [*imperium*] or "authority" [*potestas*], but as "assent" [*assensus*], for wars are waged more successfully if the assent of the priests, whose responsibility it is to judge whether or not a war is just, is added to the authority of the kings. However, he proves that "nod" is not understood as "authority" because if by chance the emperor wants to wage war without the assent of the Pontiff, St. Bernard did not attribute to the Pope any authority over the emperor, but indeed he clearly teaches that no authority belongs to him, when he says that the material sword cannot be taken out by the Church, but only by the hand of the soldier and at the command of the emperor. He confirms this opinion with the testimony of Gratian, 23, question 8 at the beginning, when he writes: "The material sword is forbidden to the Pontiffs, to whom only the spiritual sword is allowed."

My answer is that the word *nod* can signify assent, especially when we reply by nodding to somebody who asks for something, but when the nod precedes other requests it usually signifies command, or rather a command

---

157. See pp. 131–32.

so strong and effective that without an express order a nod only is enough to get that thing done. In this manner it is taken in Genesis 42, when it is said: "And Joseph was the governor over the land and at his nod the corn was sold to the people,"[158] and even more clearly in 2 Kings 17: "At the Lord's nod the good counsel of Ahithophel was defeated,"[159] where it would be ridiculous to understand "nod" as "assent," since in the Scripture it is spoken of as the "nod" of God, Who alone can change the hearts of kings whenever He pleases, and in 2 Maccabees 7 the Scripture says the same about God: "He can destroy the whole world with a nod,"[160] and in Job 26: "The pillars of heaven tremble and are astonished at his nod,"[161] and to this the poet's verse is similar: "He said; and shook the skies with his imperial nod."[162]

And that in this passage St. Bernard means "nod" as "command," and not simply "assent," is obvious from the fact that in the first passage he puts among the efficient causes the Pontiff's nod, then the emperor's command, and finally the soldier's execution. Therefore, just as in St. Bernard's opinion the soldier executes the command of the emperor, so the emperor is moved to command the soldier by the nod, that is, the command, of the Pontiff. Thus, if that nod of the Pontiff were a simple assent, St. Bernard would not say that the Pontiff has both swords, but that the Pontiff has one, the emperor the other. Therefore, when he says: "Both are yours, but both must not be taken out by your hand," he clearly teaches that both are in the power of the Pontiff, but one immediately, and the other by means of somebody else, but to be taken out at his nod or command.

"But," Barclay says, "what if the emperor does not want to unsheathe the sword at the priest's nod, or indeed what if he shall unsheathe the

158. Genesis 42:6. This is my translation of the Vulgate, for in the King James Bible this verse is: "And Joseph was the governor over the land, and he it was that sold to all the people of the land: and Joseph's brethren came, and bowed down themselves before him with their faces to the earth."

159. 2 Samuel 17:14. Again, this is my translation from the Vulgate, for in the King James Bible this verse is: "For the Lord had appointed to defeat the good counsel of Ahithophel."

160. The first and second books of the Maccabees were not included in the King James Bible because they were considered apocryphal. The translation is my own.

161. Job 26:11. Again, the King James Bible translates the Latin *nutus* as "reproof," and thus it does not give the sense of Bellarmine's argument about the word *nod*.

162. Virgil, *Aeneid* 9, v. 106. Dryden's translation.

sword openly against the priest's nod? Did St. Bernard attribute some temporal authority to the priest over the emperor in this case?"

If the emperor does not want to unsheathe the sword at the priest's nod, or if he unsheathes the sword against his nod, and this is necessary to the spiritual good, the Pontiff with the spiritual sword, that is, with ecclesiastical censures, will oblige him to unsheathe or to put back in the sheath the material sword. If the emperor is not moved by the censures, and if the necessity of the Church requires it, the Pontiff will free his subjects from their obedience and he will take the empire away from him. Thus, he will show that one sword is subject to the other, and both swords pertain to the authority of the Church, albeit not in the same way.

"But," Barclay says, "St. Bernard teaches that no temporal authority can belong to the Pontiff when he says that the material sword (by which word the supreme temporal authority is meant) cannot be taken out by the Church, but only by the hand of the soldier at the command of the emperor, and the same thing more clearly Gratian, almost a contemporary of Bernard, reports in causa 23, question 8 at the beginning."

I reply that St. Bernard only teaches that the material sword cannot be taken out by the hand of the priest, which we gladly admit, but he does not deny, rather he affirms indeed, that the material sword is subjected to the spiritual one, and that it has to be taken out of or put into the sheath at the nod of the Pontiff. Gratian also does not teach anything else but that it is not allowed to the clergy to use the material sword, and to kill men, which he confirms with many canons of Pontiffs and councils. These things are true, but it cannot be inferred from them that the Pontiff has no authority in temporal matters.

Later Barclay adds the words of St. Ambrose from book 10 of his commentary on Luke, where these words are found: "The law does not forbid to strike: and therefore perhaps to Peter, who was offering two swords, Christ says, 'It is enough,' as if this were lawful until the Gospel, so that in the law there might be the knowledge of justice, and in the Gospel the perfection of virtue." From this passage Barclay gathers that the material sword was allowed to the priests up until the Gospel.

We do not deny, as we said just before, that to the clergy after the Gospel it is not permitted to unsheathe the material sword with their

own hand, unless maybe for their personal defense or for another reason with the Pontiff's dispensation, for the ordinary use of the material
sword belongs to the soldiers, not to the priests. And yet in this passage
Ambrose does not speak only of the priests, but of all Christians, and
for this reason Erasmus misused this passage to prove that war was prohibited to Christians.[163] But, in any case, St. Ambrose supports neither
Erasmus nor Barclay, as he teaches that in the law not only defense but
also revenge is allowed, whereas in the Gospel defense but not revenge is
allowed. These are, in fact, his words: "O Lord, why do you order me to
buy a sword and prohibit me from striking? Why do you command me
to get what you forbid me to bring out? Maybe to prepare me for an act
of defense and not authorize an act of revenge, so that I would decide
not to take revenge even if I could. The law does not in fact forbid to
strike back (in this manner, in fact, this should be read, not as 'strike' as
Barclay reported falsely) and therefore perhaps He said to Peter, who was
offering two swords, 'It is enough' as if this were lawful until the Gospel,
so that in the law there might be the knowledge of justice, and in the
Gospel the perfection of virtue." That is what St. Ambrose says, that is,
that not defense but revenge was prohibited in the Gospel, and to strike
back, not to strike, was forbidden. And when St. Ambrose says, "The law
does not forbid to strike back," he seems to look at those words of God in
Matthew 5: "Ye have heard that it hath been said, An eye for an eye, and
a tooth for a tooth: But I say unto you, That ye resist not evil, etc. . . ."[164]
There it is not meant that revenge was lawful for the ancients by their
own authority but by the authority of the public magistrate, and not
because of lust for revenge but because of love of justice, and the same
is allowed to Christians. But the good Master exhorts His people to the
perfection of life, as Ambrose says: "This perfection consists in extirpating the roots of contentions and, by supporting each other in charity, in
not giving occasions for more serious evils such as wounds and killings,
because of which it would be necessary for the public magistrate to take
revenge on the criminals."

163. Cf. what Bellarmine wrote on Erasmus and the question of war in chapter 14
in the *Controversia de laicis.*
164. Matthew 5:38–39.

Barclay adds in turn that the words of the Gospel on the two swords do not signify literally the two authorities, that is, the ecclesiastical and the political, but we do not make our argument from the words of the Gospel but from the words of St. Bernard and Boniface VIII, who, explaining the words of the Gospel in a mystical sense, taught that by the two swords the two authorities were meant. In fact, St. Bernard, whom Boniface follows, combined two passages of the Gospel: one is from John 18: "Put up thy sword into the sheath,"[165] and the other from Luke 22: "Here are two swords."[166] And certainly the former passage literally signifies that Christ did not want to be defended by Peter with the material sword and did not want His Passion to be hindered; therefore, He also added: "The cup which my Father hath given me, shall I not drink it?"[167] The latter passage depends on the words above, where the Lord said: "And he that hath no sword, let him sell his garment, and buy one,"[168] and the disciples, thinking that the Lord with these words ordered that the swords be prepared, said: "Here are two swords." But the Lord says, "It is enough," either ironically, as Theophylactus explains, as if He were to say, "What are two swords against an armed cohort of soldiers?" or, as others have it, seeing that they had not understood, He silenced them by saying, "It is enough," "You have spoken enough, be silent about this matter." Truly, then, when He said: "He that hath no sword, let him sell his garment and buy one," He did not order them to buy swords, but He meant that they were about to incur that suffering which those who think that it is good to sell garments and buy swords incur. Last, the fact that the apostles did not sell their garments and buy swords is a sign that Christ did not order them to do so. But whatever the explanation of this very obscure passage might be, St. Bernard and Pope Boniface mystically but aptly and elegantly referred what is said about the two swords to the two authorities, that is, the ecclesiastical and the political.

Again Barclay objects that even if we admit this mystical explanation, "It cannot be gathered that one sword is subject to the other, or that both

165. John 18:11.
166. Luke 22:38.
167. John 18:11.
168. Luke 22:36.

are in the hands of the Pontiff, since St. Bernard does not say this and could not say this without reproach." I reply that Boniface openly says that sword is under sword, and St. Bernard says the same, but with other words. In fact, when he affirms that both swords pertain to the Pontiff, indeed both are his, but one has to be taken out by his hand and the other at his nod, he clearly indicates that one sword is under another; that is, the material is under the spiritual, and both are in the hand, that is, in the power of the Pontiff.

Finally Barclay boasts to have subtly noted something in St. Bernard's words that Barclay does not think anyone else has noticed before, that is, the reason why St. Bernard said: "The sword has to be taken out perhaps subject to your nod, if not by your hand," and just afterward, repeating the same, he omitted the word *perhaps*. Thus Barclay writes: "It must be distinguished between the Pontiff as Pontiff, and the Pontiff as a man. In fact, the Pontiff as Pontiff not absolutely, but only 'perhaps,' nods that the sword be taken out, that is, only when it is useful to the Church, when with a sound and sober decision he thinks it expedient. But the Pontiff as a man, holding enmities against another, or wanting to satisfy his greedy lust of dominion, orders absolutely that the sword be taken out."

But this subtlety has been shown to Barclay neither by sharpness of intellect nor by knowledge of Scripture, but by hatred against the Pontiffs, since certainly that subtlety would never have come to St. Bernard's mind. For "perhaps" is not opposed to "absolutely," and it cannot be taken for "sometime," or for "when it is truly expedient," unless by him who, being perverse himself, perverts also the words. Why, then, did he say "perhaps" at the beginning, and then omit it when repeating the passage afterward? The answer is easy: because at the beginning he brought up only two certain elements, that is, the command and the execution, and since he doubted whether it would be becoming to the Pope to command the soldier to brandish the sword, he said: "Perhaps subject to your nod, not by your hand." Afterward, however, he brought up three elements, the Pontiff's nod, the emperor's command, and the soldier's execution, and since there could not be any doubt that the soldiers used the sword at his command, he omitted "perhaps" and substituted "certainly." With this we have said enough of St. Bernard's opinion.

# Bellarmine's third argument is defended

In chapter 20 Barclay examines and confutes Bellarmine's third principal argument for confirming the authority of the Supreme Pontiff in temporal matters. This was the argument: it is not lawful for Christians to tolerate an infidel or heretical king if he tries to lure his subjects to his own heresy or infidelity. Judging whether or not a king is luring his subjects to heresy pertains to the Pontiff, to whom the care of religion is committed. Therefore, it is the Pope's prerogative to judge whether a king must be deposed or not. I have confirmed this proposition with three arguments, but Barclay rebuts it in this way:

"That it is not lawful for Christians to tolerate a heretical or infidel king is as false as the falsest falsehood. For otherwise the whole antiquity, which humbly endured heretical and infidel kings trying to destroy the Church of God not only because of fear of wrath but also for conscience, that is, not because they lacked the strength to expel the impious princes but because they thought that they were not allowed to do this by God's law, must be condemned."

When among judicious and serious discussants the truth is searched for, the winner is not whoever affirms his opinion with greater exaggeration, but whoever confirms it with stronger arguments. Barclay indeed says that the proposition of my argument is as false as the falsest falsehood. However, he does not prove what he says with anything but the fact that the whole antiquity tolerated heretical and infidel kings trying to destroy the Church not only because of fear of wrath but also for conscience. But he should have proved this fact, i.e., that heretical or infidel kings trying to destroy the Church were tolerated by antiquity not only because of fear of wrath but also for conscience. We, by contrast, say that they were tolerated because the strength of the Church was not enough to expel them, but that the Church could have, if there had been strength, indeed should have removed from those kings their authority over the faithful, unless there was some reason why that removal would have to be postponed to a more appropriate time. We prove the preceding with this argument, which is the first confirmation of my proposition. The Jews are forbidden from appointing over themselves a king who is not Jewish (Deuteronomy 17), and since this is a moral law, by the same law Christians are forbidden from appointing over themselves a king who is not Christian, lest they be drawn to infidelity by him. Tolerating over themselves a heretical or infidel king trying to move the people away from the faith brings the same danger and loss as appointing one. Therefore, they are obliged not to tolerate him, but to depose him if they are strong enough to do so.

To this argument Barclay responds by admitting the proposition and the assumption, which he could not deny, and by denying the conclusion only. For he says that it is not correctly inferred from the equivalency of the danger and loss that the people have the right to remove a king just as they had the right not to admit him. That this is incorrectly inferred he proves with three arguments drawn from comparison. First, whoever is victim of a misfortune and loses his goods receives the same danger and loss that he may receive by force from a robber or by an unjust sentence from a judge. However, while he can oppose the robber with arms, he cannot oppose the judge. Second, there is the same danger and loss in deliberately stepping onto a boat knowing that its keel is weak, or entering it thinking that it is in good shape when in fact it is full of cracks and holes. Nevertheless, incurring the danger of a shipwreck deliberately, or by ignorance, is not equally sinful. Finally, marrying a woman who is very hard to please and quarrelsome, either on purpose (on account of her fortune or beauty), or by mistake and imprudence, presents the same danger and harm. Still, entering into such a marriage deliberately, or by ignorance, is not equally sinful. Besides, while it would be lawful not to marry such a woman in the first place, it is not lawful to repudiate her after the marriage.

To these arguments I reply that they are drawn not from analogies but from dissimilarities, and for this reason they do not render the deduction of my reasoning less excellent. The first argument is not drawn from analogy, because the people, when electing a king, not only can but must elect a king from their kin, as the law orders, that is, a Christian and a Catholic, and they sin most gravely if they do otherwise. However, whoever encounters robbers can, if he wishes, oppose force with force, but he can also bear that injury with calm, and he is more deserving to God if he prefers to be killed unjustly by a robber than if he kills a robber while justly defending himself.

The other example of the man boarding a ship full of cracks, risking a shipwreck, has no point with respect to what we are dealing with. For we do not ignore that it is not equally sinful if one exposes himself to danger knowingly or by imprudence, but what we say is that it is equally sinful to deliberately elect a heretical king and to deliberately tolerate a heretical king if he tries to turn away his people from the truth of the faith and if there is enough strength to remove him. In fact, as it is never lawful to incur the danger of losing eternal salvation, so it is never lawful to persevere in a similar danger if that can be avoided: "He who loves danger will perish in it" (Ecclesiasticus 3).[169]

The third example of the quarrelsome wife is not much to the point, for we, as we just said, speak of somebody who knowingly incurs a danger and designedly perseveres in that danger, whereas our adversary makes an example of somebody who by ignorance or imprudence marries a quarrelsome wife, and of another who does the same knowingly and deliberately. Thus, whoever gets married according to Christian custom, whether he does it prudently or imprudently, cannot for any reason be freed from the matrimonial bond once the marriage has been consummated: what God joined man cannot separate. On the contrary, the people who elect a king can be freed from their obedience and oath of allegiance through the pontifical authority. Therefore, if Barclay wants to draw an appropriate example by analogy with matrimony, he should use the example of the marriage of a faithful man with an infidel. As, in fact, it is not lawful

169. Ecclesiasticus 3:27, my translation.

for a faithful man to marry an infidel, because there is the danger that she may drive him away from the faith, so it is also not lawful to remain with an infidel wife, not only because that marriage is not legitimate, but also because there is the same danger in marrying an infidel wife as there is in remaining with an infidel wife. In fact, even if the marriage was legitimate, as is the marriage of an infidel with another infidel, nevertheless if one of them converts to the faith and the other does not want to live with the spouse without doing any wrong to the Creator, the marriage legitimately celebrated can be legitimately dissolved, from the apostle in 1 Corinthians 7. Also the custom of the Church now holds that, because of the great danger for the faith, it would not only be lawful that such a marriage be dissolved but would also be unlawful for a man converted to the faith to live with an infidel spouse.

## CHAPTER 21

# The confirmation of the third principal argument is defended

In chapter 21 Barclay tries with great zeal and no less argumentative aggressiveness to rebut the other confirmation of my third principal argument. This was the confirmation. If Christians in the past did not depose Nero, Diocletian, Julian the Apostate, Valens the Arian, and others like them, this was because the Christians lacked temporal strength. For the fact that otherwise they could have done it rightfully is clear from the apostle's first epistle to the Corinthians, chapter 6, where he orders that new judges of temporal causes be appointed for the Christians, so that Christians would not be obliged to plead a case in front of a judge who was a persecutor of Christ. Therefore as new judges could have been constituted, so also new princes and kings, for the same reason, if there had been strength.

Barclay says that this confirmation can be refuted in many ways, and first he objects to the fact that I said that the Christians in the past did not depose Nero, Diocletian, Julian, and Valens because they lacked the strength, and he refers the reader to what he wrote before on this issue in chapters 6, 7, and 8. We too refer the reader to what we wrote in chapters 6, 7, and 8, and at this point I make just one warning, that what I said there has been said before by St. Thomas in 2a 2ae, question 12, article 2, to the first [objection]. Therefore, Barclay does not blame me only but also St. Thomas, but whoever wishes to read the passages already quoted will easily judge on which side truth stands.

Then he tries to rebut what I said, that the apostle ordered Christians to constitute Christian judges of civil controversies for themselves, from which I deduced that in the same way he could have ordered the Christian peoples to elect Christian princes for themselves, after having removed the infidels and persecutors, if the strength to accomplish it had been available. But Barclay says that those judges about whom the apostle speaks were mere arbitrators, or voluntary judges, without power to command [*sine imperio*], and from their appointment no part of jurisdiction was taken away from the pagan princes under whom Christians then lived. And to confirm this interpretation he brings forth St. Thomas and Nicholas of Lyra in his commentary on that passage of the apostle.

Surely I admit that those Christian judges appointed at the apostle's command did not have coactive power in the external forum, and if the Christians had been called either by pagans or by Christians to the tribunals of the pagan judges they certainly would have had to present themselves, and only this is what St. Thomas and Nicholas of Lyra teach. However, I deny that they were mere arbitrators or voluntary judges, for arbitrators are elected by the quarreling parties, and they have no authority to judge other than that which the quarreling parties grant them at the beginning by a mutual agreement. Those judges, however, were constituted by the public authority of the people, and those who had civil causes were obliged to go to them and were prohibited from going to the tribunals of the pagans. This can be easily proved by the words of the apostle: "Dare any of you, having a matter against another, go to law before the unjust, and not before the saints?"[170] There he shows that it is not commendable to go to the tribunals of the pagan judges whom he calls "unjust." Moreover, the apostle talks about a true judgment and not about an arbitration only, since he forbids them to "go to law before the unjust," and since he orders them to "go to law before the saints," that is, before the Christians. The apostle adds: "Do ye not know that the saints shall judge the world? and if the world shall be judged by you, are ye unworthy to judge the smallest matters? Know ye not that we shall judge angels? how much more things that pertain to this life?"[171] There he demonstrates the authority of the Church, which by its own right can judge secular matters,

---

170. 1 Corinthians 6:1.
171. 1 Corinthians 6:2–3.

since it will judge with Christ the whole world and even the fallen angels in the day of the last judgment. Certainly Christ and the Church will not judge the world as arbitrators without power to command and jurisdiction. He continues: "If then ye have judgments of things pertaining to this life, set them to judge who are least esteemed in the Church,"[172] where he concludes from what was said that since it is evil to be judged by impious pagans and since the Church has the authority to judge, by universal consent they should appoint some members of the Church to be the judges of such secular controversies. He does not say that each should select arbitrators for himself, but "You as a congregation in unity set them to judge." He advises (Cardinal Cajetan says on that passage) that a wise man should be appointed as judge of the multitude of the brethren, and he adds, "I speak to your shame. Is it so, that there is not a wise man among you? no, not one that shall be able to judge between his brethren? But brother goeth to law with brother, and that before the unbelievers."[173] There he makes clear that what he had said, "Set them to judge those who are least esteemed in the church," he did not mean that they should appoint foolish people to judge, leaving aside the wise ones, but so as to rebuke those who went to the tribunals of the infidels as if there were no wise man in the Church who could be appointed as judge, since, by contrast, the least esteemed, that is, the lowest Christians, should be more apt at judging than the highest and wisest infidels.

Now from this principle—that is, that by the testimony of the apostle the Church has the right and the authority to appoint judges for itself—the theologians, *in primis* St. Thomas in 2a 2ae, question 10, article 10, rightly infer that the same Church has authority to abolish the dominion of the infidel princes over the faithful. And it is not a hurdle that St. John Chrysostom, explaining this passage, makes mention of an arbitrator, for neither he nor any other interpreter, as far as I know, says that the apostle here speaks of arbitrators chosen by the parties, but Chrysostom only says that great wisdom is not necessary for an arbitrator of controversy among brethren. There he calls the judge an "arbitrator of controversy"

172. 1 Corinthians 6:4.
173. 1 Corinthians 6:5–6.

even if he would have a public authority to judge. Likewise, Justinus at the beginning of his *Historia* writes that the arbitrations of the princes were considered laws, for although true princes were also judges, nevertheless their judgments were called arbitrations because they did not judge from the precept of the laws but from their natural judgment. Likewise also the judges appointed by the Church in the civil causes of the Christians were true judges, but they were not obliged to follow the letter of the civil laws, and therefore they were called "arbitrators" by Chrysostom.

But Barclay objects and says: "In that passage the apostle orders nothing that either removes or diminishes or in any way prejudices the jurisdiction and authority of the infidel judges over the Christians. Indeed, he could not rightfully order anything against such subjection, since this is of natural law confirmed by the authority of God, as St. Ambrose attests that the apostle teaches in Romans 13."

I reply that the apostle does not prejudice the jurisdiction and authority of the pagan princes through the appointment of Christian judges, since he does not order the Christians not to appear in front of an infidel judge if called, but he instructs them only not to go in front of that judge spontaneously. But that the apostle could have not exempted the Christians from the subjection to infidel princes if he had thought it useful or necessary and if he had had strength to accomplish it, this, I think, cannot be said without a grave error, and the reason that Barclay offers for his opinion is completely weak. In fact, what is of natural law confirmed by God's authority and declared by the apostle is that every soul should be subject to the higher powers. But that a higher power could not be removed by another higher power and through that it could happen that subjection and obedience would not be owed to the former anymore is not of natural law, neither is it confirmed by God nor declared by the apostle. For one must obey by divine law the authority of inferior magistrates, not only for fear of wrath but also for conscience; nevertheless, the prince can remove or replace an inferior magistrate, and then no one owes subjection and obedience anymore to that person from whom the magistracy is taken away. Thus also when a king is removed from his throne either by the supreme spiritual authority in case of heresy, or by another king in case of conquest, what the apostle says, that every soul should be subject to the higher powers, does not apply to the king anymore. The same can be said about the paternal and the despotic authority, since it is of natural law confirmed by God and declared by the apostle in Ephesians 6 that children should obey their parents, and servants their masters, and yet children can be emancipated and servants can be granted freedom and through this it can happen that the former should not be obliged to obey their parents, and the latter their masters. Therefore, unless Barclay demonstrates that it is of natural law confirmed by God and declared by the apostle that secular princes, either faithful or infidels, in certain cases could not be deposed through the ecclesiastical authority, so far he has adduced nothing to the point, no matter with how many words repeated over and over again he has tried to prove his opinion in this chapter.

Afterward Barclay adds another solution, by no means more solid than the previous one: "Moreover, if one does not glance at this passage of the apostle obliquely, he will notice that the apostle attributes to himself the task of educating Christian souls to evangelical perfection, which is more of a counsel than a precept, and he exhorts them to suffer an injury and be victims of a fraud rather than quarrel among themselves, etc."

My reply is that when the apostle exhorts the Christians to avoid quarrels among themselves and to prevent the occasion of lawsuits by means of mildness and patience, he teaches a counsel of perfection, not a precept of justice. But when he orders them to go to law in front of Christian, not infidel, judges if they have indeed quarrels among themselves, then indeed he most clearly appears to give not a counsel, but a precept, when he says, "Dare any of you, having a matter against another, go to law before the unjust, and not before the saints?" and "Set them to judge who are least esteemed in the Church."

Barclay proceeds, and after passing Bellarmine he attacks St. Thomas by saying: "But since we are dealing with issues one by one, it is necessary to warn that Dr. Thomas in 2a 2ae, question 10, article 10, is of the opinion that the right of dominion and of preeminence of the pagan princes can justly be taken away from them through the sentence or the order of the Church which has the authority of God, as he says. The authority of Dr. Thomas is great for me, but not so great that I consider all of his disputations as canonical Scriptures, or so great that it beats reason or the law. Therefore, I worship and admire his ghost, but nevertheless there is no reason why one should be persuaded by his opinion, since he does not offer any appropriate and effective argument or authority for it, and since in explaining Paul's epistle to the Corinthians he clearly thinks quite the opposite, and, finally, since none of the ancient Fathers support him, and many arguments and authorities are available in support of the contrary. The argument he offers, in fact, is that the infidels because of their infidelity deserve to lose their authority over the faithful, who become children of God. This is a faulty argument and unworthy of such a man, as if anybody who deserves to be deprived of his office, benefice, dignity, authority, or another right that he possesses could then be immediately deprived by another person rather than by the person from whom he received it and because of whom he now possesses it, or by another who has an express mandate and authority over him."

The relentlessness of this Aristarchus[174] is to be marveled at, for he blames the prince of the theologians so shamelessly as to say: this is a faulty argument and unworthy of such a man, while he professes himself a jurist and has not even advanced to the portal of the sacred precincts of theology. I do not marvel, however, that he says he worships Thomas's ghost, as his book is absolutely full of inappropriate words: the spirit of that most holy scholar does not enjoy eternal life with the ghosts among the dead but with the angels among the celestial creatures. And what Barclay says, that St. Thomas's opinion is not strengthened by any efficacious argument, is false, even if it is true that the force of St. Thomas's argument could not have been penetrated in the least by Barclay's mind. What he adds, that St. Thomas himself in his commentary on the epistle to the Corinthians wrote the contrary, proves Barclay's clear ignorance, since in that commentary St. Thomas writes that it is against divine law to prohibit one to stand for judgment in front of an infidel prince, and that one owes subjection even to infidel princes, both things being absolutely true. But

---

174. Bellarmine is referring to Aristarchus of Samothrace, a famous grammarian, Homeric scholar, and librarian of the library of Alexandria, who lived in the second century. Because Aristarchus was considered one of the fathers of textual criticism, his name was ironically used as an insult for someone who is judgmental and excessively critical.

from these it does not follow that the Church had no authority to deprive the infidel princes of the dominion they have over the faithful. Therefore, saying that one owes subjection to an infidel prince as long as he is prince, and saying that an infidel prince can be deprived of the dominion he has over the faithful through the authority of the Church, are not in opposition to each other, and Barclay, since he thinks that those are contrary, either never learned dialectics or forgot its rules. Likewise, Barclay clearly hallucinates and is mistaken when, after this, he says: "But Thomas in his explanation of Paul's epistle which we quoted in the previous chapter shows clearly enough that the Church does not have the authority with which it could depose pagan princes, for he says that it is contrary to divine law to prohibit subjects to stand for judgment in front of infidel princes." For even if it is indeed against divine law to deny obedience to the prince as long as he is prince, nevertheless it is not against divine law that the Church have the authority to depose a prince. For it is against divine law to prohibit the children from obeying the parents while they are under the paternal authority, but it is not against divine law that sometimes the children be exempted from the paternal authority, as in fact a son is exempted when he is elevated to the episcopal dignity. Moreover, this argument by St. Thomas, "The infidels, because of their infidelity, deserve to lose their authority over the faithful, who become children of God, and therefore the Church can deprive the infidel princes of the dominion they have over the faithful," is not such a weak argument as Barclay says. The truly weak argument is that with which Barclay opposes St. Thomas's: "The infidels deserve to lose their authority over the faithful, but nobody can deprive them of their authority except whoever gave that authority or whoever has an express mandate from him. Princes receive their authority from God and are inferior to God alone. Therefore, they can be deprived of their authority by God alone, and not by the Church, which neither gave that authority to the infidels nor has an express mandate of God by which it should or could remove it."

I say that this argument has no strength, for it is false that political princes receive their authority from God alone, as they receive it from God to the extent to which God planted in the souls of men the natural instinct of wanting to be governed by another. But how men should be

governed, by kings or consuls, by one or many, by a perpetual or a tempo-
rary magistracy, this depends on men's will, and likewise whether this man
or that man should be king is not a specific command of God but rather
the will of the men making the decision. Whereby St. Thomas in the
quoted passage, 2a 2ac, question 10, article 10, and question 12, article 2,
poses as a certain and well-established issue that political dominion and
authority are not of divine law, but of human law, and no learned man
denies this, and neither would Barclay if he applied reason, not passion,
in his discussion.

Moreover, even if we conceded that the king is immediately appointed
by God and receives authority from Him alone, which however we do not
concede, still Barclay's argument would not accomplish anything against
St. Thomas's. For St. Thomas would reply that the Church has authority
from God through His rector and pastor to take away, in certain cases, the
authority from those to whom God gave it. In fact the Supreme Pontiff is
the Vicar of God, and because of this he has from God the authority to arrange and change many things according to the will of God, of which the
Pontiff is the interpreter. In this way the Pontiff grants dispensations in
vows and oaths that God Himself ordered to be sworn, and whose annul-
ment is of divine law, but the Pontiff grants dispensations not because he
himself is above the divine law, but because he interprets that it is the will
of God that in such and such a case the oath or vow be annulled. Likewise,
even the apostle in 2 Corinthians 2 says: "For if I forgave any thing, to
whom I forgave it, for your sakes forgave I it in the person of Christ."[175]
There he says that in the person of Christ he excused the unchaste Corin-
thian from the punishment by which he should have made atonement, by
divine law, either in this life or in purgatory, and this is what St. Thomas
in the quoted passage says, that the Church has the authority of God with
which it can deprive the pagans of the power they have over the faithful.

Then Barclay, not to leave anything untouched, picks also on what
St. Thomas says in 2a 2ae, the same article 10, question 10, that the
Church does not always exercise its right in deposing infidel princes, in
order to avoid scandal, just as the Lord paid the tribute, which He was not

175. 2 Corinthians 2:10.

obliged to, in order not to scandalize those who collected the money, and as the apostle admonishes servants to obey their temporal masters so that the doctrine of the Lord be not blamed.

Barclay says: "He did not refrain from it only because of the scandal, as Thomas in that passage thinks, but because of the lack of authority, because he was not the judge of the infidels, according to what the apostle says in 1 Corinthians 5: 'For what have I to do to judge them also that are without?'[176] and because princes, appointed by God, have as judge above them God alone; by Whom alone they can be deposed. And it does not pertain to this issue that Paul, when he commands Christian servants to show every honor to their infidel masters, adds this, only that the name and the doctrine of the Lord be not blamed."

The lust of picking and pinching of this persnickety censor is intolerable! When St. Thomas says that the Church does not exercise its right because of scandal, he does not add the word *only;* therefore this holy scholar, who mentions one reason and a very true one and the same as the one that Christ himself and the apostle mentioned, even if there are other reasons, must not be blamed so much. For the Lord did not say that He paid the tribute because of scandal "only," and the apostle did not command that masters must be honored by servants for that reason "only," that the name and doctrine of the Lord be not blamed. What Barclay adds, that the Church did not have any authority over infidel princes because what the apostle says, "For what have I to do to judge them also that are without?" is not against St. Thomas, who in 2a 2ae, question 12, article 2, declares that this passage of the apostle is intended as regarding the infidels who never accepted the faith, insofar as they are infidels, not insofar as they rule over the faithful, for the Church cannot judge the infidels because of their infidelity only, since this does not pertain to its government. But when they rule over the faithful, and especially when they try to draw faithful subjects away from their faith, then the Church has the right to deprive them of the dominion they have over the faithful. But the Church does not always exercise this right, either because it lacks the strength or because it wants to avoid scandal. And regarding what he

176. 1 Corinthians 5:12.

says, that princes are appointed by God and they have no judge above them but God, this is an old little song of Barclay, repeated ad nauseam, and rebutted in this chapter and in the previous ones.

In the last point Barclay, after passing over St. Thomas, comes back to Bellarmine, whom he says he can refute out of his own writings, and he presents some passages from book 2, chapter 29, of *De Summo Pontifice*, in which Bellarmine admits, together with Albert Pighius, that the apostles were subject *de iure* and *de facto* to infidel princes in every civil cause and that the infidel princes were not subject to the apostles either *de iure* or *de facto*. From this passage Barclay deduces that Bellarmine thought that in those times the Church had no right to depose infidel princes.

I have already warned in the *Recognitio* of my works that Pighius's opinion, which I once had followed myself, is improbable, and that one must think, following better scholars, that the apostles were *de iure* exempt from every subjection to earthly princes.[177] But even if Pighius's opinion were true, it would not follow that the Church then had no right to deprive the infidel princes of the dominion they had over the faithful. In fact, Pighius would say that the Church and the apostles themselves were subject to the infidel princes for as long as they were princes, but if they had been deposed by the Church, which holds its authority from God, then they would not be subject to them *de iure* any longer. In fact, even a people is subject to a king as long as the king governs, but if he, beaten by another king in battle, ceases to reign, the people will not be subject to him anymore.

Finally Barclay adds another phrase of Bellarmine in book 2, chapter 29, of *De Summo Pontifice*, that is, that to judge, to punish, and to depose pertains only to the superior. This is certainly most true, but nevertheless from it Barclay builds this syllogism according to his own dialectic:

"Subjects cannot by right judge, punish, and depose a superior. All Christians were subject to Nero, Diocletian, and the other pagan emperors and kings. Therefore, they could not depose such emperors and kings. The proposition is granted, as well as the subsumption, and they are supported by a most certain truth. But the conclusion follows by deduction from the

177. Cf. pp. 163–64 and n. 45.

antecedents, and it is diametrically opposed to what Bellarmine says, that the Christians then could have deposed Nero, Diocletian, etc., but since they lacked temporal strength, they refrained from this plan. Therefore, this is false and worthy of blame, just as affirmations and negations cannot both be true at the same time. Hence also the falsity of Thomas's opinion, which we have rebutted above in this chapter, appears."

But Barclay, who with just one syllogism knocked down not only Bellarmine but also St. Thomas, who for the outstanding brilliance of his knowledge is rightly honored with the name of *Doctor Angelicus,* is an absolutely great master in the art of dialectics! I reply to his syllogism in the proper form: the proposition that subjects cannot by right depose superiors is true, but for the syllogism to be legitimate it should be universal. Moreover, it must be understood formally; that is, the subject as subject, or as long as he is subject, cannot depose a superior as superior, that is, as long as he is superior. But the assumption that all Christians were subject to Nero, Diocletian, etc., is false because the apostles and their successors, who were spiritual princes, were not *de iure* subjects of the earthly kings. Second, a Christian people, even if otherwise subject to pagan kings and emperors, nevertheless in the case of the danger of losing the divine faith, could by the right of just defense shake off the yoke of an infidel prince, especially if the Church through the Supreme Pontiffs determined that this should be done. From this it follows that Barclay's conclusion is manifestly false, and St. Thomas's doctrine and that of Bellarmine, who followed St. Thomas, are most true.

# The second confirmation of the third principal argument is defended

In chapter 22 Barclay attacks the second confirmation of the third principal argument that I put in my book to prove the authority of the Supreme Pontiff in temporal matters. This was the confirmation: to tolerate a heretical king or an infidel who tries to drive men to his sect is to expose religion to a very clear danger. The Christians are not bound to, indeed they must not, tolerate an infidel king who poses a clear danger for religion, since when divine and human laws clash, divine law must be preserved and human law discarded; and to preserve the true faith and religion, which is only one and not many, is of divine law, whereas that we have this king or that king is of human law.

Barclay replies to this confirmation, first, that this argument is not in the form of a syllogism. But this is a cavil, for I neither wanted nor thought to reduce the argument to the form of a syllogism, as can be understood from the fact that I did not posit the conclusion expressly and that I inserted many things from the sacred Scripture and from pagan authors and from old and new examples, which Barclay omitted. Then, having disregarded the cavil of the form of the syllogism, Barclay tries to weaken the very strength of the argument by saying: "Let us grant that he has constructed his reasoning in the perfect form, and let us respond to the strength of the argument. Thus I say that his proposition is false; that is, I say that it is not true that to tolerate a heretical king or an infidel who tries to drive men to his sect is to expose religion to a very clear danger, but it is simply to allow religion to be in the danger which it incurred because of the impiety of the heretical or infidel king and to which it has already been exposed without guilt on the part of the people, since no just and legitimate remedy to save religion remains to the people but constancy and tolerance."

I reply that when the Church has not enough strength to shake off the yoke of infidel tyrants, as truly there was not enough in the times of Nero, Diocletian, Constantius, Julian, and Valens, then it is true that to tolerate a heretical king or an infidel who tries to drive men to his sect is not to expose religion to danger but to allow it to be in danger. But when there is enough strength and the Church can, if it wishes, deprive the heretical or infidel king of the dominion he has over the faithful through the authority of the Vicar of Christ, then if the Church does not do it, truly and properly the Church exposes religion to a very clear danger, since the Church does not want to apply the remedy that is at hand, unless maybe there should be some reason for deferring this remedy and in the meantime trying other milder remedies.

What Barclay adds here, that it was very easy for the Christians then to depose Julian, Constantius, and Valens, has been refuted abundantly above in chapters 6, 7, and 8, and I do not wish to imitate Barclay in repeating the same things often.

Barclay proceeds, and he adds: "And now to that which he deduces from the clash between divine and human laws, I briefly reply that he is mistaken in thinking that here there is a fight or clash between divine and human laws. For to preserve the true faith and religion and to tolerate a heretical or infidel king are not contradictory, and it is not that one is of divine law and the other of human law, as he thinks. Rather, to worship God by the true religion and to serve and obey the king are two precepts of divine law which can be preserved and fulfilled at the same time, as the Jesuits themselves teach."

I did not ignore that to serve and obey the king is of divine law and therefore I did not deny it in my book, but I said that it is of human law to have this man or that man as king, whereas it is of divine law to preserve the true faith and religion. And even though we are held by divine law to be subject to the king as long as he is king, nevertheless nothing in divine law prescribes that the king could never, for any reason, be removed from the kingdom; otherwise the kings who from the beginning of the world have been deprived of the kingdom would have all been deprived unjustly and there would be no commonwealth, or almost no commonwealth, justly instituted, since the commonwealths for the most part have been constituted after the removal of the kings. This is, then, what we say, that in order for divine law to be held with respect to preserving the true religion, it is allowed sometimes to modify human law and to transfer a kingdom from an infidel to a faithful person when either it is not possible or hardly possible for the true religion to be preserved otherwise.

But again Barclay takes exception: "This is all true, that is, that by human law it happens that this or that man is king. But beware, reader: do not be deceived. Bellarmine omitted the main point; he should have added, 'but once we have this or that king, it is of divine law to obey that person in civil matters with every honor and reverence.' With this addition, which no Catholic can deny, his argument is completely destroyed."

I have already taught that once we have this or that king, by divine law we must obey him as long as he sits on the throne. But it is not of divine law that he should sit on that regal throne as long as he lives, for it can happen that either he himself abdicates his authority, or that he falls from his kingdom after having been overcome by another king, or that he is deposed because of heresy; and in whatever manner he may cease to be king, also obedience to him ceases to be owed.

But, Barclay says, "From Bellarmine's opinion in *De Summo Pontifice*, book 2, chapter 29, the council is not allowed to judge, punish, or depose a Pope who is trying to upset and destroy the Church of God, but it is allowed only to resist him by not doing what he commands and by preventing his will from being executed. Why do we not think the same, and with even better reason, about kings? Since they too are superior to their peoples (as the same author attests in *De Summo Pontifice*, book 1, chapter 9, and book 3, chapter 19) and have no judge on earth? And since, moreover, some theologians of great name have thought that the ecumenical council is provided with a larger authority over the Pope than that which the people might have over the king?"

I reply that if the Supreme Pontiff became a heretic and tried to destroy the Church by driving it away from the Catholic faith, without a doubt he could be deposed or certainly he could be declared deposed by the council, as is gathered from the canon "Si Papa," distinction 40,[178] and neither Bellarmine nor any other Catholic denies this. Therefore, from this very point Barclay could have understood that it is not surprising if kings can be deposed because of heresy, even if they have no superior in temporal matters, since the Pope could be deposed for a similar cause, and he has no superiors on earth either in temporal or in spiritual matters. As to what I wrote in book 2, chapter 29, that the Pontiff cannot be judged or deposed by a council, this is meant aside from the reason of heresy, that is, if he should seem to be wanting to upset or destroy the Church with his way of living and his morality only. In fact, there is a difference between the Pontiff and the king: the Pontiff has absolutely no superior on earth, since he is the principal servant whom the Lord placed above all His household (Luke 12), of whom the Lord himself says in that passage that if that servant behaves impiously and starts to beat the menservants and the maids, and to eat and drink, and to be drunken, then the Lord will come in a day when he looketh not for him, and He will punish him most severely,[179] and therefore the Lord does not wish him to be punished by the household or by one of its members, but He reserves to Himself judgment of that servant. The king, however, did not receive the kingdom from God immediately, but the people transferred the authority to him, and moreover, if the king is or was Christian, he is subject to the Pontiff as a sheep is to the shepherd, and even if he does not have any temporal superior in temporal matters, nevertheless he has a spiritual superior whose authority extends also to temporal matters; thus he can be deposed by the Supreme Pontiff as the Vicar of Christ. As to the fact that some learned men thought that the council is above the Pope to a greater degree than the kingdom is above the king, we are not much troubled by their opinions, since the contrary can be gathered from Scriptures and even from the decrees of general councils, and on this topic we wrote enough in the second book of *De conciliis.*

But maybe somebody will ask: if the Pope has absolutely no superior

178. This is canon 6, distinction 40, of the first part of Gratian's *Decretum* (text in *Corpus iuris canonici,* vol. 1, col. 146).

179. This is Bellarmine's paraphrase of Luke 12:45–46.

on earth, by what right can he be deposed by a council or by the Church for heresy? The answer is ready: while men can be expelled by the Church through excommunication for other crimes, heretics exit and separate themselves, and, in a sense, they excommunicate themselves, as St. Jerome noted, explaining those words of the apostle in Titus 3: "A man that is an heretick . . . being condemned of himself."[180] Therefore, if the Pontiff became a heretic or an infidel or an apostate—which I do not think can happen—he would be not so much deposed as declared deposed by the council.

180. Titus 3:10–11.

# The third confirmation of the third
# principal argument is defended

In chapter 23 Barclay tries to refute the third confirmation of my third principal argument, and this is the confirmation: finally, why cannot a faithful people be freed from the yoke of a king who is an infidel and who draws the people to infidelity, in the same way that a Christian wife whose infidel husband refuses to remain with her is free from the obligation of cohabitation without any wrong to the faith, as Innocent III in chapter "Gaudemus," title "De divortiis," deduces clearly from the first epistle of Paul to the Corinthians 7?[181] This is not a greater issue.

To this confirmation Barclay responds in such a way that he seems to be purposefully unwilling to understand in what the force of the reason consists, and he does that so as to have an occasion, by much writing, either to show off his doctrine or to enrich his book. But the wise reader will easily perceive that he goes off topic. At the beginning he imagines me to be speaking of matrimony between two Christian spouses, one of whom later falls into heresy, which marriage cannot by any means be dissolved, and it cannot rightly be compared with the bond between king and people.

But it never came to my mind to speak about such matrimony. I spoke of the matrimony between two infidels, and when one of them converts to the Christian faith, she is free from cohabitation and a bond with the infidel spouse. That I spoke of this matrimony is clear from the apostle and

---

181. This refers to chapter 8, title 19, of the fourth book of Gregory's *Decretales*, which concerns a series of rules on the legitimacy of marriages contracted by heretics who have converted to the faith (text in *Corpus iuris canonici*, vol. 2, cols. 723–24).

from Innocent, whom I quoted, for neither the apostle nor Innocent declares free from matrimony somebody who, after being baptized, marries a Christian. Rather, they declare free from matrimony somebody who, after being baptized, marries an infidel and later converts to the Christian faith even though the spouse remains an infidel.

"But," Barclay says, "you did not say that the Christian spouse is free from the tie or bond, but from the obligation to remain with the infidel spouse."

I said what the apostle said, and I meant what the apostle meant. These are the apostle's words: "If any brother hath a wife that believeth not, and she be pleased to dwell with him, let him not put her away. And the woman which hath an husband that believeth not, and if he be pleased to dwell with her, let her not leave him. For the unbelieving husband is sanctified by the wife, and the unbelieving wife is sanctified by the husband: else were your children unclean; but now are they holy. But if the unbelieving depart, let him depart. A brother or a sister is not under bondage in such cases."[182] There he speaks of the obligation of cohabitation in the same way as I spoke, but the apostle by freedom from the obligation of cohabitation did not mean only freedom from the obligation of cohabitation while the matrimonial bond or tie remained, but total freedom with the power to enter another marriage, since the bond and tie with the other spouse would have been severed, and I wanted my words to be understood in this same manner as all the theologians understand the words of the apostle. Therefore, Barclay could have omitted more than half of this chapter 23.

Then he comes closer to the matter, but, in order to disprove my argument, he ties himself in a most serious mistake. He speaks thus: "But if he means this as an argument for later spouses, the reply is available from the same decretal letter of Innocent, that is, that between such spouses matrimony is not unalterable insofar as it pertains to an indissoluble bond of union, and therefore such spouses have full freedom to dissolve the matrimony so that they may separate either by mutual consent and good grace, or with anger of heart and offence, and one spouse, when the other does

182. 1 Corinthians 7:12–15.

not want the separation, may dissolve that bond through repudiation and divorce whenever he likes." And later: "It is not surprising that a spouse, led to the faith, is free from the union with and the authority of the other spouse who remains in his infidelity, since even if both had remained in their infidelity, each of them would have been equally free to separate from the other and to dissolve the matrimony by repudiation, because from the beginning there was no unalterable and firm bond of obligation." And later: "Since, then, there is no unalterable union between those, and the political subjection and regal dominion among all the people and in every law is fixed and proved both by divine and human law, what can be said that is more absurd or vain than to compare these things and to use the unity and bond of infidel spouses, which can be arbitrarily dissolved, as an argument in support of the dissolution of the regal bond, thereby making the same judgment on both cases as if they were quite similar?"

It is surprising that such a jurist rushed into this mistake from one word of Innocent, badly understood, since when Innocent says in chapter "Quanto," title "De divortiis,"[183] that the matrimony between infidels is not unalterable, he does not mean that it can be dissolved *ad libitum,* but that it is not absolutely indissoluble, as is the matrimony between Christians, for it is only dissolvable in the case mentioned by the apostle, with the apostle himself declaring the will of God in that matter. But apart from that case the marriage between infidels legitimately contracted is clearly firm and indissoluble, first, from Innocent himself in chapter "Quanto," already cited, where he says that marriage between infidels is true matrimony, and true matrimony is defined as the union between a man and a woman in undivided communion of life in chapter "Illud," title "De praesumptionibus";[184] and the canonists generally approve that definition, as also the theologians along with the Master [Peter Lombard]

183. This is canon 7, title 19, of the fourth book of Gregory's *Decretales,* which, like the previous one, is taken from a letter of Pope Innocent III and deals with issues of matrimony between an infidel and one of the faithful (text in *Corpus iuris canonici,* vol. 2, cols. 722–23).

184. This is chapter 11, title 23, book 2, of Gregory's *Decretales:* it was issued by Alexander III, and it declared as a legitimate matrimony that between a man and a woman who lived together as husband and wife even if there were no witnesses to the wedding (text in *Corpus iuris canonici,* vol. 2, col. 355).

in *Sententiae,* book 4, distinction 27. Second, Innocent in chapter "Gaudemus" expressly teaches the same, that repudiation even among infidels is not licit, which likewise he holds in canon "Si quis Iudaicae," causa 28, question 1,[185] where it is said that among infidels repudiation is valid by law of the courts [*lege fori*], not by law of heaven [*lege poli*]. Third, the Council of Trent, session 24, at the beginning says: "The first progenitor of mankind by inspiration of the divine Spirit declared the bond of matrimony perpetual and indissoluble when he said: 'This is now bone of my bones, and flesh of my flesh: she shall be called Woman, because she was taken out of Man. Therefore shall a man leave his father and his mother, and shall cleave unto his wife: and they shall be one flesh.'"[186] And certainly Adam was not talking of matrimony among Christians only but of matrimony in general; therefore, he considers every true matrimony as a perpetual and indissoluble bond. Fourth, there is the common opinion of the scholars, since Master [Peter Lombard] in book 4, distinction 33, of the *Sententiae,* and with him St. Bonaventure, Richard of Middleton, Domingo de Soto, and many others teach that repudiation was granted to the Jews by God through Moses as the lesser evil, but it was never licit either among the Jews or among the Gentiles. Others, not few, such as St. Thomas, Scotus, Durandus, and Pierre de la Palude, teach that there was such a dispensation regarding repudiation for the Jews, but that nevertheless that dispensation was removed by Christ, so that later it was not licit any longer either to the Jews or to the pagans, for Christ's words are clear enough, in Mark [Matthew] 5: "Whosoever shall marry her that is divorced committeth adultery," and Mark 10: "Whosoever shall put away his wife, and marry another, committeth adultery against her. And

185. This is canon 17, causa 28, question 1, of the second part of Gratian's *Decretum,* issued at the Council of Arverne (535 A.D.). It excludes from the communion with the Church those who had contracted matrimony according to the Jewish ceremony. In his commentary for this canon, Gratian introduced the distinction between a wedding "legitimate but not ratified," one "ratified but not legitimate," and one "legitimate and ratified" (text in *Corpus iuris canonici,* vol. 1, col. 1089).

186. This is the beginning of the Tridentine formula of doctrine for the sacrament of matrimony, issued during the 24th session of the Council of Trent on 11 November 1563 (text in *Conciliorum oecumenicorum decreta,* pp. 729–30; the biblical quotation is Genesis 2:23–24).

if a woman shall put away her husband, and be married to another, she committeth adultery."[187] Therefore Barclay, who following the mistake of the Turks wanted it to be licit for infidels to sever matrimonies *ad libitum,* cannot be excused, for even if the Turks do this, nevertheless they do it clearly by mistake. From these considerations our argument, which Barclay attempted in vain to attack, is proved to be absolutely solid. In fact, if it is licit to the faithful spouse on account of faith and religion to break the bond, otherwise indissoluble, with which he was tied to the infidel spouse before his conversion to the faith, how much more will it be licit for the faithful people on account of faith and religion to break the bond with which the people were tied to the infidel prince, especially if he strives to pervert them? For it is clear that the bond by which a people is tied to their prince is weaker than that by which a wife is tied to her husband, since the bond of the people to the prince could, and up to now can, be dissolved for many reasons, but the bond of the wife to the husband among Christians cannot be dissolved in any case, if it is ratified and consummated, and among the infidels it cannot be dissolved rightfully unless through one spouse's conversion to the faith with the other persisting in infidelity.

187. The first reference given by Bellarmine is Matthew 5:32; the second is Mark 10:11–12.

---

# Bellarmine's fourth argument in support of the authority of the Pontiff in temporal matters is defended

In chapter 24 Barclay relates the fourth argument that I used to establish the authority of the Supreme Pontiff in temporal matters to the point of removing the princes themselves in certain cases. This is the argument: when kings and princes come into the Church to become Christian, they are received with the explicit or tacit pact that they submit their scepters to Christ, and they promise to serve and defend the faith of Christ even under pain of losing their kingdoms. Thus, when they become heretics or when they hinder religion, they can be judged and even deposed by the Church, and if they are deposed no injustice is committed against them. Barclay relates my argument up to this point, even though in my book many more things are added to confirm this reason. He responds, however, by admitting the antecedent and by denying the consequence: "In fact, even if it is true that the princes who come to the Church submit themselves and their scepters to Christ, and voluntarily make those promises—either tacitly or explicitly—that Bellarmine mentions, nevertheless it is not true and it does not follow from this that they can be judged and deposed by the Church or by the Supreme Pontiff if they move away from the faith and neglect the pact that they swore. For that supreme jurisdiction and temporal authority over all kings and the whole world which Christ has as the Son of God does not belong to the Church or to the Pontiff, but only that authority which Christ assumed for himself while He lived as a man among men. Christ, however, did not usurp any temporal dominion or authority while He lived on earth as a man among men, and therefore neither the Church as the Church nor the Pope as the head of the Church and the Vicar of Christ has any temporal authority, as this very learned man himself explains and proves in many passages of book 2, chapter 4, of *De Summo Pontifice*."

Barclay's argument, with which the consequence of my argument is refuted, has a fallacious consequence and a false antecedent; therefore, he fights with no strength and with only the noise of his words. I say that his consequence is fallacious because even if the Church or the Pope would not have by themselves the authority to depose heretical princes, nevertheless they would have it from that sworn promise and from the pact contracted with those princes when they were admitted into the Christian Church. This can be illustrated with an example. When kings made an alliance with the Roman empire and swore an oath of allegiance, and if afterward an allied king moved to the side of the enemies of the Romans, the Romans did not think they would be committing an injustice to that king if they deprived him of his kingdom, even though before the alliance the Romans did not have any authority over that king; nevertheless, the promise made and sanctioned with an oath gave them that authority.

Moreover, the antecedent of Barclay's argument is false, as up to this point we have shown sufficiently by such a lengthy demonstration; and from the things that Barclay himself at this point admits this can be demonstrated with no effort. In fact, he admits that the Supreme Pontiff as the Vicar of Christ has the same authority Christ had while He lived as a man among men. But even though Christ did not want to take away any temporal kingdom from those who possessed it, neither seizing a kingdom for Himself nor transferring it to others, nevertheless whoever denies that Christ could have done it denies the Gospel itself, for this is what Christ says in John 13: "The Father had given all things into his hands."[188] If He had all things in His hands, certainly He had authority over everything, and if He had authority over everything, why could He not dispose of the temporal things of all men? In John 17 our Lord says the same to the

---

188. John 13:3.

Father: "as thou hast given him power over all flesh,"[189] where "all flesh" means "all men." Therefore, Christ as a man on earth had authority over all men, and therefore also over emperors and kings; and He could have judged them, punished them, deprived them of their empires and kingdoms, if He had wished.[190] He showed this authority when He gave leave to some devils to rush among a great number of swine and to throw them all into the sea and drown them, and He was not afraid to commit a possible injustice against those who suffered not a small damage from the loss of such a big herd, which, as St. Mark in chapter 5 attests, amounted to two thousand swine. For the Lord judged that it was expedient to the glory of God that He dispose of that temporal thing, even with damages to its owners, so that it would be known how many evil spirits dwelled in man and how easily He removed so many devils with His command [*imperium*] alone.

What Barclay adds, saying I taught that the Church as Church or the Pontiff as the head of the Church and the Vicar of Christ cannot have any temporal authority, is a mere imposture, since I taught only that the Pontiff's authority is directly spiritual, but indirectly it is extended to temporal matters, even up to the deposition of earthly princes. And why, for heaven's sake, does Barclay expend so much effort in examining and refuting Bellarmine's reasons for confirming pontifical authority in temporal matters if Bellarmine agrees with Barclay in denying that pontifical authority in temporal matters? But my books, often attacked, are available, and the reader will easily be able to judge whether I contradict myself in that book, or whether Barclay behaves as a deceiver; as the phrase of the noble poet goes: "Let fraud supply the want of force in war."[191]

Afterward Barclay adds another response, since he was not so senseless as to fail to see that the first solution had no strength, and he says: "All these things certainly the princes promise to Christ, while the Church, as His spouse in whose womb they are regenerated, or the Pontiff, not as a

189. John 17:2.
190. On this point see Bellarmine's *Recognitio,* pp. 12–15, and the introduction to this book.
191. Virgil, *Aeneid,* 2, v. 390, Dryden's translation.

man but serving as a minister of Christ, accept the promise, and therefore the obligation is primarily obtained by Christ through the Church or through the Pope." And later: "If they afterward neglect the pact contracted, or disregard it, they can be punished only by Him in Whose name they swore, and Who is the Lord of all temporal things, and Whom alone they have as a judge over them in temporal matters, not by him to whom is committed only the responsibility of disposing of spiritual things and of receiving the promise."

I reply that the promise with which the infidel princes when they come to the Church promise to be faithful and to defend the Church and to never abandon it under pain of the deprivation of their kingdoms, this promise, I say, certainly is primarily directed to Christ, but nevertheless not only can Christ punish the transgressors directly and by Himself, but the Vicar of Christ, who, having received this authority from Christ, rules the Church, can also punish the transgressors of the pact and of the oath. Likewise, we see today that those who in the king's absence swear before the vice-regent, if they perchance withdraw from the oath, are immediately punished by the vice-regent; and the clergymen who, in the bishop's absence, promise obedience before his general vicar, if perchance they prove themselves disobedient, are thrown in prison and punished by that vicar.

"But," Barclay says, "rarely does the king himself receive an oath of allegiance, but most often that work is done through the chancellor. Therefore, the chancellor, when he swears in the vassals in the name of the king to the fief and offices in the civil administration and in temporal jurisdiction under the king, attends to those duties that the Pope attends to under Christ in the spiritual government of the Church when the Pope receives the princes who come to the Church after pledging their oath of allegiance and faith to God. And as the former certainly cannot for any reason take away the fief from the vassal once the prince has accepted him (even if afterward the vassal breaks the pact and commits a crime which they call felony), which is a prerogative of the king alone and it is absolutely not conceded to the chancellor, so the latter cannot deprive of the kingdoms and offices or punish in any other temporal manner the princes received in the Church, no matter how gravely afterward they may sin and become deserters of the faith."

I reply that this whole argument is Barclay's deception because he deduces that the Supreme Pontiff is similar to a chancellor who has no jurisdiction. This comparison is very far from the truth, since divine Scriptures attribute to the Pontiff a true authority and jurisdiction the most ample and supreme, for what Matthew 16 says, "Whatsoever thou shalt bind on earth shall be bound in heaven" refers to the office of a ruler who has jurisdiction, not to the office of a chancellor. Also John [21], "Feed my sheep," attributes to the Pontiff not the office of the chancellor in a kingdom, but that authority over Christians which the shepherd has over the sheep, who can surely rule them, tie them up, strike them with a stick, and compel them to every form of obedience. Also what the apostle says in Acts, chapter 20, "Take heed therefore unto yourselves, and to all the flock, over which the Holy Ghost hath made you overseers,"[192] does not indicate the office of a chancellor but the office of a ruler and commander. Finally Matthew 24 "Who then is a faithful and wise servant, whom his lord hath made ruler over his household?"[193] does not show us the office of a chancellor but the office of the ruler of the household, who rules over the whole household with authority. Therefore, the Pontiff should have been compared not with a chancellor but with a vice-king in a kingdom, or a vicar in a bishopric, or a regent in a city, or an overseer in a household, or the head in the body. I am saying all this in response to Barclay's opinion (if we grant that it should be admitted), i.e., that the princes, when they come to the Church, promise obedience and allegiance to Christ alone. However, this opinion is false, and we cannot admit it for any reason, since the princes promise obedience and allegiance, expressly or tacitly, not to Christ alone but also to those who occupy Christ's place on earth. And that confirmation of the argument, which I have added to my fourth reason and to which Barclay refers at the end of chapter 24, pertains to this issue—that confirmation about which Barclay says he does not know

192. Acts 20:28.
193. Matthew 24:45.

or pretends not to know to what it pertains. He says: "But what he adds here to the fourth reason—for whoever is not suitable for the sacrament of baptism is not ready to serve Christ, and to leave for Him whatever he has, as the Lord says in Luke 14, 'If any man come to me, and hate not his father, and mother, and wife, and children, and brethren, and sisters, yea, and his own life also, he cannot be my disciple'[194]—I do not see what it pertains to. Certainly nobody denies this, but so what? Such reason does not pertain to the issue more than the least-pertinent point, and not even that which follows—moreover, the Church would commit a grave sin if it admitted a king who wanted impunity to foster any sect and to defend the heretics and to destroy religion. This is most true, but, as I said, it does not pertain to the issue, for the question is not about this but about the temporal authority of the Church or the Supreme Pontiff."

To what extent these things pertain to the issue, and indeed they are perfectly to the point, I show in the following manner. Let us pretend that an infidel king comes into the Church and, according to Barclay's instructions, speaks thus: "I want to become through baptism a fellow citizen of the saints, and sacredly I promise to be willing to submit my scepter to Christ, and to defend His Church according to my strength, and to never withdraw from this holy purpose. But I protest that if perchance I break the pact, if I become a heretic, an apostate, a pagan, if I try to persecute the Catholic religion and to destroy it completely, I do not want to be punished with a temporal punishment by the Church or its ruler, but by Christ alone. And if perchance the ruler of the Church expels me from the community of the pious through the sentence of excommunication, I want nevertheless the faithful children of the Church to be obliged to serve and obey me as their king, and their obligation of obedience can never be abrogated." I now ask Barclay, could such a king be admitted as suitable for baptism? I think he will say yes, but he will be made fun of by prudent men. In fact, if anybody should want to be given an earthly estate as a present and should protest that if he became a traitor of that city he should not be punished immediately by the ruler of the city but only by the king who resided in a distant land, who would not laugh? Certainly

194. Luke 14:26.

whoever should be ready, as the Gospel says, to offer his own life for the faith of Christ, should he not be more ready to lose his temporal kingdom? For it is ridiculous to say: "I am ready to be deprived of my kingdom if I break the pact, but I do not want to be deprived of it through a human sentence; I want the sentence to be pronounced by the angels in heaven." Certainly even the Church would be greatly imprudent if it admitted to its womb somebody who would want impunity to run riot among the members of the Church and who would not want the faithful people to be able to be freed from his tyranny by any authority of mortal men.

# Bellarmine's fifth argument in support of the authority of the Supreme Pontiff in temporal matters is defended

In chapter 25 Barclay examines my fifth argument, and first he reports it with these words: "The fifth and last argument is based on pastoral care and office. When Peter was told 'Feed my sheep' (John, last chapter), he was given every authority that is necessary for the shepherd to protect his sheep. To the shepherd a threefold authority is necessary: one concerns wolves, so that he may keep them away in any way he can; the second concerns the rams, so that if they ever hit the flock with their horns he may be able to confine them; the third concerns the rest of the sheep, so that he may provide each one of them with the proper forage. And therefore the Supreme Pontiff has this threefold authority."[195]

After having reported this, Barclay adds: "From this principle and foundation three compelling arguments are deduced, as he thinks. But not to be too long, I reply first of all to this foundation: it is wholly true and supports me, and from it is most brilliantly deduced the opposite of what he bellicosely affirms." This is what he said, and after many empty words he constructed this syllogism: "Christ, commending His sheep to Peter, gave him every authority necessary to protect the flock. He did not give him temporal authority. Therefore, temporal authority is not necessary to protect the flock."

---

195. Cf. Bellarmine's use of this argument with Vitoria's *relectio* 1 "On the power of the Church," question 5, article 9.

I reply that if by temporal authority Barclay wants to mean that authority which is, in itself, properly and formally temporal, the argument can
be admitted, but I deny that from this it follows that this authority, which
even if it in itself is spiritual, nevertheless could be extended to temporal
matters insofar as they refer to spiritual matters and are subordinated to
them, is not necessary to the Supreme Pontiff. If, on the contrary, by
temporal authority Barclay means the authority to dispose of temporal
matters for the sake of spiritual matters, then I say the assumption is false,
and I add that Barclay's supersyllogism suffers from the flaw that is the
most common in the art of discussion; that is, he assumes and wants
what is in fact under discussion to be granted to him. In fact, he assumes
that temporal authority was not given to St. Peter, as if this very thing
were not what he is seeking to prove in his whole book. And certainly if
it were legitimate to dispute in such a way, I too could reason thus: Christ
gave Peter only that authority which is necessary to protect and feed his
flock. He gave Peter the spiritual authority that is extended to temporal
matters when they refer to spiritual matters. Therefore, such authority is
necessary to protect and feed the flock. But let us hear another of Barclay's
syllogisms, not different from the previous one.

He says: "Then we proceed in this way. It is absurd that the Supreme
Pontiff, insofar as he is Peter's successor, has more authority than Peter
had. Peter had no temporal authority over the Christians. Therefore, neither does the Supreme Pontiff now, insofar as he is Peter's successor."

And so that it might not be objected that he assumes what was to be
proved, he proves the assumption from Bellarmine's book 5 of *De Summo
Pontifice*, chapter 6, where he says that the spiritual and temporal authorities are like the spirit and the flesh; and just as the spirit and the flesh can
be conjoined, as in a man, and can be separate, as in angels and beasts,
so also the spiritual and temporal authorities can be conjoined, as they
now are among Christians, and can be separate, as they were in the time
of the apostles, when there was no political prince in the Church. From
this Barclay deduces: "If these authorities were separate at the time of the
apostles, which indeed they were *de iure* and *de facto*, it follows necessarily that Saint Peter had no temporal authority; otherwise it would be
false that they were separate."

Barclay thinks so much of this argument that afterward he says: "And indeed these reasons are more obvious than those which anybody could oppose and refute without fraud, so that it is surprising that other learned and pious men are blinded by such an inconsiderate zeal that they do not hesitate to embrace and follow doubtful instead of certain things, obscure instead of clear things, contorted instead of straight things, and finally things involved and tied in many controversies instead of things that are plain." These are the words of Barclay, who until the end of this chapter continues to preach his reverence toward the Apostolic See and to reproach our blindness and repeat many of the things he has said before, as is his custom.

Bellarmine most truly said that the spiritual or ecclesiastical authority is like the spirit, and the temporal or political authority is like the flesh: St. Gregory of Nazianzus, Hugh of St. Victor, St. Thomas, Alexander of Hales, Thomas Netter, and others have put forth the same comparison to explain this issue before Bellarmine did. And it was not less truly said that those authorities were separate in the time of the apostles in the same way in which the spirit of the angels is separate from the flesh, and the flesh of the brutes is separate from the spirit, but now they are conjoined in the same way in which spirit and flesh are conjoined in men. From these things it is rightly inferred that St. Peter had apostolic authority, that is, the supreme and most ample spiritual and ecclesiastical authority, and that he did not have the regal or imperial or another purely temporal and political authority. But it is not rightly inferred that the spiritual authority of St. Peter could not extend to all temporal matters and even to the ruling and correcting of kingdoms and empires if kings and emperors became Christians. Therefore, the difference between the time of the apostles and our time does not concern the authority, which has always been the same, in St. Peter and in his successors, but concerns the object of that authority or the use of that authority. The apostolic authority, in fact, was not at that time exercised in ruling kings, because there were no kings in the Christian Church, whose pastor and rector is the Vicar of Christ. Now, however, that same authority is exercised in ruling and correcting kings because there is no lack in the Church of political kings and princes.

And to illustrate this issue with examples, certainly the spirits of men, once they are separated from the bodies, are the same as they were before when they animated the bodies and have the same power they had before; yet, now separated, they do not rule the bodies as they did before, and as they will do again after the resurrection. Likewise also the spirits of the angels, both the good ones and the evil ones, until they assume a body, do not exercise power over the members of the body, but when they either assume ethereal bodies or enter into human bodies, they move those bodies at their command, and they direct and restrain them; and there will be no man so imprudent as to think that angels acquire a new power when they assume bodies. By the same token, when in the human body a limb is cut off and separated from the rest of the body, the spirit cannot move that limb and direct it, not because the spirit does not have power to do so but because there is no limb the spirit might move to exercise its power. Finally, at the beginning of the Christian Church, before the apostles ordained deacons, they could not make use of them and give them commands, but after the deacons had been ordained, the apostles made use of them and gave them commands. Shall we then concede that the apostles did not have any ecclesiastical authority before the deacons began to exist in the Church? We should indeed, if we were mad along with Barclay, who from the lack of the object over which the authority is exercised infers the lack of the authority. From this it is clear how weak Barclay's arguments are, those arguments that to his judgment seemed incontrovertible demonstrations.

# The first part of the fifth argument in support of the authority of the Supreme Pontiff in temporal matters is defended

In chapter 26 Barclay begins to refute the first part of my fifth argument, which was as follows. An authority to keep the wolves away from the sheep with every possible means is necessary to the shepherd. The wolves that devastate the Church are the heretics. Therefore, if a prince from a sheep or a ram becomes a wolf, that is, if he becomes a heretic, the Shepherd of the Church will be able to keep him away through excommunication, and at the same time will order the people not to follow him, therefore depriving him of the dominion he has over the subjects.

Responding to this argument Barclay admits everything but the last part of the conclusion, in which we said that the pastor can order the people not to follow their king anymore, for Barclay makes a distinction here and says that certainly the pastor can order the people not to follow a heretical king in his heresies, but he cannot order them not to follow him in political matters. Also, he adds that certainly a heretical king can be deprived of the communion of the faithful in sacred matters, but that this is not to be done if there is a danger of schism or scandal or more serious evils, from Augustine's *Contra epistolam Parmeniani*, book 3, chapter 2, of which issue we spoke in chapter 9. There Barclay treated these same matters in a more prolix way, and I have already warned that Barclay wanted to spend a great part of his book in repeating the same things.

Therefore, passing over these things, the whole reason why Barclay denies that the supreme pastor can prohibit the faithful from obeying a heretical king even in political matters is because obedience is owed to kings by divine law, and no man, not even the Supreme Pontiff, can make dispensation in matters of divine law. To prove this he adduces the response of Innocent III, who in the chapter "Cum ad monasterium," title "De statu monachorum," says: "A monk cannot receive a dispensation so that he may take a wife or have property of things,"[196] and at this point he discusses many things concerning divine and human law and concerning the marriage of the daughter of King Roger, Constance, who, even though she was a nun, from a dispensation of Pope Clement III is said to have married Emperor Henry VI.[197]

But we have demonstrated above that Barclay's argument has no strength, since it follows from divine law that an inferior be obedient to a superior for as long as the latter is superior, but if he ceases to be superior, then the precept of offering obedience to him ceases also. We showed this point by many examples: it is of divine law not only that the people be obedient to the king but also that children be obedient to their fathers, servants to their masters, wives to their husbands. Nevertheless, if a son is emancipated, and a servant is given freedom, and a wife is separated from the husband through divorce or repudiation, they are no longer obliged by that divine law. Likewise, even a promise sworn according to divine law has to be kept; nevertheless if the person to whom the promise is made annuls it, the person who made the promise will not be obliged to keep it. Restitution is sanctioned by divine law, but if the creditor remits the debit, there is no obligation of restitution left, and many similar examples could be adduced. Therefore, likewise by divine law the people are obliged to be subservient to the king for as long as he is king, but if he ceases to be king, which can happen in many ways, there is no obligation of servitude or obedience left. Divine law does not forbid a king's deposition for just reasons, and much less does it forbid the Supreme Pontiff's declaring that

196. This is canon 6, title 35, book 3, of Gregory's *Decretales,* in which Innocent III speaks about a series of rules for monastic life, from clothing and food to property (text in *Corpus iuris canonici,* vol. 2, cols. 599–600).

197. Bellarmine is referring to the marriage between Emperor Henry VI and Constance, daughter of Roger II, king of Sicily, celebrated in 1186 and widely contested because it could potentially have led to the unification of the Holy Roman Empire with the kingdom of Sicily.

a heretical king is illegitimate and that therefore the faithful people owe no obedience to him.

Concerning the chapter "Cum ad monasterium," the issue is easy: Innocent in fact teaches only that matrimony and property of things cannot be consistent with the status of monks, since continence and poverty belong to the essence of monastic life. Therefore, the Supreme Pontiff will not be able to make the same man a monk and a husband or a monk and a man rich in individual wealth. But it is another issue whether the Supreme Pontiff could make a dispensation regarding a monk so that he might leave the monastic life to enter a secular life and, becoming a secular man, might enter into marriage and hold property of his own. On this point, in fact, scholars have different opinions.

Regarding Constance, Roger's daughter, we think it is a tale that she, while being a nun and rather old in age, married Henry VI. In fact, Geoffrey of Viterbo, who used to instruct Henry VI in literature and in morals, writes that the marriage of Henry with Constance was celebrated in Milan in 1186 during the pontificate of Urban III, when Constance was thirty years of age. From this it follows that it would be false that Clement III or, as others say, Celestine III or, as others, Alexander III made a dispensation for her in her monastic vows; for the latter was dead already, and the others had not begun to sit on the papal throne yet. It would also be false that she married when she was old, of more than fifty years of age, and last, it would be false that she was previously a nun, since no one who lived in those times writes this. See Cardinal Baronius, volume 12 of the Annals for the year 1186.[198]

198. Cardinal Cesare Baronius, whose *Annales* represented one of the most important historiographical productions of Counter-Reformation Catholicism, was a great friend of Bellarmine's and one of his most trusted collaborators. Bellarmine read Baronius's work attentively and suggested a small but important modification (Bellarmine's censure of Baronius can be found in ARSI, Opp. Nn. 243, vol. 1, fols. 229r–v, and has been published and briefly commented on by Le Bachelet, *Auctarium Bellarminianum*, pp. 567–68). The reader should notice, once again, the relationship between historical accuracy, doctrinal orthodoxy, and polemical concerns in Bellarmine's treatment of history, both in this work against Barclay and in his role as censor.

# Whether a vow or an oath is more binding[199]

In chapter 27 Barclay, in order to get support for his cause from everywhere, compares the vow of monks with the oath with which people promise allegiance and obedience to kings. He says that the Pontiff, according to the opinion of some scholars, can make dispensations in regard to the vows of monks. But even if this be granted, it should not be admitted that he could make dispensations in regard to the oath with which people bind themselves to be obedient to the king. Therefore, Barclay seems to think that the bond of an oath is greater than that of a vow, but St. Thomas in 2a 2ae, question 89, article 8, and almost the entire school of theologians commenting on Peter Lombard's *Sententiae,* distinction 39, seem to think clearly the contrary. A vow, in fact, is a promise made to God, while an oath is the confirmation of a promise made to man. A man, however, is more obliged to keep a promise made to God than a promise made to another man. Moreover, whoever violates a vow is unfaithful to God, while whoever breaks an oath commits a crime of irreverence against God; but the crime of infidelity is more serious than that of irreverence, since every infidelity toward a superior also has irreverence joined to it, while not every irreverence has infidelity. Thus, whoever violates a vow sins more gravely than whoever breaks an oath, and therefore a vow is more binding than an oath. Moreover, a vow is an absolutely good thing; an oath is a good thing if a necessity requires it, as our Lord says in Matthew 5: "But

199. On this issue see Prodi, *Il sacramento del potere,* especially pp. 227ff.

I say unto you, do not swear at all,"[200] and James in his epistle, chapter 5: "But above all things, my brethren, swear not."[201] In contrast, we never read "Do not make vows," but rather David the king and prophet, exhorts us to make vows by saying in Psalm 75: "Vow, and pay unto the Lord your God."[202] Thus, a vow is more noble than an oath, and for this reason whoever breaks a vow sins more gravely than whoever violates an oath; hence it follows that a vow is more binding than an oath. For this reason if the Supreme Pontiff can make dispensations in regard to vows, much more will he be able to do it in regard to oaths.

But Barclay opposes this argument in the following manner: "The entire monastic order, and the other orders in the Church, as some would have it, have proceeded from human decrees and positive law, and therefore the full and complete authority of the Pope is over them, as we have just said. But the submission and obedience owed to kings and princes and to everybody placed over another in the position of a superior is of natural and divine law and is confirmed by both Testaments. For even if it is of human law that we have this or that form of commonwealth, or that we have this or that man as prince, nevertheless to pay reverence to the prince once we have accepted him and to obey him in submission in everything that does not contradict God's mandates, is not only of human ordination but also of natural and divine ordination."

This argument has cracks everywhere; it does not have anything solid and firm. In fact, declaring that the entire monastic order proceeds from human decrees and positive law is not only false but also heretical, since the precepts found in the Gospel, upon which the monastic order is founded, do not proceed from human decrees but from the mouth of God and our Lord Jesus Christ, of which issue I have treated extensively in my work *De monachis,* and no Catholic denies it. Moreover, not only do all Catholics teach that monastic vows, in which the essence of the monastic life consists, are of divine law, but Barclay himself has just admitted it. Why does he therefore now say that the whole monastic order proceeds from human decrees and positive law? Furthermore, if, as he assumes in

200. Matthew 5:34.
201. James 5:12.
202. Psalm 76:11 in the King James Bible.

his own argument, the submission owed to kings, princes, and everybody placed over another in the position of a superior is of natural and divine law and confirmed by both Testaments, then the submission of the monks to their governors and superiors is of natural and divine law, confirmed by both Testaments. From where, then, does Barclay gather that the Pontiff can make dispensations regarding the submission and obedience of the monks toward their governors and superiors and cannot do the same regarding the obedience and submission of the people toward kings and princes, since they are both of natural and divine law and confirmed by both Testaments?

Indeed, since the obedience of the monks is ratified by a vow, and a solemn one at that, and the obedience of the people is confirmed by a simple oath, it seems that in any event a dispensation can be made by the Pope regarding the obedience of the people more easily than that of the monks, since the bond of a vow is greater than that of an oath, as the theologians teach. Moreover, as Barclay attests, human law decides which form of commonwealth we have and whether we have this or that man as prince, but divine law prescribes that we obey a prince after we have accepted one as such. Likewise, human law decides which ritual and form of living the monks follow and whether they have this or that person as a superior, but divine law prescribes that the monks obey with submission him whom they have accepted as a superior. Therefore all these things are the same, and there is no reason why the Supreme Pontiff could make dispensations in one case but not in the other; that is, why he could absolve monks from the bond of obedience promised to their superior but not absolve a subject from the bond of obedience promised to his king.

Barclay proceeds, and he constructs an argument from the nature of the vow and of the oath. Since this argument is not much to the point, though it is set forth by him in a most verbose way, I will reduce it to a few words so that it may be evident what the force of the argument is.

He reasons thus: a vow is a promise made to God and to the Church; therefore God is the principal creditor to Whom the promise is entrusted. The Pontiff, however, who is the Vicar of God and the head of the Church in place of Christ, can declare that God and the Church are not displeased if the promise, because of a just cause and one more pleasing to God than the fulfillment of that promise, is remitted and whoever had made the vow is released from it.

On the other hand, an oath by which a pact or a promise is sealed does not make God the proper creditor but rather the man with whom the pact is made and to whom the promise is sworn. This is very clear from the fact that a man, as the creditor, can even without any reason free the debtor and annul the oath if he wishes to voluntarily remit the promise made to himself. Here the interpretation or declaration of the Supreme Pontiff has no place, since the man himself as creditor would speak for himself. Therefore, the Supreme Pontiff cannot absolve men from an oath, since he would deprive the creditor against his will of the obligation acquired by him with the best right and permitted by every divine and human law.

I reply that when the Supreme Pontiff absolves men from an oath, he does not remove the right obtained by just and licit obligation, but either he declares that an obligation or a promise was or has become illicit, as when he absolves peoples from an oath of allegiance offered to a heretical prince or to a prince who afterward has fallen into heresy; or he removes the bond of the oath, leaving the promise in its force, only to the end that whoever had made the promise could without danger of sacrilege pursue his right in front of legitimate judges.

But these things were not unknown to Barclay, as one who especially professed the skills of the law, and so he adds: "But even if he could for cause remove and release the promise from the bond of the oath (not to fight with the canonists over this issue), let him remove it, but what is the consequence of this for our matter? You will say that the people will be immediately free from dominion and subjection to the prince and will be absolved from the bond of the oath. Is it so? Don't you see that this oath is nothing but an addition that only confirms the obligation by which allegiance and obedience were promised to the prince? And don't you know that such additions can be removed and lifted without erasing the principal obligation? Thus, the obligation to which the oath was added, up until this point, remains, and since this is of natural and divine law, it does not bind men's minds and consciences with God any less than if it were supported by an oath."

Certainly, as I said before, the bond of an oath can be removed, even if the obligation of the promise is not. But when the Supreme Pontiff absolves the people from an oath of allegiance because of heresy or for another just cause, at the same time he usually absolves them also from the bond of the promise and orders them not to be obedient anymore to the person to whom they had made the promise of obedience. Also, that the Pontiff as the Vicar of Christ could do this, we have shown above from the authority of scholars and councils and also from divine Scriptures, and many years ago we showed this very thing with five theological arguments, and Barclay with all his arguments and cavils could not rebut those arguments.[203] In fact, regarding what he repeats and pushes in this passage, that the obligation to be obedient to the kings is of natural and divine law, it has been explained by us more than once that this has to be understood as concerning the obligation to be obedient to the kings as long as they are kings, and a clear reason and the frequent practice have most clearly demonstrated that neither natural nor divine law prevents the king from being deprived of his kingdom if he becomes a heretic.

"But," Barclay says, "Bellarmine supports his arguments especially with this axiom when he wants to show that the Pope cannot submit himself to the coactive sentence of the councils (he says in *De conciliis,* book 2, chapter 18): the authority of the Pope over everybody is of divine law, and the Pope cannot make dispensations in divine law."

I say that if the Pope subjected himself to the coactive sentence of the councils or of any prince whatsoever, truly he would be subjecting a superior to inferiors, and for this he would be fighting against divine and natural law. The Pope is by divine law Shepherd, Father, and Ruler of all Christians, and for this he is superior to all who are his flock and children and subjects; and also by divine law a superior cannot be judged by an inferior at least with a coactive sentence. But indeed when the Pope judges a king, or even deposes him, he does nothing against divine law, since a superior judges an inferior, a shepherd judges a sheep, a father judges a son, a ruler judges his subjects, which is very consistent with divine law and natural reason. Even if kings in temporal matters do not recognize any temporal superior, or anybody else directly apart from God, nevertheless

---

203. Bellarmine is referring to the arguments he made in book 5 of the *Controversia de Summo Pontifice.*

they must recognize a spiritual superior whose authority extends to temporal matters insofar as they are subordinated to spiritual, as has been said before more than once.

At the end Barclay speaks thus: "So as to avoid mistakes, it must be held that the plenitude of the apostolic authority encompasses only that authority which our Lord Jesus Son of God wanted when He lived in this world as a man among men, and to this extent the Pope represents Christ for us and is His Vicar; but it does not encompass that authority which He had and reserved to His divine omnipotence as the Son of God, and God himself equal to the Father from eternity, when He said 'All power is given unto me in heaven and in earth.'"[204]

I do not only admit what Barclay postulates here, that the plenitude of the apostolic power is not the same as Christ's divine omnipotence, but I also add that it is indeed not the same as the power that Christ wanted to have, and had, on earth as a man. In fact, Christ, while He lived as a mortal among mortals, had the power that the theologians call *potestas excellentiae,* through which He could institute sacraments and remit sins without sacraments and other things of such kind, to which the plenitude of power of the Pope does not arrive. Therefore, I am not one of those of whom Juan de Torquemada has written in his comment on the canon "Coniunctiones," causa 25, question 2,[205] that it is something to be marveled at that the Supreme Pontiffs speak moderately of the power given to them, and some minor scholars without any real ground, wanting to flatter them, almost make them equal to God. Nonetheless, I affirm with certainty that our Lord Jesus Christ during His mortal life could dispose of all temporal matters and deprive kings and princes of their kingdoms and dominions, and without a doubt He granted this power to His Vicar so that he may use it when he judges it necessary for the salvation of souls, which must be his principal responsibility.

---

204. Matthew 28:18.

205. This is canon 2, causa 35, question 2, of the second part of Gratian's *Decretum.* It forbids marriage between consanguineous partners because such practice was forbidden by "the divine and secular law" (text in *Corpus iuris canonici,* vol. 1, col. 1264).

## A digression on the opinion contained in the chapter "Inter corporalia," title "De translatione episcopi"[206]

In chapter 28 Barclay declaims against the canonists, who, he says, attribute to the Pontiff all the divine and human authority based on the words of the true opinion of Pope Innocent III, which is contained in the chapter "Inter corporalia." There, in fact, Innocent says that the bond of the spiritual union between the bishops and the Church is stronger than the bond of the carnal union between a husband and a wife. And since a man cannot dissolve the bond of the carnal union, according to Matthew 19, "What therefore God hath joined together, let not man put asunder,"[207] but the Pope has not infrequently dissolved the bond of the spiritual union, it seems to follow that either Innocent wrote false things or he wanted to make the Pope like God.

But because this discussion does not pertain to our issue, and Barclay inserted this digression into his book only so that he would have an opportunity to criticize the canonists—in this chapter he writes with temerity that nobody is more incompetent than mere canonists and in the following chapter he is not ashamed to write that Innocent IV and

206. This is chapter 2, title 7, of the first book of Gregory's *Decretales*. It was taken from a letter written in 1199 by Innocent III to the dean and chapter of the Church of Angers, and it established that only the pope could transfer bishops (text in *Corpus iuris canonici*, vol. 2, cols. 97–98).
207. Matthew 19:6.

Johannes Andreae, easily the princes of the canonists, have explained most incompetently this passage of Innocent III—for these reasons I will not be too prolix in confuting him in this chapter. In fact, the canonists, among whom many very learned men can be found, do not need my defense, and I am not so well versed in the canon law as to dare to declare myself the patron of the canonists. This one thing I wish to note, that Barclay shows himself to be a calumniator when he says that the canonists attribute to the Supreme Pontiff a divine authority by interpreting incorrectly Innocent's words. This is so far from the truth that rather some of them do not fear to diminish or restrain the Pontiff because of this canon. Certainly the gloss, where Innocent says that the spiritual bond is stronger, corrects the phrase by saying "worthier," not "stronger," and Hostiensis in his *Summa*, chapter "De electione," section 21, as Barclay himself reports in this passage, says that this is not a sufficient reason, save by the authority and the reverence for him who says it. Finally, neither Innocent IV nor Johannes Andreae nor Nicholas de Tudeschis nor Petrus de Ancharanus nor any other of those whom I could peruse, attribute to the Pope a divine authority out of Innocent's words, as Barclay falsely says.

# On the true meaning of the chapter "Inter corporalia"

In chapter 29 Barclay, after rejecting other people's explanations, brings forth his own opinion on the true meaning of the chapter "Inter corporalia," and, in sum, he says that the words of this chapter contradict the thoughts of the legislator, since the Pope thought one thing and wrote another. But what is this but making the Pontiff either an ignorant man who did not know how to explain his thoughts or a malicious man who wanted to deceive the reader by lying? But Innocent was, by everybody's account, an excellent and very learned Pontiff, and he was very far from both ignorance and malice. Therefore, I will say what in my opinion the Pope in this obscure chapter wanted to teach, and, if I am not mistaken, I will show that those passages were not only most true words in themselves but were also most appropriate to explain the Pontiff's thoughts.

The Pontiff says that the bond of the spiritual union is stronger than that of the carnal union and that this is true is proved by the following argument: the bond of the spiritual union cannot be completely dissolved, not even through death, because the episcopal mark, which cannot be destroyed by any force, remains always impressed. The bond of the carnal union, however, is dissolved through death, so that if a dead husband came back to life he could not reclaim the wife that he had married while he was alive (this is the teaching of the apostle in Romans 7). Thus, the bond of the spiritual union can be dissolved only by the Supreme Pontiff and not completely, as we have said, but only in respect to the specific church to which the bishop is joined, for the Vicar of Christ only frees the bishops from the bond by which they are held conjoined with their church by transferring them, or deposing them, or granting them the possibility of renouncing the church. However, not only the Pope dissolves the bond of the carnal union, but also they who contracted such union themselves sometimes dissolve it legitimately and freely. For if one of the spouses wishes to join a religious order, that spouse can rightfully dissolve a marriage that has been ratified but not consummated, according to the Council of Trent, session 24, canon 7; and in this matter the said spouse does not have to ask for the Pope's permission.[208] Likewise, one of the spouses can dissolve a marriage contracted among infidels and consummated, which is an absolutely true marriage, if he converts to the Christian faith while the other spouse remains an infidel, from the apostle in 1 Corinthians 7. Likewise, in the Old Testament, here and there the spouses themselves dissolved even consummated marriages through the rubric of repudiation, and they did not wait for the authority of the High Priests, from Deuteronomy 24. Finally, ratified and consummated marriages among the faithful can be dissolved as to bed and cohabitation, for certain causes, by individual bishops, while the spiritual union cannot be dissolved, not even as to cohabitation, by any other than the Supreme Pontiff. From these things, therefore, it is clearly gathered that the bond of the spiritual union, which can be dissolved by the Pontiff only, is firmer and stronger than the bond of carnal union, which is dissolved by the spouses themselves and by inferior priests. And this seems to be what Innocent was referring to, for his aim in this chapter was to teach that the transferring of bishops cannot happen without the consent of the Supreme Pontiff.

208. This is actually canon 6 of the sacrament of matrimony, issued at Trent in 1563 (see *Conciliorum oecumenicorum decreta*, p. 730).

# Response is given to the objections against the first part of the fifth argument in support of the authority of the Supreme Pontiff in temporal matters

In chapter 30 Barclay, after long digressions, comes back to the first part of Bellarmine's fifth argument, which in chapter 25 he took upon himself to rebut. He speaks thus:

"We certainly grant his proposition, that an authority over wolves is necessary to the shepherd, that he might keep them away in any way possible. We also grant the assumption that the wolves that devastate the Church of God are the heretics. From this he concludes in this way: therefore, if a prince from a sheep or a ram becomes a wolf, that is, if he becomes a heretic, the shepherd of the Church will be able to keep him away through excommunication and at the same time order the people not to follow him, therefore depriving him of the dominion he has over the subjects. This is a faulty deduction, in whose place in good dialectics it should be stated: therefore, if a prince from a sheep or a ram becomes a wolf, the prince of the Church will be able to keep him away with all the means he is allowed to use."

I reply that here there is no fault, but it has been said in brief what could have been said with a longer turn of words: the method in which the pastor of the Church can and usually does keep away the heretics, as one keeps wolves from the flock, is this one, that is, to remove them from the community of the Catholics through the sentence of excommunication and to cause the Catholic people not to follow the heretical prince after that through absolution from the bond of subjection. And my aim in writing books was not to construct syllogisms properly, according to the rhetorical figures and models, as those who dispute on a proposed question for the sake of practice do in schools, but to explain and demonstrate the force of the reasons, as others, those who write books of theology, do.

But, Barclay says, certainly the pastor of the Church can by his own right excommunicate a heretical king, but he cannot rightfully absolve the people from the oath of allegiance and command them not to follow the heretical king in political matters, since this contradicts divine and natural law.

And maybe lest we complain against him that he did not maintain the proper manner of arguing, he constructs this syllogism: "The Supreme Pontiff cannot make precepts and dispensations against natural and divine law. Subjection and obedience owed to princes and to superiors is of natural and divine law. Therefore, the Supreme Pontiff cannot make precepts and dispensations in that, and consequently he cannot give to subjects the precept not to be obedient to their temporal princes in those things in which he is prince and superior. If you, as a matter of fact, do make such a precept, subjects will be allowed to refrain from obeying without being punished for that, as this would be a matter beyond the jurisdiction of the legislator. Both propositions, out of which the conclusion is inferred by a necessary deduction, are more certain than certainty itself, and I will give great credit to whoever weakens the force of this argument. As for me, by Hercules, though I ingenuously confess the weakness of my mind, I cannot see with what solid reason this can be refuted."

All these things are refuted in chapter 26, and Barclay did not present anything new in this passage but repeated the same things with other words, as is his habit. But lest he complain that we have made no response in the proper form to his incontrovertible demonstration, I make a distinction in the assumption. When he assumes that subjection and obedience owed to princes and to superiors are of natural and divine law, if he means princes and superiors who are legitimate, then his assumption is true. From that, though, he cannot draw his conclusion, since heretical princes are no longer legitimate princes and superiors after the Supreme

Pontiff has declared them excommunicated and deposed. However, if he means princes and superiors at any time, even after their authority has been abrogated, then his assumption is false, and there cannot be any doubt about that. In fact, by divine law subjects are held to obey not only the king as their superior but also the governors who are sent by the king, as St. Peter writes in his first epistle, chapter 2. Nevertheless, after the king has abrogated the authority of the governor, the subjects are not bound to obey the governor any longer, and likewise they are not bound to obey the king when he has rightfully been ejected from his throne. Therefore, if Barclay had wanted to present something solid, he should have proved that the princes of the earth, once they have obtained their political authority, are established by divine law in such a way that by no force and by no law can they be ejected from it, but he was never able to prove this point, on which the backbone of the whole question hinges.

However, he says that even though princes can be deposed, nevertheless they can be deposed only by a superior. I reply that the Pope is absolutely superior since he is the Vicar of Jesus Christ, that is, the Vicar not of a mere man, but of God and man, and for this he is the Shepherd and Father and Ruler and Head of all Christians, even princes, kings, and emperors, in place of Christ, as has been said often and as is deduced clearly from the divine Scriptures themselves.

"But," Barclay says, "the Pope is certainly superior, but not in the same kind of superiority, for he is superior to kings and princes in divine and spiritual matters, but in temporal matters the Pontiffs themselves say that they are not superior to kings, as is known from the chapter 'Per venerabilem,' where the Pontiff says that a king has no superior in temporal matters."

All these things have been treated and discussed already before; for we have shown that the Pontiff is superior to kings also in temporal matters when it is necessary to dispose of temporal matters because of spiritual matters, since temporal matters must be subordinated to spiritual ones. We have shown this from the common opinion of the scholars, having presented more than seventy testimonies, and not a few general councils of the Church, and finally from reason based on the divine Scriptures, against which Barclay did not offer anything but tragic cries and emphatic but empty words. What Innocent writes, that kings have no superior in temporal matters, is very true in that sense in which Innocent says it, that is, kings are supreme princes in temporal matters and do not have above them other kings or emperors but God, Who is the King of kings and the Lord of lords. But this does not prevent kings from having a spiritual superior endowed with so much authority as to be able to subject temporal matters to spiritual matters, for the reason of order requires that the temporal authority be subject to the spiritual when they convene in the same entity and form one Church, in the same way in which the body of a man is subject to the spirit and is directed by it and, when need be, is corrected and punished.

Afterward Barclay adds a very long invective of the people to the Pontiff, in which he, repeating himself again, puts in the month of the people the same things he himself has repeated a thousand times. This invective could perchance move unlearned and weak men, but wise and prudent men understand easily that these things are the resort of wretched men who try to seize with complaints and temerity what they are not strong enough to obtain with power. Nevertheless, lest the reader think that we want to avoid the effort of replying, or that what Barclay says through the figure of the people has more relevance than it has in truth, I will construct a response in the form of a dialogue and I will present the people as speaking with Barclay's words and the Pontiff as responding with mine.

---

# Dialogue between the people too much bound to the earthly king and the Pontiff giving beneficial counsel to the people

People: Holy Father, you are by no means superior to our king in temporal matters, and therefore you cannot stand in the way of the temporal deference that we offer him.

Pope: When your eternal salvation is jeopardized because of the temporal deference you offer the king, then I am absolutely superior to your king even in temporal matters, for I have to direct both you and him to eternal life and I have to remove all the obstacles that stand in the way of that journey.

People: Why do you prohibit what God commands us to do?

Pope: No, I do not prohibit, but rather I command you not to do what God prohibits you to do. I am the shepherd, established by Christ who is the Lord of the flock. You people are the little sheep; your kings are the rams. And therefore, as long as your kings continue to be rams, I allow them to rule and direct you, but if they become wolves, will it be right that I allow the sheep of my Lord to be directed by wolves? Therefore, rightfully I prohibit your following them, as the Lord prohibits this also, since with too great danger are the sheep ruled by the wolves.

People: Maybe because it is your prerogative to interpret the will of God contained in the divine law and in the Scriptures?

Pope: You said it.

People: But nevertheless, an interpretation which would completely annul the law and destroy the command must not be offered.

Pope: Which law of God did either my predecessors or I ever destroy and annul with our interpretation?

People: If there is anything doubtful or obscure in divine law, we recur to the See of Peter, that is, to the See that you occupy, to obtain the true interpretation, but what is clear in itself and obvious does not need to be enlightened by any interpretation.

Pope: So?

People: Since our Lord and Savior orders us to give unto Caesar what is Caesar's and unto God what is God's, and then, through the apostle, to be subject to and to obey the princes and the authorities, then you have to declare to us what is Caesar's, that is, what it is that we owe to our king and what is God's, so that we can give to each his own, and if you make this distinction we listen willingly to your voice. But when you say: "Give nothing to Caesar or your prince, you contradict Christ and therefore we do not listen to your voice."

Pope: When the Lord said: "Give unto Caesar what is Caesar's," He ordered to give tribute to him who was the ruler then, and who was not forcing the Jews to idolatry and who had not yet been deposed by any legitimate authority. God indeed ordered long before, through the Prophet Jeremiah, the same thing to be done toward Nebuchadnezzar, king of Babylon, for the same reason. But when at the time of the Maccabees King Anthioc was taking the people away from the divine faith and religion, God did not order them to continue to consider him as king, but He inspired Mathathia and his sons, very brave men, to form an army and to wage war against Anthioc as against an enemy, and to free the people. Likewise then also you, Christian people, will give to a king who is legitimate and who does not take you away from the law of God and the Catholic religion and who therefore is loved by me, Christ's Vicar, as a son, the obedience owed in those commands which he gives and which are not against the law of God and the Catholic faith. You will not consider as a king a king who tries to avert you from the path that leads to eternal life through flattery or in any other way, and who through my sentence has been cast out from the community of the pious and deprived of his kingdom; but you will offer that civil obedience to another king who will have succeeded legitimately to his place.

Furthermore, to God you will give what is God's when you worship God with faith, hope, and charity; and you will not allow yourself to be separated from Him by fear or love for any man. Therefore, you will never hear from me, "Do not give anything to Caesar or your prince," but you will hear this, "Do not be induced to consider as Caesar or your prince someone who in truth has ceased to be Caesar and a prince."

People: Certainly we say and profess that we admit Your Holiness's exposition and interpretation in the observation of divine law, but we affirm that an interpretation that mocks and almost defies natural and divine law is not admitted. For instance—lest we should move away from the issue that we are discussing, that is, we are ordered to obey princes and authorities—as obedient sons we embrace willingly your explanations and restrictions in observing this mandate if those do not annul such mandate, for example, when you say that no obligation to be obedient to kings arises but in those issues which pertain to their temporal jurisdiction, and that all spiritual matters have been reserved to the Vicar of Christ and to the Church, and likewise when you warn that one should not be obedient to the king in what he commands against divine and natural law, or what otherwise is contrary to morality. But when you simply and absolutely prescribe not to obey in any way our legitimate prince and his orders, mandates, and laws, we cannot follow your precept, since this is not to interpret God's orders, which is allowed to Your Holiness, but rather to reject and annul God's orders, which you cannot by any means do.

Pope: In the multitude of words there wanteth not sin.[209] You seem to have come from the school of one Barclay, for you multiply words without reason, but you commit a graver sin in daring to teach to your teacher and to give laws to your legislator, and you commit the gravest sin and error when you accuse the Vicar of Christ of making a joke of divine and natural

209. Proverbs 10:19.

law and of wanting to reject and abolish God's mandate concerning the obedience owed to princes. My predecessors and I never prescribed simply and absolutely not to obey in any way your legitimate prince and his orders, mandates, and laws. These are calumnies and impostures of your teacher, Barclay, for what we say and teach is that no obedience would be owed to a prince excommunicated and deposed by the Church with public authority, who therefore would have ceased to be a legitimate prince. This indeed does not contradict any divine order, since the divine order does not say that obedience should be offered to him who has ceased to be a legitimate prince. You, however, diligently listen and consider whether you should have greater faith in your father, the Vicar of Christ, and your mother, the Church, rather than in one false brother who seduces you and makes you disobey your father and your mother against God's command, when you wish to keep your zeal for obedience to the king but not according to knowledge.[210]

People: When Christ gave to Peter the keys of the heavenly kingdom, He did not give him the authority to make a sin be not a sin.

Pope: You do not know what you are talking about, as in good sense Christ did give to Peter the authority to make a sin be not a sin, and to make something that is not a sin into a sin. It is a sin to enter into matrimony in a prohibited degree of consanguinity, a sin not to fast during Lent, a sin to work on a feast day, and yet all these things and others of this kind cease to be sins with Peter's dispensation, with the authority of the keys given to him. And also, by contrast, Peter can add a new degree of consanguinity and blood relation and a new day of fast; therefore, it will be a sin if anybody contracts matrimony in that added degree, or does not fast in the added days, or does not abstain from work, which before would not have been a sin. Likewise therefore, if it had been a sin not to obey this or that king, nevertheless if through Peter's keys that king is declared a heretic and excommunicated and deposed, not to obey him will not then be a sin. It is true that Peter's keys do not extend to the point that the Supreme Pontiff could declare not to be a sin what is a sin, or to be a sin what is not, for that would be to say that evil is good, and good is evil, which is very far,

210. Here Bellarmine paraphrases Romans 10:2.

and has always been and will be very far, from the teaching of him who rules the Church and is the pillar and support of truth.

People: We therefore will follow in this part the common teaching of the canonists, who say that one should not obey the Pope's order if it is unjust or if from it many evils or scandals probably will happen and a disturbance of the condition of the Church and of the commonwealth will arise. Therefore, if the Pope ordered the regular clergy to do something which would be against the substance of their order, that is, would contradict the rule professed by them, they would not be bound to obey, as Felino explains in his commentary on chapters "Accepimus" and "Si quando,"[211] as also Innocent IV teaches in his commentary on chapter "Ne Dei," title "De simonia,"[212] whom Felino refers to, and we follow Martinus of Lodi in his treatise *De principibus*, question 498, and Felino in the said chapters "Si quando" and "Accepimus." How much less, then, must the subjects of kings listen to the Pontiff who tries to draw them away from the obedience owed to their king by divine and natural law and ratified by the most holy pact of an oath?

Pope: What the commonly held opinion not only of the canonists but also of the theologians and the experts on civil law and indeed the sacred councils themselves is, you will be able to see from the prolegomena of this book, where by universal consent it is affirmed that a king can rightfully be excommunicated and deposed by the Supreme Pontiff for just reasons, and his subjects can be freed from the bond of obedience and allegiance. It is not indeed credible that all the canonists contradict themselves, and therefore when some canonists say that one must not obey the

211. The first is canon 4, title 22, book 2, of Gregory's *Decretales*, drawn from a letter of Alexander III to the bishop of York, which dealt with the procedures for conferring ecclesiastical benefices (text in *Corpus iuris canonici*, vol. 2, cols. 345–46). The second is canon 5, title 3, book 1, of Gregory's *Decretales*, and it was taken from a letter of alexander III to the archbishop of Ravenna in which the pope established that whoever received a command from the pope should either obey or give a "reasonable cause" for refusing to obey (text in *Corpus iuris canonici*, vol. 2, col. 18).

212. This is canon 43, title 3, book 5, of Gregory's *Decretales*, drawn from a letter of Honorius III to the abbots and monks of the Cistercian Order, which regulated the procedures for the election and installation of the abbots and the relationship between them and the bishops (text in *Corpus iuris canonici*, vol. 2, cols. 766–67).

Pontiff when his order is unjust or is a cause of scandals and disturbances, first, they do not speak of the Pontiff teaching the universal Church *ex cathedra;* second, they do not speak absolutely, but conditionally, that is, if it happened, if perhaps it came to pass that the Pope would order a particular man to do something contrary to the law of God, in which case then St. Peter's teaching in Acts 5 is well known, "We ought to obey God rather than man."[213] But when the Popes my predecessors, such as Gregory VII and Innocent IV and others, wanted to excommunicate and depose great kings and to free their subjects from obedience, they did it *ex cathedra,* in a council and in a public ceremony, in consequence of the authority of God and the holy Apostles Peter and Paul, handed over to them from heaven. Therefore, whoever says that one should not obey the Vicar of Christ when he gives such an order condemns the universal Church and should be called not so much a canonist but somebody who perverts the canon law, and even though we do not think that any good canonist has fallen into such error, nevertheless if there were one, surely a prudent and faithful Christian would prefer the founders of canon law above this or that canonist. Regarding what you say, that obedience to kings is owed by divine and natural law, this is true concerning legitimate kings and those not yet deposed through the sentence of a judge. Since we draw you away from being obedient to the latter and not to the former, then either you accuse us falsely or you complain of us in vain.

People: If you order us to shake off the yoke of our king for this reason, that is, because through obedience presented to him the spiritual good may be hindered, we reply that whatever evil there is happens either in consequence of some accident or through accident, for evil of itself cannot arise out of good, and good out of evil. And we accept with grief that accident, but we cannot prevent it. We fulfill the duty owed to the king by God's command, and patiently we seek the glory, honor, and purity of a good deed; and if he should abuse the obedience owed to him and such a benefice granted by God, he will feel above him God as his judge and most severe avenger. We, however, are not allowed to abandon our

213. Acts 5:29.

duty and to disregard God's order, no matter how great is the good that may come from it, lest we get for ourselves the damnation that the apostle announces.[214]

Pope: What the Holy Spirit says through the mouth of the prophet and King David, "he setteth himself in a way that is not good,"[215] fits you rather well, for spiritual damage, that is, the danger of the ruin of souls, which follows from obedience to a heretical king, especially when this king seeks to eradicate the Catholic faith, is a sufficient reason for the Vicar of Christ, who is appointed over Christ's entire household, to strike that king with the sentence of excommunication and to deprive him of the dominion he had over the faithful. When a king, otherwise legitimate, is deprived of his kingdom because of spiritual damage through the sentence of him who rules the universal Church, not only are the people not bound to obey him, but they are bound not to obey him. For this reason, when one offers obedience to a king who has been rightfully deposed, he is the cause of evil not by accident but by himself, and in order to avoid the sin of disobedience he indeed incurs the sin of the lack of obedience. And he does not fulfill the duty owed to the king by God's order, but rather he fulfills a duty not owed to the king because of God's prohibition. But whoever denies obedience to a king, as we said, if he is rightfully deposed, does not commit evil so that a good might follow from that, but he commits a good so as to avoid a most grave evil, and he is not damned but is freed from the damnation which otherwise he would incur. And if you do not understand these things, oh foolish and unwise people, why do you not listen to me, your pastor? Why do you trust your own judgment? Why will you be seduced by another? "And when he putteth forth his own sheep, he goeth before them, and the sheep follow him: for they know his voice. And a stranger will they not follow, but will flee from him: for they know not the voice of strangers," the Truth says in John 10.[216]

214. Bellarmine is here referring to Romans 3:8.
215. Psalm 36:4.
216. John 10:4–5.

People: He Who orders us to obey kings and to give unto Caesar what is Caesar's does not make any distinction between good and evil princes, and for this reason we must not make any distinction either.

Pope: I also add, along with the apostle Peter, that one should obey not only the good and gentle, but also the froward (1 Peter 2).[217] Therefore we do not distinguish between good and evil, as long as they are superior, but our question is whether one should obey a king removed and deposed through a sentence. To such a king indeed Christ does not command us to offer obedience, and the Vicar of Christ prohibits it; therefore, whoever offers obedience to him does not worship Christ and offends His Vicar.

People : If, as St. Augustine teaches, whoever swears celibacy to God should not sin under any circumstance, even if he compensates with the fact that he believes that he must take a wife because the woman who wants to marry him promised to become Christian, and therefore he would obtain for Christ the soul of an infidel woman who was ready to become a Christian if she married him; what excuse will we use with God if, in order to make a hoped-for good happen, we should violate the religious obligation and faith of the oath given to God and to our king! Nothing is more precious than a soul for which our Lord and Savior thought it worthy to die, and therefore if it is not permitted to sin in order to win that soul to Christ, for what other reason should we ever sin?

Pope: One must not do evil that good may come, and this is the teaching of the apostles and therefore ours. Hence it is not permitted to violate the vow of chastity to win souls for Christ, and it is not permitted to do anything against the religious obligation of an oath to save the whole world; nevertheless it is not prohibited to me—to whom Christ said in the person of Peter, "Whatsoever thou shalt loose on earth shall be loosed in heaven" —to make dispensations in vows and to absolve someone from the bond of an oath. But whoever is absolved from a vow or an oath by the apostolic authority does not sin against the vow or the oath if he does something that before, when he was tied to the vow or oath, he could not do. Likewise also among men, whoever owes money to another sins if he

217. 1 Peter 2:18.

does not give the money back, but if the creditor absolves the debtor from the obligation to pay back, the latter will not sin anymore even if he never pays back the money. Likewise, a vow or an oath binds while it is in force, but if the Vicar of God, by the authority received from God and in the name of the same God, loosens the obligation of the vow or oath, whoever does not fulfill it does not sin anymore. Therefore, your question, for what other reason should we sin, is foolish, as if a priest would need to learn it from the people.

People: What you say, moreover, that you absolve us from the bond of this duty and declare us absolved, does not remove every scruple from our consciences but makes us less secure and more doubtful about your authority, since we should know that the command which you promise to absolve us from is ratified by the law of God and nature, and that Your Holiness cannot absolve anybody in matters of divine and natural law, not even on the basis of the plenitude of your power.

Pope: As you return to the same issues, you show yourself completely ignorant! I do not absolve you from a natural and divine precept when I absolve you from the bond of obedience, since I do not allow you to be disobedient to the king, which would be against divine law, but I make him who was your king not be your king anymore. Likewise whoever grants freedom to a slave does not allow the slave to be disobedient to the master, which would also be against divine law, but frees the slave from having to obey a master; and whoever, emancipating his son, exempts him from the paternal authority, does not teach that it is allowed for sons to be disobedient to the parents but makes him who was a son not be considered a son anymore; and whoever loosens a vow or oath does not give permission to violate vows or oaths but makes the vow or oath nonexistent.

People: So then we will follow you in spiritual matters and the king in temporal matters, for God orders both, and we will obey both.

Pope: If (as you were saying before) you were insecure and doubtful, why did you appoint yourself as the judge of a doubtful case, and why did you make such a conclusion? Certainly God, in Deuteronomy 17, in doubtful and obscure matters remits men to the priests, and He does not want any man to be the judge. And earlier you said yourself that in doubtful issues one should recur to the See of Peter. So why in such a grave doubt didn't you recur to the place that the Lord designated, that is, the See of Peter? And so as to make you understand that you have accomplished nothing with your conclusion, pay attention, first, to the fact that God certainly orders you to be obedient to the Pontiff in spiritual matters, but He does not order you to be obedient in spiritual matters alone. Also, consequently, God orders you to be obedient in temporal matters to a king, however one who rules legitimately, not a king who has been deprived of his kingdom because of heresy or for another just cause. Indeed, you should not be obedient to the Pontiff himself in spiritual matters if perhaps he, having fallen into heresy, was declared by the Church to be deprived of his pontificate (which we piously think cannot be possible). Pay attention also that the doubt regarding the Pope's authority, whether, that is, it extends to temporal matters, is not a doubt regarding a temporal issue but a spiritual and supernatural one, which depends not on the will and judgment of men but on the understanding of Scriptures and the interpretation of the will of God. Therefore, in such a grave doubt you should have stood not on your judgment, but on the Church's. The Church, then, both through its Head, that is, the Vicar of Christ, and through the councils, that is, its principal members, and through the scholars, theologians, and canonists, that is, its tongues, taught clearly that the temporal authority is subject to the spiritual, as the body is subject to the soul, and therefore the temporal authority, even the regal one, can be directed and corrected and judged and changed, if it errs, by the spiritual authority, which resides at its fullest in the Pope.

People: Last, indeed we respect and also, to a degree, we fear your threats, but we are not so fearful as to be scared of them more than we should, nor are we so terrified by them as to deny the just and rightfully owed obedience to our king for fear of an unjust excommunication. For even if it is commonly cried out that every excommunication must be feared, nevertheless it should be known that an unjust excommunication does not damage him against whom it is declared but rather damages him who declares it. Therefore, if you strike us with the sword of anathema because we do not want to pass over God's order at your command and to commit evil, the curse will change into a benediction so that even if we seem to be bound outwardly, we will remain free and innocent inwardly.

Pope: It is no wonder that the wise man says, "When the wicked cometh, then cometh also contempt, and with ignominy reproach."[218] Your pride has made you fall into this pit, since you have appointed yourself as judge of divine and heavenly matters; and sunk in the depth of this pit you despise not only the judgment of the Vicar of Christ but also the judgment of Christ Himself. In fact, even if you say that you fear the threats of ecclesiastical censures, nevertheless when you dare to affirm that you will not submit to them, you not only deny your fear but clearly add contempt, for whoever truly fears at least out of fear will follow the orders. And what you say, that an unjust excommunication does not damage him against whom it is declared, is true when he against whom it is declared suffers and abides by it with humility until its injustice or rather invalidity manifests itself openly. But when he against whom it is declared despises it with arrogance and dares to transgress the orders, if the unjust or invalid excommunication does not damage him, nevertheless the pride and arrogance with which he despises the pastor's orders will.

We should say these things if the censures and orders of which we speak now showed some appearance of injustice or invalidity, but when the Vicar of Christ commands the people under pain of excommunication not to obey a heretical king or a king otherwise justly excommunicated and deposed, what suspicion of injustice can arise? In fact, the Pontiff strikes you with the sword of anathema not because, as you falsely affirm, you do not want to ignore God's order at his command, and to commit an evil, but rather because you want to transgress God's order while the Pontiff prohibits you from doing so and to commit the evil of disobedience. God never ordered the people to offer obedience to a heretical king who has been excommunicated and deposed, but He ordered the people to avoid heretics, and to not even speak to them, and to obey their pastor and to listen to his voice.

218. Proverbs 18:3.

And these are the things that Barclay was pleased to say through the figure of the people, to which I replied, not without making an effort, since it annoys me greatly to waste time and effort in replying to the same things so many times, and yet at the end of this childish apostrophe, Barclay cries out that the discussion has been concluded with most firm demonstrations and incontrovertible arguments.

## CHAPTER 32

# Some false things babbled in a
# digression by Barclay are refuted

In chapter 31 Barclay first repeats many things that he had already said before about our predecessors who patiently tolerated pagan princes even if they were able to overcome them easily, and also about the disturbances raised in the Church because of Gregory VII and Boniface VIII, who either actually deposed, or tried to depose, Christian princes. Also he adds a reproach against Clement VII and Paul III in these words: "Of the last two Pontiffs I would dare to affirm (it is indeed a very well-known fact in the world) that they were the reason why religion was lost in England, because they tried to seize for themselves and exercise an odious and far-reaching authority against the king and people of that kingdom.'[219]

But this is such a manifest and notorious lie and calumny that it is surprising that it could have been pronounced by a man who professes himself an expert in history. Clearly the hatred against the Pontiffs and the lust for slander does not only blind the mind but corrupts the memory also. Who, in fact, does not know that Clement VII sought to show his favor in every way to Henry VIII, king of England, who was most dear to him, provided that justice and religion should permit it? But he hit Henry with the anathema—Clement's sentence against Henry is extant in the first book of *De schismate Anglicano* by Nicholas Sander. The truth is,

219. Pope Clement VII refused to allow Henry to divorce his wife, Catherine of Aragon, and, later, refused to recognize Henry's marriage with Anne Boleyn as legitimate. Clement finally excommunicated the king in 1533; Pope Paul III, who succeeded Clement in 1534, reiterated his predecessor's sentence.

he was forced to do so, and the reason for the anathema was so just that not even Barclay could reproach it even if he wanted so much to do so. Evidently Henry repudiated his legitimate wife, Catherine, and married Anne Boleyn who was related to him in many ways, against all laws, with a very great scandal in the whole world while the case was still pending in the tribunal of the Supreme Pontiff and while the Pontiff himself was clearly prohibiting it and threatening ecclesiastical censures. Therefore, he separated what God had joined and joined what God ordered to be separated. Thus, I ask Barclay whether Clement could have done any-thing other than what he did, acting piously? Certainly, sinning for the sake of gaining a good is not allowed, but how could the Pontiff not have sinned if he had annulled the marriage of the king with Catherine, law-fully contracted, and if he had approved the king's matrimony with Anne, who was the king's sister-in-law? And Nicholas Sander in book 1 of *De schismate Anglicano* demonstrates that this was the case by the king's own acknowledgment. Therefore, the cause of the loss of England was not the just sentence of the Pontiff but the violent lust of the king.

Indeed, Paul III pronounced an even more severe sentence against Henry, after the king had already moved away from the Catholic faith and constituted himself the head of the Church through a new and unheard-of heresy and had separated his kingdom from the community of the mysti-cal body of Christ. Therefore, Paul III could not have been the cause of the loss of England, which had already perished, and the Pontiff's aim was no other than to recover the lost flock and king in any way he could and to bring them back to the path of truth and to recall the king, who was dead in his sins, to the path of grace, so that it could be said about him, "This my son was dead, and is alive again; he was lost, and is found."[220] See Sander at the cited passage on the desertion of the king and kingdom in the year 1534 and on the sentence of Pope Paul III in the year 1535, a sentence that the Pope did not want delivered immediately out of hope for the king's conversion, as Sander notes in the same passage.

Afterward he adds another falsity not in history but in the Catholic faith and religion, which is more serious. He says: "Kings are not in the

220. Luke 15:24.

same position but are above all human laws and all positive laws, and they will give account of their government to God alone; and the later they are to be punished, the more severely they must be punished. Against private citizens execution has been prepared, and they cannot avoid it unless by the prince's indulgence. Against princes, what execution can be carried out, since princes are held by no sanction of the human laws and by no law are they called to be punished, safe in their power of dominion [*imperii potestas*]? In fact, since it is affirmed in jurisprudence that the prince is absolved from the laws, this is meant as concerning all the laws, especially penal laws, and thus the prince cannot be punished by the laws even if he is delinquent."

First of all, this opinion of Barclay's contradicts itself, for if the kings are absolved from all human laws, certainly they are not delinquent when they do not behave according to those laws. "For where no law is, there is no transgression," as the apostle says in Romans 4.[221] How is it then that Barclay said in his last words that the princes are not punished even if they are delinquent? He admits in fact that they are delinquent when they do not respect human laws, but nevertheless he affirms that they are not bound by the laws. Whoever is not bound by the laws is in no case delinquent, even if he does not respect them. Perhaps Barclay will reply that the princes are not bound by laws as to coercion but they are as to direction. Yet even if his words seem to free the princes from every obligation to human laws, nevertheless, admitting the reply given just before, I ask again whether Barclay would want princes to be absolved from the coercive force of all human laws both civil and ecclesiastical, or from civil laws only. For if he says that they are absolved from the force of civil laws only, certainly he thinks one thing and says another, since with clear words he says that the princes are above all human laws and all positive laws and they are not bound by any sanction of human laws. But ecclesiastical laws, which are issued by the Supreme Pontiffs and by the episcopal councils, are doubtless human and pertain to positive law. If, however, as the words sound, Barclay wants princes to be absolved from the ecclesiastical laws of the Pontiffs and councils, he errs openly in doctrine of faith, and he con-

221. Romans 4:15.

tradicts what he repeated before more than once, that all Christian princes are subject to the spiritual authority of the Supreme Pontiff as sheep to the stick of the shepherd, and that they can be punished with ecclesiastical censures and with excommunication. In chapter 32 he adds that princes can be deprived by the Supreme Pontiff of all means of regeneration in Christ and also be handed over to Satan for legitimate punishment of their error and contumacy. And since to be deprived of so many things and to be handed over to Satan is a most grave punishment by everybody's consent, it must be said that execution has been prepared against princes and that they also are called to punishment by the laws, which is absolutely contrary to what Barclay wrote in that passage. But let us come to things that properly pertain to our discussion.

## CHAPTER 33

# The second part of the fifth principal argument in support of the authority of the Supreme Pontiff in temporal matters is defended

In chapter 32 Barclay, coming back home after a long digression, proposes, discusses, and tries to rebut the second part of my fifth principal argument, which was articulated in the following manner: the shepherd can separate and *recludere* the raging rams trying to destroy the flock. The prince behaves like a raging ram trying to destroy the flock when he, despite being a Catholic by faith, is so evil as to gravely hurt religion and the Church, as if he were selling bishoprics or despoil churches, etc. Therefore, the Shepherd of the Church will be able to *recludere* him or to lead him back to the ranks of the sheep.

Barclay, in order to attack this argument, begins by criticizing the words and says the right word is *excludere* [to exclude] rather than *recludere,* because *recludere* means "to open up." I did not mean "to exclude," but rather "to shut in," since shepherds usually shut raging rams in some place so that they cannot assail the lambs with their horns or trample them with their feet. But, Barclay says, *recludere* means "to open," not "to close." This is certainly true when we say *recludere* the gates, or a house, or a prison. But when we say *recludere* something within the gates, or a man into a house, or into prison, then *recludere* is taken to mean "to close" or "to enclose in"; and in this second manner I meant that a ram is shut by the shepherd in a narrow and protected place, from which it cannot easily get out. And lest Barclay think that I have spoken without authority, he should read Hincmar in *Vita Sancti Remigii,* Ivo of Chartres in his epistle

49 [104], and Aimoinus in book 4 [3] of the *Historia,* chapter 57 [45]; and he will find here and there *recludere* used by good authors to mean "to shut in," in the same manner in which *religare* is used not as "to loosen," but "to tie again." And so that we may shut completely Barclay's mouth, he should listen to St. Jerome, a first-rate author, in his book *Adversus* [*Contra*] *Vigilantium,* speaking in this way: "You say that the souls of the apostles and martyrs have settled either in the womb of Abraham or in a place of rest or beneath the altar of God, and that they could not be in their tombs or where the living would have wanted them to be: that is, they are of senatorial dignity and thus they are not shut in [*recluduntur*] in a most disgraceful prison among the murderers, but in a free and honest dwelling, in the isles of the blessed and in the Elysian fields." These are the words of St. Jerome, to whom Barclay will not dare, I think, to say that *recludere* means "to open" and that therefore it should have been said *includuntur* and not *recluduntur.* And to refer Barclay to the grace of fraternal correction out of the same St. Jerome, he should remember that in chapter 30 he had sworn by Hercules when he said: "By Hercules, etc." Now he should listen to St. Jerome in his epistle to Damasus, speaking of the prodigal son: "Let no Christian mouth utter 'by Hercules' or 'by Castor' or such like creatures, which are monsters rather than divinities." But leaving this aside, let us come to the serious issues.

Barclay admits my whole argument and all things which are deduced from it by good deduction. But he denies that from this anything could be gathered other than the fact that the Shepherd, that is, the Pope, could exclude a raging ram, that is, a wicked king, from the flock and deprive him, through excommunication, of the spiritual benefits of the sacraments and of the prayers, but he could not proceed further to any temporal punishment, such as the deprivation of temporal jurisdiction and authority.

But Barclay does not perceive the strength of the argument from the comparison proposed, which he admitted as appropriate and suitable to explain and prove this point. In fact, not only does a shepherd exclude a raging ram from the flock, but also he ties it up and shuts it in or closes it up in some corner so that it will no longer be able to act as the leader of the flock. And following the comparison with this shepherd, the successor of St. Peter and Vicar of Christ ties up the Christian prince who is destroying the church by using the bond of excommunication, and in a certain way he closes him up in a corner so that he will no longer be able to rule the Christian peoples.

What Barclay says is surprising, that a prince can be excommunicated but he cannot be deprived of anything except spiritual goods, and therefore he cannot be deprived of his temporal authority or jurisdiction or dominion, and his subjects cannot be absolved from the allegiance and obedience that they owe him. In fact, it is clear that the sacred canons, whose knowledge Barclay professes, include among the effects of excommunication not only the privation of sacraments and prayers but also the privation of the prerogative to act as a legitimate member of the social and legal system. Thus, an excommunicated man would not be able to sit and judge in a tribunal, and the subjects would not be able to present themselves for judgment in front of an excommunicated man, as is the common opinion, from the chapter "Ad probandum," title "De sententia et re judicata" and from the chapter "Decernimus, de sent. Excommunic." [*Liber sextus*].[222]

Likewise the deprivation or suspension of the jurisdiction and the absolution of the subjects from their allegiance, of which issue in Gratian's *Decretum,* causa 15, question 6, next to the last canon, we read: "We, upholding the statutes of our holy predecessors, by the apostolic authority absolve from their oath those who have been bound to excommunicated men by an oath of allegiance, and we prohibit them in every way from offering obedience to such men until they come to make amends"; and in the last canon: "it shall be prohibited that the soldiers who have sworn allegiance to Count Hugo be servant to him so long as he is excommunicated, and if they hold their oaths as a pretext, they should be admonished

---

222. The first is canon 24, title 27, book 2, of Gregory's *Decretales,* in which Alexander III annulled a sentence because one of the judges who pronounced it was an excommunicated man (text in *Corpus iuris canonici,* vol. 2, col. 409). The second is chapter 8, title 11, book 5, of the *Liber sextus,* promulgated by Alexander IV, which established that the ecclesiastical judges can force the lay judges to forbid excommunicated men from initiating or participating in a lawsuit in civil tribunals (text in *Corpus iuris canonici,* vol. 2, col. 1101).

that they must serve God rather than man."[223] Finally, in case of heresy St. Thomas teaches that they can also be deprived of their authority in 2a 2ae, question 12, article 2, with these words: "As soon as somebody by sentence is declared excommunicated because of his apostasy from the faith, immediately the subjects are absolved from his authority and from the oath of allegiance by which they were bound to him." And even if, apart from the case of heresy, the privation of temporal possessions, either individual property or realms and dominions, does not follow from the force of the sentence of excommunication, yet we have proved before, with many testimonies and reasons, that kings and other princes can be deprived of their kingdom or dominion by the Supreme Pontiff for just causes. Barclay was not able to overthrow those testimonies and reasons in any way with his cavils.

"But," he says, "the temporal goods which are possessed by civil and human authority are received by the hand of a political prince, and therefore they cannot be taken away through excommunication, which is a sentence of a spiritual judge."

I reply that temporal goods, even though they are possessed by civil and human authority, are nevertheless subordinated to spiritual goods, and temporal authority itself is subjected to spiritual authority. Therefore it is certainly true that spiritual goods cannot be taken away through the sentence of a temporal judge and that spiritual authority is not subjected to temporal authority, but it is not true that some temporal goods cannot be taken away through excommunication, which is the sentence of a spiritual judge. And this cannot be called into doubt, since it is clear enough that the prerogative to act as a legitimate member of society represents a temporal and civil good and yet the excommunicated men are indeed deprived of these temporal goods, especially after a public denunciation or declaration.

---

223. Bellarmine is quoting chapter 4, causa 15, question 6, of the second part of Gratian's *Decretum,* issued by Gregory VII at the synod of Rome, and the following chapter 5, issued by Urban II (text in *Corpus iuris canonici,* vol. 1, col. 756).

## CHAPTER 34

## Barclay's error on the exemption
## of the clergy is refuted

Afterward Barclay moves to the exemption of the clergy, having seized the opportunity to do so from what he had said, that temporal goods cannot be given or taken away but by a temporal prince, and that nobody can avoid the judgment of the prince in temporal matters. And since somebody could object that the clergy has been exempted from the authority of the princes, and thus the clergy can avoid the princes' judgment in temporal matters also, Barclay replies that the clergy has been exempted by the favor of the princes, for otherwise by common law they would be subject like everybody else. In this chapter and in the following one, then, Barclay makes a digression on the exemption of the clergy, and he says many things that are averse not only to truth but also to the common opinion of the authors.

First he says that before the clergy was exempted by the favor of the princes, they were subject by common law to the judgment of the temporal magistrates. He proves this with a twofold argument: first, from the fact that clergymen are not only clergymen but also citizens of the political commonwealth, and he quotes my book, *De clericis,* chapter 28. Second, from the fact that at one time, under excellent and most pious princes, the civil and criminal cases (except ecclesiastical cases) of the clergy were litigated in front of political and temporal judges, and he quotes the fifteenth chapter of this book, where he thinks he has demonstrated it.

I answer that clergymen were exempted not only by the favor of the princes but also by the decrees of the Supreme Pontiffs and, which is most important, by divine law, and through this they had been exempted before they were exempted by the privilege of the princes. As to the fact that they are citizens and a certain part of the commonwealth, this proves that they are obliged to observe the civil laws by force of reason [*vi rationis*] and not by force of law [*vi legis*]. In order to prove this I adduced the argument that now Barclay abuses in his effort to demonstrate that by common law the clergy were subject to the civil magistrate, which however is not rightly proved from it. As to the fact that under pious princes before the time of Justinian sometimes the civil and criminal cases of the clergy were litigated in front of political magistrates, I say that in the Justinian Code at the title "De episcopis" are certainly found laws of princes which prescribe that the cases of the clergy be determined in front of secular judges, but one can find also canons of councils of that same period in which access to the secular tribunals is prohibited to the clergy, such as canon 9 of the Third Council of Carthage, canon 19 of the Council of Milevum, canon 9 of the Council of Chalcedon, and others.[224] Therefore, the exemption that the clergy had by divine law was not yet sufficiently well known and explained to the pious princes, and the holy Fathers tried gradually to explain it and introduce it.

Second, Barclay says that he is surprised that Bellarmine affirms that the Pope could simply exempt clergymen from subjection to temporal princes by his own authority through the canon law, and says: "This, I shall say, *pace* such a man, is more false than falsehood, since the law of Christ does not deprive anybody of his right and authority, and the law of Christ would do so if the Pope by means of such law could take away against the will of the princes the temporal right and jurisdiction that princes had over clergymen before they became Christian."

But so that Barclay may be more surprised, not only Bellarmine and those theologians and jurists who seem to be greatly in favor of the exemption of the clergy, but also those who seem not to support it much, say entirely the same. These are the words of Domingo de Soto in his

224. The title "De episcopis" is the third of the Justinian Code (text in *Corpus iuris civilis*, vol. 2, pp. 19–39). The councils mentioned by Bellarmine were held between 397 and 451. For more information on those councils and for the text of some of their canons, see Denzinger, *Enchiridion symbolorum*.

commentary on the fourth book of the *Sententiae,* distinction 25, question 2, article 2, conclusion 6: "Even without consulting the princes, the Pope could, and should, exempt the clergy from paying the tributes to the princes and going to the princes' tribunals, and they cannot oppose this exemption." And this same thing Diego Covarrubias, a noble jurist, following Soto, teaches in his *Practicae quaestiones,* question 31, conclusion 3, with these words: "The Supreme Pontiff could exempt the clergy and their possessions from secular jurisdiction, and that was and is appropriate to the Christian commonwealth not only in spiritual matters, because it had been already established by divine law, but also in temporal matters"; and conclusion 4: "Even if the exemption of the clergy from the jurisdiction of secular people has been introduced only by human law, nevertheless a secular prince, no matter how great, will not be able to repeal this immunity or exemption by his laws or by his authority." Therefore, Barclay should stop being surprised if Bellarmine says what nearly everyone says, and he should not want to deny what nearly no one denies, as if he were the only reasonable one.

But, he says, the law of Christ does not deprive anybody of his right or authority. This is in itself properly true, and it should mean this, "unless somebody by his own blame should deserve to be deprived." But nevertheless, when the law of Christ raises laymen to a higher order, that is, that of clergymen, it is not surprising if consequently it should deprive princes of the authority they had over those new clergymen when these men were in the inferior order of the laity, and there is no lack of examples in other instances, both profane and sacred. The king raises a private man, who was subject to a count, up to the degree of prince, and consequently he deprives the count of the right he had over that man and perhaps he subjects that same count to the prince now appointed, over whom the count had ruled before. The Pope raises a simple priest, otherwise subject to the bishop, up to the degree of Metropolitan, and for this, without injury to the bishop, he makes the priest, as Metropolitan, come to rule over that bishop, to whom just before he was subject. An infidel husband had right over an infidel spouse; the wife converts to the faith, and consequently she is freed from subjection to the infidel husband, and without any injury the law of Christ deprives the infidel husband of the right he had over his wife. By the same token, in a marriage contracted *per verba de praesenti* a Christian man acquires a right over a Christian wife, and yet if in the time prescribed by law she wants to rise to the profession of a higher life and to become a nun, the law of Christ deprives that man of the right he had acquired, not in itself, but consequently, for the law of Christ does not mean to deprive the man of his right but to honor the woman raised to a higher degree.[225] Finally a son is raised to the episcopate, and his father is deprived of paternal authority, not so that he may be wronged but because it is not becoming for a spiritual father to be subject to the authority of a carnal parent.

But again Barclay objects to this, saying: "Then since the Pope himself has obtained his own exemption by no other right than the generosity and favor of princes (in fact, as our adversaries say, he was subject *de iure* and *de facto* to the pagan princes like the other citizens), it is absurd to say that he could free others from this subjection; otherwise, to him this would apply: 'He saved others, himself he cannot save.'"[226]

Barclay's argument suffers from two flaws: it has a false antecedent and a flawed deduction. First of all, it is false that the Pontiff has obtained his own exemption by no other right than the generosity and favor of princes, for He who constituted His Vicar on earth by this very act exempted him from every authority of the earthly princes. But even if the Pope by law had been subject to the pagan princes and emperors, it would not follow that he should be subject also to Christian princes and emperors, unless he was exempted from this by their generosity and favor. In fact, since he has been appointed over the entire household, and kings and emperors are co-ordinated by him in the same household so that they might be ruled and directed by him, certainly no reasoning allows that he be subject to them, over whom by divine law he rules. But it is indeed fitting that Barclay thought that the Vicar of Christ should be despised in the same way in which the wicked Jews despised Christ; indeed they even unwillingly con-

225. Here Bellarmine is referring to one of the many regulations on the sacrament of marriage that were put in place at the Council of Trent. For an overview of how post-Tridentine Catholicism regulated marriage and on the social impact of such reforms, see Lombardi, "Fidanzamenti e matrimoni."

226. Mark 15:31.

fessed that many were saved by Christ from death itself, and they lied in a sacrilegious way when they said that He was not able to save Himself.

Third, Barclay says that it is not true what many say, that clergymen were exempted from the authority and jurisdiction of the civil magistrates by the ancient councils. He also adds that the Fathers who participated in the councils prohibited the clergy from going to the tribunals of the secular judges, but they did not prohibit the clergy, once they had been summoned, from appearing in court, and in no way did they prohibit the temporal judges from discussing the cases of the clergy; indeed there was no reason why they would have issued such a prohibition. First he tries to show this from the Third Council of Carthage, canon 9, where we read: "Likewise we decree that any bishop, priest, deacon, or clergyman to whom a crime is imputed or against whom a civil case is moved, if he wants to forsake the ecclesiastical tribunal and be judged by secular judges, even if a sentence has been given in his favor, should leave his place, and this applies to a criminal trial. In a civil trial, however, if he wants to keep his place, he should lose what he had obtained. For he who clearly has the authority to select judges from anywhere judges himself unworthy of the fraternal judgment if he, having a poor opinion of the universal Church, requires the help of the secular tribunal, since the apostle commands that the cases of private Christians be deferred to the Church and there decided." Barclay reported the words of that council up to this point, and in them he was not able to see anything in favor of the exemption of the clergy. Rather, he says that the Fathers did this only in order to curb the inconstancy and imprudence of their clergymen who, after their case has begun to be discussed in the Church, despise and forsake the ecclesiastical judges and commit themselves to the will and judgment of laymen.

But we see many things in the words of this council in support of the exemption of the clergy. First, the Fathers openly condemn recourse to the tribunals of secular magistrates, which certainly they would not do if the secular magistrates had been in all respects legitimate judges of the clergymen. For what crime was it to appeal from the tribunal of the bishop to that of the government of the province or of the prince himself, if the governor or prince was the legitimate judge not only of the clergyman but also of the bishop? Second, the council annuls the sentence given by the secular judge to the clergyman, when it judges that in a criminal trial a clergyman absolved by the secular judge should still lose his place, and in a civil trial he should lose what he had obtained; that is, in neither case would a sentence given by a secular judge in favor of that clergyman be advantageous. Even if these things were decided as a punishment, nevertheless the punishment would have been unjust if it had not been a crime for a clergyman to acknowledge secular judgment. Last, Barclay says that the council blamed only those clergymen who, after a case in an ecclesiastical tribunal had been started, transferred that case to the tribunal of the secular authorities, an action that could be injurious toward the ecclesiastical judges. Barclay should listen to the Council of Milevum celebrated in the same period and in the same place, Africa, for it speaks thus, in canon 19: "It has been decided that whoever asks the emperor for a legal investigation by the public courts should be deprived of his office, but if he asks the emperor for an episcopal court, there should be no impediment against him." Here we see that the prescription does not simply concern cases that have already started, but rather that the council forbids clergymen, absolutely and under a most grave punishment, from asking the emperor to be judged in a secular court. However, the council does allow clergymen to ask the emperor for judgment in an episcopal court.

Then Barclay moves to the Council of Chalcedon, in which it is established in canon 9: "If a clergyman has a case against another clergyman, he should not leave his own bishop out of it and turn to the secular tribunals. Rather, the case should first be discussed in front of the clergyman's own bishop. Alternatively, with the bishop's approval both parties can obtain a hearing in front of whomever they wish. If anyone disregards this procedure, he will be subject to canonical censures." From this canon Barclay says nothing is gathered but that first a case should be discussed in front of the bishop, and then, if need be, it might be deferred to the secular judge. But Barclay's gloss destroys the meaning of the text, for never in this entire canon is mention made either explicitly or implicitly of the secular judge, and in this canon it is expressly said that clergymen should not recur to secular tribunals. Moreover, in the same passage the council adds: "If a clergyman has a case against his own bishop, or against another clergyman, it should be judged in the provincial synod. But if a clergyman or a bishop has a complaint against the Metropolitan of that province, this person should have recourse to the primate of the diocese or the See of Constantinople for judgment." Here, even though there was an excellent occasion to mention the governor of the province or the emperor himself, no mention of them was made. Barclay asks, what does the following statement mean then: "But the case should first be discussed in front of the bishop"? He says that "first" refers to later, and since it has not been explained in the council what should be done "later," reason requires us to understand that later the person must have recourse to the secular tribunal, as afterward Justinian establishes in *Novella 83*.[227]

My response is that first the case of a clergyman should be discussed in front of his own bishop, but if the case is not settled then, the clergyman must have recourse to the superior mediators, that is, the Metropolitan, the Patriarch, or the Pope. The council did not point this out because it was already well known, both from the practice of other tribunals, where always from a minor judge one appeals to a superior one, and from the General Council of Sardica, canons 4 and 7, where it is declared that the final appeal of a clergyman is to the bishop of Rome.[228] Looking back to those canons Pope Gelasius I in his epistle to Faustus writes: "These canons decree that the appeals of the whole Church be deferred to the examination of that See, but those canons determine that nobody can ever appeal against that See," and in his epistle to the bishops of Dardania he says: "The canons decree that an appeal be made to that See from every part of the world, but nobody is permitted to appeal against that See." And we should not explain the canons of the Church through Justinian's *Novellae*, since we can explain them through other canons or through the practice of the Church.

Afterward Barclay adduces the Council of Agde against himself, since in its canon 3 it is established: "No clergyman should presume to bring a complaint against anybody in front of the secular judge without the bishop's permission," and he protests that this canon has been corrupted

227. Text in *Corpus iuris civilis*, vol. 3, pp. 409–11.
228. The Council of Sardica, called mainly to solve the Arian question, was held around the year 343.

by Gratian, who in causa II, question I, canon "Clericum," put it thus: "Nobody should presume to bring a complaint against a clergyman in front of a secular judge without the bishop's permission," and he is also surprised that Bellarmine in citing this canon preferred to follow Gratian's corruption rather than the truth of the council.[229]

But it is in no way credible that Gratian, an honest man and one striving for Christian perfection, wanted to corrupt the text of the council, but rather one should believe that Gratian had another version of that canon, different from the one we have. But be as it may, both versions demonstrate clearly enough the exemption of clergymen. In fact, in the council, even if those first words, "No clergyman should presume to bring a complaint in front of the secular judge," do not seem to accomplish much in support of the exemption of the clergy, the following words do indeed appear to support the exemption: "But if a clergyman is arraigned, he should not appear." Thus, a clergyman who is summoned to appear in a trial before a secular judge should not do so, and nothing clearer than this could have been said. What is in Gratian's version has the same meaning, that nobody should presume to bring a complaint against a clergyman in front of a secular judge. In fact, if a clergyman is not allowed to appear in a secular tribunal, neither will a clergyman or a layman be allowed to summon a clergyman to a secular tribunal.

In the second part of the canon Barclay notes that a serious punishment is imposed on a layman who attacks a clergyman or the Church with a calumny. This does not mean, however, that laymen are allowed to bring a clergyman or a case of the Church to the secular court provided they do so without calumniating them. Rather, it means that it is a crime far more serious and one to be punished with a most grave punishment if calumny is added. But it is not certain that here the council speaks of the secular court, since it can happen that a layman could accuse a clergyman in front

229. Bellarmine is quoting canon 17, causa II, question I, of the second part of Gratian's *Decretum*, drawn from the Council of Agde (held in 506). The text of the canon as well as the critical *apparatus* of the different versions of the canon can be found in *Corpus iuris canonici*, vol. I, col. 631.

of the latter's court, that is, the ecclesiastical, and still attack him unjustly through a calumny.

Then Barclay adds the eighth canon of the first Council of Mâcon, where we read the following: "That no clergyman should presume to accuse any other brethren among the clergy in front of the secular judge or to bring any clergyman to court in any place whatsoever, but that all cases of the clergy should be determined in the presence of their own bishop, or presbyter, or archdeacon." He also adds the thirteenth canon of the Third Council of Toledo, in these words: "The long-lasting lack of discipline and a growing presumption of impudence have cleared the way even for illicit actions for clerics who, having abandoned their bishop, bring their fellow clerics to public courts; and therefore we state that this should not be done, and if anybody presumes to do it, he should lose the case and should be excluded from communion."[230]

After bringing forth these testimonies from the councils, Barclay adds: "These are the solemn and almost only decrees of the sacred canons, on which they who falsely think that the councils could exempt, and in fact did exempt, the clergymen from laymen's authority base their errors. But indeed the canons themselves refute them so clearly that there is no necessity of bringing up anything else to overthrow that opinion."

I reply that, first, these are not the only councils that declare the exemption of the clergy, but there are many others, among which I thought the following should be briefly remembered. In the Lateran Council under Innocent III, chapter 43, we read the following: "Some laymen try to usurp too much of divine law when they oblige clergymen who do not receive any temporal goods from them to swear oaths of allegiance to them." In the Council of Constance, session 31, these words can be found: "Laymen have no jurisdiction or authority over clergymen." In the Lateran Council under Leo X, session 9: "Since no authority is attributed to laymen over clergymen by either human or divine law, we renew each and every decree, etc." In the Council of Trent, session 25, chapter 20, "De

230. The First Council of Mâcon was held in 585, and the Third Council of Toledo was held in 589.

reformatione": "Immunity for the Church and for the clergy has been established by God's ordinance and by the sacred canons."[231] To these and to similar proofs that speak all too clearly Barclay replied nothing, but he glossed over them as if he had never read them.

Second, we do not say that clergymen have been properly exempted by the councils, but that by the councils their exemption has been declared and confirmed with the addition of punishments. Finally, it is surprising that Barclay would dare to say that the opinion in favor of the exemption is confuted and overthrown by the alleged canons, since that opinion is confirmed and strengthened in many ways. In fact, if lay magistrates were legitimate judges for clergymen, by what right would the Council of Mâçon, above quoted, establish that all the cases of clergymen had to be determined in the presence of the bishop, or presbyter, or archdeacon? And why would the Council of Toledo, also quoted, with such harsh words call a recurrence to the secular court a presumption and an illicit action? And how, finally, would the same council dare to impugn the sentence of the secular judge and excommunicate a clergyman who recurred to the court of the secular judge? This is in fact what these words mean: "He should lose the case and should be excluded from communion."

231. All the canons quoted by Bellarmine from those ecumenical councils can be found in *Conciliorum oecumenicorum decreta,* at pp. 229, 412, 585–601, and 771–72, respectively.

## CHAPTER 35

# Barclay's powerful assertion with which the exemption of the clergy is destroyed is refuted

In chapter 33 Barclay, leaving behind any fear or scruple, declares: "I will say more and I will say the truth, even if it may provoke hatred against me from those to whom everything that even slightly opposes their zeal and desire is hateful. Therefore, I will say, and say with a powerful assertion, that either nobody remembers anymore, or if anybody remembers, maybe that assertion did not stick as it should have in the minds of those who should know: clergymen of the whole world, of any order and degree whatsoever, up to now have not been in any way exempted and freed from the temporal authority of the secular princes in whose kingdoms and regions they live. Just like other citizens, they are subject to secular princes in all things that pertain to the political and temporal administration and jurisdiction, and princes have the right of life and death over them, as over every other subject."

This powerful assertion of Barclay is nothing but a great temerity and intolerable error of one man who, in order to flatter kings, is not afraid to oppose himself to truth and to all theologians and canonists, among whom we have already quoted two, Soto and Covarrubias. To these we could have added innumerable other authors and, what is more, the four general councils quoted just before, that is, the two Lateran Councils, the Council of Constance, and that of Trent, in which it is affirmed in general terms that laymen have no authority over clergymen, and neither emperors nor kings are an exception. And we have no difficulty in demonstrating the novelty of this doctrine, for Barclay himself says that he is about to pronounce a powerful assertion that no one perhaps remembers anymore.

But let us see what arguments Barclay would use to try to convince the world of such a powerful and unheard-of assertion, and I will summarize briefly his whole reasoning so that it may more easily appear what strength his argument lacks. Here is Barclay: "Christians, both laymen and clergymen, were subject to pagan princes and they could be judged by them, since Christ's law does not deprive anybody of his right and authority. Also, Christian princes by their privileges exempted clergymen from the authority of inferior magistrates, but they did not exempt them from their own authority, since no author has even recorded the fact that the princes who gave those privileges to clergymen set them free to the point that the clergymen were not subject to them anymore. Rather, the princes could not, and they still cannot, without abdicating their sovereignty by this very act, give to clergymen established in their kingdoms that freedom by which the clergymen would not be under them regarding their temporal authority or by which the clergymen would not be judged and punished by them if the clergymen should commit a crime. For it is the prerogative of the prince to be able to judge the citizens and members of his commonwealth, and clergymen, insofar as temporal matters are concerned, are citizens and members of the political commonwealth, whose head and ruler is the prince. Therefore, Emperor Charles V ordered that Hermann, the archbishop of Cologne, be brought to court before him to purge himself of the crimes attributed to him by the clergy and the university, as Surius testifies in the *Commentarius* of the year 1545. And many princes reserved especially for themselves vindication of certain crimes of the clergy and entrusted these crimes to their magistrates to be punished, as for example those crimes which in France are called 'privileged,' such as treason, bearing arms, counterfeiting coins, etc." From all these things, Barclay affirms, it follows that clergymen are not exempted from the authority and jurisdiction of temporal princes.

Now I will reply in order to the individual propositions. To the first, regarding the subjection of the clergy to pagan princes, there are two opinions, as we said before, neither one of which supports Barclay. The true opinion is that the clergymen *de iure* were exempted also from the authority of the pagan princes, even though *de facto* they were subject to them, for He who in Apocalypse 1 is truly called "the prince of the kings of the earth"[232] exempted them as His own ministers. Therefore, on the basis of this opinion, Barclay's first proposition, which he never proved and does not prove here, but which he assumes as granted, and which more important authors do not grant, that is, all those who teach that this exemption is of divine law, must be denied.

But even if this were granted, Barclay would not gather anything from it, since its deduction, "Therefore the clergymen are subject to the judgment and authority of Christian princes," would be denied. For all Catholic authors, both theologians and canonists, deny this proposition, which is Barclay's second point. Moreover, the deduction is denied because the Supreme Pontiff absolutely exempted clergymen from the authority of Christian princes, who recognize the Pontiff's authority, but he did not absolutely exempt them from the authority of the pagan princes, who do not recognize his authority, since he could not coerce them with ecclesiastical censures. The Christian princes themselves exempted the clergymen, understanding how great the dignity of the clergy is, which the pagan princes did not do since that spiritual dignity was not known to them.

To the third proposition, that the law of Christ does not deprive anybody of his right and authority, I have already responded in the previous chapter, where I showed that the exemption of the clergy does not properly and essentially deprive princes of the right they had over clergymen before such men became clergymen, but consequently and, as it were, by accident. Likewise, when a son is brought up to the episcopal dignity, he is exempted from paternal authority and no injury is made to the father, since the father is not deprived of his right as such, but as a consequence, for the Church does not mean to deprive a father of his right of paternal authority, but to bring that person up to the status of which he is worthy, even if from it that privation of paternal authority follows. See many other examples in the previous chapter.

To the fourth proposition, which was that no author had ever recorded the fact that the princes exempted clergymen from their authority but

232. Revelation 1:5.

only that they exempted them from the authority of inferior magistrates, I reply that it is clear that whoever says this is either ignorant or deceitful. In fact, Rufinus in *Historia,* book 10, chapter 2, writes that Emperor Constantine declared openly that it was not allowed to him to judge priests, but that he himself should rather be judged by them. There he declared clearly enough that the priests are exempted not only from the authority of the inferior judges but also from the dominion of the supreme prince. And consistent with this declaration is the seventh law of the same Constantine in the Theodosian Code, title "De episcopis et clericis": "The lectors, subdeacons, and other clergymen who are called to court because of a wrong done by heretics should be absolved, and besides, according to the example of the East, they should by no means be called to court but should enjoy the fullest immunity."[233] These are the words of Constantine, who, since he prohibits absolutely that clergymen be called to court and wants them to enjoy the fullest immunity with no exception, clearly does not want clergymen to be called to the court of the prince himself as well, for there would not be the fullest immunity if they were subject to the authority of the prince. The law of Theodosius and Valentinian in the Theodosian Code, the last one of the title "De episcopis et clericis," is similar: "The wretched usurper decreed that clergymen should be brought indiscriminately to the secular judges, but we defer them to the episcopal court. In fact, it is not lawful that the ministers of the divine office should be subjected to the decision of the temporal authorities."[234] Since there is no exception made in this law, everything seems to be included, unless, perhaps, the authority of the prince should not be called temporal. Also, Justinian himself in his *Novella 83,* which is often quoted by our adversaries as if in it the clergymen would not seem to be exempted from the secular court in criminal matters, has these words: "First he is despoiled of the sacerdotal dignity by his beloved bishop, and then he finds himself in the hands of the laws." There we see that clergymen, as long as they remain such, are not under the authority of the laws, but only after they

233. Bellarmine is referring to the law promulgated by Constantine in 330 (text in *Codex Theodosianus,* vol. 6, pp. 34–35).

234. This is law 47, title 2, of the Theodosian Code, promulgated in 425 (text in *Codex Theodosianus,* vol. 6, pp. 104–5).

have been deprived of the clerical dignity by the bishops. And thus they are not only exempted, as long as they are clergymen, from the authority of the inferior judges, but also from the laws of the princes, as far as coercion is concerned, and this is what the council of Constance, session 31, said: "Laymen have no jurisdiction and authority over clergymen." And certainly the word *laymen* includes the supreme princes, since they are laymen too. Finally, and not to mention many other things, Emperor Frederick II in his first *Constitutio* speaks in general terms when he says: "We also decree that nobody should presume to bring a cleric to a secular court in a criminal or civil case against the imperial decrees and the sacred canons," and here by "secular court" is meant not only the courts of the inferior judges but also of the supreme ones, since all are equally secular. And in fact we see this observed where reverence for the sacred canons thrives.

To the fifth proposition, which was that the supreme prince could not exempt clergymen from his sovereign authority, we reply that It is clearly false. In fact, even if the supreme prince could not exempt from all his authority all the people who live in his kingdom unless he abdicated his sovereignty, nevertheless he can exempt some of his people from a part or all of his authority, and still be called, and be truly, a prince. For it is the prerogative of the supreme prince to exact tribute from the people subject to him, as the apostle says in Romans 13: "For this cause pay ye tribute also: for they are God's ministers, attending continually upon this very thing."[235] But a king can also exempt whomever he wants from the tributes, as is said in 1 Kings 17: "And it shall be that the man who killeth him, the king will enrich him with great riches and will give him his daughter and make his father's house free in Israel."[236] Likewise, even if a great king frees or entirely donates to somebody a city in the middle of his kingdom, he will still be called king of the entire kingdom, especially if he protects and defends that city and if the citizens willingly respect the laws of that kingdom. Similarly, therefore, a king could exempt from his regal authority clergymen living in his kingdom but nevertheless be king not

235. Romans 13:6.
236. 1 Samuel 17:25.

only of the laymen but also of the clergymen, who willingly respect the political laws and who as plaintiffs will bring to court cases they have with laymen and submit to the king's sentence in such cases. And since a king makes efforts for and attends to the defense not only of the laity but also of the clergy, then not only the former but also the latter must show him the honor that is owed to kings according to the precept of the apostle Peter, 1 Peter 2: "Fear God, Honour the King."[237] Last, they pray to God for the king, as the apostle admonishes in 1 Timothy 2 when he says: "I exhort therefore, that, first of all, supplications, prayers, intercessions, and giving of thanks, be made for all men; For kings, and for all that are in authority; that we may lead a quiet and peaceable life in all godliness and honesty,"[238] and they not only pray to God for the kings in general, but specifically they say, "for our king X," or "for our emperor Y."

"But," Barclay says, "all the members have to submit to the head, and all the citizens to the ruler of the city, so that the head and ruler could punish all the members and citizens, and clergymen are members of the political body and citizens of the earthly city as far as temporal matters are concerned."

I respond that in a natural body it is necessary that all members be subject to the head, since in such a body exemptions are not possible. But in a political body, in which exemptions are possible, it is not necessary that all members, that is, all citizens, be subject, strictly speaking, to the authority of the head, that is, of the ruler. Therefore, it is not necessary that the princes be able to punish all citizens, just as it is not necessary that all citizens pay tribute or that all serve the cause of the commonwealth in battle. "But the commonwealth will be upset if clergymen transgress with impunity the laws of the princes." They will not transgress with impunity, I say, since they will be punished by their bishop or by the Supreme Pontiff. But, Barclay says, "Charles V called to his court Hermann, the archbishop of Cologne." It is true, but he called him as one of the princes of the empire, and Pope Paul III called the same archbishop to his court as an archbishop, by the testimony of the same Surius in the same passage.

237. 1 Peter 2:17.
238. 1 Timothy 2:1–2.

Surius later writes that in the year 1547 Hermann was moved from his position by order of the Pope and the emperor. The sentence of deposition was given by the Pope, and that Charles V diligently observed the ecclesiastical immunity can be understood from the fact that in the year 1520, after an atrocious conspiracy against Charles, in which some clergymen were involved, had been discovered, Charles punished the laymen and remitted the clergymen to their ecclesiastical superiors for punishment, as Molina testifies in *De Hispanorum primigeniorum origine et natura,* book 9, chapter 21.[239]

Barclay added that there are some grave crimes that in France are called "privileged" and that are reserved to the supreme princes. But this argument can be twisted against its own author: those crimes are not called privileged because the princes reserved such crimes to themselves when they conceded the privilege of exemption to the clergymen, as Barclay thinks, but are called privileged because by privilege of the Apostolic See the kings of France are permitted to investigate those crimes, which Clarus explains in question 36, last section, "Quaero," and in his commentary on the canon "Ut clericorum," *Clementinae,* title "De officio iudicis ordinarii."[240]

To the last proposition, which Barclay gathers from what has been said before, that is, that there can be no exemption of clergymen from the authority of the prince, I reply that this proposition is incorrectly gathered from what has been said, both because it has been demonstrated that supreme princes were able to and wanted to exempt clergymen from their own authority, and because even if they had not wanted it, or had not been able to do it, the Supreme Pontiff was able to do it and wanted to exempt them, or declare them exempt by divine law, and the princes, even supreme ones, cannot impede this exemption. And this is the common judgment of the scholars, both theologians and canonists, which until now nobody but heretics opposed. And certainly this is what they

---

239. This work is actually not by Luis de Molina, the Jesuit theologian, but by a sixteenth-century jurist named Luis de Molina Morales.

240. This is chapter 1, title 9, book 1, of the *Decretales Clementinae,* and it established that bishops must correct the abuses of clergymen (text in *Corpus iuris canonici,* vol. 2, cols. 1140–41).

who want the exemption to be of divine law think, and not even Barclay doubts it, and Navarrus expressly teaches it in chapter "Novit," notation 6, n. 30. But this is what they who think that the exemption is not of divine law also say and teach, as is clear from Francisco de Vitoria, *relectio* "De potestate Ecclesiae," question 6, proposition 5; from Domingo de Soto, in his commentary on book 4 of Lombard's *Sententiae,* distinction 25, question 2, article 2; from Martin Ledesma in his commentary on the same book 4, part 2, question 20, article 3; from Domingo Bañez in his commentary on 2a 2ae, question 67, article 1; and from Diego Covarrubias, *Practicae quaestiones,* chapter 31, conclusions 3 and 4, whose words, like those of Soto, we have adduced in the previous chapter. Hence the question of whether the prince is allowed to revoke the privilege of the exemption of the clergy, which Barclay in the last chapter left unanswered, is settled, as the alleged scholars respond that it is not in any way allowed.

# The second and third parts of my fifth principal argument in support of the authority of the Supreme Pontiff in temporal matters are defended

In chapter 34 Barclay, after a long digression on the exemption of the clergy, returns to refute the second part of my principal argument, which he had proposed at the beginning of chapter 32. This was my argument: it is the duty of the shepherd to separate and shut in the raging rams that try to destroy the flock. A prince behaves like a raging ram trying to destroy the flock when he, despite being a Catholic by faith, is so evil as to gravely hurt religion and the Church, as if he should sell bishoprics or despoil churches, etc. Therefore, the Shepherd of the Church will be able to shut him in and bring him back to order.[241]

To this argument Barclay replies in that same chapter 32 that the whole argument can be granted, since from it nothing is gathered but that a prince who is evil and harmful to the Church can be separated from the community of the flock through the sentence of excommunication. We, however, have refuted this reply in chapter 33, to which we refer the reader. Then in chapter 34 Barclay adds:

"I now go back to the argument which was proposed at the beginning of chapter 32 and I reply that it does not pertain to the deprivation of any

---

241. For the use of this argument in Francisco Suárez, see Skinner, *Foundations*, vol. 2, pp. 180–81.

temporal goods, let alone of a kingdom. It is certain, in fact, indeed more certain than certainty, that the excommunication, by which act alone the perverted Christians are separated and excluded from the community of the faithful and the communion with the Church, does not take away anyone's patrimony and temporal goods." These are the words of Barclay, who after many words spent in explaining the matter, concludes that if the Pope could not take away the patrimony of private men through excommunication, much less through the same sentence could he deprive kings and princes of their empires and kingdoms.

Barclay says: "Can it be that more authority has been attributed to the Pope by the law of God over princes than over private citizens? Or that princes have to live in a worse and more difficult condition than private citizens, so that what the Church cannot do against a private man it can do against a prince?"

But when I said that a raging ram can be separated and shut in by the shepherd, by "separating and shutting in" I did not mean excommunication only, but excommunication and deposition. Not only does the shepherd separate the ram from the flock, but he also locks up the ram in a sort of prison, so that he may cease to be the leader of the flock. Similarly the Supreme Pontiff separates, through excommunication, a king who destroys the Church from the community of the faithful and also deposes the king and demotes him so that he may cease to rule the people. Therefore, that whole very long disputation with which Barclay tries to prove that through excommunication men are not deprived of their patrimony is superfluous, and Barclay has not understood the strength of our argument, which is evident from the fact that he incorrectly translated the word *recludere* as "to open" while it should have been "to shut in," as we showed in chapter 33.

Moreover, I add that there is a great difference between private possession and public jurisdiction, as also there is between substance, i.e., wealth, and power, i.e., authority; for a man can be very poor in terms of private wealth but have public jurisdiction, and a very ample one at that, and by contrast a man can be very rich in gold and silver and in fields, vineyards, and cattle, but have no political authority over other men. From this difference it results that even though excommunication does not deprive a person of his own patrimony and resources and wealth, nevertheless it deprives him of right and authority in social relationships, elections, contracts, and the like, and at the same time it hinders the public and juridical jurisdiction, for an excommunicated person is not allowed to involve himself in juridical trials, to hear cases, give sentences, and punish the guilty, as we proved before, from the chapter "Ad probandum."

The loss of the kingdom or the empire does not follow from the force of the excommunication alone, unless in the case of heresy or apostasy. Nevertheless, the Supreme Pontiff, who can suspend through excommunication a person's jurisdiction, as we have said, can also through deposition deprive a person of every jurisdiction and regal authority, and this, as we showed in the prolegomena, is the common judgment of scholars and of the Church itself. It does not mean, however, that the Pontiff has more authority over princes than over private citizens, for private citizens cannot be deposed from the kingdom, because private citizens have no kingdom, not because they are less subject to the authority of the supreme Pastor than kings are. Private citizens can however be deprived of their possessions, which happens when they must pay a pecuniary fine, or when they must go into exile or into prison, or when other corporeal punishments are imposed on them. In fact, what Barclay repeats all too often, that corporeal punishment has been placed in the power of the political magistrate only, is false, for the practice shows the opposite, especially in the tribunal of the Holy Office.[242]

Afterward Barclay adds another argument, which he puts in the form of a syllogism: "The Supreme Pontiff does not now have more authority over temporal princes than he had before he was a temporal prince. Before he was a temporal prince, he had no temporal authority over temporal princes by any means. Therefore, even now he has none over them by any means."

---

242. The range of corporeal punishments that the Inquisition could impose, as well as the relationship between the Holy Office's punitive jurisdiction and that of the secular states, was complex and changed in many ways over the course of the sixteenth and seventeenth centuries. For an overview of the Inquisition's procedures, see J. Tedeschi, "The Organization and Procedures of the Roman Inquisition: A Sketch," in Tedeschi, *Prosecution of Heresy,* pp. 127–203.

And since the proposition seems clear, he proves the assumption in this way: "Nobody who is an inferior and a subject has authority over his superior and master; therefore, the inferior cannot judge the superior in the very same matter in which the former is subject to the latter. The Pope, before becoming a temporal prince, was inferior and subject to kings and emperors insofar as temporal matters were concerned. Thus, the Pope does not have temporal authority over kings and emperors and cannot judge them in temporal matters."

My answer is that the assumption of the first syllogism is false; therefore, the conclusion is also false. Indeed the Supreme Pontiff did not obtain the right that he has in temporal matters over Christian kings and princes from the temporal realm he now possesses, but he received it from Christ when he received from Him the apostolic and supreme authority over the whole Church, to be its general Vicar, head and ruler and pastor and prince of all the faithful. Even if, as has often been said, that authority is in itself spiritual, nevertheless it is extended to temporal matters in the same way in which the human spirit, even though it is truly and properly a spirit, and not a body or corporeal, yet rules the members of the body which it commands, and it chastises and punishes them to the extent to which it realizes that such actions are necessary for salvation. Therefore, the proof of the assumption in the second syllogism has no strength, and the assumption of the second syllogism is false, and therefore also the conclusion of the whole syllogism is false. It is false that the Supreme Pontiff was ever subject *de iure* to kings and emperors, and Barclay did not prove what he assumes he has proved.

But, Barclay says, his adversaries admit that the exemption of clergymen was introduced by human law. Bellarmine, who is quoted in the margin, does not say that it was introduced only by human law, but by human and divine law. Then, even those who say that the exemption of clergymen is of human law add that it is very consistent with natural and divine law as far as the persons of the clergy are concerned, as is clear from Domingo de Soto in his commentary on book 4 of the *Sententiae*, distinction 25, question 2, conclusion 5. Moreover, those authors who deny that the exemption of clergymen is of divine law affirm clearly that the Supreme Pontiff could and should exempt clergymen, even without consulting the temporal princes, and that the temporal princes cannot establish the contrary with their own laws, as we noted before from Vitoria, Soto, Ledesma, Bañez, and Covarrubias. Thus, what Barclay repeats here with so many empty words regarding the exemption being conceded to clergymen only by the privilege and concession of the princes is false.

Afterward Barclay moves to the third part of the fifth principal argument in support of the authority of the Supreme Pontiff in temporal matters—I omit what he repeats from chapter 15 which is refuted in my own chapter 15—and Barclay says: "Bellarmine's last argument remains, its refutation requiring little effort. The third argument is that the shepherd can and must feed his sheep in such a way as is appropriate for them. Therefore, the Pontiff can command and oblige Christians to carry out those actions to which any of them are held according to their status; that is, he can oblige everybody to serve God in the way in which they must according to their status. The kings must serve God by defending the Church and by punishing heretics and schismatics, and therefore the Pope can and must command kings to do so, and if they do not, the Pope can force them to do so through excommunication or other suitable means."

To this argument Barclay replies that if we talk about spiritual feeding and punishing, then the whole argument can be granted, for the Supreme Pontiff is bound to feed all Christians with spiritual food, since his faculties, however ample they may be, are not by any means sufficient to feed them with corporeal food. Similarly he is held to compel all to their own duty with spiritual punishments, the most grave of which is excommunication, but he cannot go further, and to prove this Barclay alleges John Driedo in *De libertate Christiana,* chapter 4.

But this response of Barclay has been refuted before in many places and now can be refuted from the words of the same Driedo whom Barclay quotes. Barclay quotes Driedo, arguing that no other punishment of papal sentence and correction against delinquent emperors is given but excommunication. But John Driedo opposes Barclay and confutes him with these words, in *De libertate Christiana,* book 1, chapter 14: "But it should not be passed over in silence that the Pope, out of his plenitude of power over all Christian princes, can deprive kings and princes of their kingdoms and empires because of the crime of heresy, and he can also exempt the

Christian people from their obedience and subjection in temporal matters." These are the words of Driedo, whom Barclay alleged as a supporter of his opinion, and certainly the famous scholar John Driedo could not refute more clearly the lie and imposture of Barclay. What we said then, and what all Catholics teach, that the supreme Shepherd of Christians can oblige everybody to do their own duty in honor of God, is not meant with respect to coercion through excommunication only but also through the deprivation of kingdoms and dominions, if the Shepherd himself has judged it necessary for the salvation of the flock.

# The first example adduced in support
# of the authority of the Supreme Pontiff
# in temporal matters is defended

In chapters 35 and 36 Barclay relates and rebuts certain arguments of Nicholas Sander, and I thought that this whole disputation should be omitted because my purpose is not to prove that all the arguments proposed by Catholic authors are irrefutable demonstrations. I know that sometimes many probable arguments are mixed with more solid ones, which even if by and in themselves they may not have the strength to persuade, nevertheless once they are added to firmer arguments they help considerably to confirm our discussion. Therefore, I took it upon myself to defend Sander's conclusion, which is common to all Catholic authors, against Barclay, whose hand will be against every man, as the Scripture says of Ishmael.[243] At the same time I thought I should reply to the arguments in my writings to which Barclay specifically objects.[244] Thus in chapter 38 he relates my first argument from the example and the figurative representation of the Old Testament. Here is the summary of the argument. As we read in book 2 of the Paralipomena, chapter 26,[245] King Uzziah usurped the function of the priests. The priests removed him, but he refused to submit to the priests' judgment. For this reason, the king was immediately stricken with leprosy, and by the priests' sentence he was separated from his people

243. Genesis 16:12.
244. On the relationship between Sander and Bellarmine, see Tutino, *Law and Conscience,* chapter 6.
245. 2 Chronicles 26.

and lived in a solitary house until his death. From this it came about that the king was deprived of the administration of the kingdom and his own son became the judge of the people in the city. Hence such an argument is built: if a priest could punish a king and deprive him of his kingdom on account of a bodily leprosy, why shouldn't a priest be able to do the same thing on account of a spiritual leprosy, that is, heresy, which was represented as a leprosy, as St. Augustine teaches in book 2 of *Quaestiones,* question 40, especially since in 1 Corinthians 10 Paul says that all these things happened unto the Jews figuratively for examples?

To this argument Barclay replies that by the priests' sentence King Uzziah was separated from the rest of the people because of his leprosy, and in the same way the Supreme Pontiff, through the sentence of excommunication, can separate the king from the faithful because of the king's heresy. However, Barclay denies that King Uzziah was deprived of his kingdom, and therefore he also denies that a king can be deprived of his kingdom because of heresy by the Supreme Pontiff. That Uzziah was not deprived of his kingdom he proves from what Scripture (4 Kings 15 and 2 Paralipomena 26) attests: "Sixteen years old was Uzziah when he began to reign, and he reigned fifty and two years in Jerusalem";[246] hence, he ruled from when he was sixteen years old until his death. Barclay also proves this from what the same Scripture says: "And Jotham the king's son was over the house, judging the people of the land";[247] from this Barclay infers that the son of the king administered the kingdom not by his own authority but in the name of his sick father.

I respond that Uzziah, after being stricken with leprosy, certainly retained the title of king, but indeed his son, without the title of king, administered the kingdom with full authority. Josephus in *Antiquitates,* book 9, chapter 11 [10], attests this clearly when he says: "Uzziah lived as a private citizen in a solitary house and his son administered the commonwealth." Also the Scripture indicates this clearly enough when it says that the son "judged the people of the land" and it does not add "and he did it by order of the father or in the name of the father"; and in all the time

---

246. 2 Kings 15:33, 2 Chronicles 26:3.
247. 2 Kings 15:5.

in which the king remained in the solitary house stricken with leprosy he had no part in the government in any way. And I meant this when I said in my argument that Uzziah was forced to give over the kingdom to his son, for by "kingdom" I did not mean the title of king, but the authority, which the father did not retain, because he now lived as a private citizen, as Josephus says. And the force of the argument drawn from this example resides in this, that just as King Uzziah, stricken by leprosy, by order of the priests was forced to live in a solitary house and to live as a private citizen and give up the administration of his kingdom, even so a heretical king, by order of the Supreme Pontiff, can be separated from the community of the pious through excommunication, not only insofar as the communion of the sacraments and the prayers are concerned, as Barclay admits, but also as regards the juridical actions and the administration of the king-dom, which Barclay denies.

But to Uzziah the title of king was left. This is certainly true, yet this is not a good reason for leaving the title of king to a man excommunicated and deposed for heresy, given that spiritual leprosy is worse than corporeal leprosy, and a Christian priest is stronger than a Levite priest, and the thing represented is more perfect than the representation. Similarly, the paschal lamb was not equal to Christ crucified, and the manna was inferior to the Eucharist, and circumcision is not the same as baptism.

What Barclay says on the difference between the authority to rule and the administration of the kingdom is not to the point, first because Uz-ziah is said to have been deprived not only of the administration but also of his authority, since Josephus says that he lived as a private citizen in great sorrow after being stricken with the plague of leprosy, and second because Barclay does not grant that a heretical king can be deprived of the administration of the kingdom. For at p. 312 he says: "What I said, that the Pope can separate a heretical king from the communion of the faithful through excommunication, must be understood in the sense of the spiri-tual separation of souls, not of bodies; indeed, the subjects of an excom-municated king must not deny him obedience." These are the words of Barclay, who without a doubt and as he has shown before does not grant that the administration of the kingdom can be forbidden to a heretical king by the Pope and that a regent can be given for him, but he says himself that to King Uzziah was given a regent, who was his son. Therefore afterward he says falsely that the images of Uzziah, of leprosy, of separation, beautifully correspond to the king, to heresy, and to excommunication, and that from this representation the temporal authority of the Pontiff is demonstrated to be completely fictional, usurped, and alien to divine law. How, then, can the representation correspond to the real thing if in the representation we put a king who is obliged to live in a solitary house and not to deal with any affair of the kingdom, and in the real thing we put a king who is free to reside in the regal city and to dispense justice, as he was doing before? And if the truth of the representation requires that something more, not less, should be found in the real thing than is found in the representation, then it is necessary that a heretical king be deprived through the Pontiff's sentence of the administration of the kingdom and also of his authority. This being the case then, how can Barclay say that from this representation the temporal authority of the Pope is shown as fictional, usurped, and alien to divine law? Therefore, let us assert that our argument was appropriately drawn from the example and could not be overthrown by Barclay.

# The second example in support of the Pontiff's authority in temporal matters is defended

Then Barclay in chapter 28 [38] proposes a second example, adduced by us from the second book of the Paralipomena, chapter 23, where it is narrated that Queen Athaliah, who supported the superstition and heresy of Baal, was deprived of her kingdom and her life by the priest Jehoiada, and that Joash was appointed king in her place.

In order to refute this example, Barclay makes a little digression based on fake rumors and the usual hatred against the Pontiffs. He writes that I have alleged this example in order not to be accused by Pope Sixtus V of lack of diligence or of duplicity, if I should have omitted what others had noted. But I have written this long before Sixtus V was made Pope, and I have lectured on this in schools. Therefore, if I had glossed over so many other examples which I had read in Sander, as Barclay himself attests, why should I have feared to offend the Pontiff if I had glossed over this one? What Barclay adds, that Sixtus V had in mind to compel the order of the Jesuits to a more strict way of life and to a certain kind of clothing, these are fairy tales of men who have too much time on their hands, and it is surprising that Barclay wanted to waste his time reporting this nonsense. Barclay adds that the bull of the same Sixtus V, which grants to the Jesuits the rectorate of the University of Pont à Mousson in perpetuity, seems either spurious or added later, and also that even if the bull had truly been issued by Sixtus, nevertheless it would not be valid because it was obtained as soon as he was elected to the Pontificate. All this does not pertain to the realm of tales or nonsense but to that of calumny and hatred, as if the Pontiff would not have been able to revoke that bull in the whole five years in which he was Pope if he had learned that the bull was spurious or added later or obtained with fraud.[248]

But leaving these things aside, to the example of the priest Jehoiada removing Queen Athaliah, Barclay replies that this example is not to the point because Athaliah was ruling without authority and she had occupied the kingdom with great tyranny through force and crimes.

It is certainly true that the beginning of Athaliah's reign was tyrannical and violent, but after she reigned peacefully for six years, it is credible that the people approved her kingdom with their consent, especially since it was not known that a son of the dead king was still alive and rumor had it that all of them were dead. And it is neither new nor unusual that the beginnings of a kingdom are violent and tyrannical, but that after a while the kings are considered legitimate by the consent of the people. Augustus himself, who was considered an excellent emperor, at the beginning crushed unjustly the Roman Republic and usurped the sovereignty for himself with arms. Otto killed Galba, Vitellius ejected Otto, and Vespasian ejected Vitellius. Nevertheless all were addressed as emperors by the Senate and people of Rome. What is more atrocious than what Philip did when he eliminated the legitimate emperor Gordianus and invaded his empire? And still he was considered a legitimate emperor. I am not going to mention Odoacres the king of the Heruli, the Goths, the Lombard invaders of Italy, and innumerable others, who by force occupied the kingdom and afterward were considered nevertheless legitimate kings with the people's consent.

But, Barclay says, the priest Jehoiada did not depose Athaliah by his own authority; rather he exhorted the captains and united the troops with them against Athaliah, for the Scripture speaks thus: "Then Jehoiada the

248. The relationship between Sixtus V and Bellarmine was far from smooth, as we saw while discussing the pope's intention of putting Bellarmine's *Controversiae* on the Index of Prohibited Books (see Introduction, pp. ix–x and xv–xvi). Sixtus V had some conflict with the Society of Jesus more generally, especially regarding the Society's concept of blind obedience to the General, which for Sixtus and other important figures of the Roman Curia jeopardized the preeminence of the role of the pope within the Church. For more information on the issues at stake, see Mostaccio, "Gerarchie."

priest brought out the captains of hundreds that were set over the host and said unto them, Have her forth of the ranges."[249]

This is certainly true, but it does not hinder the fact that the queen was deposed by Jehoiada's authority. The priest alone, in fact, could not implement what he had proposed, and therefore, after having collected captains and soldiers, he exposed to them his plan of deposing the queen from the throne because of other crimes and because she was a supporter of the false religion of Baal. And the priest did not want to settle for the mere promise of the soldiers, but he made a pact with them and made them swear to cooperate bravely with his plan. Finally, he armed the soldiers by giving them the spears and the remaining weapons of King David, which were in the House of the Lord. He ordered the soldiers to slay the queen, and he crowned the new king. By his authority the people destroyed the temple of Baal and the altars of the idols and killed the priest of Baal in front of Baal's very altar.

249. 2 Chronicles 23:14.

## The third example alleged in support
## of the authority of the Supreme Pontiff
## in temporal matters is defended

I had alleged a third example from St. Ambrose, who excommunicated Emperor Theodosius because of the massacre he had perpetrated with excessive cruelty at Thessalonica. St. Ambrose then obliged Theodosius to issue a law by which the execution of capital punishments and confiscation of goods were to be deferred until thirty days after the sentence was issued. Thus, if Theodosius had issued a sentence in haste and out of anger, in that interval of time he might pacify his soul and thus revoke the sentence.[250] From this example I had gathered that the emperor, who was residing in Milan, could be judged by the bishop of Milan, from which, in turn, I had deduced that if a bishop could do that, how much more could the Pope, who is the prince of the bishops?

Barclay responds to this example thus: first, he admits that a bishop can deliberate on the crime of a prince in the external court of the Church, and the bishop can punish the prince with an ecclesiastical punishment, such as excommunication, which is among the most important ecclesiastical punishments. In this way Ambrose deliberated and judged the massacre perpetrated by Theodosius to be a sin, and once Ambrose declared

250. The incident reported by Bellarmine happened in 390, when Emperor Theodosius, in order to quell a riot that had exploded in Thessalonica after the death of the city's governor, murdered some of the inhabitants of the city as punishment for their rebellion. To put Ambrose's reaction in the context of the relationship between the Christian Church and the empire, see McLynn, *Ambrose of Milan.*

Theodosius guilty, the bishop excommunicated the emperor. Then Barclay grants that Ambrose ordrered Theodosius to issue that law as a penitence and that without a fruit or sign of penitence Ambrose would not have absolved Theodosius from the bond of anathema. From all this Barclay gathers that St. Ambrose had a spiritual jurisdiction over Theodosius but not a temporal or a political one.

But I did not adduce that example, which pertains to excommunication, against Barclay, who had not yet become known to the world, but against others, and especially against the English Calvinists who deny that a supreme prince can be excommunicated by the Supreme Pontiff, or that the Supreme Pontiff has any jurisdiction or authority over supreme princes, which indeed pertains to the political law that Theodosius issued in consequence of Ambrose's precept. Certainly we do not deny that this law represents the fruit of penitence and was ordered by the spiritual authority of the bishop, but we wanted to show that ecclesiastical princes can dispose of temporal matters for the sake of spiritual matters not only in the internal forum of the conscience, but also in the external forum of the Church. Certainly, by the same authority by which St. Ambrose could oblige Theodosius to issue that political law as a condition for absolving him from the bond of anathema, Ambrose could also oblige Theodosius to issue another political law necessary to the souls' salvation unless Theodosius wanted to be stained with the bond of anathema.

From this it is clearly gathered that with much greater reason could the Supreme Pontiff, ruler of the universal Church, command temporal princes under pain of anathema to issue political laws necessary to the spiritual good, and, by the same token, the Supreme Pontiff could command temporal princes to abrogate those laws that hinder the spiritual good, and in this way the temporal authority is subject to the spiritual authority.

## CHAPTER 40

## The fourth example is defended

The fourth example was drawn from the privilege of St. Gregory, granted to the monastery of St. Medard,[251] which can be found in book 12 [14], at the end of his epistles, in which we read these words: "If a king, nobleman, judge, or any secular person violates or contradicts the decrees of this apostolic authority and our injunction, no matter his office or high position, he should be deprived of his office, etc." Also similar words can be read in another privilege of the same St. Gregory, book 11 [13], epistle 10 [8] to a Senator Abbot.

Barclay speaks of this example: "If today blessed Gregory were alive and understood the previous words to be taken in the sense that he would have had authority to deprive a king of his office and dignity, he would cry indeed that this is a false interpretation and that he never thought of it, not even in his dreams. Indeed, the words written by him elsewhere do not give credit to this interpretation. For those words by which he advises and urges all kinds of people not to violate the privilege given by him are the words of somebody who prays, not somebody who commands. With those words he admonishes and beseeches all people not to violate the privilege given by him, and if they do violate it, God will take revenge and will deprive them of their office. And this kind of admonition and prayer now is always added at the end of bulls and pontifical decrees in this way: 'Therefore, let nobody modify this paragraph and if anybody should presume to do so, he would incur or should know that he will incur—which

---

251. On this document see p. 175, n. 64.

is the same—the indignation of God omnipotent and the blessed apostles Peter and Paul.'"

The interpretation of St. Gregory's words I presented is not mine, but that of another St. Gregory, equal in dignity and not much inferior in sanctity. I say, St. Gregory VII in his epistle to the bishop of Metz, which is epistle 21 of book 8, adduces this passage of St. Gregory to prove that he had rightly deposed Emperor Henry: "Blessed Gregory the Pope decreed that kings who presume to violate the decrees of the Apostolic See fall from their office, and Blessed Gregory wrote to a Senator Abbot in these words, 'If a king, nobleman, etc.' If St. Gregory, a very mild teacher, declared that the kings who violated the statutes were not only deposed but also excommunicated and condemned in the eternal tribunal, who could blame us for having deposed and excommunicated Henry, who not only despised the apostolic sentences but also trampled Mother Church herself as much as he could and was a most impious robber and the most evil destroyer of the whole kingdom and churches?" These are the words of Gregory VII, and if Barclay does not want to give way to him in the interpretation of St. Gregory's words, then Barclay will be excessively impudent, but if Barclay gives way to Gregory VII, he will have to admit that St. Gregory did not ignore the fact that the authority given to him from heaven extended also to the deposition of kings and princes.

But let us add another interpreter of Gregory's words, so that every word may stand in the mouth of two witnesses.[252] Thomas Netter, a most learned man, in his *Liber doctrinalis fidei antiquae*, book 2, article 3, chapter 75, says: "Certainly Blessed Gregory did not prejudice in any way the eminency of his status over that of the emperor when he put the king before himself nominally, once we consider attentively the matter that they were then discussing, which we will properly see if we examine his later actions and writings. Consider whether he did not think himself the master of emperors and kings when, after giving certain privileges to a senator presbyter and abbot of the Hospital of the French, under threat to the dignity and office of every violator of such privilege, he concluded:

252. This is Bellarmine's reference to Deuteronomy 19:15; cf. also Deuteronomy 17:6 and Aquinas's *Summa*, 2a 2ae, article 2. For a stimulating discussion of this principle in historiography see Carlo Ginzburg, "Just One Witness," 82–96.

'if a king, or a nobleman, etc.'" How well did this scholar confute Barclay who was not yet born! Barclay says that from other writings of St. Gregory it is gathered that he did not think that he had authority over secular kings, even if his words would seem to signify that he had; Thomas Netter by contrast says that St. Gregory subjected himself to the emperor nominally, but in fact he did not ignore the eminence of his status over that of the emperor. Barclay says that the words of St. Gregory sound like a prayer which any private man can add to his writings; Thomas Netter, by contrast, says that the words of St. Gregory sound like a threat to the office and dignity of anyone who might violate his decrees: no one but a supreme prince can add such a threat to his writings. But it is foolish to ask whether more credit should be given to Barclay alone or to two men of so much eminence and doctrine. But even assuming that we should ask such a question, we are able to answer it effortlessly, out of St. Gregory's own words. In fact, St. Gregory mentions in the same sentence three consequences for anyone who might violate his decree: let him be deprived of his office, let him be separated from the communion of the faithful, and let him be condemned to eternal punishment in the divine judgment. But the last two do not express a prayer, but a decree or a declaration, as the prelate who says, "Let whoever does this be excommunicated," does not pray for, but orders, excommunication, and the prelate who says, "Let whoever does this be condemned to eternal punishment in the divine judgment," does not pray for eternal damnation (who in fact is so cruel as to pray for this?) but declares that whoever does it will sin most gravely and will deserve eternal punishment in the divine judgment. Therefore in the same way the phrase "Let him be deprived of his office" is not a prayer but a decree that this man is deprived of his office, and a declaration that the people are not required to obey such a king as one deprived of his office and dignity. By the same token, the last words of the apostolic decrees do not signify a prayer, as Barclay foolishly explains (for the Supreme Pastor and Vicar of that Good Shepherd Who offered His own life for his sheep would not pray for the indignation of God omnipotent against his sheep). Rather the last words of the apostolic decrees contain a declaration and an announcement of the most grave punishment that will without a doubt happen to the violators of the apostolic precepts, for the words,

"He should know that he will incur the indignation of God omnipotent and of the blessed apostles Peter and Paul" clearly mean this. Therefore, if St. Gregory were now alive, without a doubt he would cry that Barclay's interpretation is a calumny and he never thought of such a thing, not even in his dreams.

## CHAPTER 41

# The fifth example is defended

The fifth example is that of Gregory II, who prohibited Emperor Leo, whom he had excommunicated, from collecting the revenues from Italy, and therefore he took away from the emperor a part of his empire.

Barclay puts before his refutation of this and of the following examples a rather long admonition against the arguments that are sought from examples, forgetting the arguments that he himself drew from the examples of old Pontiffs and emperors, from which he said it was most clearly known that the Pontiffs have no authority to dispose of temporal matters. But since these are common tropes that can be adapted to every disputation, I will pass them by and come to the proposed issue. Thus Barclay denies decidedly that it is true what the historians report, that the inhabitants of Italy were forbidden by the Pope to pay revenues to a heretical and excommunicated emperor. His entire reason is that Platina in his biography of Gregory II writes that Gregory opposed the people who wanted to abandon the heretical emperor, and by his own authority he held them in allegiance and obedience to the emperor. But as to why more credit should be given to Platina than to the other historians, who are more ancient and more numerous, Barclay gives as a reason that Platina wrote the history of the Pontiffs by order of Sixtus IV and had many old documents in Rome, and also that Pope Gregory, since he was excellent and most just, never would have ordered, against the Gospel, that tribute be denied to Caesar, who up until his death remained Caesar and Imperator Augustus.

But this disputation of Barclay is so shaky and weak that it is not surprising that just before in a long preface he attempted to diminish the authority of examples, since he saw that he could not produce anything firm that would refute such an ancient and relevant example. Therefore, first I say that if we take chronology into account, Platina does not contradict the other historians. It is true that for many years Gregory had opposed the Italian people who wanted to abandon the emperor, and he had hoped that with his assiduous encouragement the emperor would change his ways, come back to his senses, and listen to more sane advice. This is what Platina really reports. But when the Pontiff saw that his efforts were in vain and that the emperor was getting worse every day, the Pontiff extirpated the root and excluded the emperor from the community of the pious, ordering the Italian people not to obey him because of his impiety and not to pay him revenues. This indeed Platina does not deny, and neither do many historians, Greek and Latin, whom I quoted in my book. On this whole issue see Cardinal Baronius, vol. 9 of the *Annales* for the years 726 and 730.

Second, I say that even if Platina contradicted the other historians, one must believe the other historians rather than him, for these historians are many and are more ancient and diligent, and they write the history of the period, not the life of one Pontiff only, as Platina does. And how little diligence Platina showed in examining the documents of the Roman archives can be understood from the fact that Onofrio Panvinio, in his additions to Platina, shows many things in Platina that were either omitted or wrong. For instances in his addition preceding the biography of Gregory II, Panvinio declares that Pope Gregory II rightfully deprived the heretical emperor Leo III of his empire in Italy, which had been given him by the Pope.[253]

Third, I say that Gregory, a most holy man, did not commit a sin against the Gospel when he prohibited the Italian people from paying the rev-

---

253. In his role as censor, Bellarmine dealt at length with both Platina's and Panvinio's works in the late 1580s and early 1590s. In writing his censures of both, Bellarmine employed the same principles that he did when he censored other works of history: historical accuracy should be respected, even when it leads to writing unflattering things about the popes, and philological or historical mistakes are especially to be avoided if they in any way might offer support to the opinion of heretics (see Le Bachelet, *Auctarium Bellarminianum*, pp. 554–64, for Bellarmine's censure of Panvinio; and Godman, *Saint as Censor*, pp. 250–59, for his censure of Platina).

enues to a heretical emperor, since what the Lord says, "Give unto Caesar what is Caesar's," is understood to mean that Caesar is the legitimate ruler. But Leo, who had been publicly excommunicated and deposed from the empire by the Supreme Pontiff because of the crime of heresy, was not truly and rightfully Caesar, but a tyrant and a persecutor having the title of Caesar.

But, Barclay says, Leo remained the emperor until his death. I reply that among the Greeks, especially heretics, he remained emperor *de facto,* not *de iure;* among the Latins, and especially the Italians, he did not remain emperor either *de iure* or *de facto.*

## CHAPTER 42

# The sixth example is defended

The sixth example is of Pope Zachary, who deposed Childeric, king of the Franks, and substituted Pippin.

To this example Barclay opposes many things, which must be refuted one by one in order.

First, he contends that Childeric was king only in name, such as, he says, the king of Chess.

Even if it cannot be denied that Childeric did not do anything in the kingdom by himself, and that he administered the kingdom and its affairs through the princes and especially through the prefect of the palace, as Aimoinus reports in book 4, chapter 61, yet it is not true that he was king in name only, for he was king by law of succession and he was anointed and crowned as a true and legitimate king and had received the oath of allegiance from his people. Barclay cannot deny this unless he wants to contradict himself, for shortly afterward he writes that a most grave injury was done to King Childeric by Pontiff Zachary and Prince Pippin when Childeric was deposed from the kingdom. But what injury could have been done to Childeric if he carried a false title of king without any right? And why had Pippin been inflamed with hope of getting the kingdom and why was he aspiring without dissimulation to the title of king (as Barclay says shortly before) if Childeric had nothing but an empty title?

Second, Barclay says that Childeric was deposed unjustly, and in this he has an ally, John Calvin, book 4 of the *Institutiones*, chapter 7, and Illyricus in *Historia Magdeburgensis, centuria* 8, chapter 10.

But we prove that he was deposed justly first from the testimonies of all the authors, for they all relate this story with praise (see Cedrenus in *Vita Leonis Isaurici;* Paulus Diaconus in *De gestis Longobardorum,* book 6, chapter 5; Einhard in *Vita Caroli Magni;* Regino in *Chronicon,* book 2; Marianus Scotus in book 3 of his *Chronica;* Otto of Freising in *Historiae,* book 5, chapter 55; Ado of Vienne in his chronicle; Aimoinus, book 4, chapter 61; Burchard of Ursperg; Sigebert in his chronicle; Biondo in book 10 of the *Historiarum prima decas;* Paulus Aemilius in *De gestis Francorum,* books 1 and 2; Robert Gaguin; Jean Papire Masson; and all the others, except the heretics). Second, we prove that Childeric was deposed justly because not only were Childeric and some of his predecessors not taking care of the affairs of the kingdom, but the Christian religion, because of their inertia, was suffering greatly in the kingdom, as St. Boniface, bishop of Mainz, writes in his letter to Pope Zachary. Third, we prove this because of the virtue of the author and executor, Zachary, by whose authority this was done and who by everybody's consent was a man most holy and learned. Indeed, St. Boniface, who by Zachary's order anointed and crowned Pippin, was not only a famous scholar but also a most glorious martyr. Last, we prove this because of the outcome, as the transfer of the kingdom of the Franks from Childeric to Pippin, with God's blessing, was most felicitous and advantageous both to the kingdom and to the Church.

"But," Barclay says, "in no case is it allowed to do evil in order to attain a good, no matter how great, and that a legitimate king be deposed by his own subjects, or that they consent to his deposition, we have already shown above is in itself simply evil, since the king has God alone over him to Whom alone he is obliged to render account for his actions."

I say that not his subjects, but the Pontiff, who was his superior, deposed Childeric justly, for Zachary not only offered his consent to the deposition of Childeric, but he deposed him by his own authority, as we will soon show. And Barclay has not proved above with any solid argument that kings have nobody over them but God to Whom alone they are obliged to render account of their actions. Let the reader see what we said before and judge for himself.

Third, Barclay laughs at that argument which I drew from the felicitous outcome to prove that Childeric was justly deposed, and he says it is a base and childish argument and cites the poet, saying: "Let success elude whoever judges the deed from its outcome."[254] He also adds that the transfer of the kingdom of the Franks from the Carolingians to the Capetians had the same felicitous outcome, and nevertheless it is well known that Hugh Capet deprived the Carolingians of their kingdom and transferred it to the Capetians by the greatest crime.

I admit that an argument based only on a fortuitous outcome has little value without a doubt, as if somebody should condemn the prudence and skill of a commander only because he did not win a battle, since often loss in battle happens for other reasons than the commander's lack of prudence and skill. However, an argument based on a felicitous outcome in consequence of God's providence has not a small value, especially when it is added to other arguments, for God usually favors justice, unless on account of His wisdom it would seem that it should happen otherwise.

As to the fact that Barclay reproaches Hugh Capet for the greatest crime and for the usurpation for the kingdom and adduces the author Gaguin, we oppose to him Cardinal Baronius, who in the tenth volume of the *Annales* for the year 987 proves that Hugh was a legitimate king and in him Charlemagne's stock did not end but was propagated. And there is no lack of others who defend Hugh, such as Jean Papire Masson and others, and Gaguin does not say that Hugh did that with the greatest crime. And certainly a good argument for this can be that Robert the Pious, who ruled together with his father Hugh and after him, was a most pious and holy man, and such a great piety could not have been consistent with the unjust usurpation of another's realm.

Fourth, Barclay says that St. Boniface did not sin in executing Zachary's mandate, even if Zachary sinned by issuing that mandate. His justification is that he was held to execute the Pope's sentence even if he had known it was unjust. Therefore although the injustice of the command made Zachary guilty, the order to serve and the necessity to obey showed

254. Ovid, *Heroides*, 2, vv. 85–86. The translation is mine.

that Boniface was innocent, and he adduces the chapter "Pastoralis," section "Quia vero," title "De officio et potestate iudicis delegati"; canon "Quid culpatur," causa 23, question 1; and canon "Miles," causa 23, question 5.[255]

Barclay's statement is not base and childish, but clearly heretical, since it contradicts the express word of God, that one ought to obey God rather than man (Acts 5), which St. Augustine and other Fathers also declared, who are quoted in the canon "Iulianus," causa 11, question 3, and in many other canons on the same question.[256] In that chapter "Pastoralis," section "Quia vero," where it is said that an unjust sentence must be executed by an inferior, the gloss rightly teaches that what is here called an unjust sentence is intended to mean an unjust sentence which in absolute terms is actually just, because it is correctly inferred from the law that a sentence should be issued against a person who does not appeal in the prescribed time against something that he would have otherwise every right to appeal against. In the same passage the same gloss declares most correctly that one must not obey a mandate of one's superior if this mandate is evidently unjust. And regarding the canon "Quid culpatur," causa 23, question 1, St. Augustine contradicts Barclay, since St. Augustine says that one must obey a superior either when it is uncertain that what is commanded is not unjust or when it is not certain that what is commanded is unjust. From this it follows that when it is certain that what is commanded is unjust one

255. The first canon is canon 28, title 29, book 1, of Gregory's *Decretales,* issued by Innocent III in 1204, which deals with the office of the papal delegate. The section quoted by Bellarmine establishes that the delegate has to execute the sentence of his superior even if he knows that it is unjust (text in *Corpus iuris canonici,* vol. 2, cols. 172–75). The second is canon 4, causa 23, question 1, of the second part of Gratian's *Decretum,* and it sums up (with some significant variations) Augustine's opinion in *Contra Faustum,* bk. 22, chaps. 74–75, on what can be considered a crime and should be punishable in war (text in *Corpus iuris canonici,* vol. 1, cols. 892–93). The third is canon 13, causa 23, question 5, of the second part of Gratian's *Decretum,* and it decrees that a soldier who kills a man by order of his superior cannot be considered a murderer (text in *Corpus iuris canonici,* vol. 1, col. 935).

256. This is canon 94, causa 11, question 3, of the second part of Gratian's *Decretum.* It was taken from Ambrose, and it decreed that the Christian soldiers who were fighting under Emperor Julian the Apostate should not be considered guilty if they were obeying Julian's orders "for the defense of the commonwealth" (text in *Corpus iuris canonici,* vol. 1, col. 669).

must not in any case obey. Finally, the canon "Miles," causa 28 [23], question 1 [5], does not deal with the justice or injustice of the mandate, but in it this only is decreed, that it is a sin to kill a man by private authority, but not if this is done by public authority. Therefore Barclay, blinded by the love for his own opinion, either did not want to, or was not able to, understand the laws.

Fifth, he says that Pope Zachary concurred with the Franks who wanted to depose Childeric and to appoint Pippin as king, but the Pope did not depose Childeric from the kingdom nor did he transfer it to Pippin by his own power or authority, and therefore nothing can be drawn from this example to demonstrate the authority of the Roman Pontiff over kings, either in deposing them or in appointing them.

But this is excessive temerity, since the contrary is manifestly proved by the testimonies of all historians:

1. The most ancient Annals of the Franks have this: "Given his [Zachary's] authority, he ordered that Pippin be appointed as king."

2. Einhard in *Vita Caroli Magni* says: "Pippin was made king from prefect of the palace through the authority of the Roman Pontiff."

3. Aimoinus in *De gestis Francorum,* book 4, chapter 61, says: "The Pontiff by his own authority ordered that Pippin be appointed as king."

4. Regino, in book 2 of his chronicles, says: "Zachary, through his apostolic authority, ordered that Pippin be made king and he anointed Pippin with the oil of the sacred Unction."

5. Lambert of Hersfeld in his history says: "Pippin was declared king by the decree of Pope Zachary and was anointed by St. Boniface."

6. Sigebert in his chronicle says: "In the year 750 Prince Pippin was consecrated king by St. Boniface through his apostolic authority and the election of the Franks, and in the year 752 he was again anointed as king by Pope Stephen."

7. Hermann Contractus in his chronicle says: "In the year 752 Pippin was appointed king by the authority of Pope Stephen after Childeric had been deprived of his authority and deposed."

8. Marianus Scotus in book 3 of his chronicles says: "Pope Zachary from the authority of St. Peter the Apostle commanded the Frankish people that Pippin, who was exercising the regal authority, be allowed to also enjoy the dignity of the title. Therefore King Childeric, who was the last of the Merovingians to rule the Franks, was deposed and sent into a monastery."

9. Burchard of Ursperg in his chronicles says: "In the year 750 Pippin, elected to the kingdom through the authority of Pope Zachary according to the custom of the Franks, was elevated to the throne of the kingdom by the hands of St. Boniface." And later: "Pope Stephen confirmed Pippin in the honor of the regal office with sacred unction."

10. Otto of Freising in *Historia,* book 5, chapter 22, says: "Pippin is elected to the kingdom by the authority of Pope Zachary."

11. Albert Krantz, in *Metropolis,* book 1, chapter 14, says: "Rightly the Supreme Pontiff and the king of the Gauls exalt each other with mutual favors, when from the beginning this See was responsible for the House of Charles having the regal dignity."

12. Paulus Aemilius, speaking of Childeric, says: "Zachary absolved the Franks from their oath of allegiance to the said Childeric, and when the Franks gathered they greeted Pippin as the king."

We have twelve testimonies, some of which attest that Childeric was deposed and Pippin elevated by the apostolic authority, other say by the authority of the Pontiff, or by the authority of St. Peter, yet others by decree of the Pope. The last one writes that the Franks did not dare to greet Pippin as king unless they were first absolved by the Pontiff from the oath of allegiance by which they were bound to King Childeric. Nevertheless Barclay with his usual temerity denies that this was done by the Pope's authority or decree. The only thing we need now is for Barclay—along with Matthias Illyricus, a very well known heretic of our time and a very untrustworthy historian—to say that it is a lie and a falsity what our historians affirm, that the kingdom of the Franks was transferred by Pope Zachary from Childeric to Pippin (see Illyricus, at the beginning of his book *De translatione imperii*).

# Epilogue

After having tried in vain to refute six of the examples, Barclay either willingly glossed over the remaining six because he realized they were too clear to be obscured by the shadows of his cavils, or, overtaken by death, he was forced to leave his work unfinished. Be that as it may, finished with his work and with his life, Barclay has taken a stand in front of the Judge Whom nobody can deceive and with Whom the favor of princes never helps anybody. And I, who will have to stand in front of the same Supreme Judge soon, trust that I can with good conscience attest that I have written nothing either in favor of or for hatred of anybody, but I wrote what I considered to be the truth, what I have learned from the Church, what many before me, not only learned but also saints, have written. And I did not come to this battle of my own accord, but, challenged by a man whom I did not know, I was forced to defend as an old man what I wrote as a young man. And if I have defended the pontifical authority and my own writings as was fitting, which I strongly wanted to do, I most humbly thank God, in Whose hand we and all our discussions are. But if, by contrast, it has happened otherwise and I have failed in one thing or many, because of human weakness, I ask for mercy from Him Who is good, and ready to forgive, and plenteous in mercy unto all them that call upon Him.[257] I also willingly and gladly submit not only this present small work but all my writings to the censure of the Church and to the Supreme Pontiff, the Vicar of Christ.

---

257. This is Bellarmine's paraphrase of Psalm 86:5.

*On the Primary Duty of the*
*Supreme Pontiff*

The Supreme Pastor holds three roles [*personae*] in the Church of God: he is the pastor and rector of the universal Church, the bishop assigned to the city of Rome, and a temporal prince of an ecclesiastic dominion. But among all his duties the care for the universal Church comes first: indeed this is his first, unique, and greatest duty. It is the first because the apostle Peter was nominated pastor of all God's flock much earlier than he was named bishop of Rome or Antioch. It is unique because while there are many bishops of very illustrious cities, and also many temporal princes, he alone is the Pontiff of the world, general Vicar of Christ, and pastor of the universal Church. Moreover, this first role is the greatest because the bishopric of Rome has its limits, and rather narrow ones at that, as also does the temporal realm of the Church; but the Supreme Pontiff has no limits in the world, apart from the limits of the world itself.

Now the Supreme Pontiff could easily fulfill this duty, so ancient, so great, so exclusive, so specific, so necessary for the Church, if he assigned good bishops to every church, and if he saw to it that they fulfilled their duty, and if he compelled them, if necessary, to do their duty. Because good bishops appoint good priests, good preachers, and good confessors, therefore the assurance of the salvation of souls will depend on them. But if, due to the bishops' or the priests' negligence, some souls perished, the local priests would have to render account for this, and the Supreme Pontiff, if he had done what was necessary to prevent the souls from perishing, would have freed his own soul. If, however, the Supreme Pastor had given less than good bishops to the local churches or had failed to ensure that the appointed bishops did their jobs properly, then the Pope would have to render account for those souls.[1]

1. Bellarmine is here using the Latin expression "sanguinem de manu alicuius requirere," a paraphrase of Genesis 9:5, which I have translated as "to render account for."

The Council of Trent, session 24, chapter 1, comments on this with these words: "Finally, the sacred synod, moved by so many extremely serious inconveniences in the Church, cannot fail to call attention to the fact that nothing is more necessary to the Church of God than that the Most Blessed Roman Pontiff devote that care which he owes to the universal Church as a duty of his office, first of all to appoint excellent cardinals and then to assign very good and appropriate pastors to the individual churches; and this all the more because our Lord Jesus Christ is going to ask him to render an account for those sheep of His flock who perished because of the bad government of negligent pastors forgetful of their duty."[2]

This consideration strikes me with so much terror that in my soul I pity no man as much as I pity the Supreme Pontiff, whom everybody usually envies. Indeed, what St. John Chrysostom writes very discreetly in his third homily on the Acts of the Apostles, that few bishops are saved because it is extremely difficult to take good care of the many souls in their charge, without a doubt applies even more to the Popes. And we cannot delude ourselves by referring to good conscience, or good intention, or saintly deeds, for the apostle Paul says: "I know nothing by myself; yet I am not hereby justified";[3] and the apostle James terrifies us with that dreadful phrase: "Whosoever shall keep the whole law, and yet offend in one point, he is guilty of all."[4] Our topic is precisely a matter in which it is very easy to sin and for which it is very difficult to find a remedy. Therefore, relying on apostolic benevolence, I will place the scruples that, to tell the truth, keep me up at night, into the arms of the most pious Father, or rather at his feet.[5]

2. Bellarmine is quoting from the first canon of the decree "De reformatione," discussed on 11 November 1563 (text in *Conciliorum oecumenicorum decreta,* pp. 735–37).

3. 1 Corinthians 4:4.

4. James 2:10.

5. The pope's response: "This terrifies us too, but since men's hearts are open to God alone, and since we cannot but choose men, two examples often offer us some comfort. The first is that when Jesus Christ our Lord chose the Twelve Apostles, after spending the night in prayer—which we do not know whether He did before choosing anybody else—Judas was nonetheless one of those chosen. The second example is that

It seems to me that there are six issues that need to be reformed and they cannot be neglected without harm. The first is long-term vacancy of churches, and on this issue there is an epistle by St. Leo to Anastasius, bishop of Thessalonica [14], in which he urges that churches be provided for immediately so that God's flock not lack the care of a pastor for too long a time. There is also a decree by Innocent III [canon "Ne pro defectu"], title "De electione," in which it is written: "In order to prevent a rapacious wolf from attacking God's flock for the lack of a shepherd, or to prevent a church, deprived of its functions, from suffering a serious loss, and in order to try to avoid any danger for the souls and to prevent damages to the churches, we decree that neither a cathedral church nor a regular church should be vacant for more than three months."[6] This decree was issued together with many others in a timely resolution by a very large general council. There are also a number of letters by St. Gregory in which those who are in charge of selecting pastors are urged to do so very quickly, and if some inevitable delay were to happen, it was customary that the Pope himself would assign the vacant church to the neighboring bishop, not in order to collect the revenues, as happens nowadays, but in order to manage temporarily the needs of that church. Indeed, those most saintly and prudent Popes continuously sought to provide for the vacant churches, so as not to render themselves accountable for those souls that happened to get lost because of the lack of a pastor. It would be difficult indeed to explain in a few words how much damage vacant churches suffer; what abyss of vices the flock of God sinks into when there is no pastor; how much God's vineyard goes to waste when there is no farmer.[7]

---

when the Twelve Apostles, all full of the Holy Spirit, chose seven deacons, one among them was Nicholas, a famous heretic. We think that God omnipotent left those examples in his infinite goodness to comfort those who are in charge of choosing in the Church."

6. The canon quoted here was ratified during the Fourth Lateran Council called by Innocent in 1215. It became the twenty-third of the *Constitutiones* of that council and chapter 41, title 6, book 1, of Gregory IX's *Decretales* (text in *Corpus iuris canonici*, vol. 2, col. 88).

7. The pope's response: "In this first issue or first chapter we admit that we have sinned and that we continue to sin; but the reason for this is for the most part the difficulty in finding suitable people, and even though many people are often proposed to us, since we cannot seek information by ourselves, sometimes we have found that

The second problem is the advancement of less than useful prelates: churches should be provided with good people, and not people with good churches. I think that the advice of combining the interests of a deserving person and a vacant church at the same time is excellent, if that is possible. However, the interest of the church should always come first.[8] Indeed, in book 6 of his commentary on 1 Kings 3, St. Gregory writes that in many other issues exemption can be a salutary decision, but if the exemption is allowing an unworthy person to be promoted to a bishopric, then the exemption is deadly. And the same Gregory, in book 2 [3] of his epistles, chapter 68 [epistle 29], says that he himself had decided to avoid participating in elections of bishops out of fear of committing a sin by his choice. Moreover (not to mention other instances), the Council of Trent, session 24, chapter 1, affirms clearly that those who are in charge of promoting bishops commit a mortal sin if they do not see to it that only the people whom they judge worthiest and most useful to the Church are advanced. This is the general opinion among the theologians.[9]

I was terrified on two or three occasions when I saw people promoted to bishop in the sacred Consistory who, either because of senility, or because of a serious physical impediment, or because of the lack of any episcopal virtue, were not the most useful but indeed were hardly useful or suitable at all to administer to souls. Yes, there is the argument that it is "custom" for such churches to be given the oldest cardinals, whoever they might be, but I do not think that we would ever accept a custom prescribing that our bodies should be cured by the oldest doctors, if, because of senility or

---

those to whom we have entrusted this charge either have deceived us or have themselves been deceived by others. Sometimes we have thought it safer to postpone the decision in order not to be deceived, remembering that phrase of St. Paul's, 'Lay hands suddenly on no man' (1 Timothy 5:22). Nevertheless we also remember that in the time of St. Gregory the Great there were churches that were vacant for a long time, and because of this he used to entrust to a bishop another church, so that he could provide for that church in the meantime."

8. The pope's response: "We know that, and we have always before our eyes the need to provide as much as we can for the churches, not for the prelates, unless the case is such that we think we can provide with fairness for both churches and prelates."

9. The pope's response: "This is true, but if we must always choose the worthiest people, churches will never be provided for, because we do not know how we can know who the worthiest is."

some other reason, they are unable to cure us! If we act in this way for the sake of the physical health of our bodies, why don't we do likewise for the eternal health of our souls?[10]

I do not even want to mention those who nowadays aspire to, or rather openly ask for and demand, a bishopric, knowing not what they ask, as Our Lord says.[11] If, in fact, even in the judgment of the civil legislators no one is worthy of the dignity of priesthood unless he is appointed against his will,[12] how would a man who imposes himself not be unworthy? St. Gregory, in book 6 of his commentary on 1 Kings, last chapter, says that the right order is that men should be invited to, and should not ask for, the office of bishop. Furthermore, St. Bernard in book 4, *De consideratione*, chapter 5 [4], says: "He who asks for himself is already judged," and later: "Force and compel to come in those who hesitate and refuse."[13]

The third issue is the pastors' absence from their churches. What is the advantage of electing the right pastor if he is not there? And, not to mention old statements, the Council of Trent, session 23, chapter 1, declares that by divine precept pastors of souls are required to know their flock, preach the word of God, administer sacraments, and maintain their flock by example of all the good works.[14] It is both self-evident and has been explained by the said Council that those who do not assist their flock cannot

10. The pope's response: "Regarding those bishoprics we will speak later."

11. Cf. Luke 23:34. The pope's response: "This issue tortures us too, because if we do not want to give bishoprics to those who ask for them or to those who are proposed to us by others, we do not know how we would be able to provide for the churches, especially churches that are not too big and that offer a small income, and if Your Lordship [*Dominatio vestra*] knows a way [to deal with this], we will be happy to listen and to take it into consideration."

12. Bellarmine here refers to the law in the Justinian Code, 1, 3, 30, promulgated by Emperor Leo in 469, which prescribed that the office of priesthood was not to be bestowed on people who offered money for it, since "non pretio, sed precibus ordinetur antistes. Tantum ab ambitu debet esse sepositus, ut quaeratur cogendus, rogatus recedat, invitatus effugiat. . . . profecto enim indignus est sacerdotio, nisi fuerit ordinatus invitus" (text in *Corpus iuris civilis,* vol. 2, p. 22).

13. This is a reference to Luke 14:23. The pope's response: "These considerations can be made, but when we come to the practical aspects of the issue, we encounter many difficulties."

14. Bellarmine is referring to the first canon of the decree "Super reformatione," discussed on 15 July 1563 in section 23 of the Council of Trent (text in *Conciliorum oecumenicorum decreta,* pp. 720–22).

accomplish these things. Because of this, the council concludes that those cardinals who are bishops of churches very far away from Rome should be required to personally reside in those churches. I fear that those who are in charge of having the bishops reside in their churches fail especially in this regard.[15] In fact, I see in the churches of Italy such great desolation, more perhaps than in many years, that residency now would appear to be a prescription of neither divine nor human law.[16] First, today we count eleven cardinal-bishops who do not reside in their churches: Gesualdus, Florentinus, Veronensis, Asculanus, Gallus, Boromeus, Senensis, Bandinus, Vicecomes, Tuschus, Ossatus.[17] Second, we could mention even more

15. The pope's response: "In this issue we admit we have sinned, because we have allowed bishops to come to Rome too easily, and it is most difficult to send them away from Rome."

16. The pope's response: "Before, if Your Lordship cares to remember, maybe one in a thousand, as they say, did not reside."

17. Bellarmine is referring to the following prelates: Alfonso Gesualdo, cardinal of Calitri (in the archdiocese of Naples) from 1561 to his death in 1603, an active papal diplomat serving as vice-protector of Hungary in 1584 and later papal legate of Marche and protector of Portugal; Alessandro Ottaviano de' Medici, archbishop of Florence (1574) and cardinal (1583), papal diplomat in France, elected to the papacy, less than a month before his death, as Leo XI (1605); Agostino Valier, bishop of Verona (1565) and cardinal (1583), active in Rome and prefect of the Congregation of the Index; Girolamo Bernerio, elected both bishop of Ascoli-Piceno and cardinal in 1586 and active in the Roman Curia; Tolomeo Galli, also known as Cardinal di Como, bishop of Martorano (1560), promoted to the metropolitan see of Manfredonia (1562) and then to cardinal (1565), one of the most influential clergymen in the Roman Curia; Federico Borromeo, cardinal (1587) and bishop of Milan (1595), a member of the Roman commission in charge of editing the documents of the Council of Trent; Camillo Borghese (from the branch of the Borghese family in Siena), created cardinal in 1596, secretary of the congregation of the Inquisition from 1602 to 1605, and elected to the papacy as Paul V in 1605; Ottavio Bandini, bishop of Fermo (1595), cardinal (1596), and active papal diplomat in central Italy; Alfonso Visconti, bishop of Cervia (1591) and cardinal (1599), until 1598 Papal Nuncio in Hungary and active in politics after that; Domenico Toschi, bishop of Tivoli (1595) and cardinal (1599), an active officer in the Roman Curia; Arnauld d'Ossat, bishop of Rennes (1596) and cardinal (1599), who never left Rome to visit his own diocese.

The pope responded to this list by saying: "Gesualdo does not reside because of some conflicts, and maybe Your Lordship knows whether it would be better if he did reside. The bishop of Verona has a coadjutor. The bishop of Ascoli-Piceno is talking about resigning and he is a theologian. Galli came on the occasion of the *Annus Sanctus*. Your Lordship knows the problems that Borromeo has in his diocese. Regarding Borghese, his illness is the reason. Bandini resides because his church is in the province

bishops who serve as apostolic nuncios, some of whom have not seen their own churches for many years. Third, some occupy a political office, having neglected the office of nurturing the souls under their care; and I do not know how this can be justified. For the apostle prohibits the soldiers of God from entangling themselves with the affairs of this life,[18] and St. Gregory in book 7 [10] of his epistles, chapter 2 [epistle 10], vigorously reproaches one bishop Basilius who was dealing in legal affairs as if he were a layman. In the past some individuals from the secular judicial profession have been raised to the rank of bishop, which, as we read, was the case of Ambrose, Nectarius, Chrysostom, Gregory; but nowhere in past authors have I read of anybody descending from the episcopal dignity to take care of political offices; and this for a reason. For how can it be that those whose very duty it is to urge with words and speeches, and whose hands are consecrated to bless, are surrounded by guards and are in charge of torturing and killing people?[19] Fourth, having abandoned their flock, some either waste their time in Rome or occupy themselves with things that could be easily taken care of by somebody else. I acknowledge that certain bishops can be excused for not residing in their churches because of obedience; I don't deny that the Pope may have reasons to excuse some bishops from their duty of residence for a certain period; but I doubt that God would be pleased that so many bishops are absent from their churches for such a long time and with so much detriment to the souls, and it is rather obvious that those bishops certainly do not fulfill their duty. In fact, if bishops who are regularly present in their churches devoting all their resources to the care of souls and who do not engage in other activities still can hardly

---

in which he rules and he is in his church very often. Visconti is now returning to his church, and he has few parishioners. Toschi resides because he can be in Tivoli every week. D'Ossat does not reside because of some business regarding the king."

18. This is Bellarmine's paraphrase of 2 Timothy 2:3–4.

19. The pope's response: "Regarding nuncios, we think that it is most appropriate that the nuncios are bishops, because they command bishops and they have a greater authority with the princes and peoples, and if it weren't for the lack of men, we would replace them more often. Regarding those who hold a political appointment, if we are talking about those who hold a magistracy in the ecclesiastical state, there is only one in Spoleto [Fabrizio Perugino] and there is another, the bishop of Camerino [Gentile Delfino], who is pro-legate in the province of the Marca, so that every day, and not just every week, he can be in his church, and almost every hour he can be in his diocese."

carry the burden of their government (as St. Augustine said of himself in book 10 of the *Confessiones,* chapter 4, and as is evident from St. Gregory of Nazianzus's *Apologeticus,* from St. John Chrysostom's dialogue *De sacerdotio,* and from St. Gregory's *Liber [Regulae] Pastoralis*), how can those not be deceived who are confident that they can fulfill their episcopal duties though they are absent from their flock for a long time and take on many other tasks that have nothing to do with their bishopric?[20]

The fourth problem is spiritual polygamy, that is, when many churches are assigned to one person. St. Bernard in his epistle to Theobaldus solves this question with three words, when he says that this "is not allowed," unless with an exception justified by an urgent need of the Church. St. Thomas, *Quodlibet* 9, article 5, writes that a multiplicity of benefices requiring pastoral care is contrary not only to the canon law but also to the law of nature: not because this multiplicity is intrinsically evil, so that it cannot in any circumstance be made morally right, such as adultery, lying, and so on; but because it is absolutely evil, and yet it could be made morally right in certain circumstances, such as because of the Church's need. From this St. Thomas gathers that whoever is granted an exemption and governs two churches is not safe in his own conscience, unless because of the Church's need, for the exemption alone takes away only the impediment of the positive law; and every theologian approves Thomas's doctrine on this issue. For this reason it must be feared that maybe even those who administer an *ecclesia cardinalitia* together with an *ecclesia non cardinalitia* are not safe in their own conscience, since the reason why cardinal-bishops are allowed to govern two churches does not seem to be either the need or the advantage of the Church, but larger prestige or income for that person. St. Thomas utterly condemns both of those reasons. Nor can this be justified by saying that a cardinal-bishop runs one church completely and only administers the other provisionally. It cannot even be justified by saying that the custom of many years allows such spiritual polygamy, for not only do cardinal-bishops today in fact want to be seen as bishops, not administrators, of both churches, but also the Council

20. The pope's response: "In truth we do not retain [in Rome] for a long time absentee bishops unless they are nuncios, who cannot easily be replaced because of the importance and sensitive nature of their affairs."

of Trent, with the approbation of the Apostolic See, certainly rejects the distinction between those two functions, stating, in session 7, chapter 2: "Nobody must be assigned two cathedral churches, no matter in which capacity, neither fully nor provisionally, nor in any other way," and in session 24, chapter 17, the council states that two benefices requiring pastoral care should not be given to the same cardinals.[21] The same Council of Trent abolished that custom, introduced many years ago, not to mention the fact that what is considered evil except in a specific circumstance cannot be made good by any argument resorting to custom, but only by the presence of the said specific circumstance.[22]

The fifth issue is the easy transferring of bishops from one church to another, which can be seen especially in six cardinal bishoprics and in the Spanish bishoprics.[23] According to the canon law and the custom of the primitive Church, in fact, the transferring of bishops should not happen except for a greater need or advantage to the Church; indeed, bishops are instituted for the sake of the churches, and not churches for the sake of bishops. Today we witness daily the transferring of a bishop for no other reason but the increase of his prestige or wealth. Moreover, it is well known from the canon "Inter corporalia," regarding the transferring of bishops, that the bond of spiritual matrimony is, in a sense, greater than that of

21. Bellarmine is referring, respectively, to the second chapter of the decree "Super reformatione," discussed in the seventh session of the council (3 March 1547, text in *Conciliorum oecumenicorum decreta*, p. 663), and to the seventeenth canon of the already mentioned 1563 decree "De reformatione" (text in ibid., p. 745).

22. The pope's response: "Regarding this polygamy, we do not see it unless in six cardinal bishoprics, which we decided not to change, since this issue also has been examined and decided in this manner by our predecessors after the Council of Trent; and to upset the orders of the *Collegium* and to revise what has been done by our predecessors and many cardinals did not seem to us something that could be done without scandal, as Your Lordship will understand if you examine this issue properly."

23. The question of the relationship between the Spanish episcopate and Rome was a long and troubled one, starting with Isabella and Ferdinand's attempt to deprive Rome of jurisdiction in the appointment of bishops—the privilege of appointing bishops was in fact granted to Charles V by Pope Adrian VI in 1523. During Bellarmine's own time the question was much discussed, in particular by the Jesuit Juan de Mariana in his controversial *De rege et regis institutione*. For background on the question of the royal authority to appoint bishops, see Elliott, *Imperial Spain*, pp. 99ff.; on Mariana see Braun, *Juan de Mariana*, especially chapter 6.

corporeal matrimony, and therefore it cannot be severed except by God, or by God's Vicar on behalf of His Lord;[24] and who can believe that God would want to sever the bond of that sacred union only for wealth or prestige? Especially because severing this bond cannot happen without much damage to souls, as experience shows, and bishops seek those churches that they can quickly abandon to move up to other, wealthier ones. The poor church of Albano has changed bishops four times in a few months,[25] and six cardinal churches, whose prestige surpasses that of all the other churches, are behind all of the other churches in terms of pastoral care and diligence, especially now that three of those churches have polygamous husbands who are busy having more profitable intercourse with other wives, and the remaining three have husbands who are so weakened by their age or their sickness that they give no hope for a good education of the children, not to mention the conception of those children.[26]

The sixth problem is that bishops resign without legitimate cause; indeed, if the bond between a bishop and his church is as tight and almost indissoluble as canon law shows, how is it that every day we see that bond being severed so easily? Some bishops leave their church but keep the benefices, as if a man who repudiates his wife would keep the dowry; others leave their bishopric to be able to start a more prestigious career after getting rich from the revenues of their church; others leave their church to their nephews, so that they may maintain possession of God's sanctuary under pretext of resigning; others prefer to become papal referendaries [*referendarii*] or other minor officers in the Roman Curia, rather than great priests outside of the Curia; some find excuses such as the unhealthy climate, or the limited resources, or the people's impudence. But God knows whether these are legitimate reasons to resign, and whether bishops

24. On the canon "Inter corporalia" see pp. 331ff. and n. 206.

25. The details of the quick succession of bishops in the city of Albano (near Rome) to which Bellarmine refers can be found in the edition of *De officio summi Pontificis* by Le Bachelet, *Auctarium Bellarminianum*, p. 517, n. 3.

26. The pope's response: "We do not transfer [bishops] easily. Regarding the six cardinal bishoprics, we have already spoken above. Regarding the Spanish bishoprics, Your Lordship should consider in what difficulty we would find ourselves if we took that faculty away from the king now; nevertheless we did not fail to warn the king on this issue, both ourselves and through our nuncio."

who behave in such a manner are looking after their own cause or that of Jesus Christ.[27]

These are, most blessed Father, the issues that I think should be brought to Your Holiness's attention so that my conscience can be in this respect satisfied. And just as I wrote these reflections with sincerity, so I pray with the utmost reverence and humility that they be read by your Beatitude with benignity.[28]

27. The pope's response: "We accept resignations in very rare cases, and in general we do not accept them unless we have examined the reasons in the Sacred Consistorial Congregation, and sometimes we accept them because of the ineptitude of those who wish to resign."

28. The pope's response: "We said these small things quickly not in order to offer a justification of sins but so that you can pity the difficulties in which we find ourselves in these afflictions; indeed we admit that we have sinned not just in these but in many other instances, indeed in everything, and we have not fulfilled and do not fulfill completely any of our duties. Therefore, you should pray to God omnipotent that either He may assist us with His divine and most efficacious grace or, which we wish more, that He may absolve us from this mortal bond and substitute another man who could fulfill the duty committed to him in all accounts."

# INDEX OF WORKS
## CITED BY BELLARMINE

This section is intended as an aid to the reader, and as such its primary purpose is that of providing a complete list of works cited in Bellarmine's treatises rather than a list of the works which Bellarmine actually consulted. The places and dates of publication given for these works refer almost always (with some notable but obvious exceptions) to the first edition available in print. I have also indicated whenever an English translation is available, and whenever there is more than one English translation, I have chosen unabridged over abridged versions. I have provided English translations of non-English titles.

Ado of Vienne. *Chronicon* [Chronicle]. Latin text ed. in PL, vol. 123.

Adrian (of Utrecht). *Commentarius in lib. IV sententiarum Petri Lombardi* [Commentary on the Fourth Book of Peter Lombard's *Sententiae*]. Paris, 1512.

————. *Quaestiones quodlibeticae* [Various Discussions]. Louvain, 1518.

Aegidius Bellamera. *Commentaria . . . in Gratiani decreta* [Commentaries on Gratian's *Decretum*]. In *Remissorius*. Lyon, 1550.

Agrippa von Nettesheim, H. C. *Dialogus de vanitate scientiarum.* Cologne, 1534. *Of the Vanitie and Uncertaintie of Artes and Sciences* is a sixteenth-century English translation ed. by C. M. Dunn (Northridge: California State University, 1974).

Aimoinus. *Historia Francorum* [History of the Franks]. Paris, 1514, and PL, vol. 139.

Alexander of Hales. *Tractatus de officio Missae* [Explanation of the Office of the Mass]. In *Summa universae theologiae.* Nuremberg, 1481–82.

Alexander of St. Elpidio. *De auctoritate Summi Pontificis et iurisdictione imperii* [On the Authority of the Sureme Pontiff and Jurisdiction of the Empire]. Turin, 1494.

Alfonso de Castro. *De iusta haereticorum punitione* [On the Just Punishment for Heretics]. Salamanca, 1547.

―――. *De potestate legis poenalis* [On the Authority of Penal Law]. Salamanca, 1550.

Almain, J. *Expositio . . . de potestate ecclesiastica et laica* [Exposition . . . on the Supreme Ecclesiastical and Temporal Authority]. Paris, 1518.

―――. *Libellus de auctoritate Ecclesiae* [A Book Concerning the Authority of the Church]. Paris, 1512. English translation in *Conciliarism and Papalism*, ed. by J. H. Burns and T. M. Izbicki (Cambridge: Cambridge University Press, 1997).

Alvarus Pelagius. *De planctu Ecclesiae* [On the Lamentable State of the Church]. Ulm, 1474.

Ambrose. *Apologia David* [Apology of David].

―――. *Commentarii* [Commentaries].

―――. *Epistolae* [Epistles].

―――. *Orationes* [Orations].

―――. *Sermones* [Sermons].

[Ambrose's *Opera omnia* can be found in PL, vols. 14–17. A selection of Ambrose's works in English can be found in *A Select Library of the Nicene and Post-Nicene Fathers of the Christian Church*, second series, by P. Schaff and H. Wace (Grand Rapids, Mich.: W. B. Eerdmans, 1974–79).]

Anonymous. *Annales Francorum* [Annals of the Franks].

Anselm of Canterbury. *De fermentato et azymo ad Waleramum* [To Waleramus about Unleavened and Fermented Bread].

―――. *Epistolae* [Letters]. In *Opera omnia,* ed. by F. S. Schmitt (Edinburgh: Nelson, 1946–71). English translation: *The Letters of St. Anselm of Canterbury,* trans. by W. Frohlich (Kalamazoo, Mich.: Cistercian Publications, 1990–94).

[The complete theological and philosophical works of Anselm are available in English in *Complete Philosophical and Theological Treatises of Anselm of Canterbury,* trans. by J. Hopkins and H. Richardson (Minneapolis: A. J. Banning Press, 2000).]

Anselm of Lucca. *Contra Guibertum* [Against Guibertus]. Latin text edited in PL, vol. 149.

Antonino of Florence. *Chronicon* [Chronicle]. Venice, 1474–77.

―――. *Summa theologiae moralis* [*Summa* of Moral Theology]. Venice, 1477.

Antonius Cordubensis. *Quaestionarium theologicum* [Theological Questions]. Venice, 1604.

Aquinas. *See* Thomas Aquinas.

Aretius, B. *Valentini Gentilis iusto capite supplicio . . . brevis historia.* Geneva, 1567. *A Short Historie of Valentinius Gentilis,* a seventeenth-century English translation, was published in London in 1696.

Aristotle. *The Nicomachean Ethics.* English translation by R. Crisp (Cambridge: Cambridge University Press, 2000).

————. *The Politics.* English translation in *Aristotle: The Politics and the Constitution of Athens,* ed. by S. Everson (Cambridge: Cambridge University Press, 1996).

Astesanus from Asti. *Summa Astensis.* Lyon, 1519.

Athanasius. *Ad Marcellinum* [Letter to Marcellinus].

————. *Ad solitariam vitam agentes* [Letter to Those Who Lead the Solitary Life].

————. *Apologia de fuga sua* [Apology for His Escape].

————. *Apologia secunda* [Second Apology].

————. *Vita S. Antonii* [Life of St. Anthony].

[Athanasius's *Opera omnia* can be found in PG, vols. 25–28, and in Athanasius, *Werke,* ed. by H. G. Opitz (Berlin: Walter de Gruyter, 1934–35). A selection of Athanasius's letters, including *Ad solitariam vitam agentes* and *Ad Marcellinum,* can be found in English in *A Select Library of the Nicene and Post-Nicene Fathers. The Life of Anthony and the Letter to Marcellinus* (New York: Paulist Press, 1980) is an English translation by R. C. Gregg of those two works.]

Augustine of Hippo. *Confessionum libri tredecim* [Confessions].

————. *Contra Adimantum* [Against Adimantus].

————. *Contra epistolam Parmeniani* [Against the Epistle of Parmenianus].

————. *Contra Faustum* [Against Faustus].

————. *Contra Gaudentium* [Against Gaudentius].

————. *Contra Iulianum* [Against Julian].

————. *Contra litteras Petiliani* [Against the Epistles of Petilianus].

————. *De baptismo parvulorum* [On Infant Baptism].

————. *De civitate Dei contra paganos* [The City of God against the Pagans].

————. *De correptione et gratia* [On Correction and Grace].

————. *De Genesi ad litteram libri duodecim* [Commentary on Genesis in Twelve Books].

————. *De gratia et libero arbitrio* [On Grace and Free Will].

————. *De haeresibus* [On Heresies].

————. *De sermone Domini in monte* [On the Sermon on the Mount].

————. *De spiritu et littera* [On the Spirit and the Letter].

————. *Enarrationes in Psalmos* [Commentaries on Psalms].

————. *Enchiridion de fide, spe et charitate* [Manual on Faith, Hope, and Charity].

————. *Epistolae* [Epistles].

————. *Expositio quarumdam propositionum ex epistola ad Romanos* [Exposition of Certain Propositions from the Letter to the Romans].

————. *In evangelium Ioannis Tractatus* [Treatises on the Gospel of John].

————. *Quaestionum evangeliorum* [Questions on the Gospel].

————. *Quaestionum in Heptateuchum libri septem* [Seven Books of Questions on the Heptateuch].

————. *Retractationum libri duo* [Reconsiderations].

————. *Sermones* [Sermons].

[There are, of course, many editions and translations of Augustine's writings. His *Opera omnia* is available in PL, vols. 32–47. One Engish translation is *The Works of Aurelius Augustine, Bishop of Hippo,* ed. by M. Dods, 15 vols. (Edinburgh: T. & T. Clark, 1871–76). For recent translations of two of his major works see *Augustine: The City of God against the Pagans,* trans. by R. W. Dyson (Cambridge: Cambridge University Press, 2003 [1998]), and *Confessions,* trans. by F. J. Sheed (Indianapolis: Hackett, 2006).]

Baconthorpe, J. *Quaestiones in quatuor libros sententiarum* [Questions on the Four Books of the *Sententiae*]. Cremona, 1618.

Baldus de Ubaldis. *Super feudis* [Commentary on the *Libri feudorum*]. Rome, 1474.

Balsamon, T. *Photii . . . Nomocanonus . . . cum annotationibus Theodori Balsamonis* [Photius's *Nomocanon* with Annotations by Theodore Balsamon]. Basel, 1561.

Bañez, D. *Scholastica commentaria* [Scholastic Commentaries]. Salamanca, 1584–94.

Barclay, W. *De potestate Papae.* [London], 1609.

————. *De regno et regali potestate adversus Buchananum, Brutum, Boucherium & reliquos Monarchomachos, libri sex* [Six Books on Monarchy and Regal Authority against Buchanan, Brutus, Boucher, and the Other Monarchomachs]. Paris, 1600.

Baronius, C. *Annales ecclesiastici* [Ecclesiastical Annals]. Rome, 1588–1607.

Bartolus from Sassoferrato. *Super primam partem Codicis* [Commentary on the First Part of the Codex]. Lyon, 1505.

Basil. *Oratio in laudem SS. 40 Martyrum* [Oration in Praise of the 40 Martyrs]. Basil's works can be found in PG, vols. 29–32.

Bellarmine, R. *Controversia de clericis* [Controversy on the Clergymen].

———. *Controversia de conciliis* [Controversy on the Councils].

———. *Controversia de monachis* [Controversy on the Monks].

———. *Controversia de Summo Pontifice* [Controversy on the Supreme Pontiff].

———. *De translatione imperii* [On the Transfer of the Empire].

———. *Recognitio* [Examination].

——— [Franciscus Romulus]. *Responsio ad praecipua capita Apologiae, quae falso catholica inscribitur* [Response to Some Parts of an Apology Falsely Called Catholic].

[Among many editions of Bellarmine's *Opera omnia* I mention here the edition on which my translations are based: *Ven. Cardinalis Roberti Bellarmini Politiani S.J. Opera omnia,* ed. by J. Fèvre, 12 vols. (Paris: Vivès, 1870–74).]

Bernard. *De consideratione* [On Consideration].

———. *De praecepto et dispensatione* [On Precept and Dispensation].

———. *Epistolae* [Letters].

———. *Sermones* [Sermons].

[Bernard's works are available in Latin in PL, vols. 182–85, and in English in *The Works of Bernard of Clairvaux* (Spencer, Mass.: Cistercian Publications, 1970).]

Bernold of Constance. *Chronicum* [Chronicle]. A selection is available in English in *Eleventh-Century Germany: The Swabian Chronicles,* ed. by I. S. Robinson (Manchester, U.K.: Manchester University Press, 2008).

Beza, T. *De haereticis a civili magistratu puniendis* [On the Heretics Who Should Be Punished by the Civil Official]. Geneva, 1554.

Bibliander, T. *De ratione temporum . . . liber unus* [Chronology]. Basel, 1551.

Biel, G. *Canonis missae expositio* [Exposition of the Canon of the Mass]. Reutlingen, 1488.

Biondo, Flavio. *Historiarum . . . decades* [History in Decades]. Venice, 1483.

Bonaventure. *Commentaria in quatuor libros sententiarum* [Commentary on the Four Books of *Sententiae*].

———. *De ecclesiastica hierarchia* [On the Ecclesiastical Hierarchy].

[Bonaventure's works are available, among other editions, in Latin in the Quaracchi edition (Florence, 1882–1902) and in English in *The Works of Bonaventure* by J. de Vinck (Paterson, N.J.: St. Anthony Guild Press, 1960–70).]

Boniface [Archbishop of Mainz]. *Epistolae* [Letters]. These can be found in *Monumenta Germaniae Historica,* Hannover, 1826– and in English in *The Letters of St. Boniface,* trans. by E. Emerton (New York: Columbia University Press, 2000 [1940]).

Brenz, J. *Prolegomena*. Frankfurt, 1555.

Brunus, C. *De legationibus* [On the Office of Ambassadors]. Mainz, 1548.

Burchard of Ursperg. *Chronica* [Chronicle]. In *Die Chronik des Propstes Burchard von Ursberg* (*Scriptores rerum germanicarum*). Hannover: Hahnsche Buchhandlung, 1916.

Cajetan, T. *Apologia . . . de comparate auctoritate Papae et Concilii* [Apology Concerning the Authority of the Pope Compared with That of the Council]. Rome, 1512.

———. *De comparatione auctoritatis Papae et Concilii* [On the Comparison of the Authority of Pope and Council]. Rome, 1511.

———. *In Summam theologiae* [Commentary on the *Summa theologiae*]. Venice, 1508.

[The first two works by Cajetan listed here have been translated into English in *Conciliarism and Papalism,* ed. by Burns and Izbicki. *See* Almain, J.]

Calvin, J. *Institutiones Christianae religionis* [Institutes of the Christian Religion]. The first Latin edition appeared in 1536, with the last revisions completed in 1559. In more modern times it appeared in *Opera selecta* (Munich: Kaiser, 1926–36), among other editions. J. T. McNeill and F. L. Battles translated it into English in *Calvin: Institutes of the Christian Religion* (Philadelphia: Westminster Press, 1960).

Cassander, G. *De officio pii . . . viri* [On the Duty of the Pious Man]. Basel, 1561.

[Cassiodorus]. *Historia tripartita* [History in Three Parts]. Latin text in PL, vol. 69.

Castaldi, R. *De imperatore* [On the Emperor]. Rome, 1540.

Cedrenus, G. *Chronica* [Chronicle].

———. *Vita Leonis Isaurici* [Life of Leo the Isaurian].

[The works of Cedrenus can be found in PG, vols. 121–22, among other editions.]

Chrysostom. *Homiliae* [Homilies]. Chrysostom's works are available in PG, vols. 47–64, and in English in the Oxford Library of the Fathers series (Oxford: J. H. Parker, 1839–1977). See also *Homilies on Genesis 46–67,* trans. by R. C. Hill (Washington, D.C.: Catholic University of America Press, 1992).

Cicero. *De inventione* [On Rhetorical Invention]. English translation: *De inventione,* trans. by H. M. Hubbell, Loeb Classical Library (Cambridge, Mass.: Harvard University Press, 1949).

———. *De natura deorum.* English translation: *The Nature of the Gods,* ed. by P. G. Walsh (Oxford: Oxford University Press, 1997).

Gambari, P. A. *De officio atque auctoritate legati* [On the Office and Power of the Legate]. Venice, 1571.

Gelasius I. *De anathematis vinculo* [On the Bond of Anathema].

———. *Epistolae* [Letters].

[Gelasius's texts can be found in PL, vol. 59.]

Gellius, A. *Noctes Atticae. The Attic Nights of Aulus Gellius* is a Latin edition and English translation by J. C. Rolfe, Loeb Classical Library (Cambridge, Mass.: Harvard University Press, 1970).

Gerson, J. *De vita spirituali animae* [On the Spiritual Life of the Soul]. Paris, 1493.

Giles of Rome. *De ecclesiastica potestate.* Printed for the first time in *Un trattato inedito,* ed. by G. Boffito and G. U. Oxilia (Florence: Successiori B. Seeber, 1908). *Giles of Rome's On Ecclesiastical Power* is an English translation by R. W. Dyson (New York: Columbia University Press, 2004).

Giovanni of Anagni. *Commentaria supra prima et secunda parte libri quinti Decretalium* [Commentaries on the First and Second Part of the Fifth Book of *Decretales*]. Bologna, 1479.

Gregory VII. *Registrum.* Text in PL, vol. 148. *The Register of Pope Gregory VII, 1073–1085* is an English translation by H. E. J. Cowdrey (Oxford: Oxford University Press, 2002).

Gregory of Nazianzus. *Orationes* [Orations]. Gregory's works are available, among other editions, in PG, vols. 35–38, and in English a number of translations exist, including B. Daley, *Gregory of Nazianzus* (New York: Routledge, 2006).

Gregory of Tours. *Historia Francorum.* Gregory's text is available in PL, vol. 71. *The History of the Franks* is an English translation by L. Thorpe (London: Penguin, 1974).

Gregory of Valencia. *Commentariorum theologicorum tomi quatuor* [Theological Commentaries]. Ingolstadt, 1592–95.

Gregory the Great. *Cura pastoralis.* English translation: *The Pastoral Care,* trans. by I. Carlson (Stockholm: Almqvist and Wiksell International, 1975–78).

———. *Dialogi.* English translation: *Dialogues,* trans. by O. J. Zimmerman (New York: Fathers of the Church, 1959).

———. *Epistolae.* English translation: *The Letters of Gregory the Great,* trans. by J. R. C. Martyn (Toronto: Pontifical Institute of Mediaeval Studies, 2004).

———. *Homiliae XL in Evangelia.* English translation: *Forty Gospel Homilies,* trans. by D. Hurst (Kalamazoo, Mich.: Cistercian Publications, 1990).

in PG, vol. 7, and in English in *The Ante-Nicene Fathers*. *Contra haereticos* has been translated into English by D. J. Unger and J. J. Dillon in *Against the Heresies* (New York: Paulist Press, 1992).

Isidore of Seville. *De viris illustribus* [Illustrious Men]. Text in PL, vol. 83.

Isidoro from Milan. *De imperio militantis Ecclesiae* [On the Dominion of the Militant Church]. Milan, 1517.

Ivo of Chartres. *Epistolae* [Letters]. Text in PL, vol. 162.

James VI and I. *Triplici nodo, triplex cuneus* [A Threefold Wedge for a Threefold Knot]. 2nd ed. (which included "*A premonition to all most mightie monarches, kings, free princes and states of Christendome*"), 1609. A translation of *Triplici nodo, triplex cuneus* can be found in *The Political Works of James I*, edited by C. H. McIlwain (Cambridge, Mass.: Harvard University Press, 1918), and in *King James VI and I: Political Writings*, edited by J. P. Sommerville (Cambridge: Cambridge University Press, 1994).

Jean de Selve. *De beneficio* [On Benefice]. Paris, 1504.

Jean Quintin. *De iuris canonici laudibus* [Praise of Canon Law]. Paris, 1550.

Jerome. *Commentaria* [Commentaries].

———. *Contra Vigilantium* [Against Vigilantius].

———. *De viris illustribus* [On Illustrious Men].

———. *Quaestiones, ad Hedibiam* [Questions, to Hedibia].

[The text of Jerome's works can be found in PL, vols. 22–30; a selection is available in English in *A Select Library of Nicene and Post-Nicene Fathers*.]

Johannes Faber. *Breviarium super Codicem* [Commentary on Justinian's *Codex*]. Louvain, 1477.

———. *Opus super institutionibus* [Commentary on Justinian's *Institutiones*]. Lyon, 1480.

John of Capistrano. *De auctoritate Papae* [On the authority of the Pope]. Venice, 1580.

John the Deacon. *Vita Gregorii* [Life of St. Gregory]. Latin text in PL, vol. 75.

Josephus, F. *Antiquitates Iudaicae.*

———. *Bellum Iudaicum.*

———. *Contra Apionem.*

[Josephus's works in Greek were published first in Basel in 1544, and were edited, among others, by B. Niese (Berlin, 1885–95). For a Latin edition see, among others, *The Latin Josephus*, ed. by F. Blatt (Aarhus: Universitetsforlaget, 1958). The works mentioned here have all been translated into English by H. St. J. Thackeray and published by Harvard University Press in Cambridge, Mass., as part of the Loeb Classical Library series: *Jewish Antiquities* (1998), *The Jewish War* (1997), and *The Life. Against Apion* (1993).]

Justinus. *Epitoma historiarum Philippicarum Pompei Trogi.* Latin critical edition: *M. Iuniani Iustini Epitoma historiarum Philippicarum Pompei Trogi,* ed. by Franz Ruehl and Otto Seel (Leipzig: Teubner, 1935). English translation: *Epitome of the Philippic History of Pompeius Trogus,* trans. by J. C. Yardley and W. Heckel (Oxford: Oxford University Press, 1997).

Krantz, A. *Metropolis.* Basel, 1548.

Lambert of Hersfeld. *Annales* [Annals]. Tübingen, 1525. Critical edition in *Monumenta Germaniae historica.*

———. *Germanorum res praeclare . . . olim gestae* [History of the Germans]. Tübingen, 1533.

Latomus, J. *De Ecclesia* [On the Church]. Antwerp, 1525.

Ledesma, M. *Secunda quartae* [Commentary *Secunda quartae*]. Coimbra, 1560.

Leo. *Epistolae* [Epistles].

———. *Sermones* [Sermons].

[Leo's works can be found in PL, vols. 54–56, and in English in *A Select Library of Nicene and Post-Nicene Fathers.*]

Leo Ostiensis. *Chronica monasterii Cassinensis* [Chronicle of Monte Cassino]. Latin text in *Monumenta Germaniae historica.*

Liberatus. *Breviarium causae Nestorianorum* [A Short Account of the Affair of the Nestorians]. Text in PL, vol. 68.

Livy. *Ab urbe condita* [The History of Rome]. English translation in *Livy in Fourteen Volumes,* trans. by B. O. Foster et al., Loeb Classical Library (Cambridge, Mass.: Harvard University Press, 1976).

Luther, M. *An den christlichen Adel deutscher Nation* [Address to the German Nobility].

———. *Contra Henricum regem Angliae* [Against Henry King of England].

———. *De captivitate Babylonica Ecclesiae* [The Babylonian Captivity of the Church].

———. *Resolutiones disputationum de indulgentiarum virtute* [Resolutions of the Disputations on the Virtue of Indulgences].

———. *Visitatio Saxonica* [Report on the Saxon Visitation].

[Luther's *Opera omnia* has been edited by, among others, J. C. F. Kraake et al., in *D. Martin Luthers Werke* (Weimar, 1883–). It is available in English in *Luther's Works,* ed. by J. Pelikan (St. Louis: Concordia, 1955–86).]

Marianus Scotus. *Chronica* (with additions by Dodechinus). Basel, 1557.

Martinus of Lodi. *De principibus* [On the Princes]. *Il tractatus De principibus di Martino Garati da Lodi* is an edition by G. Soldi Rondinini (Milan: Istituto editoriale cisalpino, 1968).

Masson, Jean Papire (Papirius Massonius). *Annales* [Annals]. Paris, 1577.

Matthew Paris. *Chronica.* The Latin work has been edited by H. R. Louard (London: Longman, 1872–83), and a selection is available in English in *Chronicles of Matthew Paris,* trans. by R. Vaughan (Glouchester, U.K.: A. Sutton and New York: St. Martin's Press, 1984).

Mayron, F. *Scripta in quatuor libros sententiarum* [Writings on the Four Books of the *Sententiae*]. Venice, 1520.

Melanchthon, P. *Loci communes theologici* [Theological Commonplaces]. Wittenberg, 1521. English translation by C. L. Manschreck and H. Engelland in *Melanchthon on Christian Doctrine* (New York: Oxford University Press, 1965).

Miguel of Aninyon. *De unitate ovilis et pastoris* [On the Unity of the Flock and the Shepherd]. Zaragoza, 1578.

Molina, L. de. *Concordia liberi arbitrii cum gratiae donis* [The Concordance of Free Will with the Gift of Grace]. Lisbon, 1588.

———. *De iustitia et iure* [On Justice and Law]. Mainz, 1602.

Molina [Morales], L. de. *De Hispanorum primogeniorum origine ac natura* [On the Origin and Nature of Spanish Primogeniture]. Lyon, 1588.

Montserrat, G. *De successione regum* [On the Succession of Kings]. Lyon, 1519.

Nauclerus, J. *Chronica* [Chronicle]. Tübingen, 1516.

Navarrus (Martin de Azpilcueta). *Commentaria* [Commentaries].

———. *Enchiridion confessariorum* [Manual for Confessors].

[The standard edition of Navarrus's *Opera omnia* is Venice, 1618–21.]

Netter, T. *Doctrinales antiquitatum fidei Ecclesiae Catholicae* [Doctrinals of the Faith of the Christian Church]. Paris, 1521–32.

Nicephorus. *Historia ecclesiastica* [Ecclesiastical History]. Text in PG, vols. 145–47.

Nicholas of Cusa. *De Concordantia Catholica.* The Latin text has been edited by G. Kallen (Hamburg: Felix Meiner, 1964). English translation by P. E. Sigmund in *The Catholic Concordance* (Cambridge: Cambridge University Press, 1991).

Nicholas of Lyra. *Postilla super Bibliam* [Commentary on the Bible]. Rome, 1471–72.

Optatus. *Contra Parmenianum* or *Contra Donatistas.* Text in PL, vol. 11. English translation by M. J. Edwards in *Optatus, Against the Donatists* (Liverpool, U.K.: Liverpool University Press, 1997).

Origen. *Contra Celsum* [Against Celsus].

———. *Homiliae* [Homilies].

———. *Tractatus* [Treatises].

[Origen's works are in PG, vols. 11–17, and in English in *The Ante-Nicene Fathers*, among other translations.]

Otto of Freising. *Chronica* [Chronicle]. English translation: *The Two Cities: A Chronicle of Universal History to the Year 1146 A.D.*, trans. by C. C. Mierow, A. P. Evans, and C. Knapp (New York: Columbia University Press, 2002).

———. *Gesta Friderici I Imperatoris.* English translation: *The Deeds of Frederick Barbarossa,* trans. by C. C. Mierow and R. Emery (New York: Columbia University Press, 2004).

[The text for the two works can be found in the *Monumenta Germaniae historica.*]

Ovid. *Heroides.* English translation by G. Showerman (Cambridge, Mass.: Harvard University Press, 1977).

Panvinio, O. *See* Platina.

Paulus Aemilius. *De rebus gestis Francorum* [History of the Franks]. Paris, 1517.

Paulus Diaconus. *De gestis Longobardorum.* Text in *Monumenta Germaniae historica.* English translation by W. D. Foulke and E. Peters in *History of the Lombards* (Philadelphia: University of Pennsylvania Press, 1974).

———. *Historia Romana* [Roman History]. Text in *Monumenta Germaniae historica.*

Paulus Orosius. *Adversus paganos historiarum libri septem.* Text in PL, vol. 31. English translation by R. J. Deferrari in *The Seven Books of History against the Pagans* (Washington, D.C.: Catholic University of America Press, 1964).

Peter Lombard. *Sententiae.* Text edited by I. Brady in *Magistri Petri Lombardi . . . Sententiae in IV libris distinctae* (Grottaferrata, Italy: Ed. Collegii S. Bonaventurae ad Claras Aquas, 1971–81). English translation by G. Silano in *The Sentences* (Toronto: Political Institute of Mediaeval Studies, 2007–10).

Petrus Bertrandus. *De origine iurisdictionum* [On the Origin of Jurisdictions]. Paris, 1520.

Petrus de Ancharanus. *Lecturae super quinque libros decretalium* [Lectures on the Five Books of *Decretales*]. Lyon, 1535.

Pierre de la Palude. *De causa immediata ecclesiasticae potestatis* [On the Immediate Cause of the Ecclesiastical Authority]. Paris, 1506.

Pietro del Monte. *Monarchia* [Monarchy]. Lyon, 1512.

Pighius, A. *De ecclesiastica hierarchia* [On the Ecclesiastical Hierarchy]. Cologne, 1538.

Platina. *Liber de vita Christi et omnium pontificum.* First full edition Venice, 1479, with additions by O. Panvinio in the Venice, 1562, edition. *Lives of the Popes* is an English translation by A. F. D'Elia, I Tatti Renaissance Library (Cambridge, Mass.: Harvard University Press, 2008).

Pole, R. *De Summo Pontifice* [On the Supreme Pontiff]. Louvain, 1569.

Raymond le Roux. *In Molinaeum* [Against Du Mulin]. Paris, 1553.

Raymond of Peñafort. *Summa Raymundina* [*Summa* of Raymond]. Rome, 1603.

Regino of Prüm. *Chronica* [Chronicle]. Text edited in *Monumenta Germaniae historica.*

Roger of Hoveden. *Annales.* London, 1596. English translation by H. T. Riley in *The Annals of Roger de Hoveden* (London: H. G. Bohn, 1853; New York: AMS Press, 1968).

Rufinus. *See* Eusebius.

Sander, N. *De schismate Anglicano* [On the Anglican Schism]. Cologne, 1585.

Sebadius. *Contra Arianos* [Against the Arians]. Text edited in PL, vol. 20.

Sigebert of Gembloux. *Chronica* [Chronicle]. Text edited in PL, vol. 160.

Silvestro Mazzolini da Prierio. *Summa Sylvestrina* [*Summa* of Sylvester]. Bologna, 1514.

Simancas, J. *De Catholicis institutionibus* [On Catholic Institutions]. Valladolid, 1552.

Socrates. *Historia ecclesiastica* [Ecclesiastical History]. Text edited in PG, vol. 67, and English translation in *A Select Library of the Nicene and Post-Nicene Fathers.*

Soto, D. de. *Commentarium in IV Sententiarum* [Commentary on the Fourth Book of the *Sententiae*]. Salamanca, 1557–60.

———. *De iustitia et iure* [On Justice and Law]. Salamanca, 1553–54.

Sozomen. *Historia ecclesiastica* [Ecclesiastical History]. Text in PG, vol. 67, and English translation in *A Select Library of the Nicene and Post-Nicene Fathers.*

Suetonius. *Vitae Caesarum* [Lives of the Caesars]. English translation by J. C. Rolfe in *Suetonius,* Loeb Classical Library (Cambridge, Mass.: Harvard University Press, 1914).

Suger. *Vita Ludovici Grossi regis.* Text edited by H. Waquet in *Vie de Louis VI le Gros* (Paris: H. Champion, 1929), and English translation by R. Cusimano and J. Moorhead in *The Deeds of Louis the Fat* (Washington, D.C.: Catholic University of America Press, 1992).

Sulpicius, S. *Historia sacra* [Sacred History]. English translation in *A Select Library of Nicene and Post-Nicene Fathers.*

———. *Vita Martini.* English translation by C. White in *Early Christian Lives* (London, New York: Penguin, 1998).

[Sulpicius's works have been edited in PL, vol. 20.]

Surius, L. *Commentarius brevis* [Brief Commentary]. Cologne, 1566.

Tertullian. *Ad Scapulam* [To Scapula].

———. *Apologia* [Apology].

———. *De corona* [The Chaplet].

———. *De praescriptione* [On Prescription].

———. *Epistolae* [Epistles].

[Tertullian's *Opera omnia* is edited in PL, vols. 1–2, and translated into English in *The Ante-Nicene Fathers.*]

Theodoretus. *Commentaria* [Commentaries]. Some of these are available in English translation; examples are *Commentary on the Psalms* (2000–2001) and *The Questions on the Ochtateuch* (2007). Both were edited by R. C. Hill and published in Washington, D.C., by the Catholic University of America Press.

———. *Graecarum affectionum curatio* [Remedy for the Diseases of the Greeks].

———. *Historia ecclesiastica* [Ecclesiastical History].

[Theodoretus's works are edited in PG, vols. 80–84.]

Theophylactus. *Commentaria* [Commentaries]. Text edited in PG, vols. 123–26.

Thomas Aquinas. *Catena aurea* [Golden Chain]. English translation: *Catena aurea,* trans. by J. H. Newman (Oxford: J. H. Parker, 1841–45).

———. *De regimine principum* [On the Government of Princes]. English translation in Aquinas, *Political Writings,* trans. by R. W. Dyson (Cambridge: Cambridge University Press, 2002).

———. *In epistolas S. Pauli* [Commentary on the Epistles of St. Paul]. A selection of Aquinas's biblical commentaries is available in English in the Aquinas Scripture Series (Albany, N.Y.: Magi Books, 1966–80), and in the translations of C. Baer (*Commentaries on St. Paul's Epistles to Timothy, Titus, and Philemon,* South Bend, Ind.: St. Augustine's Press, 2007, and *Epistle to the Hebrews,* South Bend, Ind.: St. Augustine's Press, 2006) and F. R. Larcher (*Commentary on Colossians,* Naples, Fla.: Sapientia Press, 2006).

———. *Opuscula* [Small Works]. *Opuscula omnia.* Edited by P. Mandonnet. 6 vols. Paris, 1927. Also see *Opera omnia,* below.

———. *Quodlibetae.* Some parts are available in English. For instance, see

*Quodlibetal Questions 1 and 2,* trans. by S. Edwards (Toronto: Pontifical Institute of Mediaeval Studies, 1983).

―――――. *Summa contra Gentiles.* English translation: *On the Truth of the Catholic Faith: Summa contra Gentiles,* trans. by A. C. Pegis (Garden City, N.Y.: Image Books, 1956–57).

―――――. *Summa theologiae.* English translation: *The "Summa theologica" of St. Thomas Aquinas,* trans. by Fathers of English Dominican Province (London: Burns, Oates and Washbourne, 1912–36).

[Aquinas's *Opera omnia* is available, among other editions, in the "Piana" or Roman edition of 1570–71 and, more recently, the Parma 1852–73 edition, the Paris 1871–80 edition, and the Leonine edition, Rome 1882–.]

Torquemada, J. de. *Commentarii in Decretum Gratiani* [Commentaries on Gratian's *Decretum*]. Lyon, 1519.

―――――. *Summa de Ecclesia* [*Summa* on the Church]. Rome, 1489. Partial translation in English by W. E. Maquire in *John of Torquemade, O.P.: The Antiquity of the Church* (Washington, D.C.: Catholic University of America Press, 1957).

Toschi, D. *Practicae conclusiones* [Practical Conclusions]. Rome, 1605–8.

Trlonfo, A. *De potestate ecclesiastica* [On Ecclesiastical Power]. Augsburg, 1473.

Trithemius, J. *Catalogus scriptorum ecclesiasticorum* [Catalogue of Ecclesiastical Writers]. Cologne, 1531.

Tudeschis, N. de. *Commentaria in Decretales* [Commentaries on the *Decretales*]. Venice, 1473.

Ulrich of Strasbourg. *Summa de bono* [*Summa* on the Good]. The text is edited by K. Flasch and L. Sturlese in *De summo bono* (Hamburg: Meiner, 1987–89), and a selection of this work is available in English in *God as First Principle in Ulrich of Strasbourg,* ed. by F. J. Lescoe (New York: Alba House, 1979).

Valerius Maximus. *Factorum dictorumque memorabilium libri novem.* English translation: *Memorable Doings and Sayings,* trans. by D. R. Shackleton Bailey, Loeb Classical Library (Cambridge, Mass.: Harvard University Press, 2000).

Vázquez de Menchaca, F. *Controversiarum illustrium . . . libri tres* [Illustrious Controversies]. Barcelona, 1563.

Vigilius. *Contra Eutychetem* [Against Eutyches]. Text edited in PL, vol. 62.

Vignier, N. *Sommaire de l'histoire des François* [Summary of French History]. Paris, 1579.

Vincent of Lérins. *Commonitorium . . . adversus profanas . . . novitates haeretico-*

*rum* [Commonitory against the Profane Novelties of the Heretics]. Text in PL, vol. 50. English translation in *A Select Library of Nicene and Post-Nicene Fathers.*

Virgil. *Aeneid.* Among the many English translations see *The Aeneid,* trans. by R. Fagles (New York: Viking, 2006).

Vitoria, F. de. *Relectiones.* Lyon, 1557, and Salamanca, 1565. A selection is available in English in *Vitoria, Political Writings,* ed. by A. Pagden and J. Lawrance (Cambridge: Cambridge University Press, 1991).

*Weß sich Doctor Andreas Bodenstein von Karlstadt mit Doctor Martino Luther.* Augsburg, 1524.

Wild, J. *In . . . evangelium secundum Matthaeum commentariorum libri quatuor* [Commentaries on the Gospel of Matthew]. Mainz, 1559.

William of Tyre. *Belli sacri historia* [History of the Holy War]. Text edited in PL, vol. 201.

———. *Historia rerum in partibus transmarinis gestarum.* Text edited in PL, vol. 201. English translation: *A History of Deeds Done beyond the Seas,* trans. by E. A. Babcock and A. C. Krey (New York: Columbia University Press, 1943.

Zonaras, J. *Compendium historiarum* [Compendium of History]. A selection of this work is available in English in *The History of Zonaras,* ed. by T. Banchich and E. Lane (New York: Routledge, 2009).

———. *Nomocanon* [Glosses on the *Nomocanon*].

———. *Vita Alexii* [Life of Alexius].

———. *Vita Leonis Isaurici* [Life of Leo the Isaurian].

[Zonaras's works can be found in PG, vols. 134–35.]

# BIBLIOGRAPHY OF WORKS
## CITED BY THE EDITOR

---

## Manuscripts

*Archivio della Congregazione per la Dottrina della Fede*
Index, Diarii I
Index, Protocolli B
Index, Protocolli DDD
Index, Protocolli I
Index, Protocolli II

*Archivio della Pontificia Università Gregoriana*
APUG 373
APUG 1363–1366
APUG 1460

*Archivum Romanum Societatis Iesu*
Opp. Nn. 243
Opp. Nn. 252

*Archivio Segreto Vaticano*
Segreteria di Stato, Francia, 54

*Biblioteca Apostolica Vaticana*
Barberini Latini 1191
Barberini Latini 2628
Ottoboni Latini 2416
Vaticani Latini 7398

*British Library*
Additional Mss. 48121

## Printed Works

Alberigo, G., et alii, eds. *Conciliorum oecumenicorum decreta.* Basel: Herder, 1962.

Barclay, W. *De potestate Papae.* [London], 1609.

———. *De regno et regali potestate adversus Buchananum, Brutum, Boucherium & reliquos Monarchomachos, libri sex.* Paris, 1600.

Barnes, J., ed. *The Cambridge Companion to Aristotle.* Cambridge: Cambridge University Press, 1995.

Bellarmine, R. *Ven. Cardinalis Roberti Bellarmini Politiani S.J. Opera omnia.* Ed. by J. Fèvre. 12 vols. Paris: Vivès, 1870–74.

Belloy, Pierre de. *Apologie Catholique.* N.p., 1585.

Bouwsma, W. J. *Venice and the Defense of Republican Liberty: Renaissance Values in the Age of the Counter-Reformation.* Berkeley: University of California Press, 1968.

Braun, H. E. *Juan de Mariana and Early Modern Spanish Political Thought.* Aldershot, U.K.: Ashgate, 2007.

Brett, A. S. *Liberty, Right, and Nature: Individual Rights in Later Scholastic Thought.* Cambridge: Cambridge University Press, 1997.

Brodrick, J. *Robert Bellarmine: Saint and Scholar.* Westminster, Md.: Newman Press, 1961.

Burns, J. H., ed. *The Cambridge History of Medieval Political Thought, c. 350–c. 1450.* Cambridge: Cambridge University Press, 1988.

Burns, J. H., and M. Goldie, eds. *The Cambridge History of Political Thought, 1450–1700.* Cambridge: Cambridge University Press, 2004 (1991).

Canning, J. *The Political Thought of Baldus de Ubaldis.* Cambridge: Cambridge University Press. 1987.

Cantimori, D. *Eretici Italiani del Cinquecento e altri scritti.* Torino: Einaudi, 1992 (1939).

Cicero, M. T. *On the Commonwealth and On the Laws.* Ed. by J. E. G. Zetzel. Cambridge: Cambridge University Press, 1998.

*Codex Theodosianus.* Ed. by J. Godefroy et al. 6 vols. Leipzig, 1736–45.

Cozzi, G. *Paolo Sarpi tra Venezia e l'Europa.* Torino: Einaudi, 1979.

Denzinger, H. *Enchiridion symbolorum, definitionum et declarationum de rebus fidei et morum.* Freiburg Brisgoviae: Herder, 1965 (1st ed. 1854).

Dyson, R. W., ed. *Aquinas: Political Writings.* Cambridge: Cambridge University Press, 2003.

———. *Normative Theories of Society and Government in Five Medieval Thinkers.* Lewiston, N.Y.: Edwin Mellen Press, 2003.

Elliott, J. H. *Imperial Spain, 1469–1716.* London: Penguin, 2002 (1st ed. 1963).

Elton, G. R. *The Reformation, 1520–1559.* The New Cambridge Modern History, vol. 2. Cambridge: Cambridge University Press, 1990.

Erasmus. *The Education of a Christian Prince.* Ed. by L. Jardine. Cambridge: Cambridge University Press, 2006 (1997).

Frajese, V. *La nascita dell'Indice.* Brescia: Morcelliana, 2006.

———. "Regno ecclesiastico e Stato moderno. La polemica fra Francisco Peña e Roberto Bellarmino sull'esenzione dei chierici." *Annali dell'Istituto storico italo-germanico in Trento* 14 (1988): 273–339.

———. *Sarpi Scettico: Stato e Chiesa a Venezia tra Cinque e Seicento.* Bologna: Il Mulino, 1994.

Giacon, C. *La seconda scolastica: I problemi giuridico politici Suárez, Bellarmino, Mariana.* Milan: Fratelli Bocca, 1950.

Ginzburg, Carlo. "Just One Witness," in Saul Friedlander, ed., *Probing the Limits of Representation: Nazism and the "Final Solution."* Cambridge, Mass.: Harvard University Press, 1992.

Godman, P. *The Saint as Censor: Robert Bellarmine Between Inquisition and Index.* Leiden: Brill, 2000.

Grotius, Hugo. *The Rights of War and Peace.* 3 vols. Indianapolis: Liberty Fund, 2005.

Haakonssen, K. "Hugo Grotius and the History of Political Thought." *Political Theory* 13, no. 2 (1985): 239–65.

Höpfl, H. *Jesuit Political Thought: The Society of Jesus and the State, c. 1540–1630.* Cambridge: Cambridge University Press, 2004.

Hsia, R. Po-chia. *The World of Catholic Renewal, 1540–1770.* Cambridge: Cambridge University Press, 2005 (1st ed. 1998).

Israel, J. I. *The Dutch Republic: Its Rise, Greatness, and Fall, 1477–1806.* Oxford: Oxford University Press, 1998 (1995).

Jaitner, K. "De Officio Primario Summi Pontificis. Eine Denkschrift Kardinal Bellarmins für Papst Clemens VIII (Sept./Okt. 1600)." In *Römische Kurie, kirchliche Finanzen, Vatikanisches Archiv: Studien zu Ehren von Hermann Hoberg,* ed. by Hermann Hoberg and Erwin Gatz, 377–403. Rome: Università gregoriana, 1979.

James VI and I. *King James VI and I: Political Writings.* Ed. by J. P. Sommerville. Cambridge: Cambridge University Press, 2006 (1994).

———. *The Political Works of James I.* Ed. by C. H. McIlwain. Cambridge, Mass.: Harvard University Press, 1918.

Kretzmann, N., et alii, eds. *The Cambridge History of Later Medieval Philosophy.* Cambridge: Cambridge University Press, 1982.

Krueger, P., et alii, eds. *Corpus iuris civilis.* 3 vols. Berlin: Weidmann, 1954.

Lampe, G. W. H. *The Cambridge History of the Bible.* Vol. 2: *The West from the Fathers to the Reformation.* Cambridge: Cambridge University Press, 1994 (1969).

Lavenia, V. *L'infamia e il perdono: Tributi, pene e confessione nella teologia morale della prima età moderna.* Bologna: Il Mulino, 2004.

Le Bachelet, X. M. *Auctarium Bellarminianum.* Paris: Beauchesne, 1913.

———. "Bellarmin à l'Index." *Études* 44, no. III (1907): 227–46.

Locke, J. *Two Treatises of Government.* Ed. by P. Laslett. Cambridge: Cambridge University Press, 1988.

Lombardi, D. "Fidanzamenti e matrimoni dal Concilio di Trento alle riforme settecenteche." In *Storia del matrimonio,* ed. by M. De Giorgio and C. Klapisch-Zuber, 215–50. Bari: Laterza, 1996.

Luther, M. *The Freedom of a Christian.* Ed. by M. D. Tranvik. Minneapolis: Fortress Press, 2008.

———. *Vermanunge zum Gebet wider den Türcken.* Wittenberg, 1541.

———. *Vom Kriege widder die Türcken.* Wittenberg, 1529.

Mariana, Juan de. *De rege et regis institutione.* Toledo, 1599.

Masson, Jean Papire. *De vitis episcoporum urbis.* Paris, 1586.

Mastellone, S. "Tommaso Bozio, teorico dell'ordine ecclesiastico." *Il pensiero politico* 13 (1980): 186–94.

McLynn, N. B. *Ambrose of Milan: Church and Court in a Christian Capital.* Berkeley: University of California Press, 1994.

Migne, J. P., ed. *Patrologia Graeca.* 161 vols. Paris, 1857–66.

———. *Patrologia Latina.* 221 vols. Paris, 1844–55 and 1862–65.

Mostaccio, S. "Gerarchie dell'obbedienza e contrasti istituzionali nella Compagnia di Gesu' all'epoca di Sisto V." *Rivista di Storia del Cristianesimo* 1, no. 1 (2004): 109–27.

Motta, F. *Bellarmino: Una teologia politica della Controriforma.* Brescia: Morcelliana, 2005.

Nelson, E. *The Jesuits and the Monarchy: Catholic Reform and Political Authority in France (1590–1615).* Aldershot, U.K.: Ashgate, 2005.

Parente, F. "The Index, the Holy Office, the Condemnation of the Talmud and Publication of Clement VIII's Index." In *Church, Censorship, and Culture in Early Modern Italy,* ed. by G. Fragnito, 163–93. Cambridge: Cambridge University Press, 2001.

Pastor, L. von. *The History of the Popes, fom the Close of the Middle Ages.* 40 vols. St. Louis: Herder, 1936–61.

Philipson, N., and Q. Skinner, eds. *Political Discourse in Early Modern Britain.* Cambridge: Cambridge University Press, 1993.

Prodi, P. *The Papal Prince: One Body and Two Souls. The Papal Monarchy in Early Modern Europe.* Cambridge: Cambridge University Press, 1987 (1982).

———. *Il sacramento del potere: Il giuramento politico nella storia costituzionale dell'Occidente.* Bologna: Il Mulino, 1992.

Prosperi, A. *Il Concilio di Trento: Una introduzione storica.* Torino: Einaudi, 2001.

Questier, M. C. "Loyalty, Religion and State Power in Early Modern England: English Romanism and the Oath of Allegiance." *The Historical Journal* 40 (1997): 311–29.

Richter, A. L., and E. Friedberg, eds. *Corpus iuris canonici.* 2 vols. Graz: Akademische Druck u. Verlagsanstalt, 1959.

Siraisi, N. G. *Medieval and Early Renaissance Medicine: An Introduction to Knowledge and Practice.* Chicago: University of Chicago Press, 1990.

Skinner, Q. *Foundations of Modern Political Thought.* 2 vols. Cambridge: Cambridge University Press, 1978.

Sommerville, J. P. "From Suarez to Filmer: A Reappraisal." *The Historical Journal* 25, no. 3 (1982): 525–40.

———. "Jacobean Political Thought and the Controversy over the Oath of Allegiance." Unpublished Ph.D. thesis, Cambridge University, 1981.

Sommervogel, C. *Bibliothèque de la Compagnie de Jésus.* 12 vols. Louvain: Editions de la Bibliothèque S.J., Collège philosophique et théologique, 1960.

Taucci, R. *Intorno alle lettere di Fra Paolo Sarpi ad Antonio Foscarini.* Firenze: Tipografia Barbèra, 1939.

Tedeschi, J. *The Prosecution of Heresy: Collected Studies on the Inquisition in Early Modern Italy.* Binghampton, N.Y.: Medieval & Renaissance Texts & Studies, 1991.

Tracy, J. D. *The Politics of Erasmus: A Pacifist Intellectual and His Political Milieu.* Toronto, Buffalo, London: University of Toronto Press, 1978.

Tuck, R. *Natural Rights Theories: Their Origin and Development.* Cambridge: Cambridge University Press, 1979.

Tutino, S. *Empire of Souls: Robert Bellarmine and the Christian Commonwealth.* Oxford: Oxford University Press, 2010.

———. *Law and Conscience: Catholicism in Early Modern England 1570–1625.* Aldershot, U.K.: Ashgate, 2007.

Ullmann, W. *The Growth of Papal Government in the Middle Ages: A Study in the Ideological Relation of Clerical to Lay Power.* London: Methuen, 1962 (1955).

———. *Medieval Papalism: The Political Theories of the Medieval Canonists.* London: Methuen, 1949.

Vitoria, F. de. *Political Writings.* Ed. by A. Pagden and J. Lawrance. Cambridge: Cambridge University Press, 1991.

Wilks, M. J. *The Problem of Sovereignty in the Later Middle Ages: The Papal Monarchy with Augustinus Triumphus and the Publicists.* Cambridge: Cambridge University Press, 1963.

Wootton, D. *Paolo Sarpi: Between Renaissance and Enlightenment.* Cambridge: Cambridge University Press, 1983.

# INDEX

This book is set in Adobe Garamond, a modern adaptation by Robert Slimbach of the typeface originally cut around 1540 by the French typographer and printer Claude Garamond. The Garamond face, with its small lowercase height and restrained contrast between thick and thin strokes, is a classic "old-style" face and has long been one of the most influential and widely used typefaces.

Book design by Louise OFarrell
Gainesville, Florida
Typography by Newgen North America
Austin, Texas